The Film Cheat

The Film Cheat

Screen Artifice and Viewing Pleasure

Murray Pomerance

BLOOMSBURY ACADEMIC
NEW YORK • LONDON • OXFORD • NEW DELHI • SYDNEY

BLOOMSBURY ACADEMIC
Bloomsbury Publishing Inc
1385 Broadway, New York, NY 10018, USA

BLOOMSBURY, BLOOMSBURY ACADEMIC and the Diana logo are trademarks of
Bloomsbury Publishing Plc

First published in the United States of America 2020

Copyright © Murray Pomerance, 2020

For legal purposes the Acknowledgments on p. xii constitute an extension
of this copyright page.

Cover design: Eleanor Rose
Photograph/illustration © Collection Christophel / ArenaPAL

All rights reserved. No part of this publication may be reproduced or transmitted in any form or by any means, electronic or mechanical, including photocopying, recording, or any information storage or retrieval system, without prior permission in writing from the publishers.

Bloomsbury Publishing Inc does not have any control over, or responsibility for, any third-party websites referred to or in this book. All internet addresses given in this book were correct at the time of going to press. The author and publisher regret any inconvenience caused if addresses have changed or sites have ceased to exist, but can accept no responsibility for any such changes.

Library of Congress Cataloging-in-Publication Data
Names: Pomerance, Murray, 1946- author.
Title: The film cheat: screen artifice and viewing pleasure / Murray Pomerance.
Description: New York: Bloomsbury Academic, 2020. |
Includes bibliographical references and index.
Identifiers: LCCN 2020013256 | ISBN 9781501364990 (hardback) | ISBN 9781501364983 (paperback) | ISBN 9781501364969 (epdf) | ISBN 9781501364976 (ebook)
Subjects: LCSH: Motion pictures–Psychological aspects. | Motion picture audiences–Psychology. | Motion pictures–Aesthetics. | Realism in motion pictures.
Classification: LCC PN1995 .P65 2020 | DDC 791.45/652–dc23
LC record available at https://lccn.loc.gov/2020013256

ISBN: HB: 978-1-5013-6499-0
PB: 978-1-5013-6498-3
ePDF: 978-1-5013-6496-9
eBook: 978-1-5013-6497-6

Typeset by Deanta Global Publishing Services, Chennai, India

To find out more about our authors and books visit www.bloomsbury.com and sign up for our newsletters.

Don't drag your tricks, but work as quickly as you can, bearing in mind the Latin proverb, "Make haste slowly."
HARRY HOUDINI

Not even the best magician in the world can produce a rabbit out of a hat . . . if there isn't already a rabbit in the hat.
LERMONTOV (ANTON WALBROOK) IN *THE RED SHOES*

For
Stanley Cavell (1926–2018)
in cherished memory
and for
Abraham Kaplan (1918–93)
Who taught us both

"*The rest is silence.*"

CONTENTS

Acknowledgments xii

Preamble: All in the Game 1

OF SCRIPTS 11

1. Yesterdays 13
2. Tomorrow and Tomorrow and Tomorrow 20
3. Narrative Transparency 23
4. The Cheating Cut 30
5. Narrative Opacity 39
6. Our Faithful Friend 45
7. Bridge from Nowhere 55
8. And Here Endeth My Tale 64
9. Only Pretending 68
10. Keeping Minutes 72

OF PERFORMANCES 79

11. Monster! 81
12. A Star, Not a Star 88
13. Pain 93
14. Measuring Up 98

15 Privacy 104

16 Dance 121

17 Keyed Up 127

18 Don't Believe It 137

19 "I Love You" 143

20 Surrender 149

OF CAMERAS 153

21 Corral 155

22 Show Me 167

23 On the Road 174

24 "Good Cinematography!" 182

25 "Picture This" 191

26 The Angle Angle 195

27 Moving On 199

28 Behind the Camera Behind 202

29 Peek-a-Boo 205

OF SCENES 211

30 No There There 213

31 Where Are We? 219

32 Walk on the Wild Side 227

33 Happy Trails 232

34 The Thing 239

35 Heist 245

36 The Reality Effect 251

37 Stand-ins 257

38 The Superuniverse 262

OF JOINS 267

39 Believe in Me 269

40 Over Thames 273

41 Sequitur 278

42 *Veni creator spiritus* 284

43 "Bite the Dust" 287

44 Reflect On That 294

45 Presence and Presentation 300

46 By Contrast 308

47 The Blood Effect 316

Epilogue: Our Cheating Heart 321

Works Cited 335
Index 340

ACKNOWLEDGMENTS

Sincere thanks to a great number of unsung helpers, advisers, interlocutors, and general dogsbodies without whom this book could not exist. One can have what seems the very slightest of conversations only to discover, suddenly, a gateway to an unseen world. A special nod of gratitude to Dan Sacco, who is unfailingly helpful with a smile, and in emergencies, too.

All of these kind people have been profoundly helpful, too: the late Reginald Bedford (Hamilton), Rebecca Bell-Metereau (San Marcos), the late Kenneth Boulding (Ann Arbor), the late Dennis Brissett (Buffalo), the late Henry Bumstead (San Marino), Alex Clayton (Bristol), the late Herbert Coleman (Los Angeles), Ned Comstock (Los Angeles), Brandon Cronenberg (Toronto), the late Evelyn Eby (Hamilton), the late C. O. "Doc" Erickson (Los Angeles), the late Leslie Fiedler (Buffalo), Jean-Michel Frodon (Paris), the late Erving Goffman (Philadelphia), the late Assheton Gorton (Montgomery), Tom Hemingway (Coventry), Dorothy Herrmann (Philadelphia), the late Arthur Hiller (Los Angeles), Jason Jacobs (Brisbane), Ann Kaplan (New York), Mark Kermode (London), Lewis Klahr (Los Angeles), Andrew Klevan (Oxford), Bill Krohn (Long Beach), Dominic Lennard (Hobart), Daniel Lindvall (Stockholm), Elliott Logan (Brisbane), Vincent Longo (Ann Arbor), Leslie Mitchner (Princeton), Polo Ornelas (Los Angeles), the late Lawrence Paull (Chicago), the late Victor Perkins (Coventry), Lisa Purse (Reading), Simon Rainville (Halifax), Stephen Rebello (Pasadena), William Rothman (Miami), Bob Rubin (Pacific Palisades), Steven Rybin (Mankato), Joshua Schulze (Ann Arbor), Matthew Solomon (Ann Arbor), David Sorfa (Edinburgh), Dean Tavoularis (Los Angeles), George Toles (Winnipeg), Daniel Varndell (Southampton), Evan Williams (Los Angeles), Linda Ruth Williams (Exeter), Jonathan Wright (Toronto), and Kat Zabecka (Brighton), as well as the staff at *Cahiers du Cinéma* (Paris), *Figaro* (Los Feliz), The Margaret Herrick Library (Beverly Hills), *The Montague on the Gardens* (London), and *Rapido* (Toronto).

ACKNOWLEDGMENTS

My enthusiasm goes out to Katie Gallof and the staff at Bloomsbury, including Erin Duffy, Leela Ulaganathan, Dhanuja Ravi, Abdus Salam, Juhi Roy, and Namkwan Cho, true lovers of the books they make and perfect companions on this journey, and to my loves Nellie Perret and Ariel Pomerance, who always see with their hearts.

Los Angeles—London—Toronto
May 2020

Preamble:

All in the Game

FIGURE *Campbell Scott and Rebecca Pigeon at Logan Airport in* The Spanish Prisoner *(David Mamet, Jasmine Productions/Jean Doumanian Productions, 1997).*

On February 5, 2007, Ricky Gervais' *Extras* program (BBC)—a collection of "interviews" in which the very celebrated are typically treated as unknowns—entertained as guest Sir Ian McKellen. Asked what it was to "act," Sir Ian gave Ricky a very patient and gentle explanation:

> What I do is, I pretend to be the person I'm portraying in the film or play. [. . .] You're confused. It's perfectly simple, a case in point: *Lord of the Rings*. Peter Jackson comes from New Zealand, says to me, "Sir Ian, I want you to be Gandalf the Wizard," and I say to him, "You are aware that I am not really a wizard." And he said, "Yes I am aware of that, what I want you to do is use your acting skills to portray the wizard for the duration of the film." So I said, "Okay," and then I said to myself, "Mm, how would I do that?" And this is what I did: I imagined what it would

be like to be a wizard, and then I pretended, and acted in that way on the day. [. . .] And how did I know what to say? The words were written down for me in a script. How did I know where to stand? People told me.

Pretend to be a person! There isn't a one of us who doesn't do this on a regular basis, pretending and thus becoming who we have to be in one circumstance after another.[1] But something the actor does that most of us do not habitually do is, develop the capacity to impersonate (some theorists would say to become) a very great number of people very unlike one another, and sometimes with relatively little preparation. A quick-change artist! The basic idea of putting on a self, dressing in a self, has long been a normal feature of philosophical speculation:

> within the hollow crown
> That rounds the mortal temples of a king
> Keeps Death his court and there the antic sits,
> Scoffing his state and grinning at his pomp,
> Allowing him a breath, a little scene,
> To monarchize, be fear'd and kill with looks,
> Infusing him with self and vain conceit,
> As if this flesh which walls about our life,
> Were brass impregnable. (*Richard II* III.ii.160–8)

Yet, beyond that cinema is positively filled with people (actors) pretending to be people other than they "really" are, which is to say, other than they would be pretending to be (outside the critical view) were they not acting in cinema. This is the much discussed actor/character formula, the transformation that occurs inside the work of art. To be prosaic to a fault, McKellen plays Gandalf quite compellingly but, as he himself knows, *he is not Gandalf*. (Actually there is no Gandalf, beyond the word "Gandalf" on Tolkien's page and the screenplay, and the figure who moves about the film thanks to McKellen's pretending—with a long white beard and a tall staff, and on a horse.) Cinema is not only filled with such performances and performers but can be imagined only in the very abstract without them.

However, cinema offers a much-repeated, and fascinating, stretching of the rules of transformation. Imagine this: for one or another dramatic reason, there is a moment onscreen in which a character (already the work of an actor pretending to be the person being portrayed) is required in the story to *act*—to pretend to be a different person, not the character we have been watching the actor achieve but someone distinctly other. In

---

[1] Following from the enlightening work on "passing" by Harold Garfinkel, I give in *An Eye for Hitchcock* an extended analysis of Roger Thornhill as "secret apprentice."

Howard Hawks's *Twentieth Century* (1934), for example, John Barrymore's eloquent, demanding, neurotic, and hilarious director/producer Oscar Jaffe, a character if ever there was one, a man whose ego has swollen past measurement (embodied for us by Barrymore as an extended cadenza), needs to hoodwink a glittering actress who has had quite enough of his tricks (Carole Lombard). He arranges that on a railway platform she should encounter a heavily whiskered, doddering, helpless old man (performed, she does not pick up, nor do we, at first, by Jaffe). The character becoming a character. At another point in the film the irrepressible Oscar pretends he is at Death's door in order to get Lily to sign a contract to satisfy his final wish. Think of these as performances-within-performance. In *Easter Parade* (1948), a naïve chorus-girl-turned-famous-dancer, Hannah Brown (Judy Garland), is onstage with her partner Don Hewes (Fred Astaire) doing an Irving Berlin number called "We're a Couple of Swells" in which she must look not like the famous Judy Garland and not like the famous Hannah Brown but like a toothless hobo. In the recent *Operation Finale* (2018), Adolf Eichmann (Ben Kingsley) is masqueraded by Israeli agents as an airline pilot, with fake mustache and full uniform, so that they can sneak him out of Argentina on an El Al jet.

A variation on this theme has the performed character doing a fully conscious dress-up while being ignorant of some telltale, some wholly central feature of the "character" being performed. In *Rebecca* (1940), for example, the new Mrs De Winter (Joan Fontaine) prepares for a fancy-dress ball. She costumes herself, with the assistance of the housekeeper Mrs Danvers (Judith Anderson) in an elaborate gown, innocently donning the image of—the one person her new husband least wants to see in the world. The masquerade itself—her fancy-dress costuming—is openly declared as put-on, but it is not until the husband (Laurence Olivier) reacts with horror and vituperation that our character grasps her performative gaffe. For a hilarious comic variation, we have E.T. in little Gertie's (Drew Barrymore) closet, hiding among her platoon of stuffed dolls and wearing a preposterous hat that has been found for him; the creature knows that if he keeps still he will likely "pass," but as an alien he has no particular knowledge of earthling habits, certainly not doll collecting, and could not for the life of him identify the various zany creatures who surround him or how funny he looks.

More contemporaneously we find a variant on this trope in which, through the careful application of some "advanced technology" not shown to the audience, the onscreen pretension is made convincing in itself, that is, made to look not like the result of pretending but instead like a very reality (a make-believe, since this is a film); at a giveaway moment the pretender—in *Mission: Impossible* (1996) Ethan Hunt (Tom Cruise)—is discovered in a secluded chamber swiftly pulling a latex mask off his face and we discover that along with dozens of others onscreen we have been fooled. Now a familiar character is "recovered from" what is plain, only now, as a masquerade.

Two distinct issues of deeper interest are raised by the film actor's pretended pretending.

Visible Seams. First, a cool, even, and revealing illumination is spread across the surface of any one film, and then of fictional cinema everywhere, showing up the delicate seam between the characters with whom we are engaged in our watching and the actors we (persistingly) act as though we do not see. The very idea of acting, of putting on, of pretending is raised explicitly to view, even spoken about. We can note that these people of the screen world generally act as though things are quite different from this, *as though we do not see them acting*, but in fact we do see. And seeing while acting as though we do not see we, too, are pretending. As an audience, we pretend to be "not in the know" yet know that we are very much in the know. At least when confronted with familiar stars it is virtually impossible not to see that they are the folk they are while earnestly proclaiming themselves to be other, Celebrated Other, especially impossible if one has spent heavy money to see the film—or time downloading it—on the basis of the actors' fame. Again, we spy on Gandalf but we know Ian McKellen is there, too. The performative fiction may be brought more fully to life, become more electric and more present, when we watch unfamiliars, men and women we have not already learned to recognize as "themselves." This is often the case with children. Christian Bale was only a pre-adolescent prodigy when he shot *Empire of the Sun* (1987), amazing to watch yet otherwise unknown. The same went for Nicholas Hoult in *About a Boy* (2002) and Patty Duke in *The Miracle Worker* (1962). And for Leonardo DiCaprio in *What's Eating Gilbert Grape* (1993).[2] With such actors, we can know superficially and generally that "acting" is going on, without actually teasing out the actor at work inside the character. With established stars it is entirely different. To watch Mankiewicz's *The Barefoot Contessa* (1954) is to see not Maria Vargas but Ava Gardner *as* Maria Vargas, not Harry Dawes who makes Maria into a star but Humphrey Bogart (who already is one). At the beginning of Minnelli's *The Band Wagon* only a year before, we had seen the famous movie star Ava Gardner *as* the famous movie star Ava Gardner; but that screened "famous movie star" inhabited a different universe than the woman who was playing her. That diegetic "Ava" was able to interact with Tony Hunter (Fred Astaire) because she knew that he and she were both in the entertainment business and had achieved fame there, but the Ava underneath "Ava" had no truck with Tony, could never touch him, although she was able to interact with, and make more than one film with, Fred Astaire (they reunite working together in *On the Beach* [1959]).

If we are constantly aware of actors putting on their characters, if we always know there is a seam, and if we can make our awareness routine

---

[2] Bale, Hoult, Duke, and DiCaprio had all done work before these breakout performances, but not with wide popular recognition.

enough that it seems to dissipate, the further step of an actor's *character* putting on a character undoes the dissipation, cues us openly and bluntly to the process of *characterization* once again, a sharp reminder, an alarm. Seeing characterization happening before our eyes, we go on the lookout for it more broadly and more deeply in all parts of the film. John Huston's *The List of Adrian Messenger* (1963) is an extravaganza play on this turn.

But the apparent revelation of a performative seam is a trick, a cheat: a door marked BACKSTAGE that does not really lead us there (that leads, one might well sense, to only a brick wall). Our perception of performance in action (that the figures of the story are being performed as such) is the centralizing trick, or cheat, cinema offers in giving us persons tacitly claiming to be other persons inside the work. As the play-within-the-play of *even a character* becoming a "character" opens activated performance to view, with literal spontaneity and presence, it offers the performance-inside-the-performance-of-a-performance without affirmation, too. Characters, and characters' characters, simply appear as such, without asking us (or giving us pause) to consider the astonishing transformation that is taking place to realize them. The cheat of film narrative is made accessible, albeit unlabeled as such, and provides grounds for thinking about narrative more broadly as a cheat as well. A cheat we adore. A cheat we adore to adore.

A Game of Charades. The second issue invoked by pretended pretending is more slippery. When characters are seen putting on characters, they "live as" (extend the performance of) those put-on characters typically for a very limited time, engendering and joining a kind of game in a bounded zone (a zone subject to the observation of diegetic bystanders). One can see a game because particular rules of engagement are being strictly adhered to, "game pieces" are in play, and the entire construction is manifestly unlike the everyday world—either the world we live in or the one the film ordinarily depicts—as long as all action is discernably transformed by game conventions identifiable as such: in short, the game boundary is palpable. Suddenly the people who seemed to be interacting are figures playing a "scenario" together, one specifically *not identified as a scenario while it is in progress, especially if we watch from up close* since from up close we are also in the "game" and we know and accept that game players do not openly identify as game players *while playing the game*, unless extrinsic circumstances render the situation untenable. In a filmed poker game, for instance, a player visible to us as such but not self-acknowledging might "pull out" a little and suspecting another of cheating call the issue; in effect, this caller would be saying, "Look, I am a rule-abiding poker player and you are not" and by calling himself a poker player actually not, at that instant, be playing poker.

A complex and elaborate play-within-the-play can be established, entirely non-evident as such until some crisis moment when, to some calculated degree, it is revealed. Indeed, consider a game in which there are quite a few players, all looking different from one another and no one of them self-identifying as a game player while playing. In sport, all the many players wear identical uniforms; in the case I wish to point to, there are no uniforms of any kind. This is the con movie, the film about an ignorant "mark" being taken in by a group of performers not recognized as such. The donning of the interior role-within-the-role is very often not shown at first, so that initially we accept the put-on "characters" as true characters themselves. Only later, for the viewer's pleasure, is the con artist revealed to have scripted, produced, directed, and often starred in a supposed "real action" that was in fact only a show within the show. In an extreme form, with the con game being elaborated at very great length and in very minute detail, the "reveal" might come so late that we barely catch sight of the performers beneath the "characters" at all. They might seem to be strangers.

At the con film's crisis moment, some high point of dramatic probability is reached as we take note of what the complicated charade was all for: a great deal of money suddenly revealed to have been stolen, a rare museum piece revealed as a clever forgery, and so on. Our noting suggests that there has been produced for the film's audience a moment of *stunning awareness* in which the guying-up of performance is put on show for itself, in the center ring of the circus as it were, with lighting apparently showing all of its parts: "Look at the little show we have given!!" Now it is undeniable that a trick has been in progress, a cheat. And not only some of the characters you've watched but you yourselves have been taken in: you, seduced and deluded, just as they were. In the con film this *reveal* is central to the emotional turn, a vital requirement.[3] The resolving mechanism is as blunt as it is curious: seeing that some onscreen characters have been duped, the viewer, feeling superior because safely outside, presumes that no duping has affected him or her. One can both know one was cheated and avoid seeing that one was cheated simultaneously. Perhaps with pleasure, one projects one's own state onto the figures of the screen.

* * *

The con film isn't the same as the heist film. In the latter, the victim typically does know he has been taken. And focus is given to elaborate methods of penetrating a defensive shield that is extremely patent to begin with:

---

[3] Erving Goffman's "On Cooling the Mark Out," a classic analysis of cons, indicates how in actual practice the discovery by the victim (the "mark") that he has been taken in, is potentially disruptive to success. So a process is put in place ("cooling out") that disengages him from social contact with those who have been running the game but in a way that is rationalized in terms of everyday discourse (someone has bought a house in another city and is moving, etc.). While cooling out is beneficial for actual con artists, it is inutile in producing audience catharsis.

vaults within vaults within vaults, uniformed guards with submachine guns, surveillance camera systems wired to a central control facility where some character has highly expanded sensory power (often a large bank of television screens) which will be disabled. The con is the manufacture of a typical social reality standing on thin air. A kind of induced psychosis. Those taken in by cons very often never know or—more pleasing to the viewer—come to learn only as a dramatic surprise.

There is a significant catalog of con films, the most popular, ironically, being a film which overtly announces itself as such, George Roy Hill's *The Sting* (1973). Some films have con-game sequences, such as *Paper Moon* (1973), *House of Games* (1987), or *The Lady Eve* (1941). But the limiting case is presented in David Mamet's *The Spanish Prisoner* (1997), of which it must be said that telling the story to a reader who may not have had the pleasure of seeing it is a complicated challenge. I will be brief and circumspect.

Joe Ross (Campbell Scott) is a brilliant young mind, and he has created a new secret "process" (about which we are never told anything) for the advantage of Klein (Ben Gazzara), his boss. Klein has brought him, along with a newly hired secretary, Susan (Rebecca Pigeon), to the enticing island of St. Estèphe for a business meeting with principal investors. Turquoise waters, green palms! On the beach there, Joe meets a very polite and apparently vastly wealthy man who introduces himself as Jimmy Dell (Steve Martin). Soon later, in the hotel bar, Susan introduces him to someone else, her drinking partner, Pat McCune (Felicity Huffman), an FBI agent on holiday. Joe has been trying unsuccessfully to get Klein to agree formally to a settlement in reward for the fabulous "formula." Just before leaving the island, Joe is accosted by Jimmy who begs a favor: take a little package to my sister in New York, a devoted tennis fan and player. The package is wrapped in brown paper and addressed to her at The Wiltshire.

On the plane, Susan gives Joe a little irritation by lecturing him, repeatedly but with the vocal tone of an uneducated innocent, on how the world is a strange place and you don't really know who anyone is. Someone might even be a drug mule. Startled, he rushes to the toilet and tears open the package, which turns out to contain not drugs but an antiquarian book, *Budge on Tennis*, the binding of which is coming apart. In New York he proceeds to an antiquarian dealer and picks up a much better copy of the identical book, keeping the damaged one for himself. He drops off the gift with the doorman of the sister's building.

Jimmy has made a dinner date with him for Friday night, but when Friday night comes Jimmy stands him up. The next morning he chances to find his new friend at an exclusive car dealership and confronts him. But Jimmy is even more irate than Joe: "You didn't *give* the book to my sister. She waited all afternoon for you." Later, he telephones Joe to apologize for his manner and takes him dining at his exclusive club. At his swank pad on the way,

Jimmy shows Joe—on a lark—how easy it is to open a Swiss bank account by creating one with Joe's puppy's name as logon and with fifteen francs deposited. They head off to the club but are informed there that, it being Saturday, entrance is for members only. Accordingly Jimmy, refusing to disappoint his guest, signs Joe up as a member, and to finalize the ceremony Joe is given to sign a gilded certificate of membership. Jimmy now informs Joe that in his opinion, Klein is going to exploit him as far as he can, and will show his "appreciation" by according Joe very rude treatment. Immediately thereafter we see that this is absolutely true, with Klein's lawyers pressing Joe to sign a new contract—basically a kiss-off—and infuriating him. He storms out. By telephone, Jimmy assures him that his own lawyer is going to help. They should meet the next day at Central Park, near the carousel. Joe should bring his contract. And the formula.

Meanwhile, sweethearted Joe buys flowers to apologize to Jimmy's sister. But delivering them to her building, he finds to his surprise that the "tennis player/fan" "sister" is in fact an extremely elderly woman with a walker and a helper. At Central Park, confused Joe is encountered and whispered to by a chain of park workers who are apparently agents in disguise. They guide him into a conference in the park men's room, where a leading agent (Ed O'Neill) is working with McCune to "get" Jimmy, who is a thief in disguise. Joe watches the agent put his formula on the window sill while he is wired with a mic. Carrying the red notebook with the formula now, Joe goes to meet (and record) Jimmy, but he is stood up a second time. He spies one of the "workers" and greets him but when the man pivots around he turns out to be a stranger. Joe runs back to the men's room and it is now completely empty. He goes to a payphone and calls the FBI, asking for Pat McCune, and a man says that he is McCune. Frozen, Joe opens his red notebook and all the pages are blank.

When he brings a team of police to Jimmy's place they discover not a residence but a totally empty space, the "shower" from which Jimmy had emerged in his robe to chat with Joe being nothing but a tiny toilet. There isn't a single fingerprint. At the "exclusive club" they discover only a restaurant. Joe finds himself arrested for the murder of a colleague, suspicion falling heavily upon him. When in interrogation he is asked if he has any undisclosed bank accounts and says no, he is shown details of his now plump Swiss account. Asked whether he was trying to escape to Venezuela (a country from which there is no extradition) he again says no, but is shown the "membership" certificate he signed, which turns out to be a request to the government of Venezuela for sanctuary.

I will cease recounting here, so as not to deprive readers of the pleasure provided by the resolution of this film, and in order to frame this discussion around a central conundrum which will help us focus on the "cheat," quite generally, as a structured and vulnerable endeavor involving theatricality in all its elements and a kind of narrative architecture: just as films do.

The question is:

How exactly does not-so-stupid (indeed, "brilliant") Joe get locked into the puzzle game of the Spanish Prisoner that is being run by slick Jimmy? Where can we put a finger down on some vital and unequivocal clue that he was offered but entirely neglected, or declined, to pick up as we believe he should have? It is worth mentioning that all the pieces of the scenario are played out in crisp, bright, gaily colored images without particular shadow or murkiness or obscurity in which some machination could be hidden. All open to view (to our view, to Joe's view), all beyond reproach. That turquoise island sea; Jimmy's nappy forest green baseball cap; Susan's red dress and matching lipstick; the light flicking off the giant lenses in Joe's eyeglasses (through which he is failing to see); Pat McCune's blond hair in the brightly sunlit Central Park men's room; the fire-engine red notebook, and so on. While the "formula" is penned in clearly visible but also arcane mathematical symbols, still we can know it for what Joe says it is. When Joe finds out that the female McCune is really a man, and that the "tennis player" is an old lady he is in a position to know something is going on, and to tear open his notebook. But how did he get into a pickle barrel this deeply?

As with this film, every detail of the cinematic cheat is offered in plain composition, attractive, gay, alluring, and without confounding our view. Every detail as it comes up is palpably credible in itself and in its context, and indeed contexts are elaborated so as to substantiate every detail. The people (the characters) behave in a completely unsuspectable way, *merely* being there, being *only* human, *just* being kind, being *naturally* generous. Everything is *only, just, merely, naturally* what it is, and yet we find, if we back ourselves up just a little for observing, that we have been caught in a trap not so dissimilar to Joe's. Was he pulled in by Pat because in the men's room she was working with a senior agent who believably wired him? Was he pulled in by Jimmy at the club, with the gilded membership certificate, with the play bank account, with Jimmy's ineffable charm, gentility, sweet affability—the reason for casting Steve Martin. Was he pulled in by Susan's obvious sexual interest in him, a kind of flattery, a stimulation that drew him off-guard? Was he intoxicated by the brief holiday on the beautiful island, all expenses paid? What did the trick?

The antiquarian book, which turned out to be, yes, an authentic antiquarian book, because here—somewhere . . . somewhere . . . oh yes, here's another copy, in better shape. Or perhaps the white card inside, on which Jimmy had penned a note to his good-looking sister to pay attention to the carrier, because he was entirely the right sort of man for you . . .

Was it, indeed, the visual intoxication? (Because the world Jimmy created had to be seductive for Joe much as David Mamet's film has to be seductive for us.) Not just an island but white sands, arching trees, the green-blue sea. Was it not just the exclusive club but the particularly sententious and somber voice of the maître d' whose unfortunate fate it was to inform Jimmy, in front of his guest, that of course it being Saturday night entré is for members only, I'm so sorry to say, if I could do anything myself I'd . . .

But still more important than understanding *The Spanish Prisoner*, catching the catch of it, is understanding the catch of *this*, why I raise the film to attention here as an exemplification of what cinema does altogether. Even in my questioning and detailing I am shedding particular light, keying one thing and moving another aside. After all, it is not the story of this film that counts. It is not merely the succession of moments—because moments will be arranged (just as Jimmy arranges them) to flow logically one after another in an unquestionable way—but the moments themselves, the quality of the voice coupled with a precise light flickering in the eyes, a casual bathrobe, the gilding around the edges of the membership certificate. The cheat in filmic narratives, and in this con film the elaborate narrative, is not the unfolding plot taken in itself as a telling but what it covers, what is much more telltale, the *telling* way of telling, the nuancing, the etiquette, the apologies, the explanations that cover all the necessary bases. Not what happens but the way that what happens is accounted for, since the accounting is the vital assurance the storyteller needs to touch the viewer. The story, in effect, is but a pretext for the touch. The events summon the accounts, but the accounts constitute the real structure.

To ask how Joe Ross can succumb to having his magical formula stolen before his eyes is similar to other cinematic puzzles, established, ornamented, brought to an apex through narrative assembly: in *Vertigo* (1958), how is Scottie Ferguson convinced when he meets Judy Barton that if he wishes and works hard enough he can work with her to bring Madeleine Elster back to life?; in *The Asphalt Jungle* (1950), how is the ex-con Riedenschneider (Sam Jaffe) brought to such a position that all he can wish for in life is the pleasure of watching a pretty girl dance?; in *Some Like It Hot* (1959), how is Sugar Cane Kowalczyk, smart enough to know she is typically stuck with the fuzzy end of the lollipop, unable to discern that Geraldine and Josephine are not really women?; in *Guess Who's Coming to Dinner* (1967), how can the respectful and dignified Sidney Poitier be brought to a condition in which he must scream at his father that he won't be able to become a man until he can get him off his back? How many events, how many contingencies, how many collisions all seemingly uncontrived, all apparently pure, occupy narrative space in such a design that the culminating moments arrive so inevitably, as though dictated by a fate that eludes us?

This journey now winds on to a close look at the accounts and the moments, some of them at any rate, that as we view cinema bring us in, keep us there, and hold us from noticing what is happening to us as we participate. Traps that look like islands of paradise, or like red-bound notebooks we must try very hard to penetrate, so daunting is the mathematics and so taunting the formula.

Of Scripts

{1} Yesterdays
Facial recognition aphasia; with and without a memory; Oliver Sacks, "The Lost Mariner"; access to "a past"; character transports

{2} Tomorrow and Tomorrow and Tomorrow
Structured foretelling; knowing while not knowing the future; *The Wizard of Oz*; *Lawrence of Arabia*; present moments

{3} Narrative Transparency
Blow-Up; Character knowledge and rehearsal; *Dial M for Murder*; chase scenes; *Bullitt*; *Grand Prix*; *District B13*; markers; *The Naked Prey*

{4} The Cheating Cut
David Bordwell, "Intensified Continuity"; *The Bourne Supremacy*; *Citizen Kane*; Luigi Galvani; *The Long, Long Trailer*; *2001: A Space Odyssey*

{5} Narrative Opacity
The Man Who Knew Too Much (1956); Thomas Scheff's "ladder of awareness"; *Vertigo*

{6} Our Faithful Friend
Omniscient voice; Michel Chion, "the *acousmêtre*"; *The Dreamers*; *Sully*; *The Day of the Locust*; *What Maisie Knew*; *The Go-Between*; *Atonement*

{7} Bridge from Nowhere
Contiguity and likelihood; Arthur Freed Unit at MGM; *The Band Wagon*; probable eventuality

{8} And Here Endeth My Tale
Arbitrary endings; *Citizen Kane*; *Singin' in the Rain*; *La notte*; *The Third Man*; *Donnie Brasco*; *The Day the Earth Stood Still*; *A Star Is Born* (1954)

{9} Only Pretending
Dr. Mabuse; *Dr. No*; overt and covert villainy; *The Girl with the Dragon Tattoo*; *Inside Man*; *Minority Report*; introducing the villain

{10} Keeping Minutes
Dr. Zhivago; *The Magnificent Ambersons*; John Carey, "Temporal and Spatial Transitions"; *The Time Machine*; *Easter Parade*; *The Entertainer*; Stanley Cavell, *Little Did I Know*; music and anticipation; *Baby Driver*; *The Touch*; Rachmaninoff

1

Yesterdays

FIGURE 1 *Margot Winkler in* The King of Comedy *(Martin Scorsese, Embassy International/Twentieth Century Fox, 1982).*

I had lunch recently with a man I've known a very long time, an old friend, who confessed something I had never realized, that he suffered from facial recognition aphasia, the manifest inability to recognize faces. Not discriminate: *recognize*. He could see just fine, but he could not absolutely be sure he would know what he was seeing. Recognize: to affix a nominal label to a face one knows one has seen before, somewhere, sometime, and a face one can certainly tell apart from other faces. He could know with certainty that he had seen a face but not be able to put a name to it. With me he had no trouble, he said, but there were many others who would approach him amicably but leave him confounded, since although he knew that somehow he knew them he could not say (to himself) who they were, could not address them by name.

Many people have trouble remembering other people's names, sometimes needing several repetitions (and perhaps even then remaining unable to retain the information), yet they know that the name is something they know, even though at the moment it is unretrieved and seems unretrievable. They *have it* but have *misplaced it*. (The mental "room" in which one stores such things is, apparently, chock full of items of all kinds, so many that Charles Foster Kane's Xanadu seems meager by comparison.) FRA produces a strange, alienating sensation in which a person's name is not unretrievable from the vaults of memory but seems instead to be absent from the vaults altogether. Instead of "I can't recall (re-call) your name," it's a case of "I don't *know* your name." (I don't know, I have never heard, your face has never been associated with a name.) A great deal of what is mentally elided, then, is the past.

Happily our lunch went; fantastic Cobb salads with cold poached shrimp! My old friend treated me warmly, as a dear familiar, and we had a splendid time chewing over our two lives, together. He never once used my name as here now I, for quite different reasons, step aside from using his.

The peculiar reason I adduce this anecdote is that it illustrates something far more widely diffused than naming and name-forgetting, a particular odd interactional situation in which, notwithstanding an aphasic's (queer, personal) *sense* that he himself did not know a person he was recognizing (from a point of view similar to what would be taken up by others), he could also present himself openly, dramatically, as someone *without a memory*: not only someone who doesn't know a name that is not on the tongue but someone who is not knowing something he reasonably should—so very reasonably should, indeed, that his not knowing is an indicator of lost time, a horrible gap between then, when the name was on the register, and now, when it is gone. Let the aphasic protest he is not exactly forgetting, forgetting is not quite the word: no matter. He becomes a notable case of someone who apparently cannot delve into his past, cannot travel backward, *when any and all of us ought to be able to do so.*

When any and all of us ought to be able to move backward at will.

"Of course," all normals routinely journey backward, one supposes; everyone and anyone can (and should show that she can) bring up a recollection. *I remember going to the Museo del Historia Natural y Cultura with you and eating queso fundido.* Such "memoryless" figures as my lunch partner could be taken to be may well give the appearance of living entirely in the present, exactly and explicitly because they do not openly stage retrievals. Note: *the open staging of a retrieval.* I am reminded some of Oliver Sacks's "lost mariner," victim of a severe Korsakov's, whose present was more or less his world: "I wondered, when I first met him, if he was not condemned to a sort of 'Humean' froth, a meaningless fluttering on the surface of life" (39). But Sacks is making a diagnosis, giving the claim to be looking in. I am referring to the individual's performance of having no memory.

Certainly to openly stage a retrieval—*I Remember Mama* (1948)—is to identify oneself as having a history (and fake retrievals can be arranged so as to accredit a newcomer to the game with the bona fides of the longtime player). Further, one transmits an open signal about such a history when one gives a notably clear and open staging of retrieval from the past, one displays knowing oneself to have been placed before, and therefore to be placed now, in a temporal context. (A) There was a before; (B) I was participant to that before; (C) I here now point directly to it and thereby (D) credit my participation then and my pointing now. The facial recognition aphasic notably fails to give this signal with specific regard to other people, is easily taken as having no subjectively accessible past in which human encounters happened. Surely there must be a past, the person could not have been born yesterday; yet there appears no regard for or access to it. The past has no present meaning for the being who is ahistorical, and the social past has no present meaning for the facial recognition aphasic.

Open retrieval of information from "historical" files, the invocation of "remembered" names, directions, warnings, estimations, preferences, pet peeves, awkward situations, glorious achievements is a signal feature of what we call "normal" behavior, and when memory of this "typical," "everyday" kind seems to be blocked we anticipate the employment of one of a limited number of permissible excuses to both explain and bandage the situation. Momentary confusion, for example: "Oh, sorry, I didn't quite get what you asked me"; understandable stress: "Oh gosh, you have no idea how bad this migraine is!"; not having had coffee yet: "I can't do anything first thing in the morning!" Part of what makes for a condition we would call "real" is a presentation of self that includes actual or demonstrably possible open retrievals or, as above, reasonable accounts for their absence. Seeming to have nothing to fall back on, a person could be displaced from the real.

But the everyday, casual reading of others, just like psychiatric and neurological diagnosis, is similar to watching movies, at least because in both cases evaluation of a (character's) personality is tagged to the way he or she gives patent signals of both perception and memory: the character can see a red light as a red light; she remembers that a moment ago it was green; she knows that while *then* she could have driven through the intersection *now* she cannot (i.e., *then is not now*). Excepting in comedic situations, and working on the assumption that names have somewhere in the story already been shared, the character who mistakes another character's name signals a quirky, but at the same time symptomatic, relation with the past. Martin Scorsese plays a marvelous take on this problem in *The King of Comedy* (1982) with the receptionist at the Jerry Langford Show offices (Margo Winkler) who is confronted by Rupert Pupkin (Robert De Niro) again and again and again and again and again but can never quite get his name right. The first time De Niro puts on a charitable smile of toleration, as though to say, "My name gives a lot of people trouble, has always done so, and I can remember that, so it's no surprise it's giving you trouble, too." But also—and here is the charity, "I am telling you this because I also know, from past experience, that you might get flustered or embarrassed or feel you have done me an offense, and I want to assure you that's not the case." Yet he is not picking up on the possibility that to her he is a nobody *already*, since only people with appointments show up at this desk; one of the legion members of the great urban crowd, whose name one is under no obligation to know. Or that she's distracted. Or that she doesn't like him for some reason. Later on, when she persists in niggling with the name, he makes a correction that is curt and demands to get past her—a clear indication that from his point of view, she has failed at a crucial task and now, yes, indeed produced some offense, so that she ought to be, not embarrassed or flustered but, reproached—not that he has the authority to go about reproaching her. Note that it is Winkler's character whose genuineness is dubious, first to us and not long later to Rupert; the actress is genuinely there throughout.

What viewers calculate about a character is a kind of diagnosis itself, a positioning of the subject on a scale of believable normality not much different from the scale we all use in everyday life. The people we meet within our "reality" are, each, more or less real, depending on how they seem placed in long time. As we might tag the people we meet with various identities, surely with the tag we would call "real," we tag film characters, and they tag one another. That means that reality is up for grabs here, particularly the reality of the artifice. The people we take to be present "really," to be fully and unquestionably sharing our reality, can show or recount (and can reveal that they can show or recount) what they have just finished doing; or what they did an hour ago; or what happened yesterday or when they were only children (or give reasonable accounts for failures at this). Winkler's receptionist isn't present "really." Those who are, move around here and now; but they also dip backward in time. This dipping into the past and reconfiguration of its content into present anecdote or reference, embedded in conversation if not in behavior more generally, is what rounds a figure out as genuine rather than ersatz and simulated. I exist now, fully and roundly, but I have also existed before, here or in other places, in like or unlike situations, versions of which I could extract, reform, and present evidentially here and now. I can "quote myself." I am here because I took a path in order to arrive, and I can recollect at least some of the landscapes visible from that path. The formula works in reverse, too. If to seem real a character must share a past in the present, when a character shares a past he or she seems real: a useful tip for writers and actors, who might inadvertently focus too strongly on what is to come: have someone just remember something; anything; just like that.

I remember sitting at a polished wooden table eating a delicious Caesar salad at the moment the idea of writing this book came up.

With narrative characters this adjudication we make is of central importance, because at their first appearance on the screen they really and truly have come out of nowhere, out of pure non-history.[1] The scripted character has no past. For the watcher, she has arrived spontaneously (albeit in close connection with a wholly made-up and carefully produced showing, of which the making-up and production are meant both to capture our attention and elude our consideration). She is, in fact, emerging out of thin air, most especially when what we are looking at is an actor who has not been seen on screens yet (or not been seen much). Yet to seem actual, to merit our belief, such a character will gesture to "remember," to own "a past" blocked to us alone. The dialogue will be cheated to effect this illusion. Here are the very first three speeches, from "Jimmy" and "Cliff," sitting with newspapers in John Osborne's *Look Back in Anger* (1956), with my emphases to show how Jimmy points backward in time directly we set eyes upon him:

> JIMMY: Why do I do this *every Sunday*? Even the book reviews *seem to be the same as last week's. Different books—same reviews.* Have you finished that one yet?
> CLIFF: Not yet.
> JIMMY: I've *just read* three whole columns on the English Novel. *Half of it's in French.* Do the Sunday papers make *you* feel ignorant?

Because for a character *The Past* is an actorial and script invention, in plain fact any character who behaved onscreen as though he or she had no access to a past would be the realest possible character, but far too real, since our game of nominating realism doesn't buy this. We expect that any and every real present—and the character is really present—has, for those who share it, a precedent that only the wounded fail to access. The presence of the character, like the presence of any one of us in a social scene, is modulated, rounded out, nuanced by memories and hopes—hopes congruent with memories.

To unmodulated extreme presence, presence in the here and now and *only* in the here and now, a kind of unreality, a phantasmal quality attaches, as was the case with his patient originally for Oliver Sacks.

To some degree I am spelling out elements of a textbook for actors. They have learned that in order to seem strange and inexplicable they need only behave as though they don't have, or cannot access, a past—that is, as though

---

[1] Except in the case of sequels (not so very frequent), where their origins are indeterminate, being recognized by some audience members and entirely unknown by others.

they are precisely what they are as scripted, floating constructs embedded inexplicably in a contrived "present" that has, and can have, no relation to any other time. Go back for one moment to those lines from *Look Back*.[2] Jimmy was found asking Cliff whether he has read this newspaper every single time the play ran, night after night, hundreds of times in total on the West End and then some two hundred and fifty times on Broadway, and, newborn each time, Cliff said he hasn't, without any memory of having been asked before and having given the same answer, verbatim. Here is the reality of the drama, now. But that each of these can invoke past time brings on the reality of character. Performance is scripted and carried out with continual flickering rear views. That a character can *seem* to have a past is the cheat of the script. Seem to have a past: give the impression of thinking back, wondering, trying to remember or speculate, frame an argument on putatively accepted (earlier) principles. (Interrogation scenes work with this reaching backward as a fundamental material.)

In most filmic scenes of transport, where a character separates the self from present diegetic circumstances in order to wonder, to daydream, to worry backward, to try against all hope to remember what is forgotten, to reach beyond this—this thing that is the present, this Now—a great deal can be accomplished by the actor playing with special genuineness two kinds of scripted lines: (a) those that bring up (supposable) memories; and (b) those attesting, with substantial reason (we are to believe) that memory is out of the question (post-traumatic scenes). And ironically, the character who is to seem vitally and dramatically present will seem to be that way if the script allows for the actor embedding a present experience in what is to seem, and what is to be claimed as, a memory—even if later that memory will be known to be entirely made up and false. "Oh God yes!, I remember now!," with the eyes popped wide open. The act of "remembering" itself makes for the "normally real."

But the central peg in such a performance, this *genuine* quality of playing a truth, this way of making, supporting, modeling, and dramatizing the simple directness of yes!, having found the lost memory!!!, is finally a quality that is always, for the actor doing the work, a forthright lie. Owing to the fact that the actor knows what it is to remember a past—his lunch today, his rehearsals, a former love affair—he can fake remembering a past quite well. But the character: no. The character only ever *claims* to have a memory, since the character is but surface. And especially in film, where we are separated by the screen even as we are brought near the screen, the claims *as claims* are

---

[2]This play was elemental in British "kitchen sink" drama of the 1950s, and is widely credited with introducing the character of the "angry young man" into culture. In 1959 Tony Richardson released a film version starring Richard Burton and Gary Raymond as "Jimmy" and "Cliff," but the stage play at the Royal Court Theatre, Sloane Square (May 8, 1956), had starred Kenneth Haigh and Alan Bates.

more pertinent as such. My friend at lunch did cheat with me a little, as he is accustomed to cheating regularly with others who must not, it seems, come to the recognition that he does not know their faces, must not take the step of finding him weird. He talked around my name, Joe?, Samuel?, Matthew?, Harry?, Murray?, and brilliantly; skipped sentences that would require him to utter it; and switched to related and demonstrably more interesting subject matter. This friend had no past, it appeared, as far as remembering my name was concerned. And his blocking me from taking explicit note was his cheat. In respect of giving over the character as a person with a past, actors are cheating, too: always, every time, since the central point of dramatic presentation is that while the character cannot remember, without claiming memory he would seem out of place.

2

Tomorrow and Tomorrow and Tomorrow

FIGURE 2 *Margaret Hamilton (with Jack Haley, Judy Garland, and Bert Lahr in the ball) in* The Wizard of Oz *(Victor Fleming, MGM, 1939).*

On quite another order than memory is foretelling, the talent for seeing what approaches from down the road, for helping us "eat the air, promise-cramm'd." To represent foretelling visually, David Lean constructs a scene in *Lawrence of Arabia* (1962) where his protagonist, led into the farthest reaches of the shining bleachy desert, stands with his guide near a solitary well. The guide makes bold to drink as Lawrence (Peter O'Toole) watches. Blazing, almost incandescent sunlight, the sands whitened past exposure limits, indistinguishable from the white sky. (We grasp why someone would thirst for a drink there; and how disciplined Lawrence is by not going along.) Suddenly, as he peers off toward the quivering horizon, Lawrence sees (we see with him) a tiny dot bouncing. Now it grows a little larger and seems, perhaps, just perhaps, a person. Dark against the white, hundreds of millions of miles away. But growing larger and larger.

A sharp, sudden, reverberating shot.

And the guide lies dead.

Closer and closer and closer, until the rider can be made out, all dressed in black, his face dark and glowing (Omar Sharif). "It was my well."

Seeing what is far away in a future unknown. Seeing it coming. A very carefully constructed shot, that took time and labor and a film stock with a wide range of exposure.

Even the Wicked Witch of the West (Margaret Hamilton) does not do this *looking ahead* as well with her crystal ball. She stares into it and it sends a (television) view of what we are to believe is happening now, somewhere far away. But to be far away *now* is not necessarily to be in the future of she who gazes there.

To see and know what *will* happen. Because canny Lawrence somehow knows to hold off from drinking.

As with any stage play, the film actor will have been given the script in advance of shooting; will have been in a position to read it through, to grasp the many nuances of action he or she will have to embody for the camera.[1] In Scene 22 I shall be meeting a person for the first time, in a hotel bar, over cocktails. In Scene 184 I shall be naked in bed with that person. In Scene 225 that person will put a bullet between my eyes.

Thus, regardless of the order in which scenes are finished in principal photography, while Scene 22 is being played the actor will act as though entirely without consciousness of, entirely without regard for—even without a hint to—what is to be done in 184 and 225. In 225, the actor facing that gun will be playing a character whose characterological "life" earlier on, in Scene 22, at that bar, had a certain removed quality (that we shared), therefore a character, now, who remembers that bar back then, that introductory moment, that first drink. The performing aspect can be simple: as memory in action can be shown only through insert shots; the

---

[1] Speaking to Jeffrey Brown about his stage performance as Atticus Finch in *To Kill a Mockingbird* (Shubert Theater, December 13, 2018), Jeff Daniels made the explicit point that after as much as two years' intense labor thinking through the character, learning all the lines, imagining one's way into the story, his method was to jettison all that as he walked onstage. Éric Rohmer was reputed to use a similar technique when he went on scene to shoot. One has it all, very securely, very intensively, and then one just walks on without it.

remembering character looks exactly like a character not remembering. When shooting 22, the actor knows that later on in the story he or she will be "remembering this," that this scene will found later action that the actor can have known about in advance and can be thinking of all through the work, can be ready for.

While characters tumble from experience to experience, and tumble notably if they are to be believable, actors take calculated steps; they know what is going to happen before it happens; they see the dot on the horizon.

Yet none of this presents exceptional difficulty on set because no matter their training, in practice actors work existentially, living out the moment as characters. They must be present in the moment, however it is designed, and must summon the energy appropriate to the moment, the attitude, the posture, and the emotional tone. If one concentrates on what is appropriate for the present scene, earlier and later scenes will not matter since the chain of appropriatenesses, scene by scene, is in the script. Thus proceeds the systematized work of the actor. But beneath that systematized work is a person, who brings a living self to the job, one whose living self is recorded, in fact. The film is a record of the action of living selves. The person beneath the actor beneath the character knows what is going on in a more complex way than his labor calls for.

How does the performer cheat the story as a whole by managing a clear-cut focus on a present moment, when he or she in fact knows more than a present moment can show? Where does the performer lay away and store the knowledge of the full script, which knowledge must never be allowed in any one scene to come fully into play? As we are looking at knowledge, not artifacts of knowledge (tape recordings, jpegs), the storage can be nowhere but inside the performative body, the selfsame body in living action before the lens. The actor's task, then, is to establish and maintain a vital bifurcation at work. The character shares the actor's body, on and off— the actor's *whole* body—but must be constrained not to share the actor's whole consciousness. The character must have a consciousness apart from the performer's, a way of knowing, a storehold of awarenesses, an expertise, a history of experience, a plan for the future. The character must give the impression of being as much a person as the performer is when not at work performing, a whole and rounded person, with the only exception that very unlike the performer the character can be terminated at will and revivified later, at will again. At the curtain call, night after night, or by means of the closing credit scrawl, the character will be excused. But the performer who made that character will not sleep quite yet, the finale being part of the performance. Performers are, and must be, very awake as they work. The performer cheats the viewer's awareness by being fully present at every dramatic moment while pretending successfully not to be. While pretending to be someone else who is fully present, now in this moment closed off to time.

3

Narrative Transparency

FIGURE 3 Blow-Up *(Michelangelo Antonioni, MGM, 1966)*, David Hemmings in far background.

It is not only the past that believable characters access onscreen. They also travel forward, relentlessly, and sometimes there is a remarkable occurrence: the beings we are watching even seem to pass through the fourth wall, cross the axis, so that they gain a point of view remarkably similar to what has been afforded to us in our seats. Point of view: knowledge, awareness, curiosity. Note that a character suddenly sharing a viewer's knowledge is not at all the same as a viewer suddenly sharing a character's.[1] We can note

---

[1] A condition outlined thoroughly by Thomas Scheff, and discussed here in Chapter 5.

the strangeness of the effect when a character seems to have recognized that in general viewers are jumping from place to place (having been made to jump), and now, hinting at where he is intending to be, aids us by leaping ahead, by being prepared to offer greeting as he arrives: we are not following the action, categorically speaking, because in this case when Joe or Helen moves from A to B we find ourselves at B beforehand. The character action is following us. And by rights, as we think, it should: if we have jumped forward to meet the character on arrival, he or she had best arrive where we wait. (How wondrous, yet how inexplicable, it might seem if we were to jump to a location where, next, nothing happened.)

An elegant example of the "transparent" jump can be found in Michelangelo Antonioni's *Blow-Up* (1966). There is a charming old junk shop in southeast London, full of dusty treasures and enticing darkness. Outside is a paved road leading up an easy slope toward a park. The entrance to this park, as we can easily see, has tall trees with slender dark trunks, side by side. A young photographer who has been scouting the junk shop goes outside to catch a breath of air and starts, quite naturally for him, to photograph the place, snip snap, snip snap, slowly backing away and up the little rise toward the park but without seeing where his body is headed. Snip. Snap. Snap. Snap.

We CUT.

We are now inside the park looking out at that little street, with the photographer's back turned our way and four trees directly in front of us, separating us from him and the world outside. He turns our way, detects the park, and walks up into it.

To make a conventional cut here, the editor would have lingered on the photographer in the street until he stopped shooting and turned around: turn the other way, see the park, then head up the rise to gain access. At some instant just before he reached the entrance we would have cut to the inside, now to be with him as he goes in—cutting inside only on the cusp of his movement. His motion would lead the cut. Here, however, we see the park before he does. We see it behind him, dwarfing him, enticing, beckoning. We are enticed by the beautiful trees, waving in the wind, so green. We want to go in there. The filmmaker (and his camera) permit us to do what we crave to do. The character comes to "know" where we are, as it were, and moves to join us. *Our desire* leads the cut.

In this way a character can behave as though he knows what we know about the circumstances—what we know from watching this film of which that character is unknowingly a part. It is not, after all, because we are there that we spy that park. In a routine, obvious, and unannounced way characters very generally open out action in front of audiences who are watching action open out, and in doing this can be said to share if not perspective at least sensibility. But here, in a specifically invoked way, a way "out of the ordinary," a character has knowledge that seems impossible or odd, surely eerie, except for the silent intervention of forces on the other side of the camera (and the other side of the screen). On the other side of the screen is to be found that viewer, divided away from the character (so that the character's pains do not become the viewer's). A sharing on the character's part of the viewer's knowledge, an awareness of where the viewer is about to be, of where he should travel in order to meet the viewer's (important) gaze, can happen only if the veil of "the screen" becomes temporarily permeable or, as I am calling it, transparent.[2] Through the screen, as it were, the character can sense us, see our moves, divine our desires, and sympathize. *Narrative transparency*. This is a cheat, of course. Arrangements have been made so that events will appear to unfold this way. As "our" camera has brought us forward in space and time, the character "magically arrives" to be met by us instead of captaining the action; and sometimes this odd dance plays out when the new (second) location is by no means obvious from the old (first) one. *Blow-Up* is a good example. The photographer did not at first appear to see the park at all, was not enchanted as we were in watching it behind his back, and could with equal diegetic logic, if he got tired shooting the junk shop, just as easily walk to his car and drive off. It wasn't a guaranteed conclusion that he would head our way. In film the character can always go "anywhere" but almost always directs herself in a way we must wait to understand. In *narrative transparency*, the character seems to have read the script and thus know in advance: this is transparency because not only can characters not read the script; they do not even know there is a script. Wondrously, moving to the spot where we wait presents no difficulties for her to overcome. Very briefly, perhaps for only a flash, it is as though he or she knows the audience—knows that an audience is there and knows the "self" of that audience, but the character must also know that the audience is watching a movie, *this* movie. This movie made by actors. Consequentially, it is as though the character knows the actor who is underneath. Apparently, both we and the actor—first we and then the actor—moved according to some plan available only on this side of the camera. We followed a friendly camera, and the actor knew how to go in our tracks.

Another version:

As part of an unfolding story—say a crime mystery—we are transported to examine the inside of a character's house or apartment. Prowling around there with our chum the camera, we discover all the boring normalities that make lives interchangeable to some degree: room hooked to room, certain interesting pieces of furniture, a sofa, a bed, a table lamp. But lo and behold, what's this?: a secret hiding place! A little nook behind the sugar jar. Fascinating! But we'd

---

[2]A transparency that goes beyond the organized puncturing invoked by Michel Chion in his book *La toile trouée*, a structuring phenomenon that gives viewers intimate access to characters' worlds. In *narrative transparency* a character has (appears to have) access to a viewer's.

better not linger too long (it somehow being the case that while we puttered around the kitchen there was no threat of the inhabitant returning but the moment we set finger into the secret chamber the return is imminent!). We have discovered the secret spot, at any rate, have gone where no one but the absent resident has gone before. We've made a step. Imagine now that we leave the scene and the film action continues. Later on, another character, one we recognize (but who, like a typical character, does not know we exist) and also someone we know as being a hunter after the secret object, gains access to the same apartment, on whatever narrative pretext, but immediately she is inside the door, instead of puttering around drawers and cabinets and under beds as we did, proceeds straight to the secret spot we found earlier, the spot we found only after considerable hunting. The discoverer shares our secret hunting diary, as it were, reads our notes that exist only "out there, beyond the screen," all in the interest of moving the story along. The detective finding the door to the hero's secret laboratory, just quickly enough to stop the murder about to take place there but far too quickly for someone who has never been there before. Take the townspeople in 1931 intuiting where to find Frankenstein's monster, up in the rocky crags.

A subtler variation of the narrative transparency cheat is used de rigueur in chase sequences, all of which, from the Keystone Kops to *Bullitt* (1968) and *6 Underground* (2019) and beyond, depend on some pursuer P hot on the trail of some evader E, moving, most often, through a fascinating warren of architectural forms urban, exotic, or labyrinthine. One need hardly catalog the celebrated chase sequences in James Bond films, which form but a microcosm within the catalog. As P(ursuer) races after E(vader), a number of considerations come into play:

- Pursuer cannot catch up to Evader too soon, for two reasons. The catch is the end of the chase, and the pleasure of watching demands prolongation as much as the proportions of the narrative can make possible. But also, if P catches E somewhat easily, then E is evidently not so spirited or talented an evader, probably doesn't merit the extravagance of the chase at all, *in the audience's eyes*. This is not a diegetic issue, since in any chase-style diegesis E will always seem to merit being chased by P simply *on the face of it*: the chase is happening, P is eager to have E and shows the eagerness; E's flight shows the hunger for freedom (Chuck Jones's *Road Runner* cartoons). For the viewer to have a sporting thrill, P and E must be reasonably matched. But the catch-up must be held off for a further, quite dominant reason: because, in the end, the chase is not about the catch, because the P-E inter-relation is not about the value of E to P or to the audience, the actual moment of the catch, if it comes, can be as deflating as it is satisfying (as would happen in *Bullitt* without a fireball explosion adding hot sauce to the soup).

- Neither P nor E can sustain an injury or succumb to an accident that vitiates the chase. Accidents must have, as in music, only *accidental* weight. See the Monte Carlo racing sequence in John Frankenheimer's *Grand Prix* (1966), where the cars represent P1, P2, P3, and so on, and the E figure is the finish line. When one of the cars goes off the track in a horrible crash, the others just keep chasing, and attention to the destruction can come only after the race is done. The chase outstrips all other action. More: as a rhythmic continuity the chase, not the catch, being the audience's pleasure, nothing can curtail the chase. Cutting it off for reasons however logical—say, a thunderstorm is making it impossible for P to see E in the heavy rain—nevertheless makes the filmmaker's invocation of the chase format seem ill-advised in retrospect (since both the chase and the thunderstorm are the filmmaker's doing). Why invoke a process (that is extraordinarily expensive, dangerous, tricky to manage, and fraught with difficulty) only to throw it away?
- Neither P nor E can behave as though the eccentricities of the locale are non-existent since only a locale with eccentricities establishes a chase as dramatic (and, as per Ruskin, Romantic). The eccentricities are all. Watch the *parkour* chase in *District B13* (*Banlieue 13* [2004]). The complicated apartment-complex environment acts as a resistance to the electrical flow of E who flashes by in the lead, with P (a gang) following: slammed doors, slick corridor halls, other people's bedrooms, transoms, window escapes, leaps from rooftop to rooftop. Without eccentric resistance, the chase is only two mad figures running. Interestingly, if the setting is featured but entirely disattended by P and E, the filmmaker looks silly. If it is disattended or altogether elided by the filmmaker, so that the chase is an interlocking and alternating series of medium close-ups of individual speeders, then the chase makes reference only to the stamina, courage, and spiritual powers of each individual; but for this sort of interaction, some kind of battle, contained and carefully staged, is more apt to show proper diegetic action than a chase would be.

The chase form will work effectively whether or not the purpose of the pursuit is made clear, whether or not we know which of the two participants, if either, means harm, or which could do more harm, and indeed whether or not we are gaining access to the full circumstances. One of the format requirements of James Bond films is a pre-credit chase sequence of astonishing speed, athleticism, derring-do, and difficulty placed in one or more environments of spectacular bizarreness or unlikeliness; the context, if given at all, will come only (much) later. The chase alone is enough, P after E, P after E again, P still after E, P closing in on E with increasing odds of success or increasing odds of failure or no perceptible odds at all. Not P after E *because*; not P after E *lest*; not *in order that*, or *owing to the fact that*, or even *catering to the whims of Z, the powerful third party*. Only P after E, nothing more. Method is relatively immaterial, too. Run by foot, drive by car, fly by helicopters, ski on a steep slope, what have you. P in pursuit of E, P wanting to possess E, the formula of capitalism. P *after* E, P wanting to do E damage, the formula of retribution.[3] A good example begins *On Her Majesty's Secret Service* (1969).

The film chase is a chain of narrative transparencies, typically, since we do not follow P (and very often not even E) but stand where they are about to be so that they can arrive after us. (As though they are but pretending to a chase, so that we can be entertained!) Now a fourth consideration:

- P and E do the dramatic event no courtesies by disappearing from view no matter how hard they struggle, no matter how hungry each is to succeed. We have to see because the chase isn't for them, it isn't for P who needs to corner E, it isn't for E who needs to evade P, it's for us.

And here arrives the fundamental cheat of the form. As far as the choreographic design is concerned, P's hunt for E will seem believable only if E is evasive, in short, if E is given plenty of opportunity to change direction, find alleyways, jump over fences, migrate through cramped spaces, fling himself into the air, dart around laundry hanging on the line, all of these obstacles unexpected and unforeseen by P. But in order that we may see these escapades, *the camera must foresee first*. (Foresee position, lens, lighting requirements, focal problems.) Must establish us there before the character comes. Must force the character to intuit where to be next (to peek at the script).

One can twist this examination yet further. Even in scenes that are not chase scenes, just simply dramatic encounters running one after another, the elements of the film are arranged in something like a chase, events constantly being pursued by characters, and here, too, we must always be placed for an ideal view. As Donald Crafton writes, it is possible to be "using the term Chase metaphorically, suggesting the linear trajectory of the narrative in general, not a specific instance" (111). One could argue it is through narrative transparency that we manage to see all of the cinematic story, since we are enabled to leap ahead of the action without noting the cheat: the action seems to be cannily following us. The pursuit sequence models what normally happens before the camera but with all the stakes raised, all the conditions extrematized for high visibility.

---

[3]What Kenneth Boulding called the exchange system and the threat system (Personal conversation, October 1966).

Before any character "knows" how to commit an action (to the extent that we can imagine a character knowing), knows where to sit, knows what to eat, knows what street to walk or race down, knows what flight to take to Tijuana, the camera must know because the camera will be there first. But no sign will be given of this foreknowledge, save that it will result in the successful vision. No character will acknowledge a bond with the camera, even in face-to-lens moments such as abound in *Alfie* (1966) where the (Michael Caine) face is aimed only at a non-lens or with Matthew Broderick's categorical adorableness in *Ferris Bueller's Day Off* (1986), but character thoughts can never seem bonded to production contingencies. The script must cheat the fact that it is always one step ahead.

Without being one step ahead, it cannot function as a script. And without being one step ahead the camera would show nothing but a kind of afterimage.

By contrast, if we know the camera is one step ahead, if somewhere it actually tells us it is—*Hello! Watch how I always know where to go!*—the tension and thrill are leached out of the film.

The more elaborate the territory, the more pitfalls it contains, the more apartments are in the corridor, the more narrow the transoms above their doors, the more restricted or even obstructed the alleyways with barbed wire fences at the end, the more contrived will seem the camera's canny placements, and thus the more artificial will seem our easy ability to see clearly—always to see clearly, even too clearly—how the character daringly moves. Yet without elaboration, territory becomes flat and tedious, fades off, and the strength of the character(s) takes over. In this light compare *District B13*, with David Belle's fabulous precarious parkour maneuvers and Manuel Teran's marvelously sentient camera, with Cornel Wilde's *The Naked Prey* (1965), where in an extended and breathless sequence an almost naked victim must flee barefoot across the African landscape while a group of marksmen, ceremonially clad and bearing sharp spears, chase after him as their prey. With both, the P-E shot sequence model is fully in use, especially involving a "sentient" camera that always knows how to signal the character where it will be, but the dangerous eccentricity in *B13* signals the technique spatially and the signals in *Prey* are characterological.

As any instant of narrative transparency could easily be a dangerous reflection of the audience to itself (the character playing to a camera; the camera rendering the picture to the viewer), it is typically edited with distracting visual discontinuity and accompanied by pulsing and exciting musical cues, also composite elements of the cheat. The character's "reading the production from behind" functions unceasingly while being unceasingly out of view.

4

The Cheating Cut

FIGURE 4 *Orson Welles in* Citizen Kane *(Orson Welles, RKO, 1941)*.

If any and every edit is a kind of cheat, undetected or unaffirmed by audiences *as itself* while they buy into the seamlessness promised by production grammar, it leads us to shift, with calculated ease, away from what we are looking at presently and from the position in narrative space we occupy in that looking. As we know well, yet do not acknowledge, there is no way to effect such easy movement other than by way of a camera-eye that moves, that is, through some effect of the filmmaking. A camera-eye that moves, which is to say, a mechanical and logical arrangement for moving the camera, some invisible and tightly planned production involving such as shots, lights, ancillary personnel, a divided script, a developing character—all the things we would prefer to claim we have no truck with while we watch and become caught up by the film. Not only that editing is set to be invisible (as it is); but that editing-set-to-be-invisible *is invisible*. And finally the moving camera—its being, its motion—is read onto the character. And actors are aware of this.

Almost all narrative film is edited, made up of numerous shots that are hooked together (on historical variations in the length of shots, see Bordwell). The shooting script is a kind of manual for fashioning the various parts that will be collected to make the film.[1] In watching a film we agree to move discreetly and unconsciously from one isolated shot to another and in moving to understand the character as moving and being moved to move. *Discreetly and unconsciously*, as in "without acknowledging our own action" (as it is prompted and made possible by what shines on the screen to be seen). We effectively move through the story, but we move thinking ourselves stationary and imagining that it is the story that moves. The fiction of cinema demands that we digest and neglect our own motion without comment, even when, as with the Moscow chase in Paul Greengrass's *The Bourne Supremacy* (2004), the shot transitions are lightning fast, even in some instants unperceivable (quarter-second) blurs. In refusing to comment on our own motion we deny it. As long as we seem ready to play by the rules of this game of secrecy, editors can reasonably expect us to put up with any transition however outlandish, our only alternative being an open (and sullying) doubt as to how one could get there from here, so quickly and with no obstruction, no traffic jam.[2]

Of course the cheater who behaves with extravagant panache will not only go scot free but also gain immense credibility as a genius, the unnoted discontinuity he or she may have presented, the chasm across which one leaps, showing off as a kind of triumphant battle scar after the unforgiving turmoil of creative work. Three marvelous edit cheats, forward motion accomplished so effortlessly it seems as natural as rain, with each of these standing upon, evidencing a script built to support it and give it display. One can write for cinema with full knowledge that the camera's jumping is a standard possibility. One can write with the invisible pen.

---

[1]The "Building an Interocitor" sequence at the beginning of *This Island Earth* (1955) is a chilling, but also wholly entertaining comment on breakdowns and constructions, multiple parts for making unified wholes. Underneath both this rendition and the studio process itself is Durkheim's "organic solidarity" (*Division* Ch. III).

[2]Excepting the one the diegesis imposes, of course at a critical moment. See *The Taking of Pelham One Two Three* (1974).

- *Citizen Kane* (1941; ed. Robert Wise). Humiliated and rejected by his wife Susan Alexander (Dorothy Comingore), who has (stridently and proudly) walked out on him, Kane enters her fabulous bedroom at the fabulous castle Xanadu and fully trashes it. There he comes upon his tiny snow globe and picks it up thoughtfully. He stumbles through the door and into the hall, where his majordomo (Paul Stewart) and servants stand anxiously waiting. Staggering, his legs like lead, he moves past them down a long hallway. We see his reflection, tiny in an immense inset wall mirror to screen right. *Then an improbable cut that somehow seems probable.* We have jumped several leaden steps ahead of Kane. He is approaching the camera from the left and around a curve, still staggering, his eyes beads of darkness, and as the camera in its new position gently pans rightward with him we follow the body passing in front of what seems a hall of giant mirrors (an effect produced by one mirror on each side of the hall, although the one behind us isn't visible). Kane appears now in boundless recursion,[3] one mirror cameo inside another inside another inside another, retreating forever and to infinity. In every one of them he is striding, beat . . . beat . . . beat . . . beat . . . beat . . . beat . . . beat . . . beat . . . beat . . . beat. The image of Kane as a multiple self, the unboundedly puissant Charles Foster Kane (Orson Welles), populating his own little universe—an Orson Welles universe, of course—all of these Kanes stepping in unison like an army on the march. An army on the march against the enemy, She of No Faith, or the outside world with its caustic gaze, or anyone who might pity him, anyone who might come to know his awful secret.[4]

But that apparently unobtrusive cut *from* the long shot of Kane walking away from us and down the corridor, his tiny reflection stalwart if wooden at right, *to* the shot of him stumbling forward *toward* the camera which will discover the hall of mirrors: the cut that confers upon Kane the inevitability of his multiplicity, that shows him marching toward a future—that cut is telltale, outlandish. Why? Because it is another thing altogether to offer a straight continuity of motion, a pickup of the moving man to follow him stepping along, and indeed the promise of "straight continuity" is what operates as a pretext for the cut. Kane moves, stay with Kane. Keep following

---

[3]Interestingly, perhaps strangely, this recursion was pictured as well, and in the same year, using Joan Crawford, in George Cukor's *A Woman's Face* (with cinematography by Robert Planck); then paid homage by Jean-Pierre Melville using Charles Vanel in his *L'aîné des Ferchcaux* (1963).

[4]Yet at the same time a scathing Wellesian reference to *Triumph des Willens* (1935) and thus allusion to the model for his character, William Randolph Hearst, as a Nazi sympathizer.

him, see what he becomes. But here, the second shot is a whole new world, in effect a whole new destination, as though in a new dimension, something marvelous in itself, something unexpected and unexpectable, calculated to give the viewer a chill and a thrill: quickly, blatantly, with quaver and reverberation. The shots until this have been cut together to follow action and characterological feeling: Kane amok in the bedroom, Kane stunned in the doorway, Kane jerking away from the scene of the crime (this bedroom has been his trysting place with Susan, no doubt), Kane dropping away from the servants down the vacuous hall. Complete coherence, even logic, and aesthetic sensibility, too. Then suddenly a jump to a perspective that is nothing short of galvanizing. An entire camera and lighting crew, among many others, had to be at work in order to effect this magic, and for the editor Robert Wise still more work, to effect the transition in such a way that no one would notice.[5]

Galvanizing from Luigi Galvani (1737–98), who was fascinated with the body's transmission of, and susceptibility to, electricity. Bioelectromagnetic pioneer. Feeling and sentiment, the muscles (of expression) as electrical. Medical electricity. The Galvanic idea is that electricity is resident in the body itself, whether or not the body is stimulated from an outside source. Seeing the Kane-mirror shot we have a *frisson* of pleasure and wonder, a jolt, and so we can say the shot is galvanizing. Yet our principal character Kane is clearly on the verge of a fugue at this point, rigid of posture, robotic even, and silent because all his language (he was a newspaper baron) is now swallowed in catatonia. The galvanization is in the viewer, not the character. Kane in the bedroom, Kane in the doorway, Kane in the corridor . . . all electrically disconnected, but then, in a cut that audiences accept without questioning, even without detecting for what it is, Kane as the depleted and progressively shrinking doll, *our* doll, the doll that with a jolt jumps away from, and into, itself. A focus of vision, surely; but in the mirror shot there is no one to look at him but the viewer outside, who looks at the whole.

An ominous musical cue helps create the ersatz effect of the earlier shots being blended, through transition, into the mirror shot, but while it develops the action, while it expands and enriches our sense of Kane's world, nevertheless that mirror shot is not about Kane as much as it is about our thrill in observation. It works as what Tom Gunning, writing of early

---

[5] I can only notice in the way that legion scholars and cinephiles notice such things nowadays, freezing a frame to study it, repeating a movement over and over and over, reading about it perhaps, certainly not being forced by circumstance, as the viewers in 1941 were, to grab whatever I could get as the movie rolled on, rolled even away from the theater and into what would have seemed then like obscurity. After initial screenings and subsequent B-exhibition in smaller venues months later, the form was that a film would simply "go," and viewers had no way at all to retrieve it until the videotape revolution of the 1970s, if then.

cinema, termed an "attraction." It seizes us improbably and draws us (away from the story plane) into a reverie.

The design here was effected by the filmmaker in consultation with his editor, his cinematographer, and his designer, because the jump shot depends entirely on the structure of the set, which had to be conjured in advance and also tested to be sure a precise effect could be given. Welles, then, with Wise, Gregg Toland, and Van Nest Polglase. Welles as performer, too, because thinking back we can see that the slow stumbling gait, the jerky hesitations, are all in place so that at the instant Kane comes in front of the mirrors he can seem to pause there (for breath, for reflection, for inspiration) thus aggrandizing our thrill at his endlessly recursive chain of selves.

- *The Long, Long Trailer* (1954; ed. Ferris Webster). Comedic pratfalls generally work through a strange admixture of narrative transparency (see Chapter 3) and character self-abasement. When a joke is set up elaborately we follow along with keen attention, eager to know in what direction we are being led for the explosive finale. We don't foresee that finale (the joke would "fall flat" if we did), but we march along desiring it and sensing its approach. For the joke to work keenly, the punch has to be unpredictable from the set-up, not so very unpredictable as to elude comprehension but not so predictable, either, as to fit comprehension too well.[6] A "bad joke," in fact, is one for which the listener or viewer can see the punch far too soon, even soon enough to imagine or state it before it happens. With comedy film, as with all film but here more expressly, more flamboyantly, we happily take a ride toward a future we do not know. *But the successful ride depends on a shift of scene.*

The successful ride takes us somewhere else, a destination entirely missing from the map. In slapstick, this movement is decidedly physical, throwing the body of the performer into turmoil but also terminating the present performer/viewer "voyage" in an entirely unanticipated way. But when something is unanticipated it surprises; and when something is a surprise it comes to consciousness. The filmmaker's cheat here is to bring off the slapstick surprise without conveying to the viewer that he is bringing off a slapstick surprise, to cause explosive surprise without permitting awareness by the surprised viewer that she is surprised. The viewer must therefore find some astounding strength to be present for the punch, call it the ability to leap, without knowing it. This means, finally, leaping without knowing how the figure onscreen makes the leap, since the viewer's attention is contractually bound to the character. As Goffman writes,

---

[6] For discussing punch lines with me I am grateful to Alex Clayton and Tom Hemingway.

> If the onlookers laugh when the clown suddenly finds himself falling like a stone it is because they had all along been projecting their musculature and sensibilities sympathetically into his walk and now find that their leaning into his anticipated conduct, into the anticipated guidedness of his doings, their framed prediction of what is to come, is disordered. (*Frame Analysis*, 381)

How does the character manage to travel to the punch, the new location apparently unplanned and unforeseen at the beginning—but still, of course, intensively planned, intensively foreseen, for the benefit of the actor and that of the camera, which must permit the audience to be there to receive the character when he arrives? This is where the narrative transparency comes into play. The character must somehow be reading the audience's mind (the audience/the camera), the traveling mind that lets the camera ride away with it. The camera is the script, so, weirdly if unnoticeably, the audience has access to the script. But now, apparently, so does the character.

As is known albeit forgotten: while actors have deep access to the script the characters they play have none. For the characters, indeed, there is no script; no camera; no audience; only plastic space and time. This is a space-time in which it is not so very easy to believe. Our thought keeps dropping back to the actor with her script, with her plans, with her foreknowledge of the scene, and must be cheated if pleasure is to ensue.

The character's apparent foreknowledge (assuming that we can countenance a character having knowledge of any kind!)—the impression we could have, were we to consider the situation quite fully, that the character had somehow read the filmmaker's mind, because at some punch line even if the floor is pulled away from the character still the character found that floor first—might reveal itself in numerous ways beyond his or her appearing in a distal location to be met by the camera. A character could appear in a proximal location, even in the same location, but, time having passed, in a way especially idealized for camera, posing as she would never have posed in other circumstances. The change of state, as it were, is the jump forward. And in that renovated pose, a character could deliver an action not only fresh and unheralded but one that the camera was ideally placed to see, an action that would lose all its oomph were it to be seen from any other place. The pose-to-camera is found through transparency, but more: when we see this climactic pose, when we respond by exploding into a laugh or a gasp, the thing as a configuration and a design will seem quite inevitable, although previously it was unimagined, improbable. Improbable inevitability.

The telling case is Desi and Lucy. Desi Arnaz and Lucille Ball, two catastrophes waiting to happen, as viewers in the 1950s happily knew. An urban couple, they have acquired a long, long trailer and set off to see the majestic countryside. They know nothing of maneuvering a trailer, and little more about driving altogether. Many hilarious and precipitous escapes line up (Vincente Minnelli going over the top with set-up jokes), including one in which Desi goes apoplectic trying to back the trailer into a suburban driveway. Finally, thrillingly and relievedly on the road, Lucy has decided to make a fancy dinner while he drives. Beef ragout, some kind of white cake iced with gentility, a Caesar Salad (in a huge bowl: "You don't cut the lettuce, you *tear* the lettuce!"). She is dressed in a lovely dark green full-length dress, looking a little like a Caesar Salad herself—a nifty foreshadowing. We know things have to go wrong—this is Desi and Lucy! He is up front idiotically singing: he believes himself an operatic tenor, and is bellowing nonsense news: "We're having beeeef ragouuuut! And Cae-e-e-e-esar Sal-l-l-l-l-l-l-ad!" The road is bumpy, the trailer rocks, left right, up down. Lucy is challenged, to put it mildly. The lettuce is flying out of the salad bowl, especially when, having cracked in two raw eggs, she makes to toss it by hand. Soon it is on the floor, and also on her head, and the cupboard door has flown open so that all the foodstuffs are flying out, unlimited quantities of white flour spraying all over her and mixing with the salad moisture to make a kind of sticky dough that clings to her hands and dress as, with increasing desperation (and increasing energy), she careens, slips, twists, jerks, and collapses around the trailer. (Nobody but Lucille Ball could do this so magnificently, not even, I beg to say, Chaplin.) But now for the silent punch. The camera "discovers" her in a tableau moment, body dumped up against a corner like a sack of flour itself, shoulders slumped in vivid now-splotched green, legs spread helplessly, head dangling as though from strings: she is a giant marionette. Her eyes look into the lens beckoning and surrendering (as in a Warner Bros. cartoon). And the body is positioned perfectly at frame-center, a frame in which the food detritus is reduced so that only defeated, deflated Lucy is visible as content. It is as though she has collapsed with intent here, just in order to be seen this way in a feature shot. The feature shot is the joke's payoff.

But there is *more*:

As we look at her in pity, from screen left the trailer door flies open and Desi pops in to say, with exquisite inanity, "Is everything all right, Lucy?," whereupon with her left hand (screen right) she quite suddenly plants what looks like a cream pie in his face. (We realize it is the remainder of the cake.) Not only was the scene constructed for a beautiful (and beautifully messy) portrait of (beautifully messy) Lucy, it was constructed ideally to show the whipped-cream gag from the perfect angle—one that gives complete access to not only the goo but also Desi's stupefied surprise. A payoff's payoff.

Here again, choreography is kept out of view and beyond suspicion. Were viewers to see arrangements, the sort of arrangements necessary for setting up this long final shot with its two-beat conclusion, the delightful haphazardness of the action would dissolve. It is Lucy's foibles apparently occurring without (or against) plan that makes them funny. What is cheated is the arrangement of action for camera, not some aspect of the action itself (since the moment we see Lucy with food we intuit that she is going to become food). The scene is a little dance, with the finale chord being the concluding pose. And the camera, we see too late, was dancing, too.

- *2001: A Space Odyssey* (1968; ed. Ray Lovejoy). One of the supremely celebrated and much-recognized edits in cinema history, for which almost no description is required. In prehistoric times, Moonwatcher (Dan Richter), a violent ape who has just picked up a tapir bone from a skeleton and brandished it as a (first) weapon now hurls it up into the sky, and just after the white rectangle reaches its apogee and begins its descent POOF! it magically turns into a white rectangular spaceship against a black star field. Robert Kolker describes it vividly:

  > The bone-white spaceship falls gracefully in the interstellar ballet that synchronizes its movements with that of the space station. Johann Strauss's waltz "The Blue Danube" plays on the sound track—nineteenth-century music accompanying twenty-first century space technology. Death (the bone) seems to give way instantly to life—the exciting future of space travel. (611)

Not only death-into-life but time-against-time. A leap forward several million years in a jump cut. To see the transparency here, consider the ship—which for the moment is the protagonist—as a sentient entity (surely it represents advanced sentience) that not only cruises through hyperspace as we find it but acknowledges itself to have been cruising through time, through eons, now both sensing the dramatic irony of this fact and adjudging the precise spot to find itself where our camera will be, so that the irony can be hammered home. (Punch line.) Imagine the cut if there was no object-on-object match . . . ! Not only does Kubrick know this spaceship, this spaceship knows Kubrick. This conjunction is achieved through nothing less than editorial acumen, since the ship must be picked up at a particular point in the rectangle and matched with the bone at a corresponding point in order for the magical metamorphosis to seem believable: these are, after all, two distinct pieces of film, each of which was framed independently. Man's long journey from the exceedingly primitive to the technically advanced, curtained off in a split-second metaphor by an edit foretold in the script. How fortunate for the aesthetically hungry viewer, and for the ship as star of a hilarious ironic moment, that the camera just happens to be present and ready to make the match, as the plans predicted it would.

* * *

Conventional sequential editing—the editing together of the pieces of a single sequence of actions—has a progressive grammar, with the shots following one another more or less as the movement within them dictates, notwithstanding that inserts can be added. A character reaches a stairway; the character is seen climbing the stairs; the character reaches the top of the stairs. With each successive shot added on, there is instigated no particular surprise that the character having been located in the previous shot now appears in this one: the action itself is taken to make a dictate. With narrative transparency, ensuing action is not logically probable and so when the camera jumps for a position to see, it jumps as a result of the director's dictate, and the character's arrival is finally, effectively, in response to the jumping camera. This, simply, is why I see it as a situation in which the character sees through the production wall to the camera itself. The editing in narrative transparency hides, as it were, beneath the grammar of conventional sequential editing, which shapes most of the film space we see and also our steadily ongoing expectation.

5

Narrative Opacity

FIGURE 5 *Outside London's Royal Albert Hall in* The Man Who Knew Too Much *(Alfred Hitchcock, Paramount, 1956).*

We may consider *narrative opacity* to be a condition in which the actual or potential establishment of narrative transparency is itself pointed to overtly and directly, a pulling back to reveal a magic now completed or a magic that, entirely within the magician's power, is held back. But this pointing undetectably cheats the coverage of something else, as in the recursive conundrum where revealing something to have been revealed hides that the revealing of the revealing is not being revealed. "Here!" the filmmaker can seem to whisper; "here is what you may have recognized as 'narrative transparency,' but look at me using it quite intentionally, without covering it up, to produce a particular effect regarding which there *is* something I'm covering, something else you don't know." Although I have looked at it before (see *Man*), here is another peek at the much-celebrated Albert Hall concert sequence in Hitchcock's *The Man Who Knew Too Much* (1956); it works upon a signal narrative opacity.

We are placed ahead of her to see Jo McKenna (Doris Day) arrive breathlessly at London's Royal Albert Hall: narrative transparency. She has been advised that Scotland Yard's Inspector Buchanan (Ralph Truman) will be found there and she is desperate to see him for assistance in finding her kidnapped son, who is tucked away she-doesn't-know-where. At this point, Jo is relatively uninterested in the concert program tonight. Her missing son is all she is thinking about, and also Buchanan, who might be able to discover where he is.

However:

We are interested in that program, and in the pertinent fact that it is to be performed here at this place and tonight. While it could possibly seem as though transparency is in play, with Jo "knowing" and "being interested" just as we are, because she arrives just at the place where we already wait to find her (at the drive-in on Kensington Gore), nevertheless she is there for one reason and we have preceded her for quite another (our interest in the Hall having little to do with Buchanan and his presumable powers). Why do we care about the program, specifically the cantata that will be featured in it? Because we received—*but Jo did not*—a briefing about tonight's concert as, in an upstairs room at Ambrose Chapel, Drayton (Bernard Miles) played an excerpt for his hired assassin (Reggie Nalder) to make plain the precise musical cue for taking the decisive shot. There will be a downbeat at this concert tonight—*we know but Jo does not*—fatal and politically incendiary. Jo's arrival is based on reasoning *different from* our own when we arrive (and catch on an outside billboard that, as expected, the "Storm Clouds" cantata is to be performed). *Different reasoning*: note that in attending the rehearsal, "flies on the wall," we could easily presume a condition of narrative transparency, as we could find ourselves doing frequently in cinema without having conscious awareness: Jo, who is not here, is somehow reading our mind, or reading Drayton's mind, or reading the Assassin's mind, or reading Hitchcock's mind, *and learning the kill cue just as we are*. But no, Hitchcock goes to lengths to assure us that Jo is not doing that. Jo is not in the Chapel, nor anywhere near enough to learn what we learn. Hitchcock shows her outside in the street (in a complex and expensive matte composite). It is so easy to forget that the narrative flow involving Jo carries the story action forward from that street, where she is finally unable to convince the police there is trouble inside, to the Albert Hall, where she hopes to find Buchanan. The filmmaker's intention *for us* is that we are carried with the "rehearsal" in mind to the Hall where, unbeknownst to Jo and every other ticket buyer, the music that was "rehearsed" will be performed to dire consequence. Parallel tracks that do not meet—at least, not yet.

All of the clues in the Albert Hall sequence are double clues, then, directed in two separate vectors at the same time, one vector aimed toward [A] Jo on her Buchanan hunt, another toward [B] the musically informed viewer (one toward an observer who knows what the future will bring, "what will be"; one toward an observer who does not[1]):

- [i] When, in Kensington Gore, she moves past the poster into the lobby [A] Jo (the American tourist who, even earlier in life, as a famous performer, never gave a show here) is certifying to herself that yes, this is the Royal Albert Hall, the place where Buchanan will be; whereas [B] oblivious to Buchanan we are noting that this is the place where the cantata will be sung (and even, thanks to Hitchcock's considerateness in showing the poster, the names of those who will perform it).
- [ii] When in the lobby Jo encounters the Assassin (whom [A] she knows to be a strange man she saw at her hotel room door in Marrakech, but not an assassin, while [B] we know him for who he really is because we watched him "rehearse") and he threatens her with the life of her son, [A] she is made especially desperate to find Buchanan; whereas [B] we confirm to ourselves that the man who practiced with Drayton, and smirked intelligently at the man's condescension, is now here in front of us, fully equipped and ready.
- [iii] When Buchanan makes his (grand) entrance along with the portly visiting Prime Minister (Alexei Bobrinskoy) and his Ambassador (Mogens Wieth), [A] Jo thinks, "Oh yes!, there is Buchanan now! Maybe I could signal to him?"; but [B] we think, "Ahhh, that plump man in Buchanan's care is the target. Alive now, dead soon."
- [iv] When the music begins, [A] Jo is swept away by the flow of it, and more deeply anxious about her son and the fact that she couldn't talk to Buchanan, while [B] we are on track for the assassination shot, listening through the score (the script) for the right moment. Jo is not listening for a cue; she is listening to the music integrally. Were she as aware as we are that a killing is planned here, and that this cantata will trigger it, her lack of action

---

[1] An underpinning irony being that Jo McKenna (Jo Conway, the famous singer) *is* musically informed, thus a very particular member of this audience, perhaps even more knowledgeable than the viewer of the film, yet Hitchcock makes her musicality seem irrelevant for the moment. When the cantata begins, her response as a listener (to the orchestra under Bernard Herrmann and the singer Barbara Howitt) becomes far more sympathetic, far more musical in the quality of its sensitivity. The many other patrons are carefully shown sitting expressionless as statues (the intended victim notably included).

as she listens, undisturbed until her husband arrives, would be incomprehensibly deplorable, not worthy of a film's hero.

If in a more conventional development the ongoing story would have been transparent to Jo, if she would have raced up to the concert hall fully intending to block the concert, here it is kept opaque instead. We have a fully unobstructed window through which to examine the opacity she faces, and her facing it, if only we recollect and acknowledge the central gearing in the mechanism, our presence and Jo's absence at that "rehearsal."

Thomas Scheff writes of the "ladder of awareness" in narrative. The characters and the audience stand together, as it were, on various rungs of such a device, it being conceivable for us to stand on a higher rung than a principal character, on the same rung, or on a rung beneath. Similarly, each character can be placed with, above, or below other characters. In Hitchcock's *Vertigo* (1958), to offer an example that has provoked considerable discussion—Hitchcock being a real master of "ladder"ing—the audience is (shockingly) placed above the central protagonist at a key moment in the film, and must now wait in anxious suspense to see whether he will ascend to share their height or not; and if he does, what will happen. Given that this protagonist suffered horribly from fear of heights, as we have all too clearly seen, the narrative problem of him climbing or not climbing a "ladder" is metaphorized and complexified! Narrative opacity, as I am calling it, is essentially produced through a differential in the "height" of the audience and a key character, the separate knowledge that belongs to the audience being significantly different from the knowledge that belongs to the character not only in its content but in terms of how crucial it is for the narrative as a whole. In the Albert Hall sequence of *Man*, Jo finding Buchanan in the concert somewhere is far less crucial to events generally than what is going to happen with the music. She would never be able to credit this, but we know with certainty. Also, for fans of the film or fans of argument: when Jo *does* come to her senses about the assassination, she is obliged to keep firmly in mind what she was told in the lobby, that she'd better do nothing obstructive because her son's safety "will depend on *you* tonight!"

The opacity in this case is a script cheat. Two interesting reasons, one positive and one negative:

Negatively,

- Were Jo to know what we know about the Royal Albert Hall—essentially that it is the scene of a forthcoming tragedy—her behavior as the music played would have had to be different, and markedly so. She would have had to distinctively *notice* the billboard advertising the *telltale* cantata (and in order that the advertisement had meaning for her, she would have had to somehow overhear the rehearsal earlier, where we learn about the cantata for the first time and from which she was utterly excluded).

- She would have to have been much more suspicious of the man in the tuxedo. Not just a memorable face (an unforgettable face, Hitchcock knew) but a face from where? The only thing Jo ever saw this man do was politely speak at her hotel room door. Nor just politely. Exquisitely.
- Regarding Buchanan, she would have to have made some attempt to get the man's attention, rather than just timidly watching him ascend a staircase. "My son is in danger! There's going to be a killing! I've just seen the killer!"—all of which we fill in, and inaccurately. Her son is in danger, yes, surely, *but not here*. She knows there will be a killing *in London* but not here. She knows the gaunt-faced stranger is bizarre-looking, *yet he is also a textbook model of etiquette and only we know he is the killer*.
- And when the music started Jo would have to have attempted to do something to stop the proceedings, instead of riding along with the melodies as she does. Yet, do what? She has not put the pieces of the puzzle together, nor would we have done so had we not been treated to that "rehearsal." (Again: treated as Jo was not treated.) And in assembling the puzzle she would have to have been willing to sacrifice Hank, dismissively, coldly, because at least ostensibly she would have more care about the prime minister of a country she does not know. None of this is conceivable, given the details of Hitchcock's demonstrated logic.

Jo's being kept out of the picture cognitively and physically is an essential aspect of the film's composition.

And positively,

- The ironic thrill we obtain as the sequence rushes to its cadence partially grows out of our sudden awareness that Jo now knows what we knew all along, that the concert, Buchanan's presence, the assassin's shot, the intended victim (and the openness of all this to our sight) work together in a tightly composed and unbreakable knot, a knot threatening, with mounting amplitude of voice and quickening pace, to come apart. To our delight she is sharing our rung of the ladder, but has very little time to rest there (the editing shortens the shot lengths as the cantata finale approaches). Were we to have known from the outset that Jo either already knew all this or would soon enough discover it, that her awareness and ours were matched all along or very soon to be matched, all this excitement would escape like air from a punctured life raft, and the music itself, nine minutes and more of it, would have been little other than a tedious delaying mechanism.

One must appreciate Hitchcock's cagey staging at the "rehearsal." The villain facing a mirror and combing his (scant) hair. The Assassin lazily strapping on his holster.[2] All of this "backstage" behavior *Heimlich*, private, personal. And the wonderful trick of repetition. The shooting cue is repeated so the Assassin might hear it twice, since he is (quite erroneously) presumed by Drayton to be musically dense, and while this happens we get a close shot of Drayton's fingers placing the needle down carefully on the spinning recording.[3] Then, after the Assassin has gone off, Drayton, himself an enthusiast of either music or murder or both, plays the cue one more time for himself, now making a visible (not just acoustic) emphasis by dropping his hand, finger curled as around a trigger, in a conductor's downbeat.[4]

---

[2]As in the family scene at the detective's house early in Nicholas Ray's *On Dangerous Ground* (1951).
[3]For the reader born in the twenty-first century: he is using a 33 1/3 rpm vinyl recording on a turntable connected to a rudimentary built-in speaker. Such devices were almost as routinely available as laptop computers today.
[4]Miles shows exquisite musicality, because his downbeat is executed with the cleanest professionalism, although this moment is cheated, of course, since the music track can be back-synced to coincide with his downbeat—the very opposite of what is happening "live" in the Hall, one might think (but, of course, what we see there is not "live" performance). As *creator and director* of London's Mermaid Theatre, founded in St. John's Wood in 1951 then shifted to Blackfriars, he had in fact given the "downbeat" for numerous productions, not least of which was *Treasure Island* in which he played a memorable Long John Silver. The Assassin's putative musical denseness is another private joke: Reginald Nalder had been a singer and dancer in Vienna before emigrating to the United States. We do see his sensitivity as he listens in the balcony later, curious to glance at his companion's pocket score.

6

Our Faithful Friend

FIGURE 6 *The precarious sound stage in* The Day of the Locust *(John Schlesinger, Paramount, 1975)*.

Not only do audiences stand at an ideal point of view in following a narrative but they are typically aware of this fact since what is spread before them has so much detail so brilliantly visible and one surely must be *somewhere perfect* in order to see all the splendor. In the omniscient narrative, the camera functions as a direct extension of the viewer's eye and consciousness. In watching we are simply transported to the various locations in which key events will take place, as though nothing else could happen to us, as though the transporter could never take a wrong turn, as though no one gazing at this incredible world ever blinks.[1] As John Belton has made crystal clear, sound after the early 1930s was, and now remains, recorded so as to make the space of the picture acoustic, not to be faithful to the shape of the diegetic space. In a related way, the picture is recorded so as to make logical the world of the story, not the world in which the recording was made. The presumption we make in being transported through filmic narrative—arrangement is made so that nothing in the film will contradict the movement that is accorded us—is that no key event will be omitted from the story, no event of significance will take place somewhere we cannot see, no significant character will fail to appear, no meaningful utterance will be unhearable. We are not only *embedded* in the ongoingness but embedded *with a completeness and totality in which we can have faith*, placed as far inside as one can be without breaking through the wall of the skin. This is a special view, and we have been accorded it not because we can rightfully claim to be worthy but because a filmmaker we do regard as worthy has made the decision to grace us that way.

When I watch Kenneth Branagh's performance of Hamlet (1996) or of Hercule Poirot (2017) I do not suffer the same nauseating doubt or intrigue we are to presume is inside the character, yet this doubting Hamlet and the intrigued Poirot are my closest chums as I watch. In the omniscient narrative that I know intimately—whatever "intimately" finally means—what they experience I share, and since I would not wish to feel nauseating doubt or intrigue myself (a little doubt or intrigue maybe, but not the Full Monty) I tell myself to remain calm and let them "carry" me and, as loyal chums, they remain calm and do just that: we go on and on. Even quintessentially private moments between characters—Hamlet confiding to Horatio (Nicholas Farrell); Poirot questioning Princess Dragomiroff (Judi Dench)—moments such as I would never be able, or ask, to see outside of cinema, are shown openly and with a tickling casualness, as though, like an invisible phantom I inhabit (and properly should inhabit) the secret space containing the action. Lovemaking and murder are two rich examples of this effected intimacy. When either occurs onscreen I am not afforded a view so very involving that I wonder whether I am somehow naked or covered with blood spatter, yet I do sense myself to be privy to something *others* are not, and would not be, privy to, and something, further, that I *should* see from up close (see Chapters 19 and 47). *Others*: even all the people sitting around me in the same space, who, though what I see is light coming from a screen, somehow do not, as I believe it—as I require to believe it—see what I see the way I see

---

[1] Rule-proving exception: *Blow-Up* (1966) features a marvelous nocturnal moment with David Hemmings skimming down Regent Street in his Mercedes with the top down. Suddenly he thinks he sees a familiar woman on the sidewalk and quickly halts, but the camera, following our delight in the movement, keeps tracking ahead until suddenly, realizing the car is no longer at its side, it turns and looks back at him looking back.

it: my belief in the uniqueness of my sight helps me integrate the viewing as a personal experience (a vital integration if I am to willingly put my personal money up, at the box office).

In an *omniscient* story, the "voice" of the cinema is taken to be, if unknown personally still entirely amicable, amicable and inviting, inviting and embracing, embracing and enriching, enriching and therefore acceptable as an object of belief. It is the voice of an unimaginable being of great generosity, who would wish to give information but also never demand interaction—any interaction, even our expression of thanks. "I give," it says apparently, "because you deserve to be given to, and only that. You above all people deserve." We are made royal by the system. If, as per Michel Chion, cinema can often invoke an *acousmêtre* ("The all-seeing acousmêtre appears to be the rule" [*Voice* 25]),

> This was apparently the name assigned to a Pythagorean sect whose followers would listen to their Master speak *behind a curtain*, as the story goes, so that the sight of the speaker wouldn't distract them from the message. (19)

then this "voice" of cinema to which I refer, the "person" not in but of the film, the presence revealing presences to us, is an *acousmêtre's acousmêtre*, a spirit behind the puppeteer. When, to introduce whole films or specific scenes the camera, elevated, swoops over a strange and notably fascinating territory (New York City's Spanish Harlem from high above when *West Side Story* [1961] begins; the solarized "mindscape" during the star voyage of *2001: A Space Odyssey* [1968]), we immediately accept and adopt the required point of view as offered by a flying *cicerone* who loves us and out of love has given us to see. We immediately agree to find the vision valuable, even indispensably so, and sense a thrill at having this particular—this particularly entertaining—exposure to something we might not ordinarily glimpse now opened up by someone so estimable (as to find us estimable), so kind, and so careful not to drip the tea. Yet the system of service works only when it can be known in advance how the motor of our satisfaction works, known how we can be tickled, known how to afford a view beyond the apogee of our imagination, and known that good service will pay off. Instead we could be watching something cryptic and fail entirely to be touched.

As to the location of the drama as set onscreen: if the camera is indeed a "magic carpet" of sorts, we are willing to let it take us anywhere, anywhere in space and time. (H. G. Wells's time machine could move through history, but always and only at one particular place; in David Lowery's *A Ghost Story* [2017] these constraints are relaxed, with profound results.) For *Hamlet*, we are swept off to the parapets of the Castle of Elsinore, hundreds of years ago, hovering in the Danish shadows there so that we can watch the night watch. "Answer me. Stand and unfold yourself."—but not bloody likely. Far, far, far more entrancing, at any rate, than most day trips from Copenhagen. For *Good Will Hunting* (1997), a corridor at Harvard where a janitor stares at a math challenge scribbled on a blackboard (a challenge intended to stymy any member of any audience). For *Titanic* (1997), a pier at Southampton, 1912, a pier like any pier in a place like any other place, except, of course, not. For *Star Trek VI: The Undiscovered Country* (1991), the Starfleet Academy somewhere in the general vicinity of San Francisco (like Lucasfilm!), hundreds of years in the future, everything clean and tidy and sensibly ordered.

Wherever we go and whenever we presumably go there, being given to see by means of whatever delicious movements, *we trust implicitly* that the narrator is wise, capable, informed, and forthcoming. And not forgetful. And having our best interests at heart. Also, if the film is indeed true to what cinema is and can do, a narrator who manages to show things, not just use words to refer to them. This "voice," as I call it (perhaps it is more a hand opening out); this personality: it is friendly because nourishing, ceaselessly. Nourishing, responsive, considerate, loving. Generally the narrative has no motive to trick us, at least finally, to make us dupes of Cartesian deception. To keep a secret, yes, as long as that secret is either finally revealed or finally left for a rather easy evening's homework. When at film's end there is a radical, shuddering turnabout, we feel we ought to be able to look back over the thing in memory and discover how, very close to the beginning, and with an insouciance immeasurable, the secret was tossed upon the table. Generally, anything and everything we would need to know we may glean from what we see; and anything and everything that we need to see our narrational chum openly, unabashedly shows. Bernardo Bertolucci's *The Dreamers* (2003) has Matthew (Michael Pitt) staring in excited amazement at the vagina of his new friend Isabelle (Eva Green), and because we are to affiliate with his moment of enlightenment we must stare, too (the filmmaker paying homage to Gustave Courbet's *L'origine du monde* [1866]). Later Isabelle will stare with a matching amazement at his penis, and we are given her point of view, too. If in the story there are vital secrets they will be fashioned to appertain to some character(s) wanting to keep things away from others, but we—oh, no no: we will not be left out; by means of Scheff's "ladder of awareness" we will know what is "not known." Or else, finding out later, even too late, we will know that, and how, we did not know.

But while we are tacitly let into the "interior" of the film's habitation the hand holding open the gate is entirely concealed from us, so that in being admitted we have the feeling of entering of our own volition. Indeed, more: we have the sensation, having divined the combination to the lock, of sneaking in transgressively out of hunger and desire. An interesting case: Clint Eastwood's *Sully* (2016) puts us in the cockpit with the pilot and co-pilot of an aircraft that after taking off from La Guardia must make an immediate emergency landing in the Hudson River (based on a true story). Important to know: the setting of the tale is contemporary, that is, after September 11, 2001. By the time of the story, and for some years before it, no passengers were allowed into the cockpits of any aircraft, not thugs with pistols and not little boys hoping the Captain will show them the Northern Lights. Logically, the only way we can experience the thrill of *Sully* is to feel our presence *as passengers*—we don't know enough to be on the crew. But we are made uncontrollably eager to go to the cockpit, the film's advertising having warned that the pilot's behavior, and only that, will be the instrumental action of the story. He will fly the plane, we will need to see how he does it. Where is the force that recognizes our need, evaluates our enforced passenger status, recognizes the prevailing countermands, and kindly opens the cockpit door just enough for us (for the camera) to slip in. That force (which is of course the writer-producer-director-cinematographer team) is unavailable to view. Thus, the cockpit orientation of the film is a cheat, a presentation entirely out of sync with the facts of everyday life, which facts, by the way, govern the graphic design, the script, and the cinematography of the film.

In *Sully*, the cheat formula works through naughtiness. (1) Flying his aircraft into the Hudson River rather than turning it back to La Guardia, Capt. Sully (Tom Hanks) is going against all the protocols and all the rules, not to say violating the air space of New York City and possibly putting at risk civilians on or near the water. Naughty naughty. (2) Being in the cockpit as he works, or at any other time, is transgression on our part. Naughty us. (3) Sully's transgression is by no means less than our own; in fact, given that we are peaceable filmgoers and he is saving the lives of all the people on board his aircraft, his transgression is supreme. It is a sublime transgressiveness. (4) Indeed Sully is a bona fide hero, and what makes him a hero is his naughtiness, not his rule keeping. (5) The vision we get in the cockpit, by comparison with what we would see if we were pinned down in the fuselage, is a notably creative one. (Naughtiness pays.) Therefore (6) our creative transgression is hardly worse than Sully's and, in fact, is tinctured with the flavor of his heroism. All of this is embedded in the architecture of the film's structure. If we were heroic, as heroic as Sully, it could hardly be wrong or unnatural for us to be watching the action as we do; watching thus makes us heroic co-pilots. Thus are we cheated into the cockpit, against FAA rules, just as Sully cheats the airplane into the Hudson, against FAA rules as well. So amicable is the narrative in giving us an ideal point of view we do not question or even notice the gesture when it occurs.

Narration, visible or invisible, means sincerely to cheat, that is, (a) to open us, without admitting it is opening us, to wanting an ongoing and unconstrained view and then (b) to actually afford us, without telling us it is affording, the view we have been opened to want. "Friendly" cheats abound in narrative film, the problem of "ideal placement" bringing the issue nicely into the light. Consider a very complex narrative space where it is necessary to leap around and see many facets of a situation before it can be fully understood: say, the soundstage catastrophe scene of John Schlesinger's *The Day of the Locust* (1975), where first we are brought into the Napoleonic Wars, and up very close, but then pulled back to see that it was only a simulation on a movie set, then taken further backward to see the director with his megaphone upon a crane dolly, high in the air with the soundstage ceiling and lights above his head. Hundreds of busy extras are being halted at work so they can do another take and get it right, damn it!, and then, under the scaffolding of the constructed redoubt we see not only the way the carpenters' 2 x 4s have been arranged but also how the "DANGER" signs have all been binned. Now the face of the designer (William Atherton) standing in frozen fear and panic as he notices. Back to the view from the top of the redoubt with extras racing up only to plunge into nowhere when the set (now, predictably) gives way. The camera is *never not* in the perfect position to see what must be seen[2]; nor is any logic implied or interposed to explain our power to hop from position to position.[3] We of course accept this offering of power, but the camera quietly empowers us to accept it. In scripting these jumps, the filmmakers know that any explanation, not of the cluster of places to which we must move but of our easily moving there, would draw the magic curtain away from the production machine, would permit us to "see that man behind the curtain," even in the ironic case where, as here, what we are seeing is exactly the men behind a camera.

Note the non-replication of our everyday experience. Were we to be present on the soundstage like that designer, we would stand at every moment in one particular spot there, or at least one area, more or less frozen, incapacitated to see (even if urged to imagine) a great deal of what was happening. Always in life we are unable to see a great deal of what is going on. There are hidden actors, actors we hear without seeing, events of which we get a bad view, movements that are sloppy, rumored happenings that we do not catch, and so on. The ideally aimed and cultured vision blocks our attention to the fact that in the story world are hidden actors, too, ones we hear without seeing; there is sloppiness; there are events not quite in view. But we are happily swept away with the generous, the exciting, the unfamiliarly violent, with the exceptionally sexy peephole a film does manage, contrivedly, to provide. Cinema will persist in seeming not only an eye but a magical eye, that goes far beyond what the human eye can do in framing and seizing a "world." Anything that would dissipate the magic will be blocked away. For

---

[2] Or to hint at, if not exactly configure, what remains out of frame but for the viewer is resonant with what the screen shows. Offscreen space, the subject of fascinated rumination, speculation, wondering, and desire is not random.

[3] This "hopping" (my language) is a key feature of "intensified continuity" as discussed by Bordwell.

Schlesinger, the cohort of assistant directors hidden all over the set, some conceivably even in costume, massing, herding, urging, moving the army of extras playing the army of extras (and the assistant directors) in this way not that way, and in so many directions to boot, so that the effect of a catastrophe can be generated. The "director" in this sequence barks away through his megaphone, but his "assistant directors" are invisible until one of them leads the charge up the redoubt to his own peril. The director is scripted to bark, "the way directors do," as if out of his lungs comes control of everything.

One goes forward not only trusting the friendly "maker of displays" but also believing in what the displays offer, with unquestioned and unquestionable acceptance, as in a dream, where we take what we see and hear as absolutely given and, regardless of how twisted it may seem, given for the Good. We are trusting, even loving, because the narrator of our dreams, although hidden, is a goodly (if not Godly) narrator who merits our full commitment of respect. As Walter Benjamin suggested, the dream has no outside (839).

More. The friendly narration, configured if not actually embodied, has identifying characteristics, so that its presence and its workings, if unrecognizable themselves, have recognizable effects, telltale stains. We notice and affirm certain narratorial characteristics without wondering how these might work to enchain us: roughly the age (perhaps older than we are and wiser as with Kane in *Citizen Kane* [1941]); perhaps younger and more innocent as with Scout in *To Kill a Mockingbird* (1962)]); roughly the social class and technical knowledge (Heywood Floyd on the moon voyage in *2001*). Narrational tics become evident as the narration acknowledges certain realities rather than others, notices some things rather than overlooking or avoiding them. More importantly, just as the narration acknowledges social realities it also staunchly avoids claiming acknowledgment but treats them, instead, as only, merely, naturally, simply, obviously present to the narrative eye because there is no other way for them to be but present, and as though any other reality isn't real. Read through Henry James's *What Maisie Knew* (1897) for a study of social knowledge openly accessed by adults but artfully concealed from a child who is in their presence:[4]

> "I say, I say: *do* look out!" Sir Claude quite amiably protested.
> "There's nothing she hasn't heard. But it doesn't matter—it hasn't spoiled her." (74)

What we feel we *know* we feel accustomed to. If we sense the narration as friendly, we are instantly accustomed to the sort of information it reveals

---

[4] I am grateful to Nellie Perret for pointing the way to both *What Maisie Knew* and its author.

and holds back and to the kind of social access one is presumably afforded through its agency. In Stephen Frear's *The Queen* (2006), we are accustomed to going into the sitting room at Bucks House, as it's called on the inside. We see the telephone in her hand. In *Empire of the Sun* (1987), we are accustomed to being sequestered in a prison camp by the Japanese. In *The Queen* we are not so blinded by opulence, nor in *Empire* so overtaken by shadow, as to have our view compromised.

Feeling accustomed to friendly narrative, we feel the comfort that comes with custom. We can relax our hold on the reins of thought. Striking us when we are relaxed this way, the writer's cheat comes as a shock and a triumph at the end of two valuable films. As they progress, *The Go-Between* (1971) at Brandham Hall, an English country house late in the nineteenth century and *Atonement* (2007), some decades later in a similar place, we have the sense of a love story being spelled out phase by phase. In both cases there is a kind of awkward (unstable) triad.

(1) *The Go-Between.* Young Leo (Dominic Guard) is the eponymous go-between, invited to a seat in the English countryside and then expected to shuttle back and forth between the entitled Mary, Lady Trimingham (Julie Christie), and the farmhand with whom she is madly in love, Ted Burgess (Alan Bates). It is a glorious summer, a time of brilliantly sunlit days, bleached haystacks, shadowy barns, trickling rivulets, emerald swards, and taking off one's clothes. For Mary the world is enchanted by her passion, but she and Ted are caught in a mad, transgressive affair, in a cultural setting and at a time when social-class boundaries were rigidly observed and a girl like her could have no purpose in cavorting with, or even acknowledging the presence of, a boy like him. For navigating assignations messages must be carried back and forth, and Leo is the innocent messenger. Things turn out badly, Mary being led to marry a man of her class and "having a son with him" (secretly a son by Ted). By the film's end a great deal of time has passed and we learn from Leo's mouth how, Mary's husband having died in the war, he was asked once again to be a go-between for her, revealing the secret love to the son. However, this forthcoming Leo of the finale is more than a neutral, disembodied voice. Our faithful friend brings us to see him sitting behind a window during a heavy rainstorm, a very old man now looking back through the long inverted telescope of cinema and of life, decades upon decades back, to the time of his own childhood when for him everything was brave and clear and sun-drenched and utterly not understood. The writer's cheat here, that provides a thoroughgoing pleasure for the viewer, lies in giving full information about the narrator only after it is too late to imagine anything being done to mend the tattered situation he helped rend—in revealing only at the film's end that the entire film was being told from only the film's end. While the film was progressing the audience had intuited itself at Brandham, in the days of the affair, and had felt a continuity of presence there and in succeeding actions elsewhere. Suddenly it becomes

shockingly clear that the whole thing was a living memory, experienced now somewhere else, in the rain, and so long afterward that it is impossible to find certainty about anything. While the film does begin with the adult Leo, we are not given enough information to position him temporally or to come quite to the realization of who he is or what his involvements will now be shown to be (that is, to have been): he is made, when first we meet him, forgettable, so that as the alluring and complex story unwinds we find ourselves fully present with Mary and Ted, oblivious, just as they are, to what is beyond themselves.

There is a verbal irony here, of course: Mary and Ted are cheating with their dalliance, in order to make life especially delightful; and the script is cheating their cheating, to make it especially delightful for us. The principal power of the cheat is in abeyance until we are confronted with the shocking irony of Leo, our Leo, having aged; of much time having passed, *without narrational comment*. The friendly narration has jumped us through a lifetime but makes no claims to having done so; or to having the power to do so; or to having considered the kind of effect such a charge might have on us. It is as though we must of course have known where we would be headed; we must of course have seen it all coming. Any other presumption of our presumption would draw attention to the radical alteration in setting, costuming, makeup, and tone, so much attention that, swept away at the finale by our own gasping grasp that we swooped forward we would fail to catch the strange pain Leo is trying to give over.

(2) In *Atonement* we find ourselves witnessing the *feux d'artifice* of love between Cecilia Tallis (Keira Knightley), a girl of the upper class, and Robbie Turner (James McAvoy), far from a nobleman but the object of her passion nevertheless. Their trysting is accidentally witnessed by Cecilia's thirteen-year-old sister Briony (Saoirse Ronan), who in her consternation tells her parents that Robbie is a thief. He is cast out of the family circle, away from the estate house, away from Cecilia. Five years pass. We meet Briony (Romola Garai), conflicted and anxious in regard to her past. Robbie becomes caught up in the war, is wounded on the beaches of Normandy, and dies a horrible death there while she fails at nursing him. It is only at the end of the film that we meet the figure who, it turns out, has been revealing this whole fabric to us, Briony (Vanessa Redgrave) as an aging author looking back on her childhood with deep regret at having destroyed her sister's chance at love. A similar cheat works here: the intelligence, sensitivity, and point of view being employed in recounting the tale is that of a very mature and reflective woman, in this case even a magician with words, but the imagery puts us so close to Robbie and Cecilia, so close to Briony who is perforcedly so close to them, so close to all the family and their friends who circulate like butterflies around the Tallis brilliance, that we feel ourselves embedded in early twentieth-century history, even suspended in time—as becomes evident with the wounded Robbie (helpless Cecilia resting by his side)—imprisoned

in events as they occur. In practical fact it is all a memory-vision, perhaps faulted, but certainly a vision from sadness and looking over a gulf.

What happens here if the audience is told from the start of the film that the whole enterprise will be a looking back upon ancient history from the point of view of one of the protagonists who made a significant mess when she was a child and is now a long way from childhood—as, say, in James Cameron's *Titanic* (1997) with Gloria Stuart? Simply, every event that presents itself in the story to engage and enchant us with, if nothing else, the purity of its presence before us, becomes instead tainted with the shadow of the long gaze, affixed to a logic of retrospective chagrin. As Robbie and Cecilia make love in the library, Briony silently creeping in and watching, they'd be, already, here, now, nothing but a pair of failures-to-be, birds taking flight doomed to be brought down by the hunters nearby. When seen through a constantly invoked retrospection, every take-off is only an impending crash, and there is no aura of glory and wonderment first to be tasted and savored, then pined for in regret, and only much later rather coldly dissected as hopeless from the start. The cheat keeps our spirits up, gives a prospect of brightness, until love is history.

* * *

As to the cheat of the "friendly narrative," as I am calling it, one more word:

The "faithful friend" was intentionally spawned for, and has been much cloned in, commercial cinema, certainly cinematic narrative, in which a certain interpretive binding holds the viewer's consciousness in registration with the imagery. In life as we know it there are very few such considerate, outgoing, unstinting, kind, and all-knowing companions who would arrange to give us boons of experience (ideally staged) without letting us see the gifting as well as the gift. Parents, siblings, spouses, lovers, perhaps. But surely not scriptwriters. It is just because the camera is no friend of the heart that all its many boons must be offered while we are unconscious.

7

Bridge from Nowhere

FIGURE 7 *Leroy Daniels (l.) with Fred Astaire, doing "Shine On Your Shoes" in* The Band Wagon *(Vincente Minnelli, MGM, 1953).*

Contiguity in process is an important feature of "reality" as we construct and understand it. When one event leads to another, or comes sufficiently close in precedence that a second gives all impression of flowing from it, we ask ourselves—this flow being insufficient in and of itself, *as flow*—whether the second event, as a type, seems a *likely* outcome of the first. *Likely*: given that we know such results have come previously from "causes" such as this "cause"; given that our theory of the world incorporates flows like this one; given that we have no reason for doubting whether an outcome such as this outcome could result from a cause such as this cause; given all of this, when we think back on the cause we do not doubt the effect *as* effect. The forward flow will always be a flow, but it can also be an *effective* flow.

It is widely understood by those who have experienced their culture that a very broad range of possibility exists as to event-to-event flows, some events being capable of leading to (preceding) virtually anything within reason, *reason*, of course, being a set of known and accepted formulae for limiting probability in a local setting. The final determination of cause-effect relationships is open to negotiation socially. I snap my fingers and the sun rises, but only in a relatively primitive culture (not my own, I suspect) would any credibility attach to that pairing as cause-and-effect. I say a *primitive* culture: certainly, let us agree, a pre-modern one. Moses stretches out his rod and the waters of the Red Sea part . . . If I had a rod to stretch out, and I stretched it, waters would not part anywhere.

Contiguity and likelihood, then. In the typical film musical, which replicates the structure of a dream more than it does the structure of the everyday (to which, thanks to designers and performers, it very often bears some resemblance), there is the scantest imaginable contiguity between events for very good structural reasons. When, say at the Freed Unit at MGM, a decision is made to produce a show, the first step is the assembly of a contractually feasible group of musical items, these very often selected from the studio library (where on most items the studio owns copyright) or coming from the catalog of a musician (and producer) like Arthur Freed himself. The songs will be "lined up" in some way that makes for an arc of musical phrasing, rhythm, and harmony, one number seeming appropriate as a kick-off and another as a finale, etc. Then a story structure is made up that will weave the songs together, or more properly, that will narrate between the songs in what seems a forward-flowing chain of contiguities, which amounts to a continuity. The narration serves to build bridges. Each narrative bit has as its primary function making the song that preceded it and the song that follows it seem more or less contiguous; and making the second song seem as though it flows from the narrative, too. But no part of this is anything but constructed, by which I mean not always already socially understood and accepted normatively (as in the "social construction of reality" [see Berger and Luckmann]) but literally put together (with art and arbitrariness) like the pieces of a kid's Lego set.

The sense viewers would have that one sung moment fluidly (inevitably) leads to another is thus an induced sense, and the manner of inducing it is a grand cheat. With certain sorts of characters—the ones who overpopulate Freed Unit musicals!—the everyday they inhabit allows for *almost anything* to happen, and so the writers are in a position to invoke almost any integument to bind musical numbers together and make the binding seem indubitably real. But a very nice example of the fragility and artfulness of this kind of cheating is to be found in the opening few moments of *The Band Wagon* (1953), one of the really glorious musicals of the Hollywood golden age.

[1] Tony Hunter's memorabilia are being auctioned off at deplorably cheap prices, nobody really seriously wanting to collect the artifacts of this once-great (indeed once-almost-regal) Hollywood song-and-dance man whose career has utterly lapsed. This is a kind of prologue, very swift. Auctioneer can't even get one dollar for the famous top hat and stick.

[2] On the train heading to New York. Tony (Fred Astaire, whose career by 1953 had indeed seemed to collapse so that, like Tony, he could do with a comeback) hides behind a menu while his seat mate, a chubby cigar smoker (the chubby and irrepressible Thurston Hall), babbles about wishing he could meet Ava Gardner and comments that Tony Hunter "hasn't made a picture in years."

[3] Arrival at Grand Central Station. Tony is nattily dressed and happy to be back in town, but a little unconfident. He stays in his seat a bit, humming a tune, about to step out of his car onto the platform. A gaggle of photographers and reporters are ready to catch a fish, and he gives them his professional smile and friendly wave[1]: "Thanks for the red carpet, I didn't expect it!" But alas, it is for the grande dame Ava Gardner (in person), stepping just after him, that they have come. She comes up to give him a warm old-friends hello, but soon Tony is left alone beside the long empty train, quiet, reflective, a little chagrined.

[4] He swings into a charming performance of that tune he started to hum, Arthur Schwartz and Howard Dietz's "By Myself" (1937)—"I'll go my way by myself/Like walking under a cloud . . ."—as he casually paces the length of the train, nappy mauve button-down, lavender necktie, pearl gray double-breasted suit, maroon pocket handkerchief crisply folded, straw boater. He finishes up as he comes to the ramp that will lead into the station.

[5] At the head of that ramp are voices calling: "Tony, Tony!! Tony! Tony Tony!" And here, waiting excitedly to welcome him, and bearing TONY HUNTER FAN CLUB signs, are his two chums Lily and Lester Marton (Nanette Fabray, Oscar Levant), putting on

---

[1] In a little gestural moment Alfred Hitchcock neatly reprises this scene in *Torn Curtain* (1966) with Tamara Toumanova.

the Welcome Show. "Tony. Hunter. Sis boom bah!" The three do a happy-smiles routine, Tony assuring Lily, "You're much too pretty to be married to that!" Lester: "There's work to be done. I have here a script.... Smell it, you can smell it's good! There's a great part in it for you and nice little parts for Lily and me." Dissolve past nocturnal street traffic to a medium-close of the three of them talking in a sidewalk crowd.

[6] Lily and Lester are trying to persuade reluctant Tony to get in on their new musical which will be directed by the fabulous Jeffrey Cordova. But, "What's happened to 42nd Street?" he wants to know, "This used to be the greatest theater street in the town. The New Amsterdam, I had one of my biggest successes there.... Noël Coward and Gertie were here in *Private Lives*[2].... First show I ever did was at the Elgin and ... and I don't believe that's even here anymore." Key action: a cigar-chomping drunk (Cigar Reprise) steps on Lester's foot. In agony, he pays the man and apologizes (typical Oscar Levant self-deprecation: "I can stand anything but pain!"). Tony sees his pals off in a cab.

[7] He is in front of an open arcade (where, had the threesome kept walking, he wouldn't be), filled with notably goofy automata, such as a fortune teller, a weight machine, a baseball throw, and a mystery machine dominating the space but all closed off. Here, and weaving among the adults and young people populating the place, and while acquiring a hot dog he doesn't want and a collection of doubtful looks from strangers, Tony performs Schwartz and Dietz's "Shine On Your Shoes" (1932), dancing through the number, as he sings, in the classic Fred Astaire fashion (the classic Tony Hunter fashion, as we are to imagine), in this way quickly showing us (but not the people around him, who seem oblivious) that *he is back* (tastefully mismatched socks and all). The number—one of the really beautiful musical numbers in the Hollywood canon, given the lilting tune, the vibrant color, and Astaire's debonair smoothness taken to an extreme—ends with him duetting with a shoeshine man (Leroy Daniels, also wearing, in the Astaire tradition, vibrantly colored socks) and finally kicking the mystery machine into life.

Two songs, then, "By Myself," which is soft and slow; and "Shine On Your Shoes" which is more rhythmical, jazzy, upbeat, and promising. Between them the intercession of Lester and Lily, their goofy show idea, Tony's

---

[2] A flicker of researched realism: original production of the Noël Coward play, January 7, 1931, Times Square Theatre, starring Noël Coward (1899–1973) and Gertrude Lawrence (1898–1952).

hesitation—less than a minute onscreen. Let us consider the elements of this little construction:

[A] *Fictional space.* Both the station and the sidewalk on 42nd Street are jammed with people heading in all directions, dressed in all colors: a twittering kaleidoscope. Yet the closeness of the shots in both locations, centering on the trio, lifting them away from their background, makes the planet of Grand Central and the planet of 42nd St. seem to fade away while a bubble of private, joking, ultra-friendly human relationship looms forward. We had a tiny hint of this spatial division on the station platform when, leaning close to her old pal Tony, Ava Gardner made a subtle comment "only to him" about how trying the "business" is, a comment only he would understand, as her confiding smile telegraphs. Tony is worried about the wounded Lester, and helps to get him into a cab with Lily, but at the same time he is caught in his own reverie, thinking about his past, the old 42nd St., the glittering distraction of the present, and generally "going his way by himself." In one pair of spaces, then: the old and the new; the more private and the more public; buoyant energy and patient reflection; the general crowd and the special talent.

[B] *Talk.* Beyond saying how happy they are to see him, the Martons are giving Tony a sales pitch. (The sales pitch is an elemental aspect of entertainment production, and this film will focus on it later, with some sharpness.) The pitch falls flat, maybe. But a telling query: is Tony-starring-in-a-new-musical, as a conversational subject, linked to what came just before (his solo train voyage in dismay) and what could come after (beginning with his play at the arcade, then his sliding into song there, then his spirits lifted, then his participation in the musical)? At least for the viewer, the pitch works as a promise of refreshment and rebirth for the admirable, the handsome, the debonair, and the sweet-voiced Tony, especially welcome for the somewhat sad Tony singing "By Myself" because he knows the adulation he got while being famous is all gone. The promise here is that Tony will be famous again, albeit his confidence isn't presently up to it. (Hopefully if Tony tastes the flavor of fame, so will we.) As he wanders among the arcade machines he is at play, and the dance-song that comes out of him is unreflective, almost unthought, a genuine show of a talent that is inherent in the personality without effort or intentful control.

[*However*]. However, any conversation on a crowded sidewalk could be forgotten and wiped away by the audience, as Tony, Lester, and Lily's is likely to be. The conversation doesn't function as information here. It is filler, realistically conceived but underplayed to much background acoustic and optical accompaniment. What is really required in the film as a whole is a breather here, between one (kind of) song and another, a breather quintessentially produced by a setting as mundane and bustling *and public* as is the area around Times Square, "a prism through which to see the twentieth century's ups and downs and reflect about its meaning as a whole. . . . Any feature of a public space that facilitates a process of mutual looking over and checking out—sidewalks, mirrors, billboards, anything—has got to represent growth and progress in city life" (Berman 41; 56). What is happening here technically is that one song number ("Shine") is being produced out of another ("By Myself") as though naturally, like sunshine following rain. But: to have the musical numbers enchained nakedly would turn the film into something more akin to a vaudeville routine than an MGM musical. The dialogue *as speaking* (*recitativo*) is essential, but becomes overwhelming if we pay too much attention to what the sayers are saying. Thus, at the peak of the sales talk Lester is grossly interrupted by an ignorant passer-by. And more: the exceeding excitement and eccentricity of Lester and Lily, not only in the rah-rah-rah but in everything they say. We catch the tonality and personality, but the content of the speech can slide by.

[*Further*]. Further, if we were to take the conversation as signal for the film (yet it is really coming too early in the film to work this way), the parenthesizing songs would fall back in prominence: we would have to note that they are selected arbitrarily for their musicality, their decorativeness, not their implications about Tony. If the dialogue were telling and important, any two pleasant-enough songs would do. "By Myself" is lyrical, "Shine" is jazzy and syncopated: nothing more need be gleaned. The two could have been reversed, indeed, had the story been written to explain or cover that.

As affected and emphatic as the musical numbers are, still, when we watch the opening of *The Band Wagon* we have a natural and spontaneous feeling, a sense of being positioned in everyday space, and thus conclude swiftly that the events occurring in sequential order here—auction, train, platform, station, street, arcade—are realistically, merely, uncontrivedly occurring this way—that is, that there is no supradiegetic producer's or director's consciousness mapping out the elements of the film and making decisions as to how to place happenings. Of course this "naturalness" appertains to cinema generally yet it is not often recognized how elaborate must be its infrastructure, the building needed in order to keep the production crew out of not only the light but also the viewer's thought. What we see fills out a "received" order of happening: *of course this would be the order of happening* (since out of our ken it was ordered that way). Once we fade from the abortive auction in L.A. to the train there is, ostensibly speaking, "nowhere the film could go except where it goes," notwithstanding that Tony, whom we find on the train, is not at the auction except by way of his photograph. To focus more tightly: "By Myself" must inevitably lead to

"Shine On Your Shoes." Just as it seems natural his getting off the train in loneliness to sing "By Myself," it seems natural for Tony to have his friends meet him and shepherd him away, and natural for him to want to be alone and find himself at play in the arcade. Natural, too, if it is Tony (Fred) playing that a shoeshine turns into a dance display. Happenstance, if we insist; but unquestionable happenstance.

[C]   *Probability.* When we experience what seems to us "real," we have a tendency to find it likely. We take real eventuality to be probable. Once we see Tony riding on the train, Tony getting off the train is probable. To zoom: not that he must get off, or that other actions cannot happen, but that *when he gets off the train* we do not wink at the surprise of it. Once we see the reporters, Tony thinking they are there to welcome him is somewhat probable until Ava Gardner manifests, looking more glamorous than ever, and he can back into the shadow (even if only out of graciousness). Once Gardner and the publicity retinue have disappeared Tony's leaving the train is probable (what is he to do otherwise, stand there all night musing?). Walking along the train singing is *not* probable, it is arbitrary and superfluous, exactly in the way that fans of musicals hope for, but Tony *did* start humming that tune as he sat disconsolately, waiting for the passengers to leave, so we can fathom how it might "still be on his mind." In another kind of film, the editor would have dissolved from Tony walking off the train to him in further motion elsewhere or arriving at a destination (as when, in film after film, after a person touches a door handle and opens the door to a room we cut to a shot from inside, of her entering). That lonely Tony might find two friends in the station is neither probable nor improbable (as we know little about how warm and how long-lived this friendship is), but it is entirely thinkable; nothing surprises us in the way that Lester and Lily surprise him. Having met up and chuffed each other's jaws merrily, they will go somewhere together, and why not 42nd Street, after all? We learn that the Martons are a song-writing team, so there is little that is improbable about their insistently pitching a new idea for a musical: they live, think, and breathe musicals. Nor is it improbable that weary Tony would be hesitant. But the arcade is entirely a surprise, set up by, yet not probably following from, another surprise, the injury to Lester. While the arcade may normatively be there to be visited it is, for us, not in focus yet; there is little probability of a sidewalk passer-by breaking off his conversation and dashing in to play with the games. Again, the arcade moment is deliriously joyous (for us as for Tony), but we had no grounds for expecting it at all. Yet also: a crowded sidewalk actually is a space one can vacate on a whim, suddenly, with no explanation, notably in spontaneous, jivey, unstable Times Square. Putting Tony on the sidewalk with the Martons is the perfect way to slide him away from Grand Central and at the same time allow for his kneejerk reaction to the arcade. A plain ordinary walk down the fabulous 42nd Street, of the kind young New Yorkers and blithe tourists take all the time.

Plain. Ordinary. Although there is no rule saying our trio must find themselves on 42nd Street.

Ordinary. What might be true for anyone.

Anyone might feel lonely and sing "By Myself" if she knew the song. Anyone might wander among the crazy machines, snag a hotdog, start dancing. What anyone would *not* do is perform with the elegance, the trim, the practice, and the extraordinary fluidity of Astaire/Tony, but by setting up the former star, Star and only a Star, as the subject of concern, the filmmaker solicits our tacit agreement to bond with this paragon of talent. This is true from the first shot, where near the desperate auctioneer is the giant photograph, a smiling, entirely benevolent, wholly lovable Tony Hunter, Tony Hunter the Famous, As Was and Ever Will Be. We may be told Hunter has aged, but to look at Astaire is to doubt that.

The sales pitch/chummy chat between the Martons and Tony is a major cheat here. It gives the impression of artlessly *bridging* the railroad platform moment to the arcade moment, since what would our focal hero do but emerge from a platform and what could he do meeting the Martons but go along, with them nudging their script all along? But there is no such thing as an artless bridge. The apparent artlessness, the "obviousness" of the connection, is what is cheated, what I am putting into question. Levant and Fabray must play the Martons as literally exploding with excitement to see their friend, quite as though they have been talking over the idea of snagging him into their project until they're blue in the face. They burst upon him, and all the eventfulness they suggest bursts too—makes a forward motion probable. The film is filled with interstitial linkages, keeping in relation to one another songs that are in actual historical and performative fact quite self-standing: "Triplets," "Louisiana Hayride," "Stairway to Paradise." We will be guided to feel that a man who was sad a few moments ago, and who, because of that, turned down a prospect of work, has now found renewed energy and hope. We can reasonably anticipate that very soon, very very very soon, Tony will be onstage again, doing the material Lily and Lester have fashioned for him to do (since if he's going on Broadway what other material could he possibly use?).

The interstitial dialogue in a musical such as *The Band Wagon* functions somewhat in the way printed text cards easeled before the audience functioned in a vaudeville show, as overt indicators that one act was closed and another about to begin. But in vaudeville the signal system was part of the basic arrangement—audiences expected to check out the cards, to accept the presence of that easel at the side of the stage—whereas here, and in the film musical more generally, the dialogue is not our point of focus; the story it furthers is. The dialogue is transparent. If the story were truly our reason for watching, there would be little sense in MGM spending (for this film alone) almost three million early 1950s dollars so it could sing and dance its way along. Song and dance, then, *isn't* a decoration of a story; it is the story, but the songs and dances are arranged so that they seem to depend on what people say and what people say is arranged so that songs and dances will seem to spring out of it like petunias.

8

And Here Endeth My Tale

FIGURE 8 Alida Valli *in* The Third Man *(Carol Reed, London Film Productions, 1949)*.

Every story comes to an end. And yet if the writer's job in fashioning a script is to arrive at an ending that seems logical, replete, appropriately sonorous, and more or less conclusive it is true, too, that no construction functions automatically as an ending, and that no matter the ending one creates there is always something that *could* come afterward if one wished it to. Always an afterthought. The ending of a film as we have it is a completely arbitrary event, then, but in order that the viewer not have access to the construction it is necessary to cheat and make it seem inevitable, conclusive, a point after which "the rest is silence."[1]

Elegant and satisfying endings have frequently been made, then extended. (1) In *Citizen Kane*, after the camera dollies into a furnace and, seeing revealed a very rich secret, we hear a stunning Bernard Herrmann musical cue, the film could be done with a fade to black, but instead we seem to travel upward to see the plume of black smoke rising into the troubled sky over Xanadu. (2) *Singin' in the Rain* (1952) could tidily end with Kathy Selden's (Debbie Reynolds) apotheosis onstage, or even with her big kiss with Don Lockwood (Gene Kelly) in the sunshine, but a piquant twist is made as the camera pulls back to show that the kiss is replicated in a massive advertising poster just behind them. (3) Michelangelo Antonioni's *La notte* (1961) ends with the married couple (Marcello Mastroianni, Jeanne Moreau) stretched out exhausted on a golf course after a night's disturbing revelries. Alone. But the camera pans to show that they are as though alone in the universe, which is all grass and trees and space in tones of gray. (4) *The Third Man* (1949) ends with Anna Schmidt (Alida Valli) striding away from Holly Martins (Joseph Cotten) and disappearing down a straight road, walking, walking, walking, walking away, walking away ... But the camera waits and waits, waits and waits and waits ... AND WAITS for her to turn back, which she doesn't do. (5) Mike Newell's *Donnie Brasco* (1997), a film about a police undercover operation, ends with the masquerading detective (Johnny Depp) pulled out of his precarious performance by a police raid that feels like a warm embrace, but we cannot depart the scene until we see him receiving a commendation along with his wife and children. (6) Robert Wise's *The Day the Earth Stood Still* (1951) ends with Klaatu taking off for his home planet, assured that the people of earth will unite in peace, but we are left with the feeling he intends us to be carefully watched, because peace may be out of our reach. (7) *A Star Is Born* (1954) ends with Norman Maine (James Mason) striding quietly into the Pacific at sunset, but we linger to see the former Esther Blodgett, now Vicki Lester (Judy Garland), accepting an Oscar after his death by looking up proudly and announcing, "I am *Mrs. Norman Maine*."

All of these films and so many others end in a way we find beautiful and compelling, like a hymn with a Plagal IV-I cadence. Also, the present endings I cite here all valorize a particular subject directly or by trace reference: a subject we are meant to consider both supreme and wonderful. In *Kane*, the private secret in public space. In *Singin'* the trumping dominance of the

---

[1] Note that while this phrase comes near the end of *Hamlet* it is not, actually, the last thing we hear from the stage.

show-business image over reality. In *La notte*, not modernist emptiness but existential tranquility and acceptance. In *Third Man*, the finality of the loss of fidelity. In *Brasco*, triumphant heroism as an individual product. In *Earth*, the illusion, call it dream, of harmony on the planet. In *Star*, the importance of the husband, even after death.

It is merely necessary to see so-called "inevitability" as "evitability" to catch the cheats. In every case, we could imagine a continuation beyond what is currently the end point,[2] a path to some other climax that would both turn the present ending into an unresolved middle and afford us reason to see how the official ending is a completely arbitrary choice, a rejection of other possibilities. (1) In *Kane* what is rejected is a careful look at the reporters ravaging Xanadu, their reaction in depth, their feelings about a man like Kane, so that finally he remains an Olympian figure, even in death. (2) In *Singin'*, what is rejected is the idea that a love like Don and Kathy's might be not eternal but wholly human, that beneath the movie-star façades there is to be found, somewhere, people. "People who need people," in fact. And what of poor Cosmo? Didn't Don and Cosmo have a bond, too? (3) In *La notte*, what is rejected is the banality of the small everyday, not the vast golf course at dawn, the spreading lawns, the interminable sand trap, and the draped bodies, but just two dignified people back in the city living life. (4) In *Third Man* what is rejected is a small display of plain civility, that Valli might pause even for a second and say goodbye to Cotten instead of just walking past him as though the moral force of his action, his essentially unfriendly action, frees her to be unfriendly, too. (5) In *Brasco*, what is rejected is the bureaucracy of police work in place of its heroics, that Donnie would now have to sit somewhere and fill in a very long report. (6) In *Earth Stood Still* what is rejected is any questioning opinion about Klaatu, that someone might call him an arrogant know-it-all, instead of sententious acquiescence to his dictates. "Who do you think you are anyway, in that *advanced* civilization of yours?" (Because it was only earthling civilization that stood behind the making of this movie, after all.) (7) And, as so many observers today would see, what is rejected in *Star Is Born* is Vicki at the microphone crying over her beloved husband but at the same time taking rather than humbly refusing credit for the career she herself made through sharply focused care and hard labor. In the film, notwithstanding that Vicki's deferral to the dominant male may have garnered some approval, at least understanding, in the audience, the emphasis in her self-identification as "Mrs. Norman Maine" suggests an audience prepared for, even already expecting, the female self-reliance she is distinctively *not* showing. Every

---

[2]Readers who are fans of music will want to listen to Malcolm Arnold's "A Grand, Grand Overture Op. 57" (1956), which nicely poses the problem of coming to conclusions.

ending valorizes, and every valorization shines because something else is cast into shadow.

More than bringing a harmonic close, the ending must seem inevitable. The writer's challenge—consider *The Barefoot Contessa* (1954), *On Dangerous Ground* (1951), *A Bill of Divorcement* (1932), to name only three possibilities—is to craft a de facto ending, but with such panache, making so ethereal a cadence, that nothing else seems conceivable: a funeral in the rain; a bonding after a death; a triumph on the keyboard. The apogee is reached; and it is singular; and it is exhausting of all hope for action. A contiguity cheat again, but this time with explosive power. "The End," not "An End."

The presence of arbitrariness in the writer's toolbox is no surprise, since those who create fictional worlds arbitrate every single aspect of them (and filmmakers rearbitrate in their own vision). But we should note the seeming finality of the end point, its tendency not only to wrap up the story but to wrap it invisibly, as though the story really is over and really *does* end this way and there isn't any more to be shown because, in truth, in reality, under the Eye of Eternity, nothing more exists. (This, when the story is only its telling.) If the first few moments of a film are those that attract the viewer's most pronounced and most vulnerable attentiveness, the ending can offer the deepest catharsis, as in the deepest and most unequivocal sense of release, not enlightenment. Catharsis, if only the culminating chord is found, as though there is *one* culminating chord awaiting discovery.

And a radical transformation is possible, too. Bernardo Bertolucci's *The Dreamers* (2003) puts an American teenaged tourist in Paris in the family life of a pair of cinephilic twins (Michael Pitt, Eva Green, Louis Garrel), where he learns the taste of feeling, love, desire, truth, and worship. But in the final moments it is 1968 and they are on the barricades. Theo (Garrel) hurls a Molotov cocktail and Matthew (Pitt) screams at him, "No, no! We don't do that. We do this," and kisses him full on the mouth while the angry mob throbs all around. But Theo roughly pushes him away, away out of his life, away out of the film, and as the youth of Paris flow toward the camera the image is suddenly frozen in apotheosis and we hear, in charged orchestrated rhythm, Edith Piaf:

Non, rien de rien
Non, je ne regrette rien
Ni le bien qu'on m'a fait
Ni le mal.

9

Only Pretending

FIGURE 9 *Max von Sydow (l.) and Robert Redford in* Three Days of the Condor *(Sydney Pollack, Wildwood/Dino De Laurentiis, 1975).*

Since Fritz Lang's *Dr. Mabuse the Gambler* (1922), a broad array of films about institutionalized villainy have been made to popular acclaim. Mabuse (Rudolf Klein-Rogge) reappears in *The Testament of Dr. Mabuse* (1933; Rogge again) and *The 1,000 Eyes of Dr. Mabuse* (1960; Wolfgang Preiss), in all three films a consummate criminal mastermind who sets in motion complex and fabulous misdeeds and perplexes the forces of law and order. The idea of the criminal confounding authorities stems from Poe, of course, but Mabuse's telltale characteristic is the megalomania behind his enterprises, his penchant for the grand scheme (that we see partially echoed today in heist films). Two aspects of Mabuse, the character, were central: first, his overall heavy negativity and secondly, his capacity for disguise. Not only a villain but a powerfully theatrical one, who could masquerade as just about anybody. Evil dressing up as Good.

The James Bond films, beginning with *Dr. No* (1962), extracted the first of Mabuse's evil traits, expanding and aggrandizing it in the character of the mysterious supervillain, a figure with a diabolical plan to, effectively, take over the universe. In comedic form this same trope appears in many superhero films as well. It would be characteristic of a descendant of Mabuse to inhabit a secret lair, to have capable assistants very often not publicly visible, to lead a virtual army of clearly uniformed serflike myrmidons who run some vast, highly technologized facility containing the superweapon he intends to unleash. Like Mabuse, the Bond supervillain is very, very, very bad, calling up the sharpest and most intelligent—not to say costly—of civilized resources aiming to bring him under control. Most filmic supervillains do not emulate Mabuse's theatricality, however. The Bond villain blatantly (and super-civilly) presents himself, very often inviting Her Majesty's noble spy to sit at the table, supping him with elegant and expensive foods, and chatting away with cultivated aplomb. In effect he is making the statement, "I am not hiding," whereas Mabuse was a genius at hiding, like Doyle's Moriarty. He could be standing next to the chief of police in complete safety.

This second strain, villainy in disguise, deeply structures a great number of late-twentieth and early-twenty-first century films about pernicious corporations, pernicious government agencies, in general the apparently normal and sleek but actually lethal social world. A purely Adornian critique, pointing to myriad ways in which our capitalist development taken to a high level compromises ethical concerns, human health, dignity, community, the sense of beauty, and other estimable aspects of our lives together. And one of the principal *and notably recurring* elements of these films is the arch-villain who, we learn only too late, has been hiding all along in the skin of a character introduced early on as powerful, dignified, wealthy, noble, charitable, and fine, in short an epitome of the species. Or else as a completely boring bureaucrat stuck behind a desk with nothing interesting to recommend him at all. We come finally to discover a blazing truth, that the "bad guy" is not the good leader with the benevolent smile, as seemed, but a warped, very often profoundly psychologically damaged monster whose smile was only a mask. We can take Martin Vanger (Stellan Skarsgård) in *The Girl with the Dragon Tattoo* (2011), ostensibly a dignified head of a family empire but latently a sadistic torturer and murderer. Or, in *The Fugitive* (1993), Dr. Charles Nichols (Jeroen Krabbé), on the surface a meticulous medical researcher heading a dignified and multivariate project but really a malevolent crook scamming a false drug trial and willing to arrange for the murder of innocents in order to succeed. In Spike Lee's *Inside Man* (2006) the ostensibly austere and dignified Christopher Plummer is a soulless Nazi exploiter. Examples of this script maneuvering are legion.

A number of "games" are in play here. The scripter (and/or script doctor) who uses the "civilized villain" trope ("uncovering of evil") is making a more or less clear statement of the audience's foreknowledge and expectation, certainly by the early 2000s, because the character type is by now well recognized as part of the equation of such fictions—as is the actor who often plays such types. There is an implication that the film is straight, that for all its claim of disguise it in fact openly avows from the start all the disguise that it claims, becoming in the process something of a carnival dress-up. We are intended to know up front that the apparently noble head honcho is actually a vicious insider undoing his own company, threatening or killing his own employees, and all this in order to bring to fruition a plan of which no one, least of all the hero, had or could have had any inkling earlier, so outlandish, so maniacal is it. You may surely guess that I am evil, but not what my evil plan is. My evil plan is greater than anything you can imagine! You will have smelled that I am the poisonous fish, but not the lagoon in which I aim to swim. The hero's exhausting hunt for this villain is thus something of a cheat, bearable only because in carrying it through he entertainingly becomes an acrobat, a wit, a social charmer, an athlete, and sometimes an actor himself.

Also cheated in such films is an interesting range of other potentially normal, good, civil, and well-meaning characters, many or most of whom must die horribly in order for the plot to advance. Just as we have a required scene in which the villainy is dumbly invoked—the hero's visit to the disguised devil who ceremonially sets him off on the quest for the bad guy (who is standing right there, shaking his hand)—Max von Sydow in *Minority Report* (2002)—so are we treated to numerous scenes in which, just like the villain, subsidiary characters behave exactly as the (decent) people they claim to be. But with these folk there is no surreptitious message: watch out, nobody is what he seems to be, and everybody around the hero is a faker. Instead of that, the hero's friends and teammates are taken at face value, and either effortlessly forgotten or horrifyingly sacrificed. Cut the throat of the best friend, shoot the girlfriend, throw the lifelong chum off a balcony. The evil villain is also *taken at face value* in the particular, peculiar sense that he is made in the script to look somewhat iffy right away. He has a stare that goes on a millisecond too long; he has a sideways leer; his tastes are far too exorbitant and lush, effete, leading to a supercilious pride. "But," screams the script, "I am not revealing him!" The script is pointing to its own use of disguise by partially stripping it away to hint (bravely) that *maybe* things are not what they seem to be, on either side of the moral spectrum: what they *deeply* seem to be, when we consider the crystal goblets, the crystal chandeliers, the crystal bracelets, the yacht named *Crystal* . . .

What must be met through the script cheat here is a double challenge:

- The villain must be introduced clearly enough early enough that when he "pulls off his mask" and shows his true colors the viewer is not so shocked and displaced as to be unable to maintain a position of engagement with the film. What is needed is "surprise" that is not actually surprise, because actual surprise is momentarily debilitating. "I only look like the nice man you see," the villain must smirk, "You will not be too surprised to learn that I am somebody else . . . but of course you will not learn that just yet." The *fact* of the Mabuse derivative using a mask is not the great secret; the depth of his depravity is. We knew he was bad, but who on earth could be *that* bad? As with the race for status by amassing wealth, a race for negative status by amassing horror; in both directions the centrality of measurement, characteristic of the Age of Science.

- At the same time, and without compromise, the viewer needs to be shown a believable, admirable, even adorable hero, someone who merits being looked up to but who, mysteriously given his strengths, cannot see until the film's climax what the audience has suspected all along. If he is so noble and so astute, how are his powers of observation so limited or so dulled? And by contrast, if he is truly so incapable, how can he be our hero? The claim could be made that in the twenty-first century we are hungry for ordinary heroes, people like you and me, fallible sorts, except that much care and expense is taken in these films to show that the hero is anything but ordinary. He is athletically, militarily, strategically, and intellectually way ahead of the crowd. Yet evil, secretly present, overrode him.

Evil ostensibly superior to intelligence, to strength, to light. The dramatic Force of Moral Purity comes from the same authorial pen that suggests bloodshed, maiming, decortication, defenestration, scarring, gouging, burning, slicing, and all the other apparently desirable traces of The Bad (for a good example see *Sabotage* [2014]). The idea that through every exercise intelligence will never match the powers of the dark (chthonic, evil, debased, or desanctified) and the idea that one should tolerate without striving to erase multiple and rabid displays of violence, are contradictory. Holding both sides of this conundrum in the palm of the hand at once is the scripter's greatest cheat.

Can it be that finally the innocence of the hero is more vital to us, to the film, to film's potentiality than anything he or she can do? Innocence floating to the top in a fetid basin of corruption, malevolence, murder, and fragmentation. Even impotent innocence, as long as it looks pretty. The hero was only pretending to strength while being, in truth, just as helpless as we are.

10

Keeping Minutes

FIGURE 10 *Ansel Elgort in* Baby Driver *(Edgar Wright, TriStar, 2017)*.

Time flies, but not in cinema as in life.

Consider that within the first seconds of David Lean's one hundred and ninety-seven-minute *Doctor Zhivago* (1965; from the 1957 novel by Boris Pasternak) we meet eight-year-old Yuri (Tarek Sharif) as he marches through the cold steppes to the funeral of his mother. Only a few minutes before the film's end we witness his death by heart attack on a Moscow sidewalk. Within just over three hours, then, we attend almost the whole life of this character, child prodigy, doctor, supreme poet, husband, father, lover. As the film unspools the little boy grows in size and maturity, the young medical student becomes hardened to life and to love. The middle-aged man struggles with his Russia and his poems. How strange is the experience of sitting before a screen and seeing all this long history pass by, before one gets up to leave. Even odder is the reflection afterward that the pieces, if one may say, of Yuri's life do not, in the film, seem equably extensive, flowing to culminations at the same rate. His arrest by partisans late in the film happens in what seems a blink; his studious regard at his mentor's side as an attempted suicide has her stomach pumped, much earlier, is slow and methodical. This elasticity of narrative time is one of the features of cinema as art, as Victor Perkins taught in *Film as Film*. The motion within which one feels oneself caught up is variable.

Plenty of other films accomplish a character's "aging" or "development" or "transition," yet not so repletely as *Zhivago*. In *The Magnificent Ambersons* (1942), for a classical and wonderful example, arrogant Georgie Minafer (Tim Holt) grows into repentant George Minafer in a swift editorial flare. In Welles's *Citizen Kane* (1941) the eponymous protagonist (Welles) surely ages, and visibly so, but we met him already in late childhood, and then with only the briefest moment to examine him, swiftly, through a window. As we watch *Zhivago*, what can we think time to be, that a poet's more than five decades might pass before us, contracted entirely within only three hours of our lives?

Contractions involve anticipations, a sense of phrasing. As one begins to be enraptured by a melody the ending hints itself, more and more firmly. Well thought at least since Aristotle is the capacity of fiction to embody and compact time, and all the rudiments of cinematic shooting and editing, the grammar of film, afford opportunities for speeding up time (*Fellini Satyricon* [1969]), slowing it down (*Umberto D.* [1952]), bringing it to a halt (*Murder on the Orient Express* [1974]), making it seem not to exist (*One From the Heart* [1981]). Life is fictionalized as a malleable material that can be drawn and squeezed, cut apart and put together, shaped and re-shaped. And there are several ways a transition can be effected from one piece of film (showing one diegetic moment) to another (at another time). As John Carey nicely showed, changing conventions have existed in cinematic history for detailing to an audience the "fact" that story time has passed.

We experience film moments and passages by way of their occupation of time, their procession. But little attention has been paid to the tempo of the movement, an element that is central to our filmic experience.

The filmmaker can cause some moments to pass very slowly and others to race, all without using those (cutesy) conventional effects: pages of a calendar flipping quickly to show months elapsing, dates flashed onscreen to show years going by, newspaper headlines flying past, or blunt references to significant cultural events or changes of fashion. If we compare, say, the voyage into the future in the 1960 and 2002 versions of H. G. Wells's *The Time Machine*, a fiction explicitly about temporality, we find that the earlier film satisfies itself with scenic change and some slight lighting effects, whereas the later film uses a full-scale computer graphic sequence to show buildings shooting up and falling down in mere seconds, wars evaporating in seconds, inventions flashing on and off, day turning into night over and over and over and over as with a strobe. The implication here is that were we to have access to a Time Machine, and were we to ride it into the far future, our optical experience would be something akin to this effect produced by (the time machine of) cinema. Or for an example very different: in *Easter Parade* (1948) there is a musical number with Fred Astaire dancing in front of a chorus, all this watched in stunned admiration by Judy Garland in the shade of the wings. Suddenly, we see something new. Astaire is dancing at half-speed in front of the chorus continuing to dance at full speed.[1] Consider as well slighter variations, subtle modulations of tempo, adjustments of the story clock that are cheated, produced in such a way as to carry action forward usefully for the storyteller but without the audience being let in on the curious stretchings of the taffy of time.

Tony Richardson's *The Entertainer* (1960) offers a double metronome, a parallel (ostensibly simultaneous) pair of dances, running against each other at different tempi (as with the *Easter Parade* number). We are probing the life of Archie Rice (Laurence Olivier), a washed-up song-and-dance man at the end of his sad career. To regain some chance of pocketing enough money to pay the tax man, he is putting his aging father to work, Billy Rice (Roger Livesey), former mega-star now in his dotage but feisty. He believes he can still catch an audience. As he gets dressed backstage Billy doesn't stop muttering about his routine and his illustrious past. We cut away from his blithering to the hot-lit stage nearby, where a salacious and notably rhythmic routine, "Put Me Among the Girls" (by Johnny Wakefield and C. W. Murphy) is in progress. Jump back to Billy coming into the shady wings, still without his jacket. Archie and the loving but exasperated daughter Jean (Joan Plowright) are both hunting around for it. Back to the stage, "Put me . . . among the . . ." Back to the wings, Billy getting his false mustache on—it's enormous, preposterous—trying faces with it. Back to the stage, "Put me . . ." Now in the wings, however, Billy is having trouble breathing. Back to the stage. Hot, hot lights. In the wings Billy is having *serious* trouble breathing. Archie tells the stage manager to signal the singer to stall and we catch her from the wings dancing offstage, a false smile on her lips, quickly demanding what's wrong. "Billy isn't feeling well, you have to go back and do another verse. Go back. You have to go back!" She goes back onstage and picks up a reprise, this time almost doubling the tempo, "Put me among . . ." Backstage Billy has collapsed. Back to the singing. ". . . among the girls! . . ." Billy is in his final moments. Billy dies. All of the cutting here is designed to give the impression that the many events occurring in different visual fields—the stage, the wings—are in a single temporal space, yet if we consider each side of this twinning alone we find the clock ticking by, the "downbeats" of expression, not matched by those

---

[1] For a discussion of this routine, including a technical explanation, see my "Bells Are Ringing."

on the other. The stage song is jerky, frenetic, wild, mechanical. What's in the wings is somber, vague, stuttering, like a candle flickering out. Billy dies between two visual phrases of the onstage song. His anxiety and palpitation is brought on, we are given to suspect, by fear of the stage moment, which for him, through the whole sequence I've detailed, is coming closer with more and more rapidity. That is: as time runs out (on his reprieve from the audience) it seems to pass more swiftly. This is a standard parallel editing situation, originated in 1911 by D. W. Griffith for *The Lonedale Operator* but here, thanks to performative talent on both ends, there is a distinct quality of variation between what the singer is doing (with false gaiety) and what is happening to Billy. The moment of Billy's death can be imagined to be a race for him, while for Archie the future is opening up to a bald and salted field in which no happiness will grow. The future opens slowly, as though tiers of curtains are being drawn away from Archie's eyes when he sees his father expire, but the song he cannot help hearing in the background has an unrelenting tempo.

But it is our proceeding through the film I wish to examine. Not the death scene alone, but how we move away from it into what happens next. The speed of happening. We move (instantaneously) to the funeral scene, on a hilltop under a gray sky. The transition is through a normal dissolve, taking about a second or two. We feel ourselves moving now as in conventional, unmanipulated film narrative, at an even and uninterrupted pace. No matter the events being narrated, the film is giving them over . . . the film is giving them over . . . the film is giving them over. But since there is a relation between diegetic events and the extra-diegetic editing pattern, we can watch *how* the film gives things over. Billy dies → We are at Billy's funeral. No time seems to pass between the two events, no distinct time: a mere inhalation. No time for Archie to sit at a table and think. No time to mourn. No time to make funeral arrangements. The film could linger over the absence of the fondly remembered Billy, or over the anxiety of nervous and nervous-making Archie, but what it does instead is direct our attention to its own forward flow through the ether.

If we think of the temporality of the backstage sequence in *The Entertainer* (wings >>>>> stage >>>> wings >>> stage >> wings > stageWINGS) and then of the temporality of the shift to the funeral, death |---| funeral, we find that felt, known, experienced, and depicted time is handled in two different ways, first in (increasingly swift) metrical steps and latterly in a leap across a gulf. Once again: not what is happening, but how it is that, in seeing what is happening followed by what is happening afterward, we breathe our way forward. In the stage sequence of *The Entertainer* and in the large arc of *Doctor Zhivago*, the underlying assumption is that so many things happen in a life, even in a few hours of a life, that each and every one of them cannot be shown onscreen: some (artful) elision must occur. But beyond elision is secretly accelerating and decelerating elision, making patient (tranquil) and anxious (jerky) elisions. In the end, elision is the control mechanism for the advancement of what is to come. It is possible to cheat the fact of the modulation of elisions.

Elision and holding off oncomingness are intrinsically and very profoundly musical. In his autobiography, *Little Did I Know: Excerpts from Memory*, our greatest contemporary philosopher, whose life was devoted to both thought and harmony, writes of the signal part played by anticipation in, as he says, "our need for music" (Cavell 400). Stanley Cavell was remembering a traumatic moment when he first came to consider this, but the nub of his suspicion was that the musical interval, a fundament of musical form, was tied in its power and effect to the very human experience of waiting for a release yet to come. It seems a wholly musical aspect of cinema, then, that scenes might move differently, some promising resolution swiftly, here, now, here, now, here; and some implying that time and life move in an *adagio*, that change will surely come but one must be patient for it. One thinks of the spluttering, egotistical Italian music teacher in *Kane* (Fortunio Bonanova) pressing Susan to get a phrase right---NOW! Her lack of vocal talent will become clear to everyone, but not quite so swiftly as that. By contrast, if we watch Baby (Ansel Elgort) sitting at the wheel of his robin red getaway car while his associates hit a bank in *Baby Driver* (2017), sitting at ease with his headphones on, singing along with the music, using the steering wheel as a drum set, twitching and gyrating in his seat all the while keeping his calm, steady eye on the doors to the bank, we see a progression that could well be an unbounded wait. In fact, he is so appealing to watch waiting that we wish the moment could go on for the whole length of the film, and feel irritated when it is interrupted by the thieves racing back with the loot. Anticipation is variable, as musical tempo is, but it is always the extension of form through tempo, the placement of event in a phrase of anticipation, that builds the musical character of a drama and fills its heart.

Audiences sense this if they do not explicitly know it. They do not expect diegetic movement to be uniform. In *Baby Driver*, immediately after the bank heist, and its culminating, very long, unbelievably catastrophic and near-catastrophic road chase—a *prestissimo staccato* adventure if ever was—we see Baby cruising happily and in an idiosyncratic little dance down a sidewalk to fetch coffee (more on this later). The pace is all new, but the shift away from a prior pace to a present one is part of the music that is expected in cinema. The building up and cultivating of this expectation, however, is a cheat: a mounting of cultivation that occurs while the viewer is blocked from noticing that she rides in a vehicle driven by someone whose foot presses down upon, then pulls away from, the accelerator.

Beyond all of this rests a still more colossal cheat.

Regardless of the tempo at which a scene's or moment's "melody" is struck, regardless of the number of beats to the minute it has (a metronome marking of sixty meaning that there is one beat every second), regardless of the stretch of action, the actual minutes of clock time, always quietly present, move by without tempo. Tempo is an artifice laid over time. The clock has no tempo, but it is through tempo that we experience what it registers. (By altering some of the words in a sentence, or its length and placement, a writer can affect the reader's sense of tempo in reading. But the ethereal page is always underneath.) Ingmar Bergman illustrates this paradox in *The Touch* (1971), where Bibi Andersson slowly walks around the thoroughly objectified body, stilled upon the bed, of her recently deceased mother. On the wall we see the hand of a clock jigging along in its mechanical life. Tick-tick-tick, time goes by as one is frozen in the face of the living and non-living bodies together.

However it is that time passes--if we can say that it actually does *pass*--as far as we are able to surmise it passes uniformly. Yet even this cannot be established. If we can presume—as we *do always* tend to presume—that there is *one time and only one time*, and that it has a certain precise density, we must see that through any pair of film scenes, any dramatic processes, where a figure moves ahead through anticipation to some resolution or partial resolution, first to one destination and later to another, through all of this sped-up or slowed-down movement time itself is uniform. The expectation of an event coming after this event produces an interval, but intervals are superimposed on time. When we go to the movies, we spend an hour and a half or two hours of our lives looking at the screen, *no matter how fast, and across what time frame, creatures on the screen appear to move*. In musical terms, when we listen to two movements of a symphony, an *adagio* and then an *allegro*, even if the first seems reflective and swellingly slow and the second brisk and urgent the clock ticks on, through both.[2]

Filmmakers are obliged to cheat this truth, and anyone's acknowledgment of it, by concocting, just as composers do, variable scenes, slow, fast, fast, faster, faster still, very slow, stationary, fast again. Failing to do this would leave the audience open to seeing how artificial even accidental scenic rhythms are; how filmic "time" and time are not the same. At that point the screen's precious illusion is broken. The changes in tempo, the accelerations and decelerations, keep us awake and waiting for what is to come as though it really is *what is to come* rather than only "what is to come." Our actual wait as cinemagoers must be the wait we endure as human beings, because it is (only) as human beings that we are cinemagoers. We wait through the drumbeats for tomorrow, knowing that Time makes dupes of us all.

---

[2] And the conductor can tell you how many minutes and seconds that movement will take. But that clock: I forbear here to include discussion of Einstein's dictum that the issue of whether one is moving with the direction of the ether, against it, or perpendicular to it actually affects the clock in use.

Of Performances

{11} **Monster!**
Lon Chaney; *The Phantom of the Opera*; *The Unholy Three*; *The General Died at Dawn*; latex; Akim Tamiroff; *Predator*; *Alien*; Jacques de Vaucanson

{12} **A Star, Not a Star**
The General Died at Dawn; Akim Tamiroff; Nils Asther; *The Bitter Tea of General Yen*; *Dragon Seed*; Gary Cooper; Andy Serkis; David Warner; Clint Eastwood

{13} **Pain**
Montgomery Clift; *Judgment at Nuremberg*; Jack Nicholson; *Chinatown*

{14} **Measuring Up**
Dustin Hoffman; Marlon Brando; Christopher Walken; Christian Bale; Sean Astin; Robert DeNiro; Vincent D'Onofrio; *Jaws*

{15} **Privacy**
Animal Kingdom; *Psycho*; *Elephant*; *North by Northwest*; *Alien: Covenant*; *Blow-Up*; *The Forsyte Saga*; *Taking Lives*; *Atonement*

{16} **Dance**
Kramer vs. Kramer; *Annie Hall*

{17} **Keyed Up**
Hercules; *Samson & Ulysses*; *Casablanca*; *Remember*; *An American in Paris*; *The Big Store*; *The Birds*

{18} **Don't Believe It**
Baby Driver; *Singin' in the Rain*; *Born Yesterday*; *Mystic River*; *The Hospital*; *The Train*; *The Gypsy Moths*

{19} **"I Love You"**
The Third Who Watches; *The Third Man*

{20} **Surrender**
Edward Scissorhands; *A Ghost Story*; *Alien*

11

Monster!

FIGURE 11 *Raymond Massey in* Arsenic and Old Lace *(Frank Capra, Warner Bros., 1944).*

Manifesto:
 It is never wholly salutary to launch an attack on other people's fantasies, though in the case of politico-military fantasies taken to extremes in everyday life (the dream of the Master Race) such attacking has more than once proved necessary and effective. But the imaginative, fabular,

mythological fantasies that distort for thrill, that effect some telltale *frisson*: these live within our darkest thoughts in a logic none of us can control or find the origin of. If conscience doth make cowards of us all, so does consciousness. In film stories, the character of the monster is everywhere, chilling, terrifying, awakening, warning, provoking us through the mask of characters' engagement.

Monstrosity is not always biological or corporeal, yet in film, which must relentlessly make shows, the body warp is the least ambiguous way of suggesting it. While in the real world there are no twistings, meldings, hypertrophies, absences, duplications, and miscolorations of the body that lack a medical explanation of one kind or another,[1] usually in film narrative the scientific rationale for monstrosity is either only hinted at or vaguely circumlocuted, or skipped entirely in favor of a disarming depiction floating without rationale. When we see disfigurement in the everyday, and without an explanatory rationale, it can be powerfully disarming, and this happened to me many decades ago when I was brought face to face with the residents of a retreat for the bodily disfigured not far from Chicago. The faces I saw there I had dreamed, or seen, onscreen dozens of times, yet I knew those cinematic faces were accomplished with makeup, while these were not. Misshaping, duplication, swelling, and, perhaps most disarmingly, misplacement of facial elements were legion, among these mostly quite young people who got along with one another effortlessly but seemed wary of outsiders coming in to visit, even with the kindliest intention.[2] If there were explanations to be had in every case, one did not have them, they were not provided. In cinema the explanation is often not provided, surely not with any accuracy of detail. Stories instead labor to regale us with the "magical potion," the "experimental technique gone awry," the "chemicals inadvertently mixed up," the "mad scientist," the "curse," and so on.

Monstrosity onscreen is typically produced by means of an actor transform, and Lon Chaney (1883–1930) is widely considered to be the first performer who accomplished this in a prodigious, elaborate, and brilliant way. His mutations, as the monster in Frankenstein, as the Phantom of the Opera, and as legion others are Hollywood legend, particularly since he designed and almost always single-handedly applied his own makeup.[3] While the general proportions of Chaney's face remained more or less constant through his work, the qualitative modulations he produced in his eyes, nose, mouth, ears, hairline, cheeks, and jaw were so radical that his

---

[1] A medical explanation that vitiates the chill of encounter, according to Fiedler.
[2] David Lynch's *The Elephant Man* (1980) will give plain illustration of the sort of kindly intention that has no weight in such circumstances.
[3] See Matthew Solomon's analysis of Herbert Brenon's *Laugh, Clown, Laugh* (1928) in "Laughing Silently."

creatures gave all signs of having genuine physiognomies of their own, and he became known popularly as the Man of a Thousand Faces.

Chaney's tricks usually included some combination of three main features. He would use tiny wires to pull or twist skin or musculature (painfully), thus producing ricti, uncontrollable slobbering, the twisted gaze (as he told me in 1986, Dick Smith used a similar technique for removing Frank Sinatra's jowls in *The Detective* [1968]). Secondly, Chaney would use make-up paints to color and miscolor parts of the body, always with a view to what the effect would be on black-and-white film (where color contrast does not function); and he would wear wigs, rings, distinctive costumes in general. Thirdly, he would use performative techniques: grimaces, postures, limps, stooping, and so on. His last film was Jack Conway's *The Unholy Three* in 1930. He died at the age of forty-seven, before the era of latex.

For Lewis Milestone's *The General Died at Dawn* (1936), Charles Gemora invented a liquid latex application for producing slanted eyelids on the Caucasian actor Akim Tamiroff (1899–1972), celebrated later for his work in *Dragon Seed* (1944), *Touch of Evil* (1958), *Ocean's 11* (1960), and *Topkapi* (1964), among many other films. The latex eyelids permitted Tamiroff's Genl. Yang to appear on camera without the actor experiencing notable discomfort (as was Chaney's lot). The success of Gemora's application promoted its use more liberally in *The Wizard of Oz* (1939) for, among many other demonstrables, the Wicked Witch's extensive nose and much of the Cowardly Lion's adorably cowardly face. Gemora (1903–61) had been a Hollywood stand-by for populating the famously popular gorilla suit (partly because he was not tall); he worked that way with Chaney in *Unholy Three*, Béla Lugosi in *Murders in the Rue Morgue* (1932), the Marx Brothers in *At the Circus* (1939), and many other films, before leaving the suit behind and turning alien, beginning with *War of the Worlds* (1953).

Latex applications are made after a face mask is taken of the actor, baked to hardening, and then used as the substrate upon a copy of which the artist applies the monster "flesh" using soft, moldable clay. When the copy and the original are superimposed, blank spots will show wherever the build-up is found and from these blanks, separate latex partial masks are fashioned. Ron Miller astutely notes how these partial masks are used even when a whole face is to be refashioned, since one of the telltale giveaways that makeup is being used is a rigidity of expression, and multiple partial masks allow the actor much more muscular flexibility. (It goes without saying that actors develop a particular facility in using the musculature of the face.) The partials are applied to the actor's face using spirit gum or other adhesive, having been fashioned in the first place with extremely thin edges so that make-up paint applied on top can blend them smoothly and imperceptibly with the actor's (normal or painted) skin. There are so many cases of supreme latex effects in Hollywood cinema it would be impossible to construct even a short list, especially considering the bizarre creatures in George Lucas's

Star Wars (1977), the Gary Oldman transform as Dracula (1992), the water creatures in *Hellboy* (2004) and *The Shape of Water* (2017), and one of the most celebrated makeup jobs in Hollywood history, Dick Smith's aging of Dustin Hoffman in *Little Big Man* (1970).

As legion movie fans know, from having grown up with the relative normality of "monstrous" configurations on their favorite screens, latex applications painted with extraordinary artistry can be used to turn any actor into virtually any sort of being or thing, as long as the producer is willing to spend the money and time and can find the make-up artists to do it. The turning is affected, however, by whatever knowledge, or half-knowledge, lies latent in the viewer. While most who watch films do not know precisely how disfigurements are created, they do know that disfigurements *are created*, and that as they watch the unspeakable movements and actions of screen monstrosities they are seeing tricks.[4] (A neat evasion is to avoid gaining knowledge of the cast in advance. With Bong Joon Ho's *Snowpiercer* [2013] the benefits can be delightful.) Whereas with stage magic prestidigitation was a central, perhaps *the* central, technique—keep the hands moving so quickly nobody can see what they're doing—with the "magic" of screen make-up the artist using latex and paint is not at work in front of the audience at all. The process can therefore be as slow and methodical as production schedules allow for. The chief skill involves hand-eye coordination: having deft skill cooking and baking the latex and then a keen eye for figuring the precise colorations to apply in blending it in (with a view to photography under specific light temperatures and against specific backgrounds).

But as in stage magic, the essential problem of cheating appears and reappears: something is being done that must be made to appear as something else, or as nothing. The latex pieces must not be seen *as latex* (Andy Serkis, *Lord of the Rings: The Two Towers* [2002]); nor the paint *as paint* (Judi Dench, *Shakespeare in Love* [1998]); nor the dental implants *as implants* (Jerry Lewis, *The Nutty Professor* [1963]); nor the special contact lenses *as contacts* (David Bowie, *The Man Who Fell to Earth* [1976]); nor there being a point where the bald cap or wig attaches to the skull (F. Murray Abraham, *Amadeus* [1984]); nor the actor's technique in modulating vocal and muscular movement (John Hurt, *The Elephant Man*). With the screen "monster," a sharp professional eye is turned not to what has been done with the body but to how this change will look once photographed, and so the make-up test is invaluable. Nevertheless, the screen "monster" walks a very thin tightrope in performance for many reasons:

---

[4]The education of many viewers, especially young ones, has been fostered by Mission Control Media's television show *Face Off* (2011), featuring Michael Westmore (of the Westmore dynasty), Ve Neill, and other artists.

- Having little or no experience with medical anomaly as rationale, still the viewer "knows" that the monstrosity on view is not, *in reality*, monstrosity. Our social organization is arranged to keep medical extremities far from public view. When physiognomic extremity is seen onscreen it is taken, de facto, as fabricated.
  In fact the audience comes to film ready from the outset to see special effects, and this is a sword that cuts two ways: they want to see something *special*, far beyond the everyday in proportion or extension; but they also want it to be an effect, and to know that it is an effect as they (safely) experience it. The effect per se is the thrill now, not the charged creation that can be accomplished through the agency of special effects. Thus, aliens are not alien, zombies are not zombies, but we take pleasure in gawking at them and we permit ourselves (within the safe darkness) to wonder.
- Challenge is an essential quality here. If the monstrous makeup must seem a concoction to some degree it must also face the viewer's accumulated knowledge head-on by suggesting, somehow, an unimagined, unheard-of step that goes beyond traditional concoction. Those other creatures were intelligible as fakes, easily recognizable; *this* has gone past the horizon, and is something we do not and cannot know. (In 1939, when the film was first viewed, the Munchkins of *The Wizard of Oz* were not read immediately as actual midgets in make-up and costume. In 1972, naïve again, audiences didn't see amputees [Mark Persons, Cheryl Spark, Steve Brown, Larry Wisenhunt] inside the drones of *Silent Running*. In 1977, naïve yet again, they didn't fathom that a dwarf [Kenny Baker] was inside R2-D2 in *Star Wars*.) Confronted with the expectation of technology at work yet also dimly aware of unknown steps-forward, the viewer is forced to take up the contradictory position, "I know at the same time that I do not know," and the contradiction is a source of excitement (excitement because it is unstable).
- Yet, too, a lapse of belief waits at the core of the experience, or a shift in the focus of belief. Chaney's Phantom (1925) seemed to skip before the eyes as a real being, much too quickly, too momentarily to be fully taken in and thus horrifyingly beyond one's ken. The movement was fluid, humanesque. Yet the being seemed inhuman. The expression on the face was agonized, the sort of expression one would have seen studying the photographs in Charles Darwin's *The Expression of Emotion in Man and Animals* (1872), except that movie adepts did not study these photographs before coming to watch *The Phantom of the Opera*. Believing in the phantom *as phantom*, watchers were displaced from the order of the everyday, carried swiftly and urgently into a dream (nightmare) consciousness. This metamorphosis of the

audience, this powerful charge, is absent when viewers know they are looking at effects: absent but also transposed. Now the wonder is for the artistry of the effect, a technological fascination rather than a mythical-existential wonder. "*How did they do that???,*" a question that could never be asked unless someone was certain an effect had been "done." The resultant thrill is similar to that of tasting something wonderful at a special restaurant and then wishing for the recipe, yet also wishing not to have the recipe so that the mystery of the taste might linger. One wishes not to have *the recipe that one knows exists in some special kitchen.*

- In order to shock the viewer, monstrosity is extended, reproportioned. It is proposed as enduring, ineradicable (Gary Oldman's Dracula). Or it moves faster than we (than screen characters) expect, or even can have expected (the creature from the crewman's thorax in *Alien* [1979]), with the result that it acts far before one is prepared to defend. Or it operates through an augmented structure: there are more parts than can be taken in by a portrait shot; parts that work in strange and unprecedented ways (the wrist control in *Predator* [1987]); or parts internally ramified or multiplied far beyond the catalog (as in the Alien's triple mouth). The monster type may also look disconcertingly human but control a vast source of power or incalculable space (Dr. No's island [1962]; the underground storage in *The Circle* [2017]). But the more outlandish the design of monstrosity, the further it climbs out upon the thinning branch of believability, the more it seems an outgrowth of cinematic production. In the constant battle to one-up the past, character designers are always daring the catastrophe of dematerializing their monster, making it a mere mechanism. One of the tricks of the cheat is to have the monster, the fabrication, perform an unlikely action, which will take the audience's attention away from the structure of the thing itself and focus it on some ironic juxtaposition of objects and events. The paragon is Jacques de Vaucanson's mechanical gilded-copper duck (early 1740s), here described by Richard Altick, citing in part Sir David Brewster and in part W. J. G. Ord-Hume Arthur's citation of Vaucanson himself:

> "It executed accurately all [a natural bird's] movements and gestures, it ate and drank with avidity, performed all the quick motions of the head and throat which are peculiar to the living animals, and like it, it muddled the water which it drank with its bill." It also quacked. But its most spectacular accomplishment was digestion. "The Duck [wrote Vaucanson] stretches out its Neck to take Corn out of your Hand; it swallows it, digests it, and discharges it digested by the usual Passage." (65)

The "discharge" proved most popular, most tellingly evidential of the trueness, the naturalness, and unaffectedness of the thing. How, if it does this, could it be constructed?[5] With the alien in *Alien*, two discrete tricks are used to cheat the audience's attention. First, we never see the entire thing top to bottom until the very end of the film—and then only far too briefly—so it is left to the imagination to specify magnitudes (as with the shark in *Jaws* [1975], where the trick is taken one step further in that the entire creature is never quite visibly shown, unless it is underwater and thrashing, at which point the thrashing action distracts us). The second is that the innermost mouth is geared and powered to run over with distracting drool when—so unbelievably swiftly—it snaps to produce death.[6] The monstrous body is doing Show Business. Before one can stand back for serious evaluation, the "show" is over.

The actor playing the monstrosity finds in the mirror that a trick of a different kind has been played, because inside the appurtenance the self is very hard to find. The movement of the face must be relearned to fit the moldings. Movement on land and in the water must be naturalized to the species— the "species"—of the thing instead of to the needs of the performer. And of course working conditions deteriorate almost always, because one is locked into gear that limits muscularity, produces sweltering heat under film lighting, is hard to eat through and so on. The point here isn't that the "monster" is uncomfortable for the performer to act but that the discomfort is a distraction and being "monstrous" in front of a camera requires intense concentration of effort, all of which must scrupulously be hidden. The monster is the veritable star of the film, and when it is onscreen audiences do not back away from inspecting its smallest features, like nineteenth-century nursemaids picking lice from the head of a child. The telltale small feature is one of the cheats of the monster trope: it distracts attention from the thing as a whole.

With monstrosities, the viewer is positioned in two discreet atria, one in which is exhibited nothing but technique, strategy, know-how, manipulation, and craft, and the other a cavern of fear and disorienting "ugliness," misshapen abysm, horrifying excesses and absences. We see the special effect we have paid to see, surely, yet are shocked by sights that go far beyond what we knew to want, sights that disarm, terrify, and rouse other screen characters just as they do us. If in this delicious and elaborate cheat our foreknowledge fails to salve, is this because in some grand *Schadenfreude* only the thought of destroying our knowledge through exceeding it, brings release?

---

[5]The Eating Machine at Hobart's Museum of Contemporary Art works in a cognate fashion, although with literal transparency.
[6]A derivation from the snap of the animated crocodile in Disney's *Peter Pan* (1953).

12

A Star, Not a Star

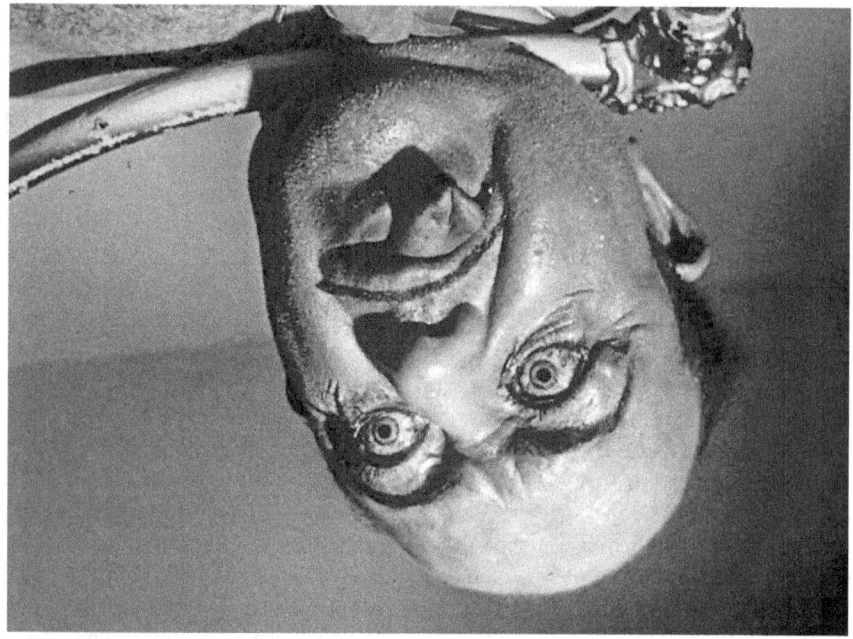

FIGURE 12 *Akim Tamiroff as a vanquished Grande in* Touch of Evil *(Orson Welles, Universal International, 1958).*

Hollywood labor practices divide the on-camera workforce, since some actors are deemed magnetic to audiences and must be highly remunerated, and others are relatively decorative and more replaceable. The star magnets bring crowds to the box office, nowadays no less than in the classical era, and must reward the viewer's investment with a glowing and plainly discernable presence onscreen. Stars thus play key roles. Character players are cast as eccentric sidekicks, bizarre villains, personable henchmen, and the like. The problem that produces the relevant cheat here is one that becomes clear when we note the differential optical allure of both types of actors.

The star must shine, indeed must appear to be the source of light that makes the whole screen shine. No matter the character in question, the star beneath has the viewer's commitment of love, and must therefore be manifested in an unquestionably recognizable way.[1] There are few exceptions to this formula. Not only will the star appear to dominate the story, he or she will on every appearance dominate the screen. But often a scene must be played with a partner who is a character actor, a persona comparatively enshadowed. Character players, in role, are as often undetectable as detectable, as often marginal as nearly central, as often accompanied by a team of other character players as alone. These actor types, stars and character players, are effectively statuses that attach to persons in an ongoingly negotiable way. In a film like *Murder on the Orient Express* (1974) (reprised in much the same form in 2017), many former big stars—Michael York, Wendy Hiller, Jacqueline Bisset, Jean-Pierre Cassel, Vanessa Redgrave, Anthony Perkins—are relegated to character-player status, albeit "star character-player" status, against the repeating (but in this case marginal) domination of Albert Finney (latterly Kenneth Branagh) as Hercule Poirot. However, given that the star is central and the character actor only (but fully) adjacent, how can the difference between their statuses be reconciled with (a) the need for the fiction to elude viewers' consciousness of status difference as such, (b) the director and cinematographer's need to compose shots including both at once, and (c) the ongoing requirement that no matter what happens, all the players onscreen should appear to belong in the same package, the same "world," yet at the same time belong there in different (classed) ways?

Return with me to Akim Tamiroff, born of Armenian descent in Russia, a student from 1918 of Konstantin Stanislavsky. A consummate professional, he was noted in America for his character parts, playing always against a dignified, handsome, or flamboyant star (Anthony Perkins, Frank Sinatra and Dean Martin, Orson Welles). The thick Slav tongue, the pouting eyes, the extraordinary bejowled cheeks made possible a kind of expressive plasticity, to which the actor's off-kilter English added tang. Like so many character players in Hollywood's golden age, Tamiroff found himself cast many times over in the same sorts of roles, it being a production practice trusted and true for directors and heads of casting departments to look at

---

[1] Although in this context, it is wise to consider Noa Steimatsky's inspired confusion watching Michelangelo Antonioni's *Il provino/Prefazione* (*The Screen Test/Preface*, 1965): It was impossible for her to know "at what level of the re-enactment we stand. Fiction and actuality, action and re-enactment, person and role are compressed" (183).

actors by way of clips from previous films, often and easily borrowed from any studio (nowadays, eager actors seeking work provide their own "reels," which are typically high-definition disks containing scenes from the films they've made). The prosthetic eyes he wore in *The General Died at Dawn* (1936) attracted attention in their own way in a white-dominated culture that doted on caricaturing other cultural types—in her book *Romance and the "Yellow Peril,"* Gina Marchetti gives a critical view of this kind of colonization, commenting, for example, on how the Swedish actor Nils Asther (1897–1981), a notably handsome face in Hollywood from 1926 through the mid-1950s, played Frank Capra's *The Bitter Tea of General Yen* (1932) in "grotesquely designed" makeup (50). Asther had no prosthetics there, but he did sport sharply defined and outrageously angled eyebrows, which consistently brought attention to his eyes. As to the easily converted Tamiroff, in the mid-1940s, when Harold Bucquet and Jack Conway were preparing *Dragon Seed* at MGM, they would have been familiar with Tamiroff's work in *General Died* and possibly even have cast him because of it. The cheat of the latex was therefore helpful not only for establishing a precise (and peculiar) caricature but also for furthering an actor's career.

The character player is faced with the challenge of unendingly transforming the self for camera, so as to be able to play one distinct type, say, at Warner Bros. for three days' shooting and a quite different one at Fox just afterward for two days' more, and so on. Make-up, hairdressing, the manner of carrying the costume, vocal modulation, quirky facial expression—all these features, taboo for the star who must always be a Self—aid in the changes. While one will find the star's portrait photograph a fairly accurate representation of the being one has been seeing on the screen, the character actor's might be unidentifiable, posed as it is in unaffected clothing, without makeup for character, and in less sculpted light. In fan magazines and other publicity, the star's head shot will gain a different kind of prominence, showing him or her off as a blemish-free, intensely expressive point of contact. Stars typically don't need to withdraw prosthetic masks for such "everyday" photography because as a rule they don't wear prosthetic masks in the first place, they show and sell themselves as being what they "actually are." In the case of Gary Cooper, a photographer will take care to light the facial bone structure prominently, to have bounce light emerge from the eyes. And assistants will see to it that the hair is not only impeccable but also harmoniously singing. Cary Grant will look debonair and relaxed, as though the camera is his mother. Joaquin Phoenix—who started out playing characters and became a star, yet maintained a preference for odd characters to bear his stardom—appears on a cover of *Vanity Fair* (for October 2019) standing at the lip of a swimming pool in a white shirt and black tie, but he is in the pool, having been doused, and is sopping wet: adventurous, daring, over the edge, serious, sincere, and calm, with dark penetrating eyes. Marilyn Monroe is photographed by Richard Avedon in a tight-fitting black spangled dress with an extended V-neck. She is fully made up but her hair is in shambles (the Hangover look) and she gazes slightly off-camera with her eyes half drawn in what seems like sadness. For Bert Stern her platinum hair explodes in waves, her eyes beckon, and her smile tickles amusingly, as though she is having a dirty thought.

All actors' head shots are cheats—they must be; their function is not to tag but to flog the person—but the star shot is an elaborately fashioned one. Studio executives don't cast on the basis of this sort of thing, since stars are either on contract with work routinely assigned or else independent contractors desired in advance by the producer. But for both the glamour figure and the character figure, advertising photographs and narrative cinematography both work to create two bonds: one of the actor with her diegetic character, the other between the characters themselves (the relation between the actors being almost always of no account on set). The identity of any actor as employee is wedded to the identity of a character and also to the ensemble of personae to be found inside the narrative. Each character abiding there must fit. Yet at the dining table of labor, only some sit at the head.

But the star's centrality and the relatively peripheral placement of character actors work together to fashion a complex cheat upon the audience's knowledge. The screen must be composed with fields of relative importance so that the viewer can have assistance in swiftly focusing and following the details of a story. This is one good reason why star players constantly have more intense lighting. But the lighting of character players in the star's surround must seem to logically derive, to be related in intensity if not to match, and all this irrespective of the "natural light" that is being simulated in the "place." Lighting does a lot to bring actors' work in line, to affiliate characters while maintaining bright star centrality, and thus the lighting hides actual working relations in a very particular way. In the world of film labor offscreen, however, hierarchical distance may not exist between workers or may exist very acutely, it being possible for a star to attend the same synagogue on Rosh Hashanah as the character actor he played with yesterday, or play poker with him on an off-work weekend, or refuse to be in the same room. Yet at the same time, and completely covered over by both script and light, one performer may be separate from another—even when both are stars, or both character actors—for reasons audiences do not surmise. One example: in *Sweet Smell of Success* (1957), Burt Lancaster and Tony Curtis share star billing, and both feature as centerpieces of any and every shot that includes either of them. But Lancaster's company was producing the film, and in effect he was paying Curtis for his labor. There is a power split between the two onscreen but it has nothing to do with the power split behind the camera. Harry Carey and later his son Harry Carey Jr. were intimate friends of John Wayne, but in John Wayne's westerns they again and again played subsidiary character parts to his star turns.

More than external manipulations—the lines in a script, the beams from an arc lamp—the professional training and astute talent of performers cheats their relations as people and in character very profoundly. Friendships are masked over. Antipathy is whipped into a delectable frosting, as we see in the ultra-smooth scenes in *State of the Union* (1948) with Katharine Hepburn and Adolphe Menjou, whom she loathed, and the testy scenes there and in *Adam's Rib* (1949) between her and Spencer Tracy, with whom she was in love. While in their relations the characters of a story will display social status and differentiation, before the lens there is fostered the illusion that the performances themselves, *as performances*, inhabit a democracy.

13

Pain

FIGURE 13 *(Top) Montgomery Clift in* Judgment at Nuremberg *(Stanley Kramer, Roxlom, 1961); (Bottom) Jack Nicholson with Faye Dunaway in* Chinatown *(Roman Polanski, Paramount, 1974).*

On a May evening of 1956, engaged in the filming of *Raintree County* for Edward Dmytryk, Montgomery Clift was in a serious car accident and sustained multiple injuries to his face. Notwithstanding the producer's fears that his star's disfigurement would negatively affect the box office, Clift himself took a stoic position, imagining that he would now be able to act better and the film would be a smash. He was interested, here as always, in the quality of the performance he could give, not the pretty face he might present to the camera for the viewer's pleasure. Of course, from a fan's point of view Clift had been showing a notably pretty face since his early work in *Red River* (1948). The smooth-faced innocence he projected there was in need of serious modulation by the time he came to shoot *Judgment at Nuremberg* for Stanley Kramer in 1960.

As Rudolph Petersen in *Judgment*, he is put up by the American prosecutor (Richard Widmark) as witness against the Nazi atrocity perpetrators on trial, and then grilled mercilessly by the defense attorney (Maximilian Schell). The testimony occupies a scene that runs some twelve minutes, with Clift onscreen throughout. He is forced to whimper self-consciously that the Nazis sterilized him, that he is now living only half a life. The defense alleges that the sterilization took place because Petersen was mentally defective to begin with, and the hesitant, stammering, out of control speech he produces in response, the gazing around and flailing helplessly in the witness box, would indeed seem to evidence a deficit (although not excuse decisions that may have been made because of it). The performance is a tour de force of vulnerability, insecurity, victimization, and loss. In the many close-ups of Clift, it is unavoidable that we notice that damage upon his face, the scar traces, the pudginess, the disproportion between his left and right sides, all of which adds to the weight of the moment.

Another vision, now. In Roman Polanski's *Chinatown* (1974), the private detective J. J. ("Jake") Gittes (Jack Nicholson) is caught prying around a Los Angeles aqueduct one night by a paid henchman (Polanski), who proceeds to teach him to stop nosing around other people's business by literally slashing his nose with a knife. From here onward, we see Gittes with a clean white bandage on his nose. Beyond it, the face of Gittes is thoroughly the face of Nicholson, tanned, smart-eyed, purposive.

Two prominent facialities, then, Rudolph's and Jake's by way of Clift and Nicholson, clearly and unmistakably presented as marred. Do we regard them with an appreciable difference, the plots that ground them notwithstanding? One face is wounded, the other is "wounded." How are the visual treatments unalike, and what responses do each mobilize? Like other actors who have been disfigured, or eccentrically figured, through birth or through accident (Joaquin Phoenix and Stacy Keach with harelips, Natalie Wood with a missing finger, Mark Hamill after his January 1977 accident) Clift brings up a hesitancy on the viewer's part to look directly, a respectful (or fearful) withdrawal in the face of extreme vulnerability on show. One is overcome by the sense that if there were any way for him to do it, Clift would cover over his scars and his reshapen face and resort to only performing a character's grotesquerie, yet also that any cover-up would bring him closer to the looker's attention not further away. The only solution is willing (even proud) acceptance of the blemish as, now, an intrinsic part of identity, a feature that belongs where it is, and hoping that the viewer will make the necessary allowances. Nor is serious wounding always a strictly visual matter. When we have a performer with a broken voice, we hear the break in every syllable of dialogue, but make allowances (Jack Krugman, Julie Andrews after her Broadway run in *Victor/Victoria*), fully aware that, unlike a false limb but very like a tortured face, it cannot be hidden. Erving Goffman notes in *Stigma* one of the effects of body repair: "Where . . . repair is possible, what often results is not the acquisition of fully normal status, but a transformation of self from someone with a particular blemish into someone with a record of having corrected a particular blemish" (*Stigma* 9). Clift's "blemish" not only resulted from but was the accident itself; his history and his presentation of self in *Nuremberg* is an indication of a repair dutifully and successfully undertaken. Goffman goes on:

> While a blemish such as a facial disfigurement might put off a stranger, intimates presumably would not be put off by such matters. The area of stigma management, then, might be seen as something that pertains mainly to public life, to contact between strangers or mere acquaintances, to one end of a continuum whose other pole is intimacy. (51)

The matter of Petersen and Clift together on the witness stand complicates analysis. Petersen has been disfigured in an invisible way, but his wail renders the sterilization at least conceptually visible; at the same time Clift, who *is* Petersen at this moment, carries a very visible and totally unchangeable stigma. Between the audience and the character, between me and Petersen as I watch his torment (and perhaps think of it as a remodeling of his torment in the car, as Clift), there is a relationship of intimacy, "public intimacy." We are always intimate with the characters of the screen but this peculiar intimacy is touched by the touch of fate.

The structuring of Rudolph Petersen as a man whose sex has been maimed and, more chillingly, as a victim at the hands of the Third Reich, gives him a stigma not only ineradicable (like Clift's facial trauma) but in a way pendulous, of great gravity. The male can think of himself as "the same" (but altered) if his face is reconstructed surgically.[1] But if his testes are removed surgically or blocked chemically from functioning his self-

---

[1] This applies to Mark Hamill's transformation and to Ann-Margret's after her stage accident in September 1972.

regard must suffer a far more grievous assault, an ongoing, repetitive, unending assault. By placing this aspect of Petersen's life into the script, and foregrounding it through the way he is treated and how he responds during testimony, the script in effect allows the performer to cheat (by outbidding) his own disfigurement, surely to cheat the otherwise overpowering effect of it, the "Something-strange-has-happened-to-the-way-he-looks" effect. We think of the face and the sex, here both wounded, as imbricated with each other. The facial structure is part and parcel of the character who wails that he was sterilized. If he is mentally deficient in any way, we can read the face as proper to that condition. In any event, we are given multiple reasons for downplaying the wounds on the face. Knowing we will be likely to respond this way, the cinematographer has no qualms lighting Clift flatly, letting the gray tones of his torso and face drop back into those of the witness box. He is only a small organic figment in a gigantic arrangement of sociopathic terror, and the vision of him testifies to this reduction and gearing of self, as he testifies to atrocity.

As to Nicholson's Jake Gittes, his is not, like Clift's, a face to be lost in performance while being remembered as belonging in a crowd of stellar presences—Burt Lancaster's, Spencer Tracy's, Judy Garland's, Richard Widmark's—but instead the principal figure and perceptual object of *Chinatown*, an embodiment to be featured always, through special, accreted illumination, central positioning, perfection of focus. Curiously, as the story winds on Jake's nose bandage continues scene after scene to appear pristine white, as though refreshed nightly (a not implausible arrangement), and because of that stark whiteness it becomes the single prominent point of concentration no matter the conversation or the action. Functionally, of course, the effect is produced by the prop and wardrobe assistants, working with the makeup people, who actually replenish that bandage routinely through the day's work. Any perspiration or staining it picks up, even inadvertently, will show and be likely to mar a shot. But the effect is to make Gittes's handicap leap into our awareness and gain identification, through the extreme clarity of its display, as constructed. An interesting side effect is produced here for aiding the narration. Jake is a sly fellow. He becomes a character who might very well, it seems, be putting on his own contrivance, distracting the attention of those he meets just as Nicholson is distracting our attention. This lends him tactical kenning, deviousness—more than the placid-looking Nicholson would convey (without overtly laboring) if his face were untouched.

The narrative is helping both actors work with facial disfigurement as they appear, one by incorporating the disfigurement itself as a metaphor for a more general debility which must be openly shown for the Clift scene to properly work, the other putting light not on the wound itself—Jake's nose—but on strategic labor to wrap it up, cover jobs. Two cheats, then. For *Judgment*, don't put any cover at all, none, not of any kind. The subject matter is so grandiosely horrible that only the deepest truth of performance can legitimately and honorably address it. Then, for *Chinatown*, put a cover and show it as the central fact at hand. Nicholson is (satisfyingly) at risk of coming across as tactical himself, something of a chameleon who hides in public view, or at least strategizes beyond our awareness. Clift becomes a model of sincerity.

14

Measuring Up

FIGURE 14 *Jon Voight and Dustin Hoffman in* Midnight Cowboy *(John Schlesinger, Jerome Hellman Productions, 1969).*

"We already and from the first discern him making this thing other," writes Norman O. Brown (8). This thing, the whole thing, the central thing as he must know it, himself, yet also the self as entity, his body. The body as sized. The body as a performance in itself.

    Acting is more or less one or the other of two possibilities, in practice. It is being, which is living, in its fullest essentiality, such as is seen with Kristen Stewart in *Personal Shopper* (2016) or Elliott Gould in *The Long Goodbye* (1973). (The camera catches it all. You cannot lie to the camera.) And this is metamorphosis. (Metamorphosis – Becoming – Transformation – Hiding.) As there is never anything onscreen but truth and whole truth, what was complete and real at the moment the aperture was open. In this sincerity of the flesh there is constant metamorphosis in that as time passes life flickers and develops and no two moments are the same. The actor must authentically feel his presence in his moment, and must negotiate secretly, that is, privately, with the character in order to give the character openness to, and access to, that mutability. In such acting one does not play a scene, one plays a life.

On the other hand we have construction, masquerade, where the character is a device the actor literally or metaphorically puts on. Anthony Hopkins as Hannibal Lecter, Mary Astor as The Princess Centimillia in *The Palm Beach Story* (1942). One finds here a notable constancy moment to moment, the constancy (almost rigidity) of a portrait in a frame, because the mask is not alive in itself. Also a strange quality of presentation: metallically articulate, burnished, intensified beyond human limit, not what we find in people but what we find in people represented.

With both kinds of acting the performer has no choice but to be, finally, in self-knowledge as well as in presentation, a body, this body and not that one, and whether the body is expressed without reserve (Brando in *Don Juan DeMarco* [1994], playing a toss-and-catch-the-popcorn game in bed with Faye Dunaway) or is affected through contortive manipulations (John Hurt as Merrick in *The Elephant Man* [1980]) still the camera cannot but show it, there being nothing else of the performative self to show. And what the camera shows must stand, hold itself, breathe, and get dressed. What is it that happens onscreen with the actorly body as the camera team contrives to shape, arrange, and show it? Especially in regards to a key aspect of the actor's body, something no actor and no person would go through life without both sensing and recognizing: size. Toooo large. Tooooo small. Jusssst right!

As to corporeal girth, overall weight (involving bone density), or bulk, essentially horizontal displacement, impressions are not difficult to manage. Pads work very well (Orson Welles as Falstaff [1965], Angelina Jolie in *Regression* [2015]) and are nicely concealed, but lens choice can be easier still, wide-angle lenses (below 50 mm) tending to spread space laterally (permitting a more closely-positioned camera) and spreading body elements (facial elements notably) outward from the center of the screen. Dream sequences, drug hallucinations, memories, and so on are very frequently established through extreme wide-angle photography, 18 mm or 20 mm. On the contrary, the longer the lens the more the body will withdraw.

Clothing may hide a body the camera finds oversized in relation to others in the scene, in construction but also in fabric texture and color in relation to the texture and color of the props and set. Color affects us strongly through contrast (on which see Albers). Coloration can cause a garment, and therefore the body encased in it, to apparently recede into or spring from the background, as a shot or character placement might require. The cinematographer can use filters to affect a coloration's distinctness and sharpness; and can use the shadows created by his lighting to hide part or all of an actor's body, as happens with the very heavy Brando as he makes an entrance in *Apocalypse Now* (1979).[1] Extreme corporeal variation can come into use for, among other possibilities, bold comedy, as with Arnold Schwarzenegger and Danny DeVito in *Twins* (1988) or Alan Hale with Errol Flynn in *The Adventures of Robin Hood* (1938).

Actors will sometimes slave to adjust their weight for a role, and some will be made legendary for their exploits. Christopher Walken filmed Cimino's *The Deer Hunter* (1978) after a six-month-long diet of rice and bananas, depriving himself until he was spindly. Christian Bale used diet and exercise to bring himself down to almost fifty-percent of his body weight for *The Machinist* (2004). Going in the other direction, Sean Astin bulked up for *Lord of the Rings* (2001, 2002, 2003), much as Robert DeNiro had done for *Raging Bull* (1980) and Vincent D'Onofrio for *Full Metal Jacket* (1987).

Actor labor, coloration, lighting, lens, and garments can work in combinations to establish girth, then. But with fully grown adult actors the length of the body is not so malleable outside of CGI today or the make-up and photographic tricks we find in, say, *The Nutty Professor* (1963). An actor who is very tall will be very tall at work; a short one not as tall as that, and these sizes will have to be accounted for. What can production do when a tall actor and a shorter one must walk side by side or hold a conversation in close-up? Or when shots of two such actors in the same setting must alternate in editing (in good match)? If a tall character and short character interact against a detailed background, both of them shot at chest height, the background will wildly fluctuate and the viewer's experience will be of a vertical bouncing when the shots are cut together. The cheat for a single shot involves cranking the camera up or down on its stand or dolly, thus getting a framing of the actor's head and shoulders roughly at chest height, and with careful attention to the kind of background present and how much of it shows. One way to avoid the background bouncing is to have the set designed from the start so that one side of it looks very different than another, each side usable as background for one of the unmatched actors; the effect of creating exchangeable backgrounds at differing heights is thus made somewhat easier. Of course when computer graphics are creating the background, or when bluescreen or greenscreen are being used, background problems of this particular kind disappear (giving way to others). And with very neutral backgrounds, a director can line each of two actors up on the same side of the location or set and later have the pieces of film intercut as though they are on opposite sides.

---

[1] My gratitude to Dan Sacco for this and related observations about actor size.

As to considerable repetition of a shot take after take, presuming that the camera position is fixed and the camera height is registered, an exposure can be redone as many times as needed; the actor usually has marks on the floor to indicate where to stand, and script supervisors will work to help the actor re-strike a particular pose, get a cigarette partially smoked at the right length, have a bead of sweat repeatedly on the brow located exactly over the center of the left eye. Paired shots usually require that the shorter actor be placed on a wooden box or a ramp, and some actors wear lifts in their shoes; thus the camera can favor the taller figure and a usable composition can be obtained (Claude Rains on an ascending ramp as from a distance he walks toward Ingrid Bergman for *Notorious* [1946]). Filming *Jaws* (1975) off Nantucket, Steven Spielberg discovered the nightmare problem of making shots that would match in editing, because here he had not only actors of differing heights (Roy Scheider distinctly taller than Richard Dreyfuss) but a boat that was bobbing on the tide. As the side of the boat went up and down, so did the horizon line, but in order to make stable editing possible the horizon has to be kept constant, a problem that here required enormous patience, long waiting times, and willingness to waste film. People who admire *Jaws* tend to overlook the astonishing coherence of the editing. Those critical spirits who flagellated Spielberg's reputation by accusing him of economic profligacy on set failed to see how any attempt to use film stock inexpensively would have made for an impossible editing job.

Between actors and their characters we find a certain elemental separation that invokes the problem of cheating in that audiences are not always to be let in:

- The actor as (i) an embodied being, one who moves about the social world in a normal way, and the actor as (ii) a characterized being, one who sparks and maintains the drama, are essentially identical twins, identical in that the person who acts and who underlies the character is the same person who made way to the studio to be filmed. Yet for the viewer these two personae neither match nor overlap. The body of the performer, viewers rarely note, is a construction for the screen, a visibility resulting from adjustments: of lighting, of clothing, of the lens, of the camera position, of other performers nearby, and so on, and through this construction the viewer imagines that body as a sized and a palpable one. Sensing the onscreen actor-character body to be coherent and present, one values its size, even believes in it, yet in the everyday world, where people reside, the same performer may well be taller, shorter, broader, slimmer, and generally other than was envisioned onscreen. The viewer is led by production cheats to an imagination of character size, alone and in relation to other characters, yet viewers can tend toward extending this reading off the screen and into real life. The imaginary character size exists in a space inviolable, the space of the story as seen, and need bear only the slightest affinity with the performer's size off-camera.

The star close-up will very often take an actor's face and magnify it so that it fills the entire screen. Spread poster-like before us will be the well-known features in sympathetic array, the parts bearing relation to one another in a predictable and pleasing manner. But in the real world, close-up lenses missing, we do not have opportunity to view the star, or anyone, with this kind of proximity mixed with sharp focal clarity. The performer is of necessity smaller in reality. On the street one can *perhaps* recognize the performer (there is a delicious scenic moment in *The King of Comedy* [1982] about precisely this: "When it's him it doesn't look like him."). But the comparison between screen persona and real personality, as embodied, goes far beyond the simplicity of measurement. For the viewer there are subjectively felt components of any perception. The screen body has a plasticity actual bodies do not present themselves as having; it seems to float in space rather than being gravitationally bounded. Onscreen there is no gravity. The screen body travels magically, is cut apart and apportioned magically (medium shots, close-ups) then magically reconstituted (long shots), touches the objects in view in an only barely discernable way. The actor's everyday body, should one encounter it in the everyday, turns away in privacy or modesty or distraction and does not present, "face-on," that recognizable star hieroglyph.

- Nor is there recognizable pathos in the screen body itself, outside of what a scripted moment might inspire us to read or imagine. The actorial face that is scarred, blemished, misshapen—all medical contingencies—is made over so that the character face can harmonize with other character faces. Extra lines are filled; pimples are covered; scars are painted just as sometimes for good dramatic reasons scars are *painted on*. The character body is entirely fashioned in coherence with dramatic requirement, and at the expense of the producer; but the performative body is kept in reserve—it operates through a history of employment. We must always remember that in the golden years, actors on the studio contract found that the way they appeared, both onscreen and offscreen if they were in public, literally belonged to the studio.

- Further, although we come to know the character in her diegetic surround, become able to effect recognition in a flash, we tend not to know the actor at all, except as a result of work. She offers a routine presence behind characters roughly like this one (*like*: recognizably covering or based upon the same actorial persona). The face goes with a name, if only a name attached to a face. We don't know the autobiographical past, the birthplace, the friends of youth, the formative experiences, the taste for color and shape and flavor, and much more. We don't know the size, whether we would have to look up to say hello or look down or look straight forward. In the classic theater, with the large screen, we always look "up." The figures are gigantic. On handheld screens, we always look "down" at figures that are figurines. This "knowledge" of a performer is in reference to the age of mega-publicity in which we now live, and in the context of which we watch films. There is so much "information" of one kind or another circulated about the people we see transmogrified on the screen (Anthony Hopkins on Instagram, September 2019, petting his tabby) that it is virtually impossible, watching them in narrative action, not to entertain some kind of imagination of their presence in (what is for us) some wholly fabular "real" world. Eating at Musso's. Giving an interview to MSNBC. Getting out of a stretch limousine with a love partner of the moment, grinning, gleaming for the cellphone cameras. We need not see these kinds of trans-diegetic scenarios to suspect they exist, yet our conception is perforce vague. In response to the strength or frequency of our imagination (publicity is aggravating that imagination relentlessly), we may be confused into thinking these are people we know. Of course, this is fetish. When I was two years old I had a much chewed-up stuffed lamb, and I gave him a name and he was my friend.

It is true, too, that once a characterization is in progress the actor finds the character and only the character, in the mirror. Perhaps for the actor the character has no size, since he or she is well aware that characters will appear great or small as the picture crafts them. When a very tall actor (Peter Graves and Alexander Siddig are two I have met, whose height was striking) works, he will make certain his character knows how to easily pass through doorways and so on. But he will know, too, that this character at ease in his body is not himself, does not watch doorways and low ceilings the way he, almost instinctively, does—not unless the watchfulness is in the script. The character merely is, but the actor works with his own bodily "equipment" and that of his co-workers to negotiate the pictorial space together. Once the film is finished, no character will be too tall or too short. Every one of them will be just right.

15

Privacy

FIGURE 15 *The cast of* Starship Troopers *(Paul Verhoeven, TriStar, 1997).*

Actors on the screen always experience a kind of privacy, a closeting, in that we cannot get at them or be with them in the same space and time (and they recognize this and feel it as they work); they are untouchables, a cast(e) aside. But characters may never find guarantee of such privacy. How they are exposed to us varies script to script, but exposed they indubitably are.

Wash

In *Animal Kingdom* (2016), teenaged orphan Josh (Finn Cole) has taken up residence with his grandmother, her chum, and her three sons, who range in age from their mid-twenties to late thirties. One of this crowd, Shawn (Andrew "Pope" Cody), is fresh out of jail, and eager to help the other three with a heist job. He is assigned to find a getaway car and wishes to commandeer the help of the young visitor. At the moment in question J.—as he calls himself—is in the shower. Important to be clear: (a) a young actor at least appears to be in front of us, completely naked, self-cleansing; and (b) a script has specified that in this scene the character called "J." will be showering. Earlier moments have explicitly not identified J. as mudstained or uncomfortable physically, that is, desperately in need of a shower, and nothing in the immediately ensuing action dictates that J. should be recently cleansed. We have to find him somewhere, and the decision has been made to put him in the shower.

Our camera is both inside the shower stall with J. (a cursory half-nod to *Psycho* [1960]) and malingering on the wafer-thin border between the stall and the bathroom, where Shawn makes his entry and presses J. to hurry up and get dressed so they can get going. In the shots of their interaction the camera is cranked up so that the images are uniformly chest-up on both sides, eyeline match being established with some care since, again as per the script, it is to be signaled to the viewer that the sudden intruder is not looking, just as the viewer is not looking (has not been given to look) at J.'s body, only at J.'s receptive face. The sound of the running water is continually present. There are intermittent, and rhythmically edited, de rigueur shots of nude J. running hands over himself as he listens (that is, Cole gives a believable show[1]).

This little scene figures for me here because it is a notably clear and uncontaminated example of a much replicated trope in contemporary television and film work. Some character of interest, alone or with someone else, is in the process of showering or taking a bath when the camera discovers the action and attends it. Eric Deulen and Alex Frost in Gus Van Sant's *Elephant* (2006) tellingly cleaning each other, an erotic and revealing moment if at the same time cheated through (typical) genital masking; Daniel Craig and Olga Kurylenko in Marc Forster's *Quantum of Solace* (2008); Virginia Gardner showering behind a heavy (but not heavy enough) curtain in David Gordon Green's *Halloween* (2018); Keanu Reeves with Ana Ularu in the bathtub in Matthew Ross's *Siberia* (2018); Scarlett Johannson simulating Janet Leigh in Sacha Gervasi's *Hitchcock* (2012); Matt Damon fingering the warm green water as Jude Law bathes in *The Talented Mr. Ripley* (1999); little Jack Dylan Grazer showering with his favorite clown in Andy Muschietti's *It* (2017); teenaged Gabrielle Anwar sucked under the

---

[1]Believable: he follows a series of steps that could be taken from a Shower Manual that all of us possess and use religiously, as though nobody could be in any doubt as to what some other person would do in a shower.

soapsuds in Abel Ferrara's *Body Snatchers* (1993); Anthony Michael Hall, Ilan Mitchell-Smith, and Kelly LeBrock in John Hughes's *Weird Science* (1985); Amy Sedaris in Jon Favreau's *Elf* (2003); Jim Carrey in Tom Shadyac's *Ace Ventura: Pet Detective* (1994); Sissy Spacek in Brian De Palma's *Carrie* (1976); Kate Beckinsale in Dominic Sena's *Whiteout* (2009); Michael Pitt, Eva Green, and Louis Garrel in Bernardo Bertolucci's *The Dreamers* (2003); Nick Robinson in Greg Berlanti's *Love, Simon* (2018); Molly Ringwald in Hughes's *Sixteen Candles* (1984). And the water drips on. All of these scenes have three features in common:

- First, a very unequivocal sight is offered to the viewer of the character(s) positioned *in* a shower or bath. That is, showering or bathing is going on without any shadow of doubt, and going on believably. The shower enclosure or bathtub is included as a distinctly marked, centralized feature of the scene. While there are exceptions, normally we see the shower or bath take place when the character does not explicitly need a shower or bath; and in the scene that follows afterward other characters normally do not trouble to mention that the bather has just discernably bathed: "Golly, you look clean! You must have showered!"
- Secondly, the view afforded the audience, unlike any view presumably afforded one of the characters who steps into the place for some reason, is foxily curtailed, this in such a way that as one watches the screen one is made conscious of not only the view being presented as an open gateway but also of its limitation: limitation of perspective here becomes a blatant subject of cinema. Not only am I seeing, but somebody has made an arrangement for me to see, because what I am seeing is *invisible stuff*, seen but not to be seen.
- Thirdly, the scenes *as set* are almost always entirely irrelevant to the narrative, the shower scene in *Psycho* being the definitive exception: whatever important and/or revealing dialogue is set under the running water could as well be spoken elsewhere, even more clearly because without the running water sound. Our young J. could be finishing his bowl of Special K at the breakfast table, for instance, when Shawn interrupts him and presses him to hurry. He could be outside, washing a car. He could be watching tv. He could be nestled on a comfortable chair under a warm light, doing his homework or even—*mirabile dictu!*—reading a book.

Are we led into the shower because, absent narrative declarations notwithstanding, the character is evidently stained or dirty, disheveled or wounded in some way, and narrative decorum requires not only that he or she clean up but that we witness the clean-up act? (In *La trêve* [2016], Joann Blanc's Inspector Peeters is often extremely out of sorts and showers for recuperation [that never comes].) Why would it not be sufficient for the showering character to say, "I'm going to shower," and then emerge cleaned up and in fresh clothing? In what way can we understand it being necessary that the shower be *evidenced*? Leaving aside the nonsensical speculation that we find the character inherently false and want to get underneath the clothing to find the true identity—since there is nothing inherently true about skin, in performance—can we think we understand ourselves entering the shower because we doubt some situational sincerity and ingenuousness, suspect the character is really using the shower or its sound for a purpose quite other than cleansing, and one we should discover (Roger Thornhill [Cary Grant] slyly deceiving Eve Kendal [Eva Marie Saint] in *North by Northwest* [1959])? Or do we imagine there is some important piece of information that can be conveyed only in the shower/bath situation, a code to be discerned in the grout between tiles? Regarding that last possibility, it's important that we keep in mind a simple fact of visual narrative: that the tiles would gain attention. No matter the content of the dialogue in a shower or bath scene, the fact of the naked body in a warm and cozy circumstance will override it. Do we enter the shower because, as the filmmakers have correctly presumed of us, we are eager to see the actor without clothes and the shower or bath is the perfect (and perfectly conventional) pretext? Thus, in watching the shower/bath scene, or at least in watching ourselves watching it, are we made conscious to some degree of our own desire to strip the performer? Do we have to make some particular self-identification in order to accede to this hypothetical situation, a self-identification that is a potential self-incrimination, and does the setting of the shower or bath assist us, prime us, in doing that? Because stumbling into a stranger bathing can be a cause of shame or embarrassment, a cheat is required in the cinematography so that we can preserve our self-esteem, and that cheat is the odd framing. Is cinema perhaps always everywhere about stripping away coverings, so that a desire to see people without clothing is no different, really, than a desire to hear them tell the secrets of their heart? What are we presumed to want always and already, that we can relish being given such spectacles?

A certain realism is built up by masked shower/bath scenes. We are systematically brought close to a stranger's body—speaking in terms of the intimacies we all allow, both the character and the actor are in fact strangers to us—and allowed, even encouraged, to participate in two optical fictions:

(a) First, that this stranger, while being rather fully unknown, is nevertheless, somehow, not quite a stranger. Not only can we apply a name, in fact two names, but this person is sharply and instantly recognizable as belonging to a type we have learned to recognize already: not only a female, say, but a female of a certain race and age, who does or does not have a job, and if she has a job who works in one kind of occupation rather than another; so that altogether she belongs on a kind of "team," containing not only her but others as well. She is an exemplar. We establish a relation that is *typical* rather than personal, encountering and swiftly accounting for aspects that accord with our general expectations of *people like this*. And we neglect, if we even detect, quirky, idiosyncratic, personal tics, gestures, and features such as birthmarks, scars, flab, tattoos, all of which could be used in typification but tend not to be, yet at the same time help mark this body as foreign, belonging to someone with whom we *might* form an idiosyncratic personal bond. The birthmark or tattoo at the top of a bicep, gleaming now with water, becomes only "a birthmark," or "a tattoo," which is to say a singular example of the broad category of colorings we would name "birthmarks" or of the broad category of designs we would call "tattoos" in full knowledge that a legion human beings have similar ones and scrub them in the same way, yet also, to some little degree, *this* birthmark or *this* tattoo, drawing us in a little or nudging us away. The shower is not the place we zoom in for deciphering. In the shower/bath we are presented with singular *examples of* types, but not individual people. Not fully and only *this mark, this tattoo, this positioning, this body, this arm, this man* but Mark, Tattoo, Posture, Person. This cataloging is a form of cheat, in that the peculiarities, the *puncta*, that describe a single unique embodiment are flattened and subsumed under types so that we can operate as though we do not see the actual solitary nude human being in the frame.[2]

(b) Secondly, that we are performing the gaze upon this body strictly in accordance with well-accepted conventional norms of behavior in such places and such company. There is a proper way to watch someone shower, and we know and obey the rules. We look at the head, the head and shoulders, the shoulders and back, even the feet, even the hands using soap upon one of the body sections just named; but we do not look at the genital area, the buttocks usually, the breasts, the armpits, the lower belly. This allows us to think of ourselves as modest, polite, authentic, and sincere rather than being forced to recognize ourselves as eager to see other people's privacies. But this opportunity to confer nobility upon our own gaze is afforded by the camera's careful placement and framing, not by our self-discipline (which in this case is a mere follower), and so it is an ethical cheat as well. We are never shown something from which the genteel person we would claim to be, would humbly turn away.[3]

The underlying question here, the question that brings the cheat into focus, relates not to our own prudish reticence to look at the naked body

---

[2] By virtue of its identificatory clarity the cinematic nude shot, notably in bathing, differs from the painted nude discussed by Kenneth Clark.

[3] The keyword here is "shown": we can much more easily be told, especially in printed fiction, since, first, the verbal mode allows full disbelief and secondly, the words on the page are not in public display—we are not seen seeing them, so that "turning away" is hardly requisite or useful. See for a particularly interesting example Bret Easton Ellis's *Glamorama* 382ff. And thanks to Jason Jacobs for pointing this out to me.

(the naked Star Body, indeed) or admit that we would like to, but to the persistent peeking that is arranged for us, and that we gleefully accept in the face of that reticence; in short, we have a hungry reticence that models itself as abstinent reticence; a reticent curiosity that insists on denying how curious we are. The requirement to direct one's emotional commitments in two opposite directions at once produces the requisite cheats that we find—cheats that help us: heavy glass shower stall doors and walls (easily penetrated by brutish tongue, as we see with *Alien: Covenant* [2017]!), extremely misty weather conditions, flagrant shower heads, copious lakes of bubble bath, or neatly positioned bodies or body parts. The neat positions work beautifully for camera, but no one would wish to suffer one of them in real life. All this notwithstanding the extreme care with which a cinematographer can compose his frame, using (very typically) the bottom cutoff line to dissect the bathing body. That cutoff line is an "offside" over which a hand or two can easily stray, as in grasping a bar of soap or other accoutrement that might attract attention; or as in reaching up to smooth water away from the eyes. The actor's face, a notably expressive zone, often acts as a body covering: that is, covers up the fact that the filmmaking team is covering up. The expressive face is endlessly fascinating, and also endlessly distracting if it belongs to someone on the marquee. It is because covering up must itself be covered up that cheats become fascinating.

There is nothing particularly new about prudery, modesty, or lascivious curiosity. What is worth attending to is the structural arrangement by which curiosity about the body and its private functions is *partially but only partially* satisfied, the limitation on satisfaction imposed in the name of some noble protection of vital interest, some show of diminishing the very curiosity motivating the style of the presentation in the first place. Without a presumption of curiosity about the body, there is no sense in visiting someone in his or her shower in the first place. Taking a shower does not beg accompaniment: it's too wet for a secret phone conversation, too humid for typing a code, too soppy for inscribing codes onto the tiles. And truth is, there are very few people who sing in the shower so well we would feel we were at a concert were we there listening to them.

At the beginning of the twentieth century, when John Galsworthy published *The Forsyte Saga*, civilized people repressed their curiosities about other people's naked bodies, sufficiently satisfied (at least as far as they felt it was acceptable to demonstrate) by the kind of hints that clothing could provide. Nowadays while curiosities of this sort are still repressed, guarded against, actively fought, there lingers a common pretense that they are not; that glimpsing, peeking, openly seeing are all commonly possible and socially acceptable exactly because they can be done. The camera's peek is taken *not* to compromise modesty because (only because) modesty can systematically not be admitted to. Thus, when the camera creeps down a hallway into a bathroom facility, and thence into a shower stall, where the water is running and a naked body is present alone or with another naked body (or, as in the case of *Starship Troopers* [1997], a platoon of them), nothing is marked in the screen image as untoward, strange, perverted, wild even though we are looking in the manner of those who are not looking. If the curiosity the camera addresses is considered a wild extravagance if not a transgression, the camera only marginally gives this the nod. Metonymic redemption: a body fragment sufficiently rounded and glistening to stand in (secretly) for the (imaginary) whole.

Copulate

Consider a relatively superficial cheat. Two naked bodies are writhing on a bed, steamed in the throes of lovemaking. By convention, one tends to hear an underscore heavy on strings and light on brass and woodwinds, a score absent the hyperbolic accents of percussion: violins as heartstrings. Or violins as nerves pulled to the breaking point. Usually in contemporary film at the beginning of the twenty-first century, the bodies and bed are photographed in color, although not a great variation in color is actually to be seen—high color contrast would separate out the bodies, give them roundness—amber light very often flooding over a bed with rumpled pink or amber sheeting and casting gleams over amber bodies. There may be a vocal track of moans and squeals, but they would be minimized in the mix and the scene would "read" just as clearly without sound as with. There is sometimes shown a (relatively swift) mounting toward climax, sometimes not. One is regaled by a virtual *Kama Sutra* of variant positions. And with some regularity one or both of the participants rises afterward and goes about doing something else. In all of this, the body *as visualized* is used as a self-cover: intertwined legs symbolize (stand in for, mask) the linked genitalia that, present or impending, are rigorously not shown and rigorously motoring the action; torsos overlap; arms interconnect to form bizarre glyphs as if while copulating the team are sending off coded intelligence. Parts of heads are visible, or whole heads severed from bodies, just enough to make sure the viewer can identify the characters and be pinioned to the drama. Of course the body parts we can see mask over the body parts we cannot. As to the point of view: the camera seems to rest just beside the bed, or perched on the sheets to the side of the bodies in play. *We are there.*[4] Sheets and duvets will decorously cover, and then salaciously uncover, parts of lithe, pink, undulating bodies, making a beautiful abstract

---

[4] A very popular weekly television series commencing in 1953, narrated by the prestigious Walter Cronkite, *You Are There* episode by episode posited direct narration of a celebrated, important historical event (the landing of the Hindenburg, the Gettysburg address, and so on)

composition that can be viewed from on high. When the upper erogenous zones of either lovemaker are shown they are used as sculptural forms for creating such abstracts, and for cheating the absence of the lower regions. Even the presentation of buttocks, seen from the side, can work as a tidy cover (the ass not as a thing to be figleafed but as figleaf itself).

Frequently climactic moments are covered over by lap dissolves, which can be multiplied to create a kind of alternating rhythm between dreaminess and awakeness in the characters and for the benefit of viewers. It is easy enough, too, to have the camera suddenly transported to another zone so that the orgasm is merely a sound effect from the distance or, indeed, substituted for by a telephone call or crowd cheer at a football game.

In cases of frenetic sex (increasingly popular after 2010) where very shortly after meeting for the first time the (entirely overwhelmed) characters race to disrobe in some private space and then conjoin vertically, say against a wall, there being no time to wait even for lowering the self to a bed, the camera dutifully shows the speedy dispensing with trousers, panties, skirts, in order to suggest boldly that erotic action is in play below the waist and of such urgency that decorum of any kind is out of the question. Urgency becomes the compositional form. The urgency is almost always further cheated through the actors' guttural expressivity. An example accomplished with some style and recognition of class priorities involves Ethan Hawke and Angelina Jolie in *Taking Lives* (2004). Another is the library lovemaking scene in Joe Wright's *Atonement* (2007), where we have Keira Knightley in a floor-length forest-green satin gown and James McAvoy in a full tuxedo. As their passion comes to the point of overflow, he has her pressed up against a burnished wooden bookcase, floor to ceiling, softly illuminated. It seems a simple—because exceptionally swift—matter for him to have her panties off and the brilliant green dress sufficiently hiked up, and his own fly (at this time in England he would say "flies") down, so that in a breath there is, presumably (because of her [virginal?] gasp), penetration: litany in the library. What we see is two otherwise dignified people, each representing a principle gender, standing and spasmodically jerking toward each other if at the same time maintaining cool British composure, all this more or less in full clothing (depending on the angle of view).

In the case of this film and this particular scene, the voyeurism conferred upon us is significant narratively, thus philosophically, because we are not the only lookers-on. A thirteen-year-old sister, Briony (Saoirse Ronan), garbed entirely in angelic white, has wandered in and is standing in frozen fascination, her eyes pried as wide open as clamshells. She will not turn out to be silent as a clam, however. Her report about Robbie and

---

with the audience "in direct attendance"; we were there. This was obviously an advertisement for television's ability to, as we were meant to sense, take us around the world.

Cecilia, however confused (we do not hear it, and have no reason at all for supposing she knows what she has seen with any exactitude), leads to Robbie being banished from the house and the love affair being destroyed. As the film progresses, this single instant has the deepest conceivable moral and emotional implications. Robbie's banishment and the tragedy of the broken love affair both expand in volume and meaning because of the authenticity, read *compelling heat*, of that lovemaking. Yet it was an authenticity that begged our belief, that demanded vicarious participation to be fully comprehensible.

Two frequent assumptions leading to cheats:

- That the personnel who make movies are the sorts of people who would believably engage in sexual activity whenever and wherever possible, with insatiable and inordinate appetites. The sex we see onscreen, therefore, leans toward the real, has a tendency, barring obstructions, to seem journalistic and hence believable; actually happening. BUT: we know, and can be presumed to know, that what we are watching cannot actually be happening. This verisimilar behavior is, and can only be, faked. And since we are known to know this (that we are knowingly looking at acting, after all), some trick must be pulled to con us out of that knowledge, to suggest that here, finally, and, thankfully, visible to us in perfect composition, is a moment of sexual *presence*. Actors, many fans assume, would always automatically want to have sex; the film system would be designed to facilitate the preferred view that they are doing so when they are not; and then finally the system would be designed *to inform us that actors are not sexually active in the manner that we think them to be*. The absence of the giveaway shot is direct evidence of this last contrivance, *because it is a discernable absence*. Even a central absence. We are openly shown that a culminating truth is being kept away from us, and in being shown that, something else is also kept out of view but not in such a way that we are aware of. That something is our shame, our overriding sense of propriety now violated with our participation. Since the orgasmic truth must be omitted, there is a sense in which we shouldn't have been there at all, not for any part of it. In *Atonement*, young Cecilia is frozen to the spot out of astonishment, curiosity, the hunger for experience, and shock; she cannot bring herself to leave. Neither can we, yet we feel we should, and when the sex builds we feel the cloister more and more. We want to see, quite desperately, but are surprised, even shocked, to note that we *can* see. This desire, fostered by what is onscreen, cheats the moral code we know we are violating. Our violation is one that, because of the helpful cheat, we need not atone for.

- Also, that we may—indeed must—be shown explicitly the outplay of an action generally (and widely) considered intimate and private, shown it without doubt—without the kind of doubt young Briony must have had—yet at the same time without untrammeled clarity. Clarity could be provided by a more clinical view—precisely the sort of view that would be labeled pornographic and avoided at all costs, yet at the same time a point of view that would in fact *show* what cinema in such moments is purporting, yet failing, to show. But the clinical view is treated as poison. The lovemaking scene is carried off in such a way as to leave the viewer with a kind of trembling modesty.

There is a far less superficial cheat about filmed lovemaking scenes. They systematically beg a certain provocative, deeply troubling question that surpasses the nature of the narrative itself and goes to the center of our film-viewing experience. We are always, by agreement, stood in for by the camera. The camera is our factotum and our simulacrum, our friend and our distanced eye. What is the camera—and what are we—doing in this place? We come to be near the bed because the camera merely moves to be near anything at all "of interest," yet how and why is this "of interest" and how and why does the camera move to it with such apparent casualness?[5] Casually, as though there is nowhere else the viewing eye could reasonably be at the orgasmic moment, nowhere any viewer would prefer to be. Even Lawrence Durrell's fascinated narrator, confronting the lovemaking moment, has a greater degree of modest self-consciousness as he finds himself describing "an indistinct mass of flesh moving in many places at once, vaguely stirring like an ant-heap":

> My sudden appearance must have suggested a police raid for it was followed by a gasp and complete silence. It was as if the ant-hill had suddenly become deserted. The man gave a groan and a startled half-glance in my direction and then as if to escape detection buried his head between the immense breasts of the woman. It was impossible to explain to them that I was investigating nothing more particular than the act upon which they were engaged. (186)

Durrell's viewer knows he was "investigating," while in our cinema watching we are held back from that knowledge, with purpose. We are merely there, not intentfully gazing, nor investigating, nor exercising curiosity, nor admittedly

---

[5] *Apparent* casualness, note. Since late in 2018 "intimacy coordinators" have been employed on-set as intermediaries between actors and directors, and choreographers of ideal sexual representations. More on the problem of achieving "comfort" in intimate scenes in Chapter 16.

feeling thrilled. The thrills pass into and out of us too quickly to be known as thrills while they are there. Our excitements are unnameable and invisible until seen in retrospect. The objectivity we find in Durrell—"They lay there like the victims of some terrible accident, clumsily engaged" (187)—is forever part of his textual narrator's talk and consciousness (the narrator is a long way off), however the very present film camera in lovemaking scenes has not penetrated, like the narrator in *Justine*, by accident. Could not have. Can do nothing by accident. Yet because of the cheat of the scene, accident seems to be everywhere.

As we pattern our interpretation of the lovemaking scene, in framing a reason for the camera's presence we also frame a reason for our own. How is it possible, how can it be rationalized, how can sense come of the fact that we are here watching this now? Watching directly, without mediation. As it occurs. Who could we claim to be, or not to be, in gazing the way the camera allows us to gaze? That the onscreen lovemakers were showing off to a third party (Georg Simmel's *tertius gaudens*) for augmentation of their own pleasure, and that the camera might silently be occupying the stance of this third seems a rather far-fetched consideration. Similarly disregardable is the thought that as watchers of this, we consider lovemaking—bluntly, sexual action—as no more interesting in itself than, and in fact not especially different from, any other perfunctory action, such as doing the dishes, cooking a pot roast, having an argument, making a bank deposit. It is simply behavior, that *only*, and we are simply observers, here and everywhere. This scene *isn't special*.

But hardly so. The special lighting, the artful compositions of form, the peremptoriness of the dramatic action all suggest this is not something quotidian at all. And, we must recall, even Durrell's narrator, adopting a quotidian point of view in order to "surprise the truth of [his] own feelings" (186), uses language with a kind of awed hesitation, as though he is aware that suddenly he is faced with something distinctly *not* banal.

It may well be with a kind of transgressive, even somewhat ashamed daring that we permit ourselves to be the seers the camera must be imagining it is photographing for. In the Durrell, the viewer-narrator's self-conscious reaction is produced by the lover's startled awareness and response; whereas in the cinematic scene the lovers have no such awareness to pique us. Indeed, the viewer who has lapsed into a thoughtless sleep while watching may well have no self-consciousness at all, but merely drink in the vision of naked flesh in the same way as everything and anything else onscreen. A true imbibition. A soporific dullness prevents even the elementary consciousness that certain truths, certain pleasures, certain eventualities are being systematically denied in the process of showing; denied without proclamation. To be offered a piquing sight and denied fullness is, after all, both an insult and a demeaning. For this to happen without indication, *quite as though it is not happening*, is an outrage.

Arise

Getting out of bed brings us from one world into another. There is narrative cogency: the character getting up is a person, persons sleep, when they have slept they get up. A character who remains alive but doesn't get up fluidly is either not well or very tired, neither condition generally useful for action narrative. Getting up is topically irrational: when we see a character do something, we do not need to be told that the night before doing it he was asleep. Principal in depictions of getting up is a coherently designed bedroom space, accurately reflecting either the private tastes of the sleeper or else those of the person whose bedroom is being shared (even if the space is a hotel room). Standard items of composition: rumpled sheets (almost never blankets); naked or semi-naked body(ies); evidence somewhere of sleeping habit (nude, shorts, pajamas); demonstrative semi-conscious attitude. By attitude we read the character's drowsiness on being drawn out of sleep, slowness to adapt to waking conditions (often by sitting up in bed for a few seconds or by sitting on the edge of the bed). And also first tasks: to march into the bathroom to pee, to march into the kitchen(ette) to put on the coffee maker (film characters almost never have their first coffee of the day at an outside emporium), to march to the window, draw the drapes, and peer outside (into the street; into the sky; into nowhere). The wake-up scene is almost always followed closely by a business scene with the character now fully dressed, fully awake, and fully aware at a workplace or else making way to some important destination; we pick up the action as he or she moves into it. We could also have picked up the action without the wake-up scene that came before.

Of this (very typical) get-out-of-bed construction, we can note two important features that seem to define narrative bounds and possibilities:

[1] *A temporal shift.* As the preceding scene will conventionally have taken place at night (often very late at night), thus in darkness, the morning wake-up is given in order to inform the viewer that time has passed, a spate of time, indeed, during which the character in play has rested safely and been entirely *uninvolved* in relevant action, in short, a rest period in every sense, a time-out. Extra-diegetic narrative time has passed, we are moving forward in (ordinary) diegetic narrational time, what we are about to see is to be taken (either fully or provisionally, until subsequent confirmation) as happing *after* what we saw happening before. We are awakening to a new day. "New," meaning: unplanned developments may occur; we may travel to a new location; we may meet unknowns. All of this is a nice reflection on the filmmaking process itself, since when a cast and crew awaken after sleeping off one long day's work and head off to a new work call, they, too, will enact new developments (unexpected by the viewer), will do this in a new location (even if the same set, still the same set *later*), will encounter strangers. One could see that in the moment of awakening and crawling out of bed, the

character is most closely affiliated with the actor beneath. Yet, not to forget: in such scenes, actors are not actually awakening from sleep, and the sleep we see at the introduction of the scene is mere "sleep," the play sleep every one of us learned to perform in childhood. The producer cannot afford for the actor to actually sleep during a "sleep take."[6]

[2] *Preparation for the day's action.* Consider the difference between (a) having a narrative move from any nocturnal scene A, where something of interest happens with the protagonist, to any morning scene C in an action setting, where time has passed and some ongoing continuity of action is being established (reflection, ensuing behavior, discussion with others); and (b) making that narrative move but inserting a transitional scene B, a morning scene in which the protagonist from the night before now awakens in bed and goes off to get ready for C. What is added logically by the addition of B, aside from humanization of the character—he or she has trouble waking up, just as I do; he or she takes a shower; he or she gulps down a cup of coffee—and a pointer to the character's design taste (which could easily have been effected already in other previous scenes). What is the narrative value of the oft-witnessed scene of a character "opening the eyes"? Do we need to *see* that the character sleeps, else we might fail to believe? Scene B gives evidence, yes, that the character spent a night sleeping; but there are so many bodily functions we do not appear to need evidence for, that are also real: the character checks a small pimple on the cheek in a mirror, applies a little alcohol; the character takes a half-open book on the coffee table and either puts it back in a bookshelf or decides to leave it alone; the character picks up the telephone, then thinks twice and decides not to make a call. On and on. Perfunctory, everyday, trivial things. How is the character rolling over in bed, sitting up, and walking off (with a small ballet of body moves to keep vital areas from showing to camera) substantially different? Won't the viewer make the assumption, all else considered, that in any scene the character comes into action prepared (in an embodied way) to do what he or she does?

Is the moment of sleeping in a bed an especially private moment, more than, say, going into one's safe deposit box or dropping a letter into a mailbox or receiving a telephone call? Is it somehow primal, elementary beyond elementary? And if it is this, what exactly is established by our being given access to the elementary-beyond-elementary? Surely that the character is just like we are--albeit that the character is *not* just like we are--at least in some respect now demonstrated before the camera: human in the same kind of way, vulnerable, feelingful, desirous, fearful exactly as could be anyone watching. Such a demonstration would of course contradict a number of scenic imperatives of cinema, including a belief carefully established and

---

[6] I give a much fuller discussion of "sleep" in Ch. 5 of *Virtuoso*.

nurtured in viewers that the characters are entirely special, entirely worth watching in some charged, elevated, transacted way. We paid to see them wake up in bed (in the way we know we wake up ourselves in bed), paid to see evidence of the everyday. Watching them behave at first light is higher, better, more delicious than going into a public square and watching strangers feed the pigeons.

In many ways, then, the bodily exploration we can make as we watch a character get out of bed is a narrative cheat in total. Artfully replicated from the real, effectively staged and photographed, emphatically timed, it almost always nevertheless takes place without performing a narrative action of significance. The scene of awakening is a filler: the shot of the character with eyes closed and head on pillow; the shot of the character groaning; the shot of the nude or semi-nude body appearing out of the sheets and standing; the shot of the stumbling action that comes next. All this is perfunctory in the extreme, narratively speaking, with only rare exceptions. A significant exception, yet one that is handled very swiftly onscreen and entirely without titillating ornamentation, is the photographer's (David Hemmings) awakening in London the morning after the pot party at the end of *Blow-Up* (1966). Here we are to feel—and the filmmaker and cinematographer do make us feel—that a vital *change* has taken place while the character slept. That the world he is awakening to is a different world (for him). He goes to sleep in a tumble, fully clothed, and when he comes awake it is merely by popping his (all-seeing) eyes open in morning light.

Douche

In the opening episode of Granada Television's *The Forsyte Saga* (2002), we are made privy to the bedchamber of Soames and Irene Forsyte (Damian Lewis, Gina McKee) as, early in their marriage, they engage in lovemaking. This is a double cheat, first in the way that all lovemaking scenes are cheats, as I discuss above; but secondly in that the diegetic logic would have us believe we are in the Victorian era, when marital sexuality was kept entirely out of strangers' view. The bedclothes are pulled over Soames and Irene, and both are clearly dressed in white muslin sleeping garments the lower parts of which, we are to presume, have been pulled aside to make genital engagement possible. The man is atop the woman and is thrusting rhythmically, then more and more quickly, then arching in an abrupt halt. Again, a series of gestural (body-gestural) moves intended as a chain of signals or indications, all this based in a gestural language ostensibly shared with the viewing audience: the thrust from above, the variation in speed, the intensification, the halt as climax. Gestures are here aimed to signal action at a distance (a distance from the perceiving eye), a fundamental function of the gesture broadly speaking.

The "distance cheat" is repeated in the ensuing moments. Irene gazes upward (as though thinking, calculating), then slips out of bed and goes into the toilet for privacy. There she has a lit candle which she carefully places on a shelf, lifting down from a hook that is positioned at shoulder height a small metal pitcher-and-tubing apparatus. We see her hang the pitcher above the tub, see her pulling the robe from her shoulders, and "testing" the "device" by holding it up so that she can see four little fountains of water emerging from the tip. She now positions herself in the tub in a way not clearly visualized by the camera, brings the tubing down below the bottom of the screen. Facial gestures indicate feelingful responsiveness to something she is doing out of sight (presumably using the tubing as a manual douche and also, we are to calculate given her general earlier expressions of distress regarding physical contact with Soames and the speed of her withdrawal to the toilet, as a device for literally displacing his semen). A great deal is left to the viewer's suspicion, imagination, and presumption to knowledge, not least the decision as to whether Irene should be read as abhorring Soames's sexuality or as wishing at all costs to prevent impregnation by him (thus, serfdom in the Forsyte family). One might make some headway arguing that at this moment for Irene, the interruption of seminal flow is a task of urgency; but the central analytical point is that whether or not this is so, we are not given an explicit statement by way of pictures. As we do not definitively see, we cannot definitively know what is going on; yet still the nosey camera makes its point of sneaking into that toilet and "watching" this procedure without actually watching.

In the original John Galsworthy novel, *The Man of Property* (1906), it is five hundred pages before one comes upon Soames Forsyte's mastery of his partner:

> The morning after a certain night on which Soames at last asserted his rights and acted like a man, he breakfasted alone.
>
> . . .
>
> He ate steadily, but at times a sensation as though he could not swallow attacked him. Had he been right to yield to his overmastering hunger of the night before, and break down the resistance which he had suffered now too long from this woman who was his lawful and solemnly constituted helpmate?
>
> He was strangely haunted by the recollection of her face, from before which, to soothe her, he had tried to pull her hands—of her terrible smothered sobbing, the like of which he had never heard, and still seemed to hear; and he was still haunted by the odd, intolerable feeling of remorse and shame he had felt, as he stood looking at her by the flame of the single candle, before silently slinking away. (509–10)

That single candle and that silent slinking: the first finds its way, filmically, into her hand, in the toilet, where instead of covering her face and producing smothering sobs she calmly proceeds through a technical maneuver, crude as it may have been made to seem as a reflection of the times; the second infects the camera-brain. Soames's "asserting his rights" and his "acting like a man" are converted as well: the former into his superior position and solitary movement within the bed, as far as, through brute gesture, we can detect, and the latter into his pressing rhythms and their startling interruption.

What an allusive marvel! The technique of allusion is well at work, optically in the television film no less than textually in the Galsworthy. Circumlocution or wholesale bypassing keeps the material from stating bluntly and unequivocally what we are to take as "happening" inside the drama, at the specific node that involves physical pleasurable engagement between persons. With a tone of haughty charity, we might nowadays look back upon writing of the very early twentieth century as formal, prudishly Victorian, for us inappropriately secretive about sex—pretending to ourselves, no doubt, that the twenty-first-century version of the story is more explicit, less restrained, and rightly less prudish. But is it less prudish, in fact, to openly invoke an action or behavior one takes great pains to avoid specifying, indeed to avoid locating in space because of the closeness of the camera's framing, and to avoid showing in the kind of detail that would render it unimpeachably clear? If, in order to be true to the spirit of the source material, the 2002 production needed only to make some assertion that Soames Forsyte took an opportunity one night to "assert his rights" and "act like a man" (whatever, in 2002, such phrases could reasonably be taken to mean), would it not have been sufficient to have someone remark casually at a garden party or at a breakfast that rumor had it he had done so? Would we really require to have *watched him* asserting and acting? Require out of some compulsion to witness the orgasm and, that being apparently insufficient, to witness as well Irene's complex reaction? Witness, that is, without actually witnessing.

To the educated eye, the movement of Soames's body looks very much like the sexual sort; but to the uneducated eye it might well pass for muscular spasms of any kind, unimaginable precisely because of the lack of education. And the self-showering utensil, the mini-douche, would, again, have been incomprehensible to the untutored except as a strange toy with a cryptic utility. We do not see the actual application of the instrument to Irene's body. Were the film produced during the era of Hollywood censorship (roughly 1933 to 1966), we might imagine these as smart strategies, allowing for a double reading without making explicit statement: but the film is produced in 2002!

A still more remarkable gap presents itself. Assuming that for some reason the filmmakers did sense a need to openly demonstrate Soames as a fully engaged, sexualized male; and Irene as a reticent, fearful, and more broadly unsatisfiable female, who needed for some reason to reject his sexual intrusion; what is gained in being coy about the demonstration? Why in the first part of the scene be certain that the bedclothes are pulled up and in the second part that the camera never shows any truly informative details? Although in the Victorian era many husbands, prudish, personally modest, would have penetrated their wives beneath the bedclothes, those bedclothes are cheated as covers for penetration *now*, in a distinctly non-Victorian era. The answer that will be forthcoming is, needless to say, "realism," as though Damian Lewis and Gina McKee are otherwise perfect representatives of the Victorian person. If it is argued that the filmmakers wished to be authentic to Victorian tradition rather than to contemporary practice, one would have to ask whether in Victorian tradition people did what we are doing, sneaking into a private bedroom for an entertaining surmise. The point about Irene's douching is that she would have hidden her device and its usage from Soames; that it is the man's eyesight from which this little performance is being masked away; and as the camera now masks it away quite efficiently, we may presume the contemporary camera is picking up the Victorian man's dominating viewpoint.

Yet why *any* viewpoint? A quite realistic approach would have been to avoid showing anything at all with respect to conjugal sex; to have the whole thing intimated, circumlocuted, altogether distanced. Here it seems necessary for the filmmakers (possibly because they sense that it will seem necessary to their viewers) to show what goes on during the sex; yet also, and crucially, to avoid showing it, because, owing to our own prudery, the offering of an actual sight would be a violation of sensibilities—-not Soames and Irene's sensibilities, but ours. It is quite all right for us to be peeking in on the activity in bed, peeking and, indeed, holding ourselves there until the culminating moment and even afterward; and quite all right, too, for us to visit the secret toilet facility; but in both the bedroom and toilet we should have our eyes either closed or turned away, or blindered, *or be able to claim that we did*.

Here, then, is an open demonstration that persists in being entirely closed. A closed "open," which is to say a complete cheat, itself covered up by the details of set design and actor behavior so as to seem anything but what it actually is. Peter Gay quotes a comment in the *Saturday Review*'s evaluation of George Eliot's *The Mill on the Floss*: "There are emotions over which we ought to throw a veil" (*Heart* 250).

16

Dance

FIGURE 16 *Woody Allen and Diane Keaton in* Annie Hall *(Woody Allen, Jack Rollins & Charles H. Joffe Productions, 1977).*

As screen sex scenes demonstrate with particular clarity, what is visible to the camera results from an involved and often complicated prior dialogue between principal agents, the actor whose body will be photographed standing most certainly among them. But a dialogue, which is to say a conversation; not touch. Words written into a contract clause here, words in a rider there, keywords especially: "ass," "top ass," "cock sock" (a miniature garment for holding the penis away from contact with other people's skin), "pubic hair," and so on. Not only an aggravated vocabulary but a chain of discussions in which it is shared, some of these being formalized ones in which scenes will be taken apart, discussed shot by shot, negotiated with pinpoint specificity so that everyone associated with every maneuver is comfortable. Military sorties work in roughly the same way, with the same kinds of minute mappings of the relevant territory and deployments. Commercial airline flight plans. Filmed car chases. Best to think of the sex scene as the final result of a long chain of tactical workups, some of them amicable, some of them perhaps contentious, yet all devoted to producing what actors and production personnel would call, in unison, "comfort," not to say the desired effect on film.

Salient features of this "comfort," a condition that will not show onscreen, since it is a different matter than the "comfort" the characters might be "feeling":

- After the arrest of Harvey Weinstein in May 2018, the problem of exploitation and abuse became well-known and much discussed. Thus a great deal of what goes on today in Hollywood filmmaking, certainly a great deal of the talk that precedes it, flows from the Weinstein shock wave and a spreading (perhaps epidemic) public concern for delicacy regarding the body and the optimal search for consent. "His right hand will be on your back, here, and his left hand won't be touching you." One can easily imagine tentative mutually agreed finger-pointing, use of a little stick as "pointer," or even full-color PowerPoint shows with body maps and arrows.

- But at the same time, the "comfort" screen that performers feel when they make (and sign) deals about action in sex scenes—again, all essentially verbalism—is not the same kind of comfort that people feel when they are engaged sexually: the comfort of anticipation, of closeness, of unexpected heat, of release. Negotiated "comfort" is a verbal commitment, hanging upon a set of designs and definitions and tantamount to a pledge. And much of what can be claimed openly as "comfortable" behavior conforms to a shared moral code, a set of agreements about what other people will (and should) find acceptable—that is, claim to find acceptable—in one's body use and movement. Proprieties, norms, conventions, patterns, routines. An actor might very well feel uncomfortable with a filmed move; or might feel less than comfortable; might even wish that for more comfort the filming should involve a move that officially one should avoid feeling "comfortable" about: "Touch me here." The word "comfort" is thus the result of a political negotiation open to public scrutiny. The actor doing "sex" is not to feel the comfort she would feel while doing sex, not, at least, admittedly.

Take the case of an actor, let us call him Joe, who (a) has filmed more than ninety percent of his shots for a picture (and who is therefore, from the point of view of a producer watching a budget, almost impossible to replace);

(b) is now and has always been the favorite choice of the director and the producing staff for the role he is playing; (c) is obliged to film a scene in which, as the script dictates, his character "masturbates"; and (d) indicates to the director, privately, that, although he knows full well the framing will be cut off at chest level and no genital configuration will appear onscreen, still, for his own *comfort* he desires to be naked and to masturbate actually (say, because he was trained in the Method Acting tradition). This is not the kind of "comfort" that would be typically assumed and negotiated in filming, although here as elsewhere, the filmmakers would try every trick to satisfy the actors they wanted to work with: yet, "satisfy," not satisfy. What if the issue is important enough to the actor that he will walk off the picture if forbidden?

- The screen images of so-called "sexuality" will not only be separated and distanced from moments of real sexuality in the offscreen world. They will be proclamations of being separated in this way. Here is what was done, here is what was agreed to, here are the lines we promised not to cross, here we are—watch carefully!—not crossing them. Sex becomes, in effect, talk and also a record of talk. Sex is words.

For clarity: I do not mean to point to chatter, discourse, or any use of language by anyone in an actual situation that has become sexual. Such a thing is the tease it is intended to be. But here onscreen, the sexual moves we see are all physical choreography of verbal scriptings—usually in legal form. "I said I would do this, and I am doing it" is the essence of the sexual act. More urgently, "I said I would *not* do that, and here I am, *not doing it*."

Because the camera does not film the vital discussions, the action in front of the lens seems to be all there is and all there ever was, when in fact it is the tip of a very large iceberg preconceived to the smallest detail. An actor whose finger is fondling the body of a screen partner will appear to be exploring, investigating, playing, whereas in the fact of it the moment will have been rehearsed several times, with both actors trying many variations until they find one they and the director think works.

More, however:

In terms of its pre-arrangement the typical filmed sex scene is like any and every other scene in motion pictures, even if more generally the hidden sensitivities of participants are not on view to be compared. In any scene before the camera, movements, touchings, pointings, alignments, brushings-against, utilization of objects, entrances, exits, the whole works all depend intrinsically on body-to-body arrangements—contacts, avoidances, angular positionings, sudden movements—that would be unlikely to show successfully on film if they happened on the spur of the moment for the first time when the camera turned. Comfort is perhaps the smallest consideration here. Money is more crucial, and every pause, every retake, every gaffe costs. The scene must be prepared. The workers must know, each, what the others are doing now and are planning to do next. She is standing there, and she will walk to here. I am here, and I will walk to there at the same time. She will move more quickly than I do. I will spit out a line of dialogue as I cross past her.

How and why do negotiated preparations make their way into filming? And by what cheat are they erased, camouflaged, tucked away from the audience's view? In general here, as with so much else in our experience of cinema, we know a great deal that we disavow; we accept and believe so much that contradicts what we know. The delight of participation is unthinkable otherwise. Are we helped somehow—and if so, how—to conceive the action we see as spontaneous and original, not negotiated and rehearsed?

[1] *Gravitational Tricks*. A glass containing liquid is knocked by a character's hand so that it falls off a table and smashes on the floor. No matter the choreography of the scene, for an actor to make a move like this very convincingly sells the spontaneity of the character's action. The legendary case is the restaurant argument scene between Dustin Hoffman and Meryl Streep in *Kramer vs. Kramer* (1979). He has a tall glass of some delicious-looking French white, perhaps a Pouligny-Montrachet—the character's money appears to have been spent. They are fighting about the custody of their child. Heat mounts. Finally a point comes (apparently so, because we are in no way given preparation for it) when Ted (Hoffman) loses his composure entirely and with a spasmodic, violent, explosive gesture smashes the glass off the table and into the air. The wine, the glass all go into oblivion, loudly, visibly, in a gasp of complete *gaucherie*. What has been said many times about this scene is that Hoffman did not tell anyone he was going to do this; and in fact it would not be difficult to imagine that he did not know himself, until he felt the action. The shock of Streep's reaction is stark. This cheat toward spontaneity is effected by breaking the rules. Yet: breaking rules inside a very tightly drawn boundary—everything must be in frame, for instance; everything must be lit;[1] no harm can come to Streep from Hoffman's maneuver; preparations must either be in place or possible in the event the shot has to be re-taken, and so on. Was it a real glass glass, or a breakaway? Was she sitting exactly in the right place and posture *not* to be hit by any of it?

[2] *Population Tricks*. As characters in narratives populate spaces together, when any one of them takes a position it will be necessary to ensure (a) that he or she does not block our view of any other character important

---

[1] Alfred Hitchcock on light in film: "We must bear in mind that fundamentally, there's no such thing as color; in fact, there's no such thing as a face, because until the light hits it, it is nonexistent" (Truffaut 183).

at the moment or any important object, and therefore the actor's position vis-à-vis the camera needs to be worked out; (2) that no person or object has already been positioned in such a way as to block a key actor's stance or move. Consider a much-celebrated comedy scene. Alvie Singer (Woody Allen) and girlfriend of the moment Annie Hall (Diane Keaton) are at a Long Island summer rental, standing in the kitchen, trying to cook lobsters. Part of the joke is that Alvie being Jewish, he doesn't know lobster from pinochle; when he holds up one, he extends his arm to keep it as far away as possible, as though it is a monster. Another part of the joke is that Annie is from the Midwest where they ain't got no lobster. Another part of the joke is that they are trying out domesticity. Another part of the joke is that the lobsters are having a revolution and seizing power, crawling all over the floor. The two people need to jump around the kitchen space, jump around one another, and jump around the lobsters without inadvertently stepping on any of them, all with rhythm and pacing to keep the scene moving.

Allen and Keaton had to know where they were to stand and move, how many beats to take on each line, and where the partner would act as well. Considerable staging, measuring the distance from each character to the lens to establish proper focus, making sure the lighting was right were all called for. Letting the character breathe, each actor tacitly follows a set of choreographic commands. The positions here had to be learned and retained without aid, because since a white floor had to be laid in order that the lobsters not disappear against the terra cotta tile floor that was part of the kitchen, and since there would be medium-long shots showing most of the room and notably that white floor, marker tapes for the actors could not be laid down.

In this scene, the untrainable lobsters crawling around throw the switch for definitive spontaneity, realism, uncontrivedness; and all the actors need to do is appear to be reacting to creature movement they cannot in fact predict.

[3] *Display Tricks*. Not only are objects touched and grasped before the lens in such a way as to make them sufficiently visible for telling the story, but actors in role make themselves sufficiently visible as workers, too. This process occurs through a translation: Actor A is playing character X; B is playing Y. In order that A get necessary exposure in a scene he sees to it that X is exposed to the right kind of light, and B counterposes by worrying about Y. Standing at a certain distance from the lens, making the smallest gesture of the head or body while not speaking, knowing how the color of one's garment will show in the scenic composition, and so on: all these tricks help actors have their characters get primal exposure; or, more importantly, not be overcome by other actors working to do this. "If you stand just there like that, you're blocking my key light a little." The director and surely the cinematographer will be conscious of such things, but actors have their own professional reasons for caring, too, and for looking after themselves. But

a nice move for gaining attention in a shot is to respond to a partner's line of dialogue with *no gesture at all*. This works especially strongly when the partner has uttered a pregnant line, something that would call for reaction. The apparent non-reaction thus becomes the reaction, and the silent character the odd sort of person—odd: noticeable—who would react this way. But this trick also conveys to the viewer a sense of directness and spontaneity, of unrehearsed reality, as though the non-responder is hearing the other for the first time, is finding the dialogue astounding or outrageous, and is truly stunned.

In all these cases—actors' self-display, actors' ways of being-in-scene, and actors' use of gravity and other physical forces—the telltale sudden or delicate move may well be an accretion upon a set of intentions, gestures, and articulations that have been worked out in detail much in advance. An accretion: something that decorates the behavior without altering it, without requiring that the scene partner get an advance signal. Sometimes it's necessary only to take a silent beat before hitting a word, as though one is thinking as one speaks (spontaneously) and searching for the right thing to say.

The tension in the negotiation-rehearsal construction is an elemental one. The actor will have made conscious arrangements to be unselfconscious, to be comfortable in the scene. The scene will be caused very intentfully to play as though it is happening out of an explosion of spontaneous feeling, in short, in a way that could be wholly comfortable for no one.

17

Keyed Up[1]

FIGURE 17 *Christopher Plummer in* Remember *(Atom Egoyan, Serendipity Point Films, 2015). Lory Wainberg is listening.*

One often sees a character sit to play the piano, but there are relatively few performers who know how to do it. And the piano opens itself to much deception, chief among instruments, since anybody can place hands upon a keyboard and almost anybody can move fingers one or two at a time. The illusion being created in "authentic" screen pianism, as we sometimes sense it, is that not only the character but also the actor beneath abounds in

---

[1] A small part of Chapter 17, "Keyed Up," was presented in a different form as "Shoot the Piano Player" at the Society for Cinema and Media Studies, Seattle, March 2019.

musical sensitivity and talent, is richly filled with the desire to express, and doesn't mind putting on a show. To stick the label "musical" upon a person is to perform a strange elevation, as though he or she now approximates some Olympus of high sensibility, tasteful refinement, and especially melodic desire, not to say athletic capability (because to play the piano is athleticism to be sure). The played tune is a kind of utterance or articulation, and in using the hands to produce it the character is making a speech beyond what words or tongue can muster.

Another feature of musical instruments, generally, is that in direct presence, the use of them cannot be faked—anymore than the use of a bat can be faked on a baseball diamond. You can either play or you cannot. Were the viewer to become aware of a character merely "playing the piano," not really playing the piano, were a viewer to notice during a musical scene that the body onscreen isn't doing what one is supposed to understand it doing, the only resolution would lie in finding reason for the character to be dramatically cheating—a cheat inside the story, a fictional cheat—but almost always such a reason is absent. Further, as actual piano playing cannot be cheated the character—living in a reality—cannot be presumed to be cheating it, and since the actor is closely allied with the character, here by way of arms and hands, we have a tendency to believe the actor isn't cheating either. Musical cheats are thus in a special category: easy to accomplish in a way that much else isn't for film, in the sense that the audience is unlikely to pick the cheat up, and this because it is notably unlikely to try. Yet cheating there must almost always be.

Shoot the Piano Player

A roundabout route can lead us to the problem of filmed hands upon keys. Consider Pietro Francisci's *Hercules, Samson & Ulysses* (1963), starring Adriano Bellini, Iloosh Khoshabe, Liana Orfei, and Enzo Cerusico, all of them orating outrageously in palpably dubbed English. As one observes the many technical operations calculated to hide this aspect of the production—lips moving emphatically but out of sync with the dialogue, compositions favoring an unusually large number of extreme long shots or medium-long shots that obscure the actors' speaking mouths, and shots in which the actors' faces are obscured during speech—it becomes evident that a kind of ventriloquism is in progress: a body, or part of a body, in physical action acoustically mobilized from without. As Kenneth Gross observes in *Puppet: An Essay on Uncanny Life*, "While a puppet's movements will seem to belong to the physical thing . . . the puppet's voice always comes from the outside. Its voice is always alien, never its own" (66–7). Of actors, slaves, and prostitutes—I think we could add puppets and almost all performers who sit at keyboards in films—Shadi Bartsch sees a "symbiotic relationship between foreignness, self-display, not being one's own master" (164). Sound cinema's separation of image from sound not only facilitates a general ventriloquism but is emblematized by it, the visualized object puppeted with an alien voice. Ventriloquism generates metonymy of a sort, one part of a moment fragmented away from, standing in for, another. Shooting the piano player is an elegant approach to this problem. Although in some rare cases an actual pianist plays in front of the camera, typically the sound of music is fed into a picture from an outside source, in order that the illusion be given, as it is in *Hercules*, that vision and melody are unified at the same time in the same place.

There is no art that is not metonymic, using a part to express the whole; nor one that does not employ fakery of one kind or another, since no matter the artistic representation of life, life is the more complex. But metonymy is not always an explicit method of trickery. To say this another way: the part need not reference a whole that is entirely nonexistent, as we see happening in onscreen piano playing, where hands at the keyboard can suggest a pianist who is not, in any way, there. As with many other physical and emotional activities, the act of playing the piano becomes reduced for cinematography; but here, as in depiction of other instrumental performance yet in pianism with more complication, the reduction has the capacity to separate what we see from what we hear, producing shots that amount to visual emblems or equivalents of sound passages only apparently being generated as we watch. There is a sense, indeed, in which we hear without seeing—hear authentically, at any rate, while not seeing authentically—thus achieving a state of relaxation addressed by Simmel in his essay on city life. This separation, this puppeting is in play notwithstanding the standard additional dialogue recording (ADR) trick, mentioned more fully in Chapter 18. Even when sound is recorded live on set, piano sound is more than likely to be fake.

Always and inevitably at stake in authentic piano performance, as authentic piano performers know from their earliest days at the piano, are three independent variables: [a] technique, [b] touch, and [c] musicality.

[a] Technique involves agility, strength, reach, and precision: getting all the right fingers on the right notes with appropriate, but easily modulated, speed and loudness; moving the fingers up and down the keyboard, note by note, octave by octave, chord by chord, fluidly and without gulps; not hitting false notes; and having a hand sized appropriately for the composition at hand, J. S. Bach not calling for the reach one would need to play Rachmaninoff, for example. Since in most filmed pianism the sound of moving fingers, the correctness of the notes, and the appropriateness of the performance to the composition are all arranged ventriloquially, nothing in the image necessarily suggests bad technique, this, ironically, even at the level of young persons playing very simple music. More bluntly: if the sound recording of piano playing is good, any hands moving on the keys will seem to show technique. In real life achieving and showing technique are supremely difficult, even taxing—as with, for example, dance.

[b] Touch involves degrees of delicacy, expressed physically, most important being the ability to sound a note without undue application of

pressure: an outside production again, although in this case one far less frequently to be heard, since the cost of acquiring the services of a first-rate musician is far greater than the cost of getting a performative filler. Touch works upon the action of a piano—the ease with which a finger might depress a key.

[c] Musicality is essentially the marshaling of enthusiasm: causing the piano to speak or sing on behalf of both the composer and the performer at once.

Only the very greatest masters of the piano are extremely technically adept, possessors of a perfect touch, and intensely musical. While some actors can play piano, there are no actors one could call great masters of the instrument; they are great masters of another instrument, that substitutes onscreen. It is worth noting further that the display onscreen of profound musicality could be overly absorbing for the audience, draw attention from the characters, the story, or the moment. Competence is required, but serious musicality could ruin a scene. In the same breath one should say that "serious musicality" must frequently be performed.

While the puppeting of the onscreen musical moment is essentially an off-camera matter acoustically—no matter what is happening on set, the actual sound is not the sound we are hearing—the added sound must be aligned with the photographed image in order to give the complete effect. Any sound dubbing moment at all will present the same kinds of challenges, except that with piano playing, if we are seeing the keyboard, there are ten sound effectors moving alone or in groups slowly or quickly at each instant and the sync has to match all of this. As with more conventional forms of the maneuver, successful puppeteering means hiding the puppeteer. Thus arise the many cinematic gestures of revelatory concealment: showing disembodied hands, or arms and hands, and adding in pre- or post-recorded piano sound; substituting the expressive face or upper body for performing hands; moving the camera to such a distance that the operation of fingers on keys cannot be ascertained; or, in an extension of puppeteering that seems to bring the puppet alive, giving very brief shots of a performer actually playing a short—and easy—passage carefully learned out of musical context: a few chords, a small scalar passage, and not necessarily something from the music we are hearing as long as there is a match. This kind of "vérité" passage will be intercut with disembodiments and expressivities to lend the impression of a holistic performance. David Sudnow recollects a process like this in learning to play the piano: "For the most part, my practice sessions were given over to playing a handful of songs, doing my improvisations. Fluent manipulations of these pathways produced *a semblance of competence*, and I was able to sustain long playing sessions" (35). We can see the same "semblance of competence" employed in filmic depictions of painters at easels, where the combination of expressive and highly skilled bodily action and technical manipulation is similarly, in the cases of most performers, impossible to show.²

In diegesis, screen pianism usually involves casual entertainments or distractions, salon moments, onstage meditations after the song-and-dance rehearsal is over, even, as in the celebrated scenes of *Casablanca*, performance for an exclusive audience by a knowledgeable club pianist, sweetly informal of manner, doing a piece that is hardly more than a soft-chord accompaniment for voice. The script will tend to eschew depiction of many aspects of piano playing familiar to those who do it seriously: use of the feet on the instrument's pedals, often enough a vital component of tonal production; discussion with other pianists or with anyone else of the music at hand, its difficulty, its challenges to the player; rehearsal of any kind, which might, if shown, lead viewers to think that, contrary to what the film naturalistically shows, actual labor is involved in playing the piano.

In both standard puppeteering and ventriloquism, both of which contain extrinsic mobilizations of what is made to seem like natural action but only the latter of which necessarily involves a tonal supplement, the cover mechanism is intended to keep the audience's thoughts away from the means by which the illusion is effected, to make a systematic cheat: hide the strings; throw the voice. I leave for further discussion the relation between the hidden ventriloquial voice and Michel Chion's *acousmêtre*. The secrecy has two key facets: frontal elimination of the actual source of musical production; and giving the impression that what one is seeing amounts to that source. What is essentially metonymical here is the presentation of a partial body not in performance to stand in for an entire body in performance; the presentation of various views of the operation of a device without showing fully that a character is operating it (since the character is not).

It might seem that using a performer who actually plays the piano would be a straightforward solution for filmmakers, but a number of production and dramaturgical contingencies get in the way, in effect force the cheat. First, there are relatively few Hollywood actors, especially star actors, who can play the piano, are known to be able to play, or are willing to give the show. Exceptions like Clint Eastwood, Oscar Levant, and James Stewart prove the rule. Even in the case of actors like these, care is regularly taken to ensure that they are seen to perform music far below the level of difficulty one associates with virtuosic pianists. But although the star persona and character strength merge onscreen to create a unified situated front, the façade of illusion is vulnerable to being overshadowed by the music itself. A bravura piano passage, even an especially touching rather simple one, captures the highlight, erasing the character and star together, and it takes a

---

²Screen performers who were off-camera painters themselves (Vincent Price, Tony Curtis, Anthony Quinn) tended not to play painter characters for the camera.

performer of exceptional sensitivity and talent to yield to the music and then quickly regain star stature at the keys: we see this with Christopher Plummer playing Wagner in *Remember* (2016). But the least effortful procedure—as in the least expensive and time-consuming—is to use the inexplicit view and the ventriloquizing offscreen musician, even, sometimes, substitute models for arm and hand work.

Most inexplicit views take up camera positions similar to what audience members would have at a concert if they did not occupy the precious few seats that afford a direct, close-up view of the keyboard. A number of energizing cheat routines are conventional:

- *Spasm*. As we see it rendered, musical passion makes (carefully cultivated) long ("authentically musician-like") hair shake, elbows pump in and out like bellows, shoulders desperately hunch with the strain of concentration. Musically untrained actors can perform expressive gestures like these quite easily, more easily than they can display artful flexibility with their untrained hands. A glance on YouTube at Daniil Trifonov playing a concerto will quickly show the folly of such "emoting."

- *Spontaneity*. We witness a production of musical performance happening, as it were, on the spot, out of a flush of momentary spirit, *with no history*, since the moment of pianism is very often inserted into the film arbitrarily and without build-up. Yet no one but the savant merely *plays* the piano, it is necessary to practice long and hard today in order to give a good show tomorrow. Scales, arpeggios, chords, close finger position, octaves, not to mention fragments of a piece played over and over at different tempi—six to eight hours a day: all of this is elided in screen representation. Except in cases where, themselves the subject of drama—*Madame Sousatzka* (1988), *The Piano Teacher* (2001)—piano lessons are substantially ornamented with emotion and conflict, practice is treated as a boring and pointless, or conflict-generating, time waster. In *An American in Paris* (1951), the concert pianist Oscar Levant, who in his real life practiced substantially, plays a character named Adam Cook who again and again merely sits and plays with aplomb. The pianism "slumbers" in his hands and need only be "awakened."

- *Centralized maneuver*. The pianist's feet are kept out of camera frame, while, as anyone who plays the piano knows, the instrument's pedals must often be involved in performance and cannot be managed other than with the feet. Upper bodies dominate the screen as much as arms and hands. Thus, screened pianism is an "upper" business, coming from the torso (the heart) and its extensions, the dexterous hands, rather than a "lower" self. If there is no lower involvement, no passion in melody or form, piano music ceases to be human.

- *Hand jobs.* Two aspects of the hand movement shot: the degree to which the camera reveals actual muscular training and flexibility; and the extent to which whatever we are seeing is in correspondence with whatever we are hearing. As to the first, in film fictions musical passages of bravura difficulty are never shown directly, so we are left to presume the strong muscularity. As to correspondence, a musically untrained viewer will be prone to seeing it even when there isn't any, and will also tend to take any movement of the hand upon the keys as a specialized index of talent. Of course, it makes no difference at all if a figure plays keys that don't sound out what we hear (sound to be synced afterward), as long as no sharply visible discontinuity appears onscreen (a scale doesn't even vaguely resemble a chord).

Nor do audiences tend to pick up the blatant continuity mismatch between disembodied hands at the keyboard and the diegetically "same" hands attached to the character's arms in other scenes. In short, one looks at the hands but one does not look at the hands. With close-up shots, hands can move in any way that won't seem incongruous with a dub-in, and indeed dubs can be designed, redone, or completely altered to suit the visual drama of the moment.

- *Optical involvement.* Coverings will effectively be covered if showcase attention is accorded a character's especially studious regard of the keyboard while the fingers presumably move off-camera: scientists looking through the musical microscope, as it were. This demonstration of eager observation sucks in viewer engagement, suggesting that in zoning in on the keys the piano player is doing what the viewer is doing zoning in on her. And the piano music seems authentic if we see somebody raptly focusing on producing it. Sometimes in a concert—but not on film—a pianist will have the eyes closed.
- *Empty reading.* In general, filmed piano playing offers the non-musical viewer a catalog of interpretable gestures: the bowed head, the head raised back, the expressive eyes, the moving arms, the flashing fingers of the right hand, those of the left, trick ornamentations (trills, glissandi, bravura ascending or descending passages). Regardless of their non-indexicality, such gestures can constitute a piano language that filmmakers and viewers tacitly agree to share, with some particular signs gaining considerable repetition from film to film: the bodily, usually facial, beauty of the pianist in elegiac melody; the augustness of the polished piano

itself: handsome and enormous like a Steinway-D, or battered and diminutive, like an old upright; the busy busy busy fingers; and *amour* between the player's body and the instrument. But piano-playing viewers will regard all of this optically gestural material quite differently than naïve viewers do: a pianist knows, for instance, that it matters not a whit how pretty one looks while playing (Farley Granger beware). The implication here is that with piano playing, an entirely spurious collection of discernable gestures can be attributed meaning; we may think of this as "empty reading." A language loses indexicality through a kind of jargon.

- *Flattening.* The first act of cinema is to erase the distinction between accomplished and unaccomplished pianism, since what appears onscreen must appeal to a largely unwitting audience and many people, competent only to recognize the wholeness or sweetness of a melody, are unable to note what the performer adds through musicality. Thus, the diegetic moment does not *depend upon* technique or musicality. Let us say the treatment is sentimental, in that the diegetic pianist's sweet "desire" to play beautifully—a matter for scripting—is taken as de facto evidence of skill. In *The Big Store* (1941), Chico Marx is typically perceived as merely comedic, even only barely skilled, whereas any pianist will note his marvelous technique and delicate touch. By contrast, in *The Birds* (1963) "Tippi" Hedren sits at an upright and plays a Debussy Arabesque apparently with sufficient technical skill, but almost entirely lacking musicality or a sensitivity of touch; the candy-wrapping of the lovely music and beautiful "musician" covers.

- *Uncertainty.* As the outside and inside of the pianistic moment cannot be seen at once we are confronted by a Heisenbergian fragmentation: in one shot we cannot see an effect being produced and also the motive of that production. Here, of course, is a feature of cinema, drama, and social life generally—that interiors must become characterological claims; but when music is the product, the artist's "inspiration"—innermost desire—becomes a central dramatic issue. If keyboard sounds cut in with images of hands or body parts become for the moment evidence of musical production, a lit disembodied face alone conveys the feeling of an inward moment of inspiration. But on both sides of this equation one finds cheats: the musical "production" isn't the thing we are seeing, and the face in ecstasy doesn't necessarily cue musical fever.

- *Performative focus.* While screen narratives do not show this, the trained performer can make music sing while thinking about something else (like any actor hard at work).

- *Tic.* The arm muscles, very frequently the objective center of a piano shot, need not come into use in order to mobilize the muscles of the hand. To play a perfectly fluid scale (a difficult challenge) covering three or more octaves; or an arpeggio over the same range; or a chord progression or octave progression, it is not necessary to lean over one way and the next, or to wave the arms; it is not required to pretend one is on a cricket pitch. Everything happens *in the hand*. In effect, much of what is seen onscreen when the hand is concealed amounts to a kind of actor's tic. Were a character to tic this way *without a piano*, he might be read as a ticquer.[3]
- *Cubism.* Attending a piano performance in the everyday world, one need not see anything. It is quite sufficient to listen. And those whose pocketbooks can afford only the cheapest seats may well be placed where no view is afforded. But if one does wish to gaze, the most productive target is the hands upon the keyboard. The power and the capability, as well as the tenderness or ferocity, are in the hands. Wherever one is placed, however, that is where one is. Cinematic pianism invariably makes the piano experience cubism by cutting (delicately!) from angle to angle, as though what is happening has so many facets it takes numerous camera positions to gather them all into one vision. The impression the editing tries to foster is that as the camera positions change we move closer and closer to the sacred fire at the heart of the music. But since it is the sound of music that rules, and the showing of piano players is a matter of arbitrary concession, the particular choreographies one finds in filmed piano scenes are telling in themselves rather than reflective of the music. The screen is made continually interesting as a vision, so the problem faced by cinema is the conversion of the sound of music to the look of music, or at least the look of what can be sold as the sound of music.
- *Musical interest.* As normal citizens, do piano-playing characters onscreen ever even show themselves interested in music, do they talk about it or worry or plan, do they have favorite composers, or favorite pieces to play, or favorite techniques to chat about? In much

---

[3]Here as in so much else of cinema we gain a clear view of Kenneth Burke's act-scene and act-agency ratios, the bias in reading an action that is given by the place in which the action is made or by the tools that are used to make it. Take a person making a repetitive movement with one hand while holding the other palm-up and it is easy to make the reading "mentally unstable," or "hallucinatory" (as we can see in Frank Perry's *David and Lisa* [1962]). Put a wooden spoon in the first hand and a bowl in the second, and place the whole thing in a kitchen, and you have a diligent cook.

dramatic piano playing, the musical character sits at the keyboard and operates as an automaton.[4]

- *Onscreen offscreen.* Piano players onscreen don't engage in routine "backstage" activities that would characterize the daily life of actual musicians. They typically do not discuss their instrument—"I much prefer a Bösendorfer to a Steinway if I can get one, but my very favorite is a Chickering"—nor refer conversationally to a keyboard's "touch"—"Heavy heavy heavy: gotta have bigger hands to play this"—or to the decision of opening, half-opening, or closing the top—"We'll do it with the top down unless that's a problem for you"—or to matters of tuning, or difficult passages, or muscular pain. The narrative piano player as emotional sprite is thus always entirely the figure, or part-figure, in view, with no life outside the frame: no consideration of the instrument beneath the fingers, no need for Epsom salts.

- *Indications or silences.* In Hollywood narrative, the piano performance given by a character at one moment will not come in for discussion by other characters later on. Someone might be encouraging at the time: "That's beautiful, Anton! Keep playing!," but evaluative conversation is eschewed, as is remarking on the piano playing having had some distinctive and overwhelming effect on the listener's life. In concert set-ups the audience of course applauds, even goes crazy, but the film cuts to the performer stepping backstage and mopping the brow, receiving a stern look from an angry lover or whomever, heading back into the light to take a bow: all business. The partner riding home in the limousine: "That went very well tonight." But never, "I don't know how you do that beautiful melodic passage near the end, you play it so magically"—all this because the audience onscreen and the one watching in the theater have just heard that melodic passage and don't require to be sententiously informed of how beautiful they already found it. This dramaturgical knot of never overinforming the viewer operates as an ongoing rationale and mechanism for cheating, because in the offscreen world people do comment to performers with the enthusiasm we must take for granted when we watch movies.

---

[4]Workers are often shown one-sidedly this way. But in *The Man Who Knew Too Much* (1956), Hitchcock interposes a short but telling scene in an embassy kitchen and the corridor outside, where slaving laborers are seen *on a break*, being only people with one another.

18

Don't Believe It

FIGURE 18 Singin' in the Rain *(Gene Kelly and Stanley Donen, Paramount, 1952)*: Jean Hagen is at the front microphone, here suddenly revealed as a mouther only, as we find Debbie Reynolds dubbing her from behind.

The centerpiece of narrative screen composition is the human act. Dramatic construction will have us looking after motive and effect, those couplers which permit that linear assemblage in which one act owes to another and begets yet another. But from the point of view of watchers observing human action there is an omnipresent feature more elemental still than motive and result, an address to the possibility of conviction. This is what we might call *credibility*. Any moment in which we see a doing, a completion, an interrelation, we take the object of sight to be authentic and believable *in itself* or else an incitement to suspicion about its production. This thing being done exactly as I see it being done: I believe it or I do not. In Frank Tashlin's *Artists and Models* (1955) Dean Martin is singing a street song with some children, one of whom is a little boy pulling a wagon onto which Martin hops. Post-sync recording aside, we can believe on the instant that Martin *is credibly singing*, but that little boy: is he really pulling that wagon all by himself?, or is a clandestine device being used, so that he need only give the impression of pulling? As we will discover, while some confusion can attach to the distinction between *credible* and *incredible* acts, typically for viewers in the act of viewing none does.

An elegant example of the problem can be found with something as simple as walking down the street,[1] bright illustration being given in Edgar Wright's *Baby Driver* (2017) in a scene that follows directly after a very long and involved car chase with Ansel Elgort's Baby pulling off *incredible* driving stunts to escape from numerous avid chasers. He races into a parking structure, stops, and abandons the car. And now we see him gliding down the sidewalk, as it turns out on his way to get coffee for his heist cohorts. He is listening to music through his earphones and dancing his way down the sidewalk. Twisting, sidestepping, pacing, twisting, with exquisite form and a vivid sense of spontaneity. When we see this, we take the body onscreen (character and actor together) to be both (a) visibly, dramatically posited as the agent of the movement and (b) authentically the mover. This action looks as though it is being done by this person and this person only. There are no cutaways to long shot, the whole thing is in medium shot with the body wholly visible. Shot distance is critical for credibility. If a character mounts a horse for a race and during the race we cut away to long shots, the riding might suddenly seem incredible, the jockey suddenly replaced by a professional or a stunt rider. If a shot is made too close-up, we might be watching a performer upon a dummy horse inside a soundstage. John Wayne's riding backward as he leaves Ed Asner's abode in *El Dorado* (1967) is a brilliant demonstration of the credible act: a character played by a performer who really did know how to ride.

When we see someone walking we take them seriously, as though they are actually and uncontrivedly walking just as appears. If by contrast a man limps, he is either seriously, actually, and uncontrivedly limping or else faking the limp for some reason: perception alone will not solve the riddle. The actor could fake a limp in order to characterize. The character might fake a limp in order to gain some advantage over other characters

---

[1] For a thorough analytical discussion of which, see Ryave and Schenkein.

in the story. But simply put, limping is *incredible*—not to be taken at face value in and of itself. There are few recognized ways in which plain walking can be produced other than by the walker (the walker riding on a dolly is one), but there are many conventionally recognized ways in which a limp can happen. Credibly, for the character, an accident onscreen. Incredibly, for the actor, a specially constructed shoe, a faked walking style. But the fully framed and unadorned walk is *credible*. When we see Elgort moving down the sidewalk we think, "Elgort is moving down the sidewalk as the camera watches." Similarly Dustin Hoffman and Jon Voight in a duo, in *Midnight Cowboy* (1969), especially, perhaps, the moment when Hoffman's Ratso (limping some) smacks the hood of a taxi and screams, "I'm walkin' here! I'm walkin' here!" There are variations that make the situation more complex, to be sure. As a camera slowly zooms in we find revealed the true status of the walker. Say it is a robot programmed to behave this way (in the story) and designed to look human: the discovery shows that the walk is something we ought to have found incredible (it wasn't a person walking, as seemed) but didn't (because from a distance it looked like a person). Or a camera pulls back and we see that the walker/dancer is not moving on the sidewalk at all, but is floating in the air in what we are to take as a dream: again, our sense of credibility was mistaken. But these exceptions are relatively rare. Usually when a character walks we believe we are seeing the banality of walking and nothing else.[2]

Talking we tend to take as credible, as long as the talker's face is visible.

Being stationary and watching or listening tends to seem credible.

Buying a little bouquet of flowers at a vendor's and carrying them: credible.

Taking a yoga pose: credible.

Kissing, chewing and swallowing, breathing—credible, credible, credible.

But a great number of dramatic actions are patently incredible, in the simple sense that we can see them without being able to determine with conviction that no special support structure is guiding, managing, and polishing the action. I have discussed playing musical instruments: we are never to be certain a technical cheat is not in use. But singing: lip syncing makes possible the secret substitution of a foreign voice, as demonstrated in the extended "dubbing studio" sequence of *The Errand Boy* (1961), where we not only see Rita Hayes dubbing Theodora Davitt, in detail, but also come upon the hilarious outcome of the protagonist's invading the facility at lunch time and tinkering with the controls. Or in the famous finale sequence

---

[2]In their analysis of first films made by Navajos given only the scantest instruction on camera loading, Sol Worth and John Adair found that walking was a signal aspect of narrative construction and cultural meaning for the filmmakers, a telltale authenticity they felt the need to explore.

of *Singin' in the Rain* (1952), where the obnoxiously controlling Lina Lamont (Jean Hagen) "sings" in front of a live audience, who suddenly see, as the curtain is raised, that Kathy Selden (Debbie Reynolds) is at a hidden microphone, singing for her.

I am forced to leave untreated here what could occupy another volume, the delicacies and tricks of artificial sound, as in ADR (additional dialogue recording), which is done after shooting, or Foley tracking (addition of object sounds, again done after shooting). In voice synchronization, sounds are made to match lip movements. In the Foleyed overlay of slapping, clacking, clumping, squeaking, burping and other sounds when doors open, car doors are smashed, and so on, lies a virtuoso orchestration, turning the everyday world into instruments of sound production. With both we have an entire second tier of cheating expressly calculated to waylay and misdirect the viewer's consciousness. The actor on the ADR stage is benefiting from a projection of a loop, watching a take and recording the dialogue (which was merely spoken in front of the camera) now with the proper rhythm and emphases—over and over as many times as it takes to get it right. For Foleying, a special stage is larded with half coconuts, framed pieces of glass attached to metal hammers for smashing, fake doorknobs, horns, sticks, smackers, brushes, leaves, and anything else on earth that can make an interesting sound. Foley artists are continually experimenting, finding, and adding to the storeroom of "magical" devices.[3] For ADR, actors must develop in secret the talent of making sound to match the movement of their own lips as seen in a loop.

Driving a car: a breakdown partial vehicle is filmed on set showing steering wheel, seat, windshield, rear seat, and so on, but the outside environment is rear projected. If we take the "driving" character to be authentically driving, still the apparently obvious link between the "driver" and the action we see is not, analytically speaking, so obvious. The credibility is up in the air, especially when, as the vehicle moves, considerable interior action must take place (an ultimate version being the mountain-car sequence of *Family Plot* [1976]). In walking, the link between the observed actor body and the observed motion is obvious. Yet presence in location is essentially incredible, since photographic tricks can place a body in any ground (William Holden and Judy Holliday standing outside the National Archives in *Born Yesterday* [1950], a rear-projection composite); and since set design is powerful enough to render any interior space believable even when it is fake (for example, the tiny apartments built by Henry Bumstead for Eastwood's *Mystic River* [2003]). Having a meal is incredible: actors cannot possibly actually eat the food the character is seen eating, since the act may have to be repeated

---

[3]For more on film sound more generally, see Altman; Beck; Chion, *Audio-Vision*; Eyman; and Weis and Belton.

as many as seventy or eighty times to get a good take (and since nobody producing a film takes for granted any actor's physical tastes or allergies).

The tactical point of the filmic cheat is to overcome the viewer's resistance, his or her proneness to considering an act incredible by conveying it in a credible mode, or by erasing features that lend toward the incredibility. The meal: the actor can't eat all that much food over and over but actually we don't see any actors eating, we see them passing food around, hear them talk about food, watch them fork food up and move it toward the mouth before a cut switches us to another diner. The production problem lies in having the food on the table diminish as the scene proceeds.

In a way, the enhancement of credibility through substitute action is a kind of stunt, and anyone on the crew might be converted into a momentary stunt person. Here are two fascinating stunts, one secretly disruptive and one openly kept from view:

Stunting voice. When he was shooting *The Hospital* (1971), Arthur Hiller told me,[4] he had a scene with George C. Scott, head of a hospital in which patients are systematically being killed, now utterly frustrated and a physical wreck for lack of sleep. The character was to stand up, walk to a window, open the window, lean out, and say in utter exasperation, "Jesus . . . Christ!"

Take after take after take after take after take Scott leaned out the window and said, almost sotto voce, "*Jesus Christ.*" A meek whisper.

No matter what he tried, Hiller could not bring the actor to change his rendition. So in the editing room, he went to another part of the picture where Scott was railing and said "Jesus . . . Christ!!!" He snipped that out and edited it into the other scene. When we see the film, albeit the character puts his back to camera when he leans out the window, nevertheless we take his expostulation to be wholly credible, to be emanating from this body we see from behind; when in fact it is wholly faked, ironically with his own voice and without his intention: unwitting self-mockery, entirely guised.

Stunting expertise. It goes without saying that whenever an act A is to be substituted by another version B, a version accomplished more inexpensively, more accurately, or even accomplished at all when the actor working to produce A simply cannot do it; whenever a cheat uses extraneous footage to make credible what would otherwise be open to question, the viewer's presumption, quite naturally, is, that the substitute performer is an expert, sufficiently to do handily what we see being done. When a character has to do something physically taxing, so that in watching we might be filled with doubt about the actor and think him "dubbed in" by a stunt person who can manage more easily, we take this stunt person to be notably expert at the activity: driving cars, leaping from heights, recoiling from gunshots, even, as in the case with body models, standing (or lying) in for the star during

---

[4]In personal conversation, Autumn 1971.

a lovemaking scene. Not only expert but *more expert than the actor being replaced*. The replacement is taken to be working, in fact, only because the actor is in some particular way relatively incompetent or blocked. And once people have seen quite a few filmic examples of such transfers, they come to automatically expect certain kinds of stunt substitutions—that is, they know their credibility is being poached. What a lovely challenge to rationality, then, is the physical stunting of Burt Lancaster's characters, almost invariably performed by Lancaster himself even in conditions of danger as in *The Train* (1964) and *The Gypsy Moths* (1969). As long as we are ignorant of Lancaster's stunt work, we read the character as amazingly accomplished and presume some even more amazingly accomplished stand-in has worked to convince us: sliding down a high ladder against the clock in *The Train*, for example—a trick the actor would have learned much earlier in life as an acrobat. Producers and actors know that the perception of "credibility" or "incredibility" is rooted much less in the accomplishment of action before the camera than in the viewer's knowledge, and the expectations that flow from it.

19

"I Love You"

FIGURE 19 *Charlize Theron and Johnny Depp in* The Astronaut's Wife *(Rand Ravich, New Line Cinema, 1999). A tiny homage, perhaps, to Edwin S. Porter's* The Kiss *(1900).*

It is eye-opening to consider how much narrative cinema is finally, climactically about two people in love, the pledge, the rescue, the tentative courting, the culminating union; and very stable is the myth that such a state of affairs is apotheosized in "the perfect kiss." The kiss of truth.

Assemble the players as we may wish, the perfect girl(s), the perfect boy(s), in the end it is the merger of mouths, the intercourse of interiors, that brings the union, the hiatus that we feel as (at least momentary) "closure."

The kiss, even in action stories that ostensibly have nothing to do with human passion, devoted instead to showing how a heroic band struggle against an assembly of social forces, against gravity, against the limits of their own endurance, against anything and everything to redeem some vital treasure. For the Good, one finds, ultimately, the hero and heroine bonding with an embrace, the two chums striding into the night, the galpals swept away from the everyday, albeit in an embrace that is played sometimes for comedy. Always, finally, the union:

>By this marriage,
All little jealousies, which now seem great,
And all great fears, which now import their dangers,
Would then be nothing: truths would be tales,
Where now half tales be truths.
(*Antony and Cleopatra* II.ii.136–40)

Very little screen action is as vulnerable to collapse as the romantic gesture, since audiences are prone to taking it as so unaffected and natural an agency, something no one has to rehearse. (Whence the comedic value of the teenager rehearsing a kiss with a pillow, or charging to a waiting mouth in the nocturnal shadows but without aim.) There is a belief, further, that a superficial look of passion is linked to, can only be linked to, real passion hidden away: that even for the few seconds of the kiss we are watching, the performers who produce it together are experiencing roughly what their characters seem to feel. When we see two stars of a film bonded together (Robert Redford and Natalie Wood in *Inside Daisy Clover* [1965], directed by Robert Mulligan; Richard Burton and Elizabeth Taylor in *Who's Afraid of Virginia Woolf?* [1966] directed by Mike Nichols; Sidney Poitier and Katharine Ross in *Guess Who's Coming to Dinner* [1967], directed by Stanley Kramer; Al Pacino and Diane Keaton in *The Godfather* [1972], directed by Francis Ford Coppola; Harrison Ford and Karen Allen in *Raiders of the Lost Ark* [1981], directed by Steven Spielberg; Johnny Depp and Juliette Lewis in *What's Eating Gilbert Grape* [1993], directed by Lasse Hallström; Jake Gyllenhaal and Heath Ledger in *Brokeback Mountain* [2006], directed by Ang Lee), and photographed close-up so that the soft gleam of one person's skin radiates against that of the other, lit to look like precious stones in a perfect setting, melodically intoning mythic epigrams, "I Love You, I Love You, I Love You," it seems automatic to think that there are beating hearts beneath the skin we see, and that in those hearts there is desire to unite this way. The fiction of movie-star romances thus stems in many ways from narrative constructions arranged by third parties. Unthinkable except as bald comedy (Han Solo egotistically shuffling Princess Leia aside) is a scene in which one beautiful, heroically strong, selfless type stands nose to nose, cheek to cheek with a second one and says, "Well, nice talking to you," and calmly walks away. The proximity must bring on the meeting of lips, the meeting of lips the opening of mouths, and the opening of mouths a coupling of more severe contingency in a planet far, far away once the lights have come up.

That kiss:

There are probably no living persons who have not taught themselves how to perform it through some reminiscence of what was seen onscreen (the motion picture operating essentially as a mannerist textbook). Getting the right interpersonal distance, as measured in inches or centimeters. Angling the head. Moving one's mouth forward at some calculable speed. Actually aiming for the partner mouth, locating it with the very blind lips (since way down there and from this angle and proximity the eyes cannot get a view). Moving into, not back out of, the touch. Deciding when the moment is done, that is, knowing how long to engage, how long and with what ornamentation. Pulling apart slightly, what to do with the eyes, which now gaze longingly into the other's eyes gazing longingly into one's longing gaze. What to say, if anything, since whole architectures have been known to collapse on a word. And then continuing to operate with what is now not only knowing but knowing-oneself-to-know more than can be known from exterior viewing alone.

The kiss! . . . . .

Onscreen it cannot but be summative. It cannot go wrong. It cannot be obscured. It cannot be scenically mishandled. And the building hunger, the itch, that is initiated and grows monumentally—this must seem actually present, which is why one speaks casually of the good or bad "chemistry" between actors. When there is "good chemistry," the two major stars appear to yearn for each other's nakedness and desire, but for real. Legion are the studio publicity stories concocted about one contracted star beginning an affair with another (even while shooting a film), these putative escapades functioning as spurs to audience belief in the chemistry which, like all chemistry, is quite beyond sight.

Onscreen the kiss, something affected as natural and easy to do—when of course it is neither—betokens the joining of the stars, a culminating moment for the drama but also for the stargazing experience. As long as the mélange of feelings is orchestrated as a finale or cadence the success of the film can depend on the accuracy of the kiss, its believability even if all else seems bogus. This is the supreme bodily touch (censorial restrictions of the times notwithstanding), the link that brings the actor and character together in their own internal "kiss," as it were. The bond that weds passion to action.

But the problem here, here and always, is the conundrum presented by what the social theorist Georg Simmel called the *tertius gaudens*. The Third who Watches. As voyeurs in reality, we would have the same difficulty as the camera has: obtaining, from any conceivable viewing position, a perspective in which the action of each party is visible wholly and fully at the same time as the action of the other. As viewers of intimacy we can but seize an illusory angle, something that charges us to imagine the coupling beyond our limiting frame. And when we look at the camera as a *tertius*, noting that it is wearing (as both enabler and prophylactic) a lens, we must see that angles become expressly, overwhelmingly important. And in physical fact it is *not* the case that the angle one person requires in order to do mouth-to-mouth with a second is the same angle that a camera requires of kissers in order that a sight be made of it. Displacement, refraction, warping, misalignment—all these potential grenades—always threaten to exaggerate features of the kiss, throw the act out of proportion, make what is intended to be graceful and accomplished look sloppy, amateurish, and hopeless, even grotesque. Actors learn, for instance, that in extreme close-ups with one another, and varying according to the size of the lens, they must not look into one another's eyes or onscreen their gazes will fly past each other. In *Virtuoso* I quote Peter Lorre revealing a lesson he gave Bogart about choosing one eye to focus on, but not both (267–8) and those two had only dialogue together. Physical engagements are more complicated still.

Mouths will frequently not touch in the way that it appears they are touching. Aimed targeting might bring a modicum of pleasure to the actors but the characters would appear to be misaiming. All this warping is because the clarity and proximity of focus most desirable for kissing scenes requires an aperture of f.2, perhaps even f1.2, and not more than f.4. At f.2 the linear depth is foreshortened intensively, the graphic planes of space are brought together. For the kiss *as kiss* to be discernable it must be shot in profile, or "cheated toward" the profile, and this means that the depth between the side of the actors' cheeks near to the viewer and, say, the distal side of their noses is contracted. When people kiss in reality they physically negotiate a space that is not contracted in this way. As well, when characters talk to each other certain slight angles must be interposed in the actors' body placements, in order that the alignments of the bodies look as though they match.

Beyond being cheated optically so that it seems optically right, the screen kiss is cheated symbolically. The character never—but never—openly makes statement about that kiss, what it felt like exactly, whether or not it seemed acceptably good, or, even more, precisely what sensations affected various body parts. "Gosh, when I kissed you my lower lip, toward the left side, felt as though it were being eaten alive." After the kiss comes silence. In that way, the kiss can be taken to be culminatingly informative, to speak the speech in the fullest, least ambiguous way, leaving "no stone unturned," no hint undelivered. There is an electrical cheat as well, almost always: the kiss moment summons and delivers extraordinary illumination, as though the mouth-to-mouth is actually running electrons through hitherto hidden lightbulbs. A glow in the eyes. A glow on the cheeks. The world opened in wonderment as a visual entity. Except in the rarest of circumstances, in everyday life when people kiss the lights do not come on except, perhaps, in the dark cave of the imagination, and the cheat in film here as elsewhere is to make the luminosity in that cave tangible. Key lighting helps a lot.

The screen kiss also cannot fail. No character can say, "Golly, I have been thinking for some time how wonderfully attractive you are, and I have been desiring beyond desire to plant my lips on yours; but now that I have done it, I have to confess it wasn't as wonderful as I hoped it would be, no offense intended." Nor can a character tell a second character, "Gee, yes I would, yes, love to kiss but I have a bad tooth infection." Or, "Gee, I'm a vegan and you eat meat so if I kiss you am I eating meat, too?" Or, "Kissing you was actually not so much at all, because in my dream last night I was kissed by an angel."

The kiss has to seem to be the universe in a grain, everything here and now, all possibility contracted into this blaze of shining penetration. If one kisses with spontaneity and release, nothing of the sort can happen on camera, since for the screen kiss, considering focal distances and hot spots of light, angles of bodies and timing, make-up and the grace summoned for movement, there is enormous work to be done. The kiss as architecture.

20

Surrender

FIGURE 20 *From* Predator *(John McTiernan, Twentieth Century Fox, 1987). Inside the costume and under the makeup is Kevin Peter Hall.*

In matters of honor and value between antagonists it may be prudent to adopt a combative position, but as one actually practices it acting is not, principally at least, a matter of honor and value between antagonists. Being combative is unhelpful and unproductive in many ways, not least of which is that in straining to gain ascendancy in a shot or scene the performer draws attention to her own urgent self-consciousness, breaking the dramatic illusion. The more obvious a dramatized confrontational situation, the more apparent can be the actor's travail, an illustrative case being the heated argument in *Marriage Story* (2019). But as to confrontation, very few situations are worse for a performer than confinement within the artificial boundary of special effects, with the accompanying obligation to restrain one's actions in line with the limitations and capabilities of the effected character. Is one subsumed by one's makeup, or does one make a distinct point of emerging as a performative self? The actor and character are in a face-off.

In diegetic surgeries, battles, alien encounters, plague outbreaks, and other like situations, the actor will typically be smeared over with an entirely artificial sheath, a suppurating make-up wound, a latex facial substitution, a scaly alien skin; or confined to a wheelchair or stretcher or bed or other mechanical device (as in torture chambers or, for Andrew Garfield in *Breathe* [2017], an iron lung). Such transformations can be felt as reductions of the self just as much as aggrandizements, aides to the creation of, as it were, *monstres par défaut* as much as *monstres par excès* (see Fiedler 20ff.). And a construction might bring experiential traumas. Actors who must wear full-body suits (Haruo Nakajima playing Godzilla in 1954 and onward, Bolaji Badejo towering in the Alien costume for Ridley Scott) or actors wearing ape costumes (David Warner in *Morgan!: A Suitable Case for Treatment* [1966]) or being locked in rubber (Johnny Depp in *Edward Scissorhands* [1990], Ricou Browning in *The Creature from the Black Lagoon* [1954]), or being turned into a kind of flexible figurine (Tilda Swinton in *The Chronicles of Narnia: The Lion, the Witch and the Wardrobe* [2005], Boris Karloff in *The Mummy* [1932], Cate Blanchett in *Elizabeth: The Golden Age* [2007], Helena Bonham Carter in *Alice in Wonderland* [2010]) may find it difficult to do the things most people don't think about at all, like sipping a glass of water, chewing a sandwich, using the toilet. The point of the taxation through confinement is only the producer's profit, in that taking the make-up off and putting it on again is an expensive process and producers would prefer to have it done only once in a shooting day.

More difficult than tolerating the get-up, however, is working with it expressively, because the actor feels a need to be seen as himself, not only as the character, and the laid-over character tends to dominate the performative self, even obliterate it. Once the studio system dissolved, actors could not count on the seven-year contract (which, a kind of imprisonment itself, did offer job security for a time) and found themselves, in many cases, continually reaching for a new job in the knowledge that "Look at me, look at what I can do!" isn't something producers would take to heart if it came from the mouth of a character instead of the mouth of an actor who could *make* characters. The best path to a successful performance in masque is to hold back from fighting the conditions, exactly as in coming to terms in everyday life with a debilitation like a broken leg. Let the mask take over . . . entirely. Become the mask, though hopefully not to the point that the mask becomes taken as the performer, that is, will not come off. One recognizes that it is the mask affecting the audience's sensibility and thought, and one's job is to service and support the mask. If it is sometimes necessary to go to extreme lengths in providing this support, one must always avoid openly competing with one's own character, however ersatz that character might seem. The more one competes against it, tries for characteristic personal expressive signals and permits tics, the more and more constructed and arbitrary seems the character mask. The more arbitrary the character mask, the more arbitrary the film altogether.

In this odd case, then, the actor's supreme cheat, his or her way of turning the viewer's critical mind *away from* the thought that the character is an artful and made-up creation, is to do nothing but play the lines and move as the constraints permit. For self-advertisement one must trust to the publicity. There are delightful, deeply engaging moments in *Scissorhands* when one senses the actor becoming acutely aware he cannot move his hands because his character has no hands to move, and Edward's little looks of surprise and wonder are telltale in convincing us of his sincerity, since the "scissor hands" fell to him, far from being a result of his will and operation. I am here, I am trapped in here, there is little I can do but I will throw myself into doing at any rate. Johnny Depp sacrifices his personality entirely here, disappearing inside Edward.

But *throwing oneself* into doing: there are ways of doing that, and ways of doing that. David Lowery told Eric Lavallee at the Fantasia International Film Festival the ironic story of shooting Casey Affleck in a ghost costume for his film, *A Ghost Story* (2016). The principal actor is in the costume for the entire movie save the opening few minutes:

> It was very clear that it was him—and it was almost surreal how much the sheet exaggerated his physical traits, because he has a very specific way of walking, a very specific way of hanging his head, he slouches a little bit, and the sheet just magnified all those things so even though we didn't see his face it was very clearly him. But the other thing that happened was that it was very clearly an actor with a bedsheet over their head. And it felt too corporeal. It felt very clunk and, to be honest, quite silly. So from that point forward we started refining the way in which the costume was utilized and the way in which he acted underneath it. And by and by we just sort of removed every bit of his body, which—and every bit of his performance, and once we had done that it became clear that we could put someone else under there, which we did do from time to time.

A case of the self effusing through the costume and making a leakage that threatened the continuity of the viewer's belief. It was necessary with the camera and costume together to "just sort of remove" every bit of his body, and then every bit of the performance that was his. Not the performance the actor was giving, but the performance that, intentionally or not, he was appropriating.[1]

---

[1] I am grateful to Brandon Cronenberg for pointing me to this interview, available online at https://www.youtube.com/watch?v=0YJ08840jhY

Because Karloff, Chaney, Lugosi, Nakajima, and others—and, later, actors such as Badejo and Depp---carried off performances in "deep costume," because their work underneath was so stellar and so convincing—that is, because they didn't seem to be there beneath the highly decorative character—it became possible after the late 1970s to film puppeted monsters that would be taken for granted in superficial terms exactly as these actors led audiences to take their characters. Servo-mechanical devices don't need to be fed lunch, after all, and they don't claim residuals. If, because Nakajima made no efforts to show himself onscreen Godzilla the giant reptile could seem a reasonable fit with his environment, a character figure ostensibly being mounted *without an actor's help*, it at first became possible, and then more and more popular, to make monsters that really didn't have or need actors' help.

To become a characterological transform is to lose oneself inside the makeup. The makeup, the plastic, the latex prosthetics are doing the performance with the help of one's nervous and muscular system. The actor becomes a motor, then a motor principle, then finally a ghost in the machine.

Of Cameras

{21} Corral
Richard Chalfen; *Pillow Talk*; *Bullitt*; *Poltergeist*; *Who's Afraid of Virginia Woolf?*; *Funny Games*; *The Guilty*; *The Bourne Ultimatum*; *The Circle*; *Zabriskie Point*

{22} Show Me
Wolfgang Schivelbusch and light; Impressionism; Nestor Almendros; *Claire's Knee*; *Pauline at the Beach*; *Rebecca*; Greta Garbo and William Daniels; *Suspicion*; *Day for Night*

{23} On the Road
Parker; *They Live by Night*; *Baby Driver*; *Lady for a Day*; *Collateral*; *Family Plot*; *Legend*; *A Stolen Life*

{24} "Good Cinematography!"
Academy Awards, 1970–2018; *Chinatown*; *The Revenant*; *Close Encounters of the Third Kind*; *Vertigo*; *Pauline at the Beach*; *Sweet Smell of Success*

{25} "Picture This"
Regression

{26} The Angle Angle
"Dutch" angles; *The Thief of Bagdad*; *On the Waterfront*; *Inside Daisy Clover*

{27} Moving On
Panoramic perception; the *coup d'oeil*; Baudelaire

{28} Behind the Camera Behind
Linwood Dunn; optical printing

{29} Peek-a-Boo
Psycho; *Mon oncle Antoine*; *The Lady in the Lake*; *The Naked Kiss*; *Up in the Air*; *Alfie*; *House of Cards*; acousmêtre/optimêtre; Walker Gibson

21

Corral

FIGURE 21 *Kristen Stewart and Jodie Foster in* Panic Room *(David Fincher, Columbia, 2002).*

The camera's biography is simple: it has always been able and ready to go anywhere the light is sufficient, has always been a creature of curiosity preferring not to face obstructing walls. And yet, regard! There are walls, and the camera cannot go everywhere. When, as in *Pillow Talk* (1959) and *Grand Prix* (1966) and *The Thomas Crown Affair* (1968) the editor makes use of optically printed camera mattes to create the "multiple screen" that at first enchants by the multiplicity of its views, by the hint that we can be in more than one place at the same time, we realize too soon that every looking requires a boundary, and we cannot apprehend without some selectivity of concentration. One is reminded of Richard Chalfen's curious dictum that we can photograph anything anywhere anytime, but we don't.

The camera does not see everything that takes place in the realm of the narrative:

- It cannot see—and so we cannot see—at one and the same time both the outside surface and the interior wellspring feeding it; and in fact we do not see that interior quite generally. It is well known that surfaces can be misleading, that appearances do not always convey or completely convey motive. It is the surface that makes it possible for us to discern an objective form: a leaf on a branch, a rolling ball, a body in conversation. Everything seen by the camera is a surface except that:
- The shadow is neither surface nor interior.
- The camera, and we, not only can see but must see. Since we must see, we must be enabled to see. The camera is there to see, and therefore no action that does not have a clear visual component can be subjected to it. Make the implicit explicit. The camera cannot see (a) belief, (b) fear, (c) adoration, (d) fascination, (e) meditation, (f) forgetting, (g) excitement, or any other emotional state that humans claim to be feeling. It cannot see someone's anticipation or drawing to a conclusion. What the camera can see is movement, action, and gesture that can be claimed to be pinned to some internal state: a sign of belief, a sign of doubt. The camera does not see happiness but when a little girl is giggling with her eyes atwinkle we can say we are seeing it. Running to, running away—the camera can show these, although in point they look exactly the same (like sunrises and sunsets) unless some further information is given by editing. Chewing we can see, digesting we cannot.
- Thought we cannot see, but words inking their way onto a page we can.
- The camera is always pricking or pinioning the viewer's consciousness. The bathtub dialogue in *Pillow Talk* (between Rock Hudson and Doris Day) is an attempt to articulate both sides of a telephone conversation at once, the speaking face on one side of the screen and the receptive hearing face on the other, and then the two persons switching.[1] As we do not with surety determine motive as the conversation gets underway, both faces are incessantly puzzling.

---

[1] As in the conversational behavior with "flappers" using "bladders" that Gulliver describes in regard to his voyage to Laputa (Swift 172): "It seems the minds of these people are so taken up with intense speculations, that they neither can speak, nor attend to the discourses of others, without being roused by some external taction upon the organs of speech and hearing . . . [the officer makes] gently to strike with his bladder the mouth of him who is to speak, and the right ear of him or them to whom the speaker addresses himself . . ."

With each character a moment arises when we are to notice a disconnect between a vocal gesture and a facial expression, as if to say, "This person does not mean what is being said." But in order to catch this—it is purely visual, as any acoustic hint would leak into the telephone—we must watch one side of the screen. Any subtle nuance provided simultaneously across the gap, to the effect that the listener is *actually* hearing one thing while *pretending* to hear another, is hard to catch clearly at the crucial instant. In car chase scenes, we flip from the lead car to the pursuer (*Bullitt* [1968] is a textbook example) but every moment we spend in the lead car, watching the driver and his thug accomplice, say, is a moment we cannot spend in the chase car, watching the good-natured cop.

- But there are also dramatic "privacies" enacted for good social form, the camera in this case standing in with just enough bravado to cover our own squeamishness. We can visit a salon or dining area but we do not typically visit closets, bathrooms, basements in normal usage, the dry cleaner taking a stain out of a shirt, that space under the covers. (On this, see Chapter 15.)

When cinema points to a space we are forbidden to enter, a certain problem of engagement arises. Seeing the forbidden space—the room at the top of the stairs in *Poltergeist* (1982) stared at by little Carol Anne (Heather O'Rourke)—and noting how it is closed to us, we detect, more than the space, the forbidding itself. We are made suddenly self-aware as persons presumably yearning to go where going isn't permitted, yearning, then, and being held back from yearning. The viewer is not only aware of herself desiring, she is aware of herself *being taken as someone who desires*, someone who is or was expected to desire. If I don't suspect you of wanting to sneak into my private locker, the one the camera has put in front of your face, I don't mount a KEEP OUT sign on it. Such a sign would index not only the privacy of my tabooed space, the space I don't want anybody but me to be in, but also, and more importantly, my presumption of *your* curiosity about it, that you have a will to invade. Without some correction, the audience, now implicitly accused, could easily be provoked to fixate on exactly the forbidden zone, even on nothing else, because *it has been pointed out as the kind of taboo that tantalizes*. The audience now being caught up with wondering about this blocked-off zone, it may fail to catch something far more relevant, and in cinema, the audience's attention and calculation are always organized and pinpointed.

- As to going: the camera cannot go everywhere, but this fact must be cheated if the illusion of plastic movement is to be preserved. The audience must have the sense that there is nowhere the camera does not go, because they are offered what seems like an unbounded collection of views. As everything we see is replete and promising, filled with potential, we are content to see it as we do, from *this* point of view, at *this* distance, with *this* clarity, rather than through the kind of denial that would propose different views not made available. The surface we see is all there is.

The framing may include at its margins passages and spaces to which the narrative does not explicitly take us—the dark alleyway—but the cinematographer can have his gaffing team light these spaces in such a way that they pass essentially unnoticed in a shot centering on something more brightly lit (and therefore more dynamic). The set designer can collaborate by planning and building a story space where some aspects are toned down through coloring or embellishment and some are keyed up. The screenwriter will take caution about mentioning places we do not see, so as not to permit distracting disappointment in the not-seeing. The point is that generally speaking we go where the story makes us feel the need to go, and our attention, satisfied, is drawn away from otherwheres. In *Who's Afraid of Virginia Woolf?* (1966), a drama taking place largely in a domestic living room, there is a point when one resident prods the other about the bedroom, and in fact this bedroom is "upstairs," in a zone to which we have hitherto had virtually no access; but in a subsequent scene we do go to this bedroom, and we can even recollect how we did swiftly and casually go there near the beginning of the film to watch a woman changing but were so fascinated by her (Elizabeth Taylor at her frowziest) we may not have paid much attention to the space.

The camera is summatively generous. No treasure is hinted at that the camera does not hold out for us to grasp. The camera itself is never (never to be seen as) held away from treasures available somewhere within the diegetic world. The camera is free. The camera is supple. The camera is magical.

To put this obversely: an Aristotelian unity holds sway, in that all the nooks and crannies opened to our view turn out (magically) to be important for the story (and what is not important is made to seem nonexistent). But of course this is a grand cheat, a method of reducing the potential complexity of a tale to the more limited range of what can be shown: what the producer can afford to show, what the designers can manage to configure, what the viewer can be presumed willing to tolerate.

- More than uniform diegetic importance, the various visible *endroits* in narrative space must compose and hold, together, a certain uniformity of reference. The designer knows that once he or she has commenced imagining and drawing out plans for any set at all, that set will offer certain reference to a fictional "reality," whether that reality is intended to be phantasmal or reportorial, whether of a wonderland or of an everyday. In whichever direction the design is to move, it must move with a uniform bearing. For a tiny example: the carefully crafted bedroom of an apartment will have to look like the sort of bedroom that would be in the sort of apartment where the living room and kitchen, if the bedroom looked like that, would look like this. The representation will need to seem to stretch into a coherent whole space, and also to continue as (narrative) time goes by (as production time went by) to appear more or less reasonably the same. There is a fictional *world* and in it the parts are logically coherent. If we are in the African veldt and we meet a tribal king (as in *Yeelen* [1987]), his throne will be something like a comfortable boulder. If we are visiting the residence of Dr. T., his personal suite, brazenly colored, will have been imagined by him no more or no less than the room in which his five hundred little piano students play on the one great keyboard (1953). Further, various limited designs (to be built in different corners of a soundstage, or on adjacent soundstages) will relate to one another in not only a proportional but also a tonal way. A set designed to represent a grand reception area, for example, will have to seem just as real— no more or less real—than sets designed earlier to represent hotel rooms, train stations, and so on. A much blunter way of seeing this: all the settings in a film will appear to have been designed by the same (nonexistent, invisible) hand—not designed at all, in fact, yet extremely believable in juxtaposition, as the editing will put them. Once the design process begins for a film, the designer is making a kind of commitment to consistency.

- Often in dramatic films, when characters name locations the story visits them subsequently, else the dialogue will be worked to dispense with the location's importance as soon as the place is brought up. The naming in fact typically operates as a preparation for narrative movement. Behind the scenes: when the script is approved, agents for the design team and the camera crew go through it and calculate what particular settings and views will be needed, exactly in the way that the casting people come to be aware what roles will need be filled by them.
- A principle and ongoing cheat is that with the actor's intelligent involvement characters proceed through stories behaving with the utmost casualness as though certain unseen spaces *simply aren't there*; as though the diegetic world the characters inhabit is fully, coherently, obviously the world they see and know, just as it is fully, coherently, obviously the world for us. Characters do not have more curiosity than the fictive world they inhabit would subtend. The space into which a character enters seems to be:

(a) ideal for the event that is to take place there—that is, nobody feels cramped or swimming in the sea unless the cramping or extreme openness are intended (the red room in *Red Desert* [1964] is a tight space but excitingly so);

(b) elegantly designed to hold and feature that event, a space that for the characters must be an optical wish fulfillment (as it is for us), regardless of how "shabby" its surface;

(c) uninteresting in itself *as a narrative space anticipated by a character for later use*, excepting for meticulous inspections that are part of the dramatic construction, as when Michael Caine visits Laurence Olivier's labyrinthine lair in *Sleuth* (1972) or when Vera Miles visits the upstairs bedrooms in the Bates house in *Psycho* (1960). Characters very often tend to move into a space and relate to other characters as though the space itself has no vital qualities that touch or distract them: *we* can be touched and distracted while they pay no heed; or they are sent into a space with spectacular visual qualities and forced to exploit these as part of the action, exploit them immediately on being present (Harold Lloyd and Jimmy Conlin on the skyscraper with the lion in *The Sin of Harold Diddlebock* [1947]; Audrey Hepburn fearful at the Palais Royal in *Charade* [1963]; John Alexander repeatedly chasing up the staircase (à la Teddy Roosevelt) in *Arsenic and Old Lace* [1944]). However it gains use or attention, the space in which we linger to watch the action is put forward as the singular and only space appropriate, available, and existent at this moment. There is no need, and no urge, to peek around and find attached secret spots, improvements, unless, again, that very peeking around is the substance of the drama. A limiting case might be *My Dinner with Andre* (1981), in which, aside from a very brief opening and very brief closing phrase, both involving the streets of Manhattan, we are settled for the entire film at one table in a corner of one restaurant, listening to two people converse; yet we are made to feel absolutely comfortable, quite as comfortable as they are with their roast quail. Indeed, many viewers of this film swear they have journeyed to the sites mentioned in the tales that comprise the conversation.

- Narrative space shows dramatic coherence, in that whatever we see happening here is just the sort of thing that could happen in a space like this, or else, with an irony the film intends us to receive and enjoy for its own sake, just the sort of thing that would never happen in such a space (a direct inversion): the gigantic Waterloo station at rush hour is exactly right as the place where Jason Bourne (Matt Damon) would flee and hide in *The Bourne Ultimatum* (2007). Or, in a flipped situation, without knowing where he is Jerry Lewis's nerdy yet very male Jerome Jerome arises, gets dressed, and goes to breakfast in a gigantic girls' sorority house in *The Ladies Man* (1962). These are examples of Kenneth Burke's "scene-act ratio." The action must not be such as to compel presentation of some other space, to which we do not go. But the naturalism of the fit between action and place (the straight fit/the ironic misfit) is a cheat against our virtual confinement where the action is. The appropriateness of setting is so rich we do not notice how it is our cell.

- All of these principles, including the cheat mechanisms, can themselves become the substance of dramatic exploration, as happens for instance in *Noises Off . . .* (1992), theatrical characters fleeing from our sight but then suddenly appearing backstage, and in *Synecdoche, New York* (2008), where filmic fiction is the subject of the filmic fiction. In *The Magus* (1968) domestic environments are lifted away in an elaborate fabrication.

- There are three kinds of fictional spaces, and film constructions work by invoking and arranging them: (i) places a character desires to visit: *idylls*; (ii) places a character is forced to visit: *dungeons*; (iii) public spaces that people move through both conversationally and physically in order to get to (i) or (ii): *neutrals*. All these have corresponding cheats.

Typically (i) the happy destination, the *idyll*, will be set up as the solution to an apparently irresolvable problem that confounds characters for whom we have already been made to feel an enthusiastic affinity. They are not quite in the "right" place, but if they can find a way to get there all will be resolved. The earlier moment—a passing phrase, a whole scene—establishing the character(s) as lovable, and the attached moment in which the problem is presented in all its daunting complexity work together to make travel to and arrival at the esteemed destination a matter of course. Often we will be brought in during the journey (for instance, in Michael Haneke's American remake of *Funny Games* [2007]) to find people (played by star actors we already know and love, Naomi Watts and Tim Roth in this case) on the road in their car, chatting, joking, or arguing about the problem they need to solve. The set designer and cinematographer might collaborate on the characters' arrival to show the destination as architecturally notable, marvelous, special, ideally located, and so on. But what does not happen, what the cheat makes unnecessary by framing the place as a mere waystation on a longer route, is any pointed reference to the place of arrival as *a singular destination which is* itself *the whole subject of this film*. We merely arrive there, merely make ourselves at home but not with such imbrication as to block us from proceeding with ongoing action. The arrival of Aziz (Victor Bannerjee) and Adela Quested (Judy Davis) at the monkey temple in *A Passage to India* (1984) is, at first, a similarly wondrous, promising event showing off a space that is marvelous. Dr. Meecham's (Rex Reason) arrival by auto-piloted aircraft at the research facility in Georgia gives a warm, welcoming tone near the beginning of *This Island Earth* (1955). Dorothy landing in Oz (1939), amazed Anna's visit to the palace of the King of Siam (1956), the travelers' chancing upon the hidden Shangri-la in *Lost Horizon* (1938)...

Clearly the idyll can function in romantic and in terrifying films, in fantasies and in nightmares, as long as it presents itself, at least initially, as a happy find. In *Ransom!* (1956) an idyll is converted by the action into a dungeon as a cozy home becomes the inutile haven for two people whose child has been abducted, and then reconverted to an idyll at the conclusion when he is returned safe and sound.

Or:

(ii) Characters suffer capture, imprisonment, debilitating discomfort, torture, degradation. The cheat here is doubled. The script implies over and over that *there is another place we are not seeing*, the normal zone of freedom outside these constricting boundaries, the "better place." In prison escape films, we are given references to a "world outside," and prisoners use the word "inside" to define their cloister, the prison. Beyond this general reference to a freeing exterior we have little or no time to take note of the space itself *as a space* because of the horrifying, wounding, or nauseating events that take place here and, for the information of the viewer, negativize it. Nor in the face of the horrors do we calmly examine the creatures who by making an appearance constitute an event: Jabba the Hutt in *The Empire Strikes Back* (1980), Col. Saito (Sessue Hayakawa) in *The Bridge on the River Kwai* (1957), the giant spider in the terrifying dank basement of *The Incredible Shrinking Man* (1957), or the horrifying kidnapper (John Goodman) in *10 Cloverfield Lane* (2016). As to unpleasant events and unpleasant spaces, it is especially interesting to consider how a thoroughly confining and undesirable situation can be produced in a routinized working environment. *The Guilty* (2018) posits an emergency call center where an operator (Jakob Cedergren) trying too eagerly to help a young woman phoning in becomes embroiled in something shockingly bad. In *Panic Room* (2002), Jodie Foster and Kristen Stewart escape home invaders in what they believe is a specially designed safe space, but because it is insufficient to their needs they are forced to visit the outside, that is, their own (fancy New York) apartment and thus the invading thugs who are lurking there with extreme malevolence.

(iii) A neutral space can be immense with respect to the size of the protagonists who go there (the cornfield in *North by Northwest* [1959]) or cozy and gemutlich (the restaurant in Little Italy where Michael Corleone carries out an assassination in *The Godfather* [1972]), but it is always used by the characters without belonging to them. It can be painfully nondescript (the nocturnal plaza outside Lincoln Center where Laurence Olivier stabs Roy Scheider in *Marathon Man* [1976]) or so elaborately filled with event that it merits a special set piece inside the film (the rainy square filled with umbrella users in *Foreign Correspondent* [1940]). The protagonist will be split apart from the space, briefly or totally, either discernably edging through a crowd there or engaged in a special way that makes the place irrelevant (Dustin Hoffman's Ratso Rizzo limping through the streets of midtown in *Midnight Cowboy* [1969]). The public neutrality leaks into the diegesis as diegetic neutrality. Hotel rooms are particularly useful as public spots—spots that only some character(s) can be found in, but that anyone can theoretically rent and visit—and when significant action takes place there it is the action and the actors committing it that gain attention, not the room itself (even, finally, in a setup where the room gets explicit identification, as in the two adjoining hotel rooms we finally visit in *The Conversation* [1974]).

In the *idyll*, a key cheat is the act of rendering the space instantly, naturally, unquestionably hospitable and right, even more for the characters than for the viewer. The character does not have to take dramatic time to make the place comfy, so that if we see a character actually taking time for this we know that the activity itself has, or will have, signal dramatic import. In the *dungeon*, the space provides an ominous pathetic fallacy, oozing with a foreboding darkness or "darkness" that acts as an unrelenting warning yet not actually warning the viewer to "stay away" by shutting the eyes. *Neutral* spaces are carefully constructed and photographed so as to give signs of only appropriateness, never welcoming warmth or ominous darkness, so that the action can stand out. If we watch a film like Spielberg's *The Terminal* (2004) we see the enormous lengths to which the visionary filmmaker, the scriptwriter, and the key performer must go in order to make rational a distinctly individualistic and much extended use of a space intended for vast publics and speedy movement.

- These spatial types are not fixed in a drama; a fictional development or turn can metamorphose any of them into one or more of the others, as with *Ransom!*. The space capsule in *Apollo 13* (1995) begins as an idyll and becomes a frightening dungeon, as does the Chunnel train from Paris to London in *Personal Shopper* (2016) or the 15:17 to Paris in Clint Eastwood's film of the same name. For a few very piggish little folk, Willy Wonka's magical chocolate factory becomes anything but a wonderland. To reverse: *Lord of the Flies* (1963) concludes with a warming transformation of a war-scarred island into a haven of safety. A computer hacker helps Emma Watson turn a silicon valley nightmare into a promised land in *The Circle* (2017). In *Zabriskie Point* (1970), one kind of neutrality becomes another as the (anti-)hero takes off in a single-engine plane from an airport that seems to him a gateway to paradise; but landing there hours later he is mortally assaulted by the LAPD; two radically different kinds of human action in the same diegetic space. With neutral space, the vital cheat is to shift attention to its appropriateness for containing the action, in this way rationalizing, normalizing, and naturalizing the background as the only or most ideal possible locale, the place we are watching *as a place* "because it is obvious"—in short, the place we are not really watching.

If the neutral space is counterperformative, in that it recedes in support of the character's attitude, feeling, and movement, and in that as action proceeds we focus our attention on what is being done rather than on the appropriateness of what is being done to the setting, idylls and dungeons are both highly performative in themselves, enunciatory, bold. Whether the space is nurturing and comforting, as in the idyll, or threatening and terrifying, as in the dungeon, it articulates its qualities openly and directly without being dependent on, or underpinning, action. In this way, idylls and dungeons not only help amplify what actors do there but also release the actor from the obligation to be extreme in gesture. Since the scene does some of the work, adds distinctive flavor to every twitch and gaze, the actor can "shrink" the performance into very small postural expressions or expressive nuances. A small number of telling examples:

- In *The Fugitive* (1993), there comes a moment when the fleeing Dr. Richard Kimball (Harrison Ford), with the contemporary Javert, Samuel Gerard (Tommy Lee Jones), hot on his tail, comes out of a dank dark tunnel and finds himself staring down a mammoth precipice, the fall of water dropping into the base of a dam. The only extremity required of Ford here (actually required of his double) is a formal posture in diving forward into the air. As to facial response when he sees the height, the Dutch angle of the water dropping away accomplishes a great deal for him. The moment is galvanically frightful, but if we concentrate on the performer not the character we see that he is curiously relaxed. In addition, any extreme gesture he made here would subtract from the power of the scenic background, a power not to be disregarded as the producer has made expensive arrangements to have shots that convey it.
- Or we can look at the secret lair of Dr. No (Joseph Wiseman) in the first James Bond film, as designed for the screen by Ken Adam. A

vast lateral space, walled by arrangements of stone boulders, softly lit, accessible by elevators through copper-sheathed doors, set with specially lit modern sculpture. Here is a brutal announcement of capacious wealth and the illusion of an unconfining space, although the script has prepared us already for the owner of this place being the villain (thus, of course, a dungeon keeper). All this conspicuous wealth will be used for nefarious purposes; and movement for Bond (Sean Connery) and his girlfriend Honey Ryder (Ursula Andress) will hardly seem (to them or to us) unconfined. The glow of the space is an antithesis of the dark inscrutability of Julius No himself. When the man makes his entrance, the performer is enabled already, instantly, to walk only with calm steps and to avoid facial gesture beyond the probing gaze. He is always already at home in a scene that bespeaks his attitude, and the visitors are always already amazed by the place, and therefore by him: amazed on scene, yet also cuing us to amazement.

- But if we look instead at the little Tennessee homestead in which Alvin York (Gary Cooper) lives with his aged mother (Margaret Wycherly) and young brother (Dickie Moore) in Howard Hawks's *Sergeant York* (1941), especially at the moment Alvin bids them farewell and mounts his steed to head off to war, we find the main character isolated in a spreading landscape, a road running off and downward, rolling hills, huge trees, all this dappled with sun, and the mother, brother, and girlfriend (Joan Leslie) waving from the house on a hill. The scene fairly radiates off the screen with a naturalness, a sense of a paradisiacal American countryside untouched and untrammeled. This is God's land, a place that is all promise and all future, an opening into a better world. As Alvin rides away there can be no doubt, no felt hesitation, that he will return to this bucolic world, that his war experience will be a safe one. We can focus on him as a character type well developed, rather than a fighting agent entering a scene of conflict, which scene would be seen as the true heart of the film. The true heart is this filmic Tennessee Eden, designed by John Hughes and effected, for this sequence, through a matte shot part of which is made at the Warner Bros. ranch and part of which is a painted picture. Cooper does not need to enunciate his comfort and good feeling at this homestead, or his regret on leaving it, since the idyllic setting conveys both ideas fully. His (somewhat normal) taciturnity is at home, and in no way dysfunctional here.

When as viewers we have the sense that we are *rightly in a place*, rightly because along with the characters we wish to be—or realize the appropriateness of being—there; rightly because along with the characters we cannot (but also would not, at the moment) free ourselves to be elsewhere; rightly because it is as good a spot as any for what is being done, simply a facility that permits action, we do not have the sense of being intentfully placed, of being corralled by the camera, though every image is a kind of entrapment.

22

Show Me

FIGURE 22 *Jacqueline Bisset and Jean-Pierre Léaud in* Day for Night *[La nuit américaine] (François Truffaut, Les Films du Carrosse, 1973).*

Wolfgang Schivelbusch details a problem associated with seeing how you work:

> As long as the work that needed to be lit up was tied to individual craftsmen and only the winter morning and evening hours required extra light, the glow provided by traditional candles and oil lamps was adequate. This changed with the introduction of industrial methods of production. Work processes were no longer regulated by the individual

worker; they became integrated, comprehensive operations. The new factories needed new sources of light. Artificial light was needed to illuminate larger spaces for longer periods of time. In the factories, night was turned to day more consistently than anywhere else. (8–9)

So much emotionally founded reification attaches to considerations of movies and movie production that it has become very easy to overlook the factory production mode through which films are produced. Indeed, as with assembly in the computer industry, sophisticated medical practice, and robotized manufacture of all kinds, film production is an intensified model of "integrated, comprehensive operations." But cinema has a particular fondness for, and hunger for, light. Schivelbusch notes that the theater was "the place with the greatest appetite for light in the nineteenth century" (50), but we can see rather easily that in the twentieth and twenty-first centuries that place is the movie set, especially in the twentieth century, I should add, when high-definition video and super-fast stock were not yet available and processes like Technicolor required immense amounts of illumination.

Regardless of the technical issues in obtaining any particular film image—managing shadows, encountering reflections, warping space, balancing colors, effecting camera movement, and keeping focus clear with movement in front of the camera—an image will not show space and the objects inside it unless light is provided.[1] Everything that appears on film appears because it is lit to do so. Even the shadows. Without light, the film stock gets no exposure at all. The slower the stock (the lower the ASA—a rating system from the American Standards Association) the more lethargically it drinks up light and thus the more light required to get a decent exposure. Early Technicolor three-strip was produced through Kodak black-and-white recording film that had a very low ASA. The more light you put in, the more depth of field you can get, but also, the more unpleasant become working conditions for people being lit, since lights produce not only glare but heat. Cinematographers have been using a number of interesting light(ing) tricks to enhance the visual quality of film while somewhat depreciating the agony of shooting:[2]

- *Sourcing.* Following from Caravaggio (1571–1610), Vermeer (1632–75), Turner (1775–1851), and Pierre-Auguste Renoir (1841–1919), cinematographers have learned to be meticulous in unifying set

---

[1] A thorough discussion of camera movement and of film lighting can be found in two books by Patrick Keating, *The Dynamic Frame* and *Hollywood Lighting from the Silent Era to Film Noir*; and in John Alton's very helpful *Painting with Light*. Nestor Almendros's *A Man with a Camera* is eye-opening.
[2] Including, Kino Flo, a high-output fluorescent system designed for Robby Müller by Frieder Hochheim and Gary Swink in 1987.

lighting according to a single-source plan. The diegetic scene has a presumable main source of light: the sun in the sky at a certain time of day in relation to the window(s) of the set, for example. When all the light replicates the angle of approach of the diegetically invoked light source, the scene must be lit to take on "natural" shadows in order to seem real. This "natural sourcing" is one of the principal tactics intensified in what is called noir film.[3] Directors have to block actor movement with a "main light source" in mind, since otherwise an actor might end up delivering a key line of dialogue while moving through shadow and for the cinematographer to brighten that shadow area enough to show the actor would ruin the scenic effect.

- *Diffusion.* The *plein-air* lighting of the Impressionists—Pissarro (1830–1903), his pupil Cézanne (1839–1906), and Sisley (1839–99) in particular—offered visions of a uniformly lit outdoors with a vast, seemingly unbounded array of color and an even, soft light suffusing every aspect of the space (Pissarro's canvases from Pontoise; Cézanne's from Provence, Sisley's from Bougival). Keenly struck by their methods, Nestor Almendros invented for *Claire's Knee* (1970) a technique for diffusing sunlight that he continued to use on films afterward, perhaps most notably *Pauline at the Beach* (1983). His idea was to seam together some white bedsheets and then suspend this makeshift canopy by attaching it at the corners to four long poles. The canopy would be erected above the area being filmed. The light flooding down from the sun would be diffused through this scrim, losing sharpness, passing a soft and evenly intense bubble of light over the whole area. Almendros was particularly happy about this invention for its extreme utility in removing weather conditions from the shooting equation, since earlier it had been vitally necessary for assistant directors to arrange all the shots taken under any particular outdoor weather conditions (cloud types and movements) to be staged with a view to lighting match; but weather is so variable it plays havoc with shooting schedules, and invariably a great deal of money is lost in waiting for the right kind of day. The canopy spread light in the same way no matter whether the sky was blue or gray, cloudy or not. A tremendous amount of freedom of movement is accorded the performers, too, since everything they do under the canopy, every pose they take, receives uniform soft lighting.

---

[3]For a clear comparison between patterned shadows created for single-source lighting and the same created for noir expressivism, see first Alfred Hitchcock's *Suspicion* (1941), the opening train sequence or the shots inside the new atrium of the Aysgarth home, and then John Huston's *The Asphalt Jungle* (1950).

- *Speed*. In the late 1950s and early 1960s, new and considerably faster stocks made it possible to shoot on the street *with available light*, even at night (on technical matters such as this, see Salt). All the potentially expressive glare, and the detectable formal sculpting, of artificial light is banished in the name of situational realism. Where are we? What does it really look like here (*really*: not in a movie)? Using available light, whenever possible, is a boon to filmmaking for other reasons. The production becomes a smaller picnic, with fewer pieces of bulky equipment to move around, less reliance on electrical sources. Nestor Almendros's nocturnal street photography for *Paris vu par . . .* (1965) is a good case, as is Raoul Coutard's shooting for *À bout de souffle* (1960). Shooting with available light can produce more splotches of darkness in scenes, relaxing the designer and decorators' need to fill in all the spaces. As well, the available light cheat might lead viewers to associate more comfortably with screen images as similar to what they see in the everyday, with, among other effects, the result that personalities teasingly remote from their audiences (Gloria Swanson's Norma Desmond in *Sunset Blvd.* [1950]) are now lowered from their heights, brought close, brushed up against (Monica Vitti's Giuliana in *Red Desert* [1964]).
- *Arcs*. The arc lamp, invented early in the nineteenth century by Humphrey Davy, operates through an electrical current leaping from one rod to another, in filmmaking rods made of carbon. The light is extraordinarily bright (thus, if not modified by filtration or other tactics, something of a giveaway), very useful in *noir* cinema for giving the harsh highlights needed to make the contrasting shadows especially ominous. It also produces a very high-temperature blue light equivalent to daylight, thus being exceptionally useful bare, or suitably filtered through gels, for simulating outdoor sunlight on an indoor shooting location. The "outside world" is a generalized cheat in cinema, almost never being a true outdoor space. Space outside the window(s) of a room or a car when we see action inside, is created by either arc lamps or skypans aimed at flat-lit painted backings.[4] Arc light angled through a built window-frame on a set will photograph as daylight.
- *Barn doors*. The various forms of tungsten (yellow-balanced) light used on sets can be fitted with metallic "barn door" shutters that allow for precisely directing the angle of incidence. As we see

---

[4] For an exceptional case of lit painted backings used as the "outside world," see my *The Eyes Have It*, Ch. 4.

the world "naturally," all objects are lit with angularity, so that uniform lighting can look false unless distractions are provided by subjects with interesting features or those engaged in dramatically vital activity. The screen world seems molded and shaped, because objects are not uniformly lit. This is just one type of mechanism that provides for precision in lighting control. It is one thing to supply light to a scene, another entirely to sculpt it so the right things (including actors' faces or parts of them) are "properly" heightened.

- *Cookies.* Decorative or especially evocative shadows are created by a device known as a "cookie." This is a piece of cardboard or Styrofoam that has been cut into a particular shape and then affixed to the end of a long slender rod of some kind. A stage hand holds the cookie up stationary or with movement between a light source and the scene itself, thus effectively sculpting the shadow. Examples: light flickering off the windshield of a "moving" car (shot on set with a breakdown vehicle on gimbels); or the notable shadows of *noir*, trees, poles, silhouettes, which have invoked such a wide appreciation among fans and critics. To see astounding and very beautiful, very large and complex cookie shots, made to emphasize single-source lighting, see the "West Wing" sequence of Hitchcock's *Rebecca* (1940).
- *Bounce.* As with diffused light, reflected light casts no shadow, and can thus be very helpful in bringing soft and uniform illumination to the star face in a portrait shot. Selective reflection, carefully aimed, can help a cinematographer *create* the roundnesses and contours of the celebrated star face, as William Daniels did with Greta Garbo. A sheet of card stock or other pallid substance (nowadays often Styrofoam) is held by a camera assistant below the performer at such an angle that light from above aimed down at it will bounce back into the face. This "bounce light" is singly responsible for much of the celebrated star images of the classical age, a significant part of what made the star seem to be beyond the human, closer in form to a Greek sculpture.
- *Radiation.* Photographing the close-ups of Grace Kelly for *Rear Window* (1954), George Barnes created a variation of a trick that had long been in use: rubbing a thin film of Vaseline on the lens in order to obtain a diffuse, softened shot of the female face. Instead of doing that, he stretched a nylon stocking over the lens and then burned a tiny hole in the center with a lit cigarette. The light on Kelly's face (considerable bounced light) now gave crystalline focal clarity directly in the center in a very small area, and then spread radially with more and more diffusion. The stunning facial portrait as Lisa leans over Jeff to awaken him shows the effect.

- *Taking sides.* There are no humans whose left and right sides are perfectly isomorphic. Any one of us looks like one person when photographed in right profile; and like someone else shot on the other side. This effect is modulated considerably when the camera shoots frontally at an angle. For profile shots, performers may have sound professional reasons for wishing to avoid certain possibilities and may even, as did Claudette Colbert, insist on contract clauses which would stipulate profiles from one particular side only. But the script supervisor has to keep careful notes of the angles used on principal players, so that shots taken at different times but meant to be edited together will match. The matching of two shots, discussed in film theory as "suture," is part of what conveys to the viewer the illusion of being enmeshed in a coherent multi-dimensional space where moments are real, but this conveyance depends on film being shot in such a way that an editor can piece it together reasonably, much later. The matching of shots can't be created in the editing, then, if it is not effected before the lens first. The "fit" has to be arranged in principal photography, through pose, through positioning, through camera placement and movement, through lens, through lighting, and through careful notation.
- *Keys.* The "key" light is a tightly focused and intense light (usually tungsten-based) that concentrates on a principal object or on some especially important feature of the performer's body (almost uniformly the star's eyes, producing that telltale twinkle). I was on a set once where the lighting of each shot took an extraordinarily long time. The scene was "the Oval Office." A long table with chairs all around and papers, both crumpled and flat; coffee cups; pens. I was told by an insider that the Japanese crew was using normal Japanese lighting techniques: first bulk-lighting the whole area, then spot-lighting various key areas where performers would be standing, and then carefully keylighting every single object that would be in frame, with a separate keylight for every single crumpled piece of paper, each keylight separately controlled for intensity, coloration, and sharpness.
- *Props.* In two ways most set lighting in cinema is arranged to be invisible as such, with the exception of "practical" lights such as table lamps, candles burning in candelabras, chandeliers, and so on, which typically do not actually light the scene. Light sources are hidden off-camera, but also the light produced by the light sources, fashioned to seem *only realistic* for the scene, has no more discrete visibility in itself than any light does for us when we use it. Light is noticed when it gets in the way: a reading lamp too glary or not angled ideally. Sun coming through a window and getting in a

character's eyes. But it can be necessary or useful to have a diegetic light, present merely as part of the décor, functioning as production light, too. An especially high-powered bulb put into a table lamp or a lighting fixture outside a residential door. In *Suspicion* (1941), Hitchcock offers what has become a celebrated example of diegetically internal keylight, as Cary Grant mounts a staircase holding a glass of what seems to be irradiated milk. It was important to direct the audience's gaze to the milk, more than to him, since the filmmaker wished to implant in his viewers the suspicion that the milk contained something like poison. Wiring ran from a battery pack on Cary Grant's body through his sleeve and up the bottom of the tray to power a lightbulb that was inside the glass. Truffaut pays a small homage to this in *Day for Night* (*La nuit américaine* [1973]) as Jean-Pierre Léaud marches slowly with a candle on a set for a film-within-the-film. As part of our trip behind the scenes into the magic-land of filmmaking, we are bluntly shown the tiny electrically powered light making the radiance of the candle possible.

Aside from specialty cases such as the milk glass above, where a light effect is designed to be expressly visible as part of the storytelling (the studio catastrophe scene of *The Day of the Locust* [1975] is another good example), it is more generally the case that lighting is subjected to a blanket and paradoxical cheat: nothing will show without it, yet it is always effected so as not to show. Not only could a glimpse of a lighting fixture at the edge of the frame ruin a shot and dispel the narrative illusion but so might a too noticeable splotch of light inside the scene, something that seems not to accord with the place as posited. In what follows next, I address one special, and especially tormenting, lighting situation for filmmakers.

23

On the Road

FIGURE 23 *Tom Cruise (l.) and Jamie Foxx in* Collateral *(Michael Mann, Paramount, 2004).*

Particular camera, lens, and lighting problems are posed by the narrative trope of characters driving in cars, a feature that goes back to before the 1930s. In Sergei Eisenstein's *Strike* (1925) we see a dark car moving through the rain, with the driver dimly lit inside. The central function of the car shot or sequence is social realism, the depictive recognition that we live, and dramatic events occur, in a world filled with automotive transit. That people use their cars in many ways, inhabit them, furnish them, perhaps most importantly relate to other people in them. It is rare that a car sequence appears depicting action that could not possibly have been shot in a stationary location elsewhere, and indeed the most typical use of the car in our culture, a means of getting from one place to another (as is shown climaxing *The Graduate* [1967]), is among the less frequently depicted uses onscreen. In movies, things happen in cars, and in such a way that they seem heightened for being placed that way.

Here are some of the problems in car shots:

- The car interior is relatively cramped as spaces—certainly typical diegetic spaces—go, and must now fit two or more characters, a camera operator, and perhaps an assistant, as well as all the necessary lighting equipment. Bus interiors, such as we see in *Speed* (1994), have more room but it is almost impossible to get a clear shot that blocks off the lighting fixtures.
- The car interior is dark on the face of it. For night shots it will seem cavernously so. The cinematographer does not want to ruin the realism by bringing in too much light, but unless there is light nothing is going to be seen.
- The world outside, through which the car is passing, must look crisply focused and colorful, sufficiently that it does not seem to exist on a different planet from that of the interior. The story will sometimes depend on some particular person or object seen outside, from within the vehicle. But: too much clarity can produce too much interest, so that as the vehicle passes, a distal place or object suddenly becomes more pressing to the viewer than a character speaking a key line of dialogue up close. Elia Kazan manages the crucial back-seat-of-the-car conversation between Brando and Rod Steiger in *On the Waterfront* (1954) by eliding views of the outside altogether, and replacing them with flashing light (as from other cars).
- For action scenes the car must appear to move quickly through space. *6 Underground* (2019) is a paradigm. Often precarious and aggressive action is required as well, such as a character in one car attempting to kill a character in another at full highway speed (*Bullitt* [1968] or some of the cavortings in the early car chase of *Baby Driver* [2017]). There is considerable inspiration for the photography of such activity—with sharp axle blades anticipating the guns of oncoming "millennia"—in the stunning chariot race of *Ben-Hur* (1959).
- Sometimes very precise control of star lighting and sound recording are required while the set (the vehicle) is "in motion," and outdoor location shooting is out of the question for getting precision shots of this type. Further, sound stages, even back lots, are not large enough to accommodate fast-moving cars, although of course there are legion film moments where slow-moving cars have been filmed indoors. Nina Foch's green limo in *An American in Paris* (1951), Fred Astaire and company showing up at the log cabin in *Swing Time* (1936), for just two cases.

Here are some pain-killers for these production headaches:

[1] *For cramped interiors*. Various types of camera rig are in use. In one type the camera is in a metal harness bolted or strapped onto the hood of the car so that shots can be made of the driver and passenger as the car moves, with characters' eyelines facing the camera. There are also tow rigs in which the entire (fictional) car is affixed in a rectangular steel grid, a kind of trailer being pulled by a camera truck. The wheels of the car do not touch the road, but the rig has wheels. From the back of the truck a camera crew films the car, which is low enough to the road to be made to appear, through an angular cheat, as though it is on it. Some film shots have been made with hand-held equipment operated by a crouching cameraman inside the vehicle. It is almost never the case that actors are actually driving the car they appear to be driving, and there are indeed stunt cars where the steering is handled from the passenger side or from the rear seat.[1]

[2] *For darkness*. Special lighting rigs are employed to highlight the star faces without changing the structure of the image by illuminating so much of the car interior that other aspects of the interior become distractingly interesting. The body lighting can be filtered to modulate the strength, and the typical outcome is a car in which the driver and passenger receive uniform—but also diegetically nonsensical—light. So much cinematography has been done with body lights inside cars that the trope comes to seem normal, although it can never be entertained as wholly logical, the only "real" light bouncing up at such a driver being dashboard light, increasingly dim and LED originated in the contemporary age. The cheat here is essentially a trade-off. The car does not require illumination, dramatically speaking, but the characters do and they are in the car. Further, the bodies being lit are star bodies and the fact of their being lit, as we apprehend it, brings notice of the star structure and thus the status of the present experience as movie-going (if not driving). To go for stark, dark realism and lose the performer seems a greater price to pay than permitting an eerie glow to run through the space as the car moves. Daylight sequences can of course be made without this effect. In Taylor Hackford's *Parker* (2013) Jennifer Lopez pulls her car up one night and stops it next to what we are led to believe is a street lamp; cool halogen illumination floods over her face to identify both her character and the scenic situation at once.

[3] *Outside*. The world outside will be seen in either of two different ways. First, it may be photographed naturally with the car seen in an exterior as it moves through. This kind of photography is done from some stationary perch that the car passes; or from a traveling car acting like a fast-moving dolly, or from a rig (as above). Or from a helicopter (in a shot that originated with Nicholas Ray's *They Live By Night* [1948]). The camera vehicle will

---

[1] Steve McQueen did almost all his own stunt driving in *Bullitt*, however.

either have larger softer tires than most vehicles, or be traveling on a special track, or have a camera setup on gimbels, so that bumps in the road do not affect the shot. Usually for a driving sequence it is not necessary to have the driver or passenger visibly identifiable in every shot of the group, as long as key shots make very crisply focused reference to the stars. Stand-ins can be used for distant shots.

In place of exterior shots, or used intermittently to accompany them, are shots from within the vehicle where the outside world is seen to pass by the windows. When a lot of traffic is involved, the assistant director will be completely in charge of all the personnel and vehicles and will more or less direct the movement by which cars on the road creep up and pass the central vehicle or lag behind, or whatever. In driving emergency sequences—*Baby Driver* has extraordinary footage of this kind, as does *The Bourne Supremacy* (2004)—the A.D. has a crew of stunt drivers, and the action is broken down into tightly choreographed very small shots where, with the help of catapults, springboards, and pull-aways vehicles and bodies can seem to twist, spin, flip, and fly through space catastrophically.

The most frequent technique for capturing the outside world through which a car moves is rear-projection photography, in which footage of the scenery, from some particular point of view meant to simulate a position in the vehicle, will be shot considerably in advance and then, on a special soundstage, projected from behind on a screen outside the window area of the partial car rig. That vehicle is most likely to be only a "car," nothing more than a cursory frame, steering wheel, seat, and window structure, often on gimbels, springs, or moving platforms. Process plates (as they are called) need to be made early on, and are usually effected by a special effects camera unit on a location. Views through the back window or the windshield of the car, angularly through the rear windows, or laterally through the side windows need to be shot with the special-effects camera car moving at a different speed for each (sixty percent of forward motion for lateral; eighty for angular; one hundred for full rear).

Rear projection can lose effectiveness the more it diverges from the main photography in terms of image quality: focus, saturation, illumination level, and blur. Yet it need not. What makes rear projection difficult to achieve with brilliance is the fact that there are legion difficulties inherent to the process no matter what kind of film story it is being used to fake. With cars, a poor quality rear-projection screen can diffuse light badly from the center to the margins so that there seems to be a hot spot (*Lady for a Day* [1933] gives a good example). The film stock used for the plate will affect the saturation and brightness, not to say the color balance. But the most perplexing of problems is the maintenance of dramatic balance, since the better the rear-projection plate, the crisper, the more colorful, and the better lit, the more clearly audiences can see outside the vehicle as well as inside, and the more likely, then, that their attention will be taken up by some extraneous but momentarily interesting feature of the landscape, while it is almost always necessary to maintain the audience's attachment to the characters, not the place.[2]

[4] *Action*. Cars in action sequences are driven far less quickly than appears to the eye, the cheat here being principally acoustic. The sound of the growling motor, the squealing tires, the shrieking brakes, the gunning of the engine—all these give a direct sense of impending threat and a racing attitude. Shoot drivers at 35 or 40 mph, or less, and fill with an intensified sound track, especially squeals of rubber, and the viewer picks up a sense of speed. The speed of the motion will seem to increase if the pace of the editing does, too, so the briefer the average shot length the speedier the action appears. For *6 Underground*, very terse lines of dialogue very quickly spoken between driver and passenger aid in the fast editing and production of "speed." In *The Bourne Supremacy* much of the chase driving is shot on location from within the vehicles, but there is no dialogue; the thundering and fast-tempo motor sounds of the music track assist in "speeding up" the action.

[5] *Featuring the star*. The optimization of lighting control and sound-recording quality by using the vehicle rig and the rear-projection apparatus is important mostly for star scenes, so that exterior shots are used principally where the character does not require mic'ing or careful facial photography. The better (and more authentically) we see the cars on the road, the less dramatically central are the people in them. When we have a complex narrative involving car travel at its center (the going-to-work sequence in *Zabriskie Point* [1970], shot on Wilshire Blvd.), or one in which the star protagonists will be present throughout the driving sequences (Michael Mann's *Collateral* [2004] for instance), a special lighting and recording rig will be used in real space, designed to make shooting possible from virtually any angle.

With studio-made rear-projection composites, what is constantly on the filmmaker's mind, but is hardly noticed by audiences unless things go wrong, is that the live portion of the action, what is being shot on set, must be lit in such a way that the levels match the lighting of the background properly. If a car is driving at night, for instance, there will not be a lot of ambient illumination flooding in through the windows, and street lighting will be distinct. So the inside of the car will have to be dim, or the radical brightness will fail to fit the picture. However, the difficulty with all of this is that the lighting of the outside was set long before the studio shooting, and is fixed in the background plate. There is thus a great deal of constraint on the set.

In car shots there may be a mixing of key dialogue bits with key visuals. In effect, the more principal characters enunciate their lines, the more attention

---

[2] See further Pomerance, "Bells."

is devoted to them at the expense of the scene. The less they talk, the more we fixate on the scene. And the longer we fixate on the scene the more likely it is that we will see some slight disjunction between the background and the foreground—a disjunction that in non-vehicular scenes we are less prone to seeing. One of the cheats of car scenes is to keep the protagonists talking enough to be a distraction in themselves.

But linguistic utterance need not be articulate. In the downhill car scene of Hitchcock's *Family Plot* (1976), where Bruce Dern and Barbara Harris are trapped racing at about forty-five degrees downhill, inside a car the brakes of which have been tampered with, we find intercut with the driver's point of view and external shots of the car on the road dozens of shots of Harris trying to climb on top of Dern to save herself and Dern trying to throw her off so he can keep eyes on the road. Many of the close-ups—his foot interfered with on the brake pedal—are made in studio. The shots are cut together rather quickly, so that the viewer, like Harris's Blanche, bounces around desperately (a carnival ride). Artfully intermixed here are perfectly lit shots of the car interior seen from below and beside the driver with rear-projected outside, and location shots of a stunt vehicle. The vocality is so aggravated and fearful that it takes our attention from the seam that joins the rear plate photography to the live footage.

Photographing car scenes faces a far different challenge today, as the car culture has become more rabid and where the car shot signals, among other things, the regularity of the everyday. Sometimes an action, especially a dialogue, heightened in believability because vehicular, will be diminished in dramatic power exactly because the car is a casual, almost too casual conversational setting, the sort of place where people go to "just talk." In police procedurals now—typically cop duo films—much more attention is paid to the types of conversation and the conversational content inside the police car, between partners, than to the car as an agency of travel: in fact, it is taken entirely for granted as an agency of travel, but the quirkiness of the partners inside it is demonstrable most succinctly through their banal conversations. The car would seem to transform all conversation into banality.

In the classical era the car signaled social class and functioned principally to convey class-bound action forward. Car scenes today are ornamental to the mechanism of the story and do not move the action forward as much as they imbricate us with the action. The realism of car shots, a popular myth, dissolves some in actual viewing. When we see people driving cars on film we know full well they don't really look like people in real life who, driving cars, don't tend by posture or gesture to proclaim that they are doing so. If on the road today one finds plenty of rude, aggressive, and incompetent driving, when any of this kind of thing is performed on film it is carried to an extreme, becoming almost comedic (Margot Winkler does a notable car-bound riff in *New York, New York* [1977]). As it is not troublesome to discern how unlike the everyday a car routine is, car scenes must be cheated through the inclusion of brazen distractions inside and outside, no matter how dramatically probable. Driving down an expressway on the wrong side of the road and heading the wrong way . . . driving near a precipice . . . driving next to a car that is trying to bump you off the road. Driving with gunshots fired. Driving wounded, as one bleeds. Driving against helicopter pursuit. And on and on. All of these eccentricities of staging wrap us so deeply into the momentary action we forget that we are being steered. Steered, too, onscreen, and in a way that no one could accomplish if the world were caving in. Perhaps the ultimate car-in-extremis moment comes with John Cusack in his limousine in Santa Barbara in *2012* (2009), racing to save himself as the urban geography comes apart under his wheels. An ultimate moment of a more tightly composed, and entirely parodic kind is the ambulance chase in Frank Tashlin's *The Disorderly Orderly* (1964), one of cinema's great action choreographies involving Jerry Lewis putting his foot to the floor.

Substitute driving is but one of the attractions of car scenes. A tender moment, designed for romantic flavor, can be worked by means of a car, too, and through an interesting substitution. There is a culminating brief scene in *Parker*, where the eponymous hero, an action figure with a strict moral code and a thoroughgoing sense of decency (Jason Statham) is parting from Leslie (Jennifer Lopez), a young real estate agent in West Palm Beach, who has been helping him revenge an especially filthy crime debacle. They are in a car together, she at the wheel. He patiently explains what she must do with the huge cache of jewels he has stolen from the robbers, and that in following his instructions she must be very patient. She listens. It is a quiet Florida night. He looks at her and gives a respectful nod. This could have been, perhaps even should have been, a smashing romance, but he is with someone already (she is not, haplessly) and love isn't in the cards. As he stands on the pave looking through the window she gives him a genuinely tearful smile of goodbye. He responds with a tiny, but genuinely profound nod. The car draws away, and we can see the regret, the release, the *Weltschmerz* in her posture and touching expression. CUT TO: a shot from behind as Leslie's white car disappears into the night. The scene works only if we accept the offer of sense and sensibility that is being offered onscreen, namely, if we continue to feel Leslie moving away, moving away forever, into the long dark night of time—and this after a very involved and swellingly sincere relation with the person being left behind. Parker gets it, as we see from his pose. And we get it, too. But a little cheat is in progress. Lopez is at the wheel as in the lateral shot she moves the car away from him, off right. In the ensuing long shot, the money shot, it is a stand-in driver. Yet we feel her there. We feel what we wish to feel, yet at the same time the wish will have to satisfy on its own.

[6] But Brian Helgeland's *Legend* (2015) illustrates a further, and fascinating complication. In the back seat of a car we are to see the two infamous Kray brothers (Tom Hardy and Tom Hardy) in conversation as their car is driven forward on the road. They are frontal to the camera, the world passing by through the rear window and rear side windows. The technique here, inspired by Sol Polito's work on *A Stolen Life* (1945) with Bette Davis, involves combined in-camera split-screen and rear projection. The twinning is accomplished with one actor on one side of the visual field playing out a scene; then the film being re-wound to the starting point, the same actor in different costume and make-up playing the same scene—the brother's part of it—on the other side. As long as the balance of content in the shot is rather dark, as in this car interior it is, the duplication in the final shot will seem clean. In what way, however, can a shot be re-wound and made twice if the world is really gliding by outside the windows? Things out there would change. Thus, a rear projection is used outside a car rig, a strip of film that can also be rewound and projected again, identically, making possible both "genuine" passage in a vehicle and "twinning." Here and in other effects work of the kind, two issues are examined by the viewer for veracity—the viewer never stops examining the world for veracity: the doubling of personality as authentically believable, a problem for the actor to confront as he invents his tactics for handling each brother's distinctiveness of appearance and manner and as he works the complexity of the two-sided gab; and the believable presentation of geophysical reality in its own right: the car interior, the outside passing by, the bodies placed on the seats. To emphasize the curiosity of the sequence: Reggie and Ron could have this conversation in a sitting room. And the decision to set it in a moving vehicle, while it does little to make the actor's work more difficult, is far more complicated photographically, far more expensive, far more finicky to get absolutely right (because more takes would have been required, each of them costing money). To go one tiny step further: The Krays actually seem more believable as living beings who beat other people up, when they are in stationary locales—a sitting room at the mother's, a pub. The car trip does make them seem able to scoot around town, although for the viewer the ability to use a car for scooting is, by 2015, entirely received. A complicated scene, then, presumably about the viewer's incurable itch to be on the road.

24

"Good Cinematography!"

FIGURE 24A *(Top) Big Basin State Park in* Vertigo *(Alfred Hitchcock, Paramount, 1958). Photography by Robert Burks; (Bottom) Amanda Langlet (l.) and Arielle Dombasle in* Pauline à la plage *(Éric Rohmer, Les Films Ariane, 1983). Photography by Nestor Almendros.*

Viewers who are not in the business of making pictures often credit a film they have seen with having "Good cinematography!" The images brought pleasure. The images had clear (enough) focus and interesting subject matter. The pictures taken as a whole gave the viewers a "good" feeling, morally speaking, and through their appraisal the goodness of the feeling is projected outward as a feature of what is on the screen.

{READER ALERT FOR THOSE WHO BELIEVE IN SANTA CLAUS}

Virtually everything that cinematographers do—all cinematographers—has elements of the extraordinary, and the fastest way to learn this is to take up a camera and try to make beautiful pictures of the world. Yet, to win accolades extraordinary accomplishment is not required of cinematographers: an astutely written, or exceptionally witty script can do the trick; or a set of well-crafted performances; or someone's celebrated stardom plainly shown; or eye-catching set design and decoration, a haunting musical accompaniment, an editor's genius. Good producing is almost never credited, like good hairdressing or good continuity, but it's amazing how much a producer can do to foster the development of a film (or to stifle it). Viewers may be struck by a director's infusion of pace, the feeling that events are rhythmically ongoing. And as to the cinematography, it may be evidence of nothing more than the most routine aspects of professional accomplishment on the part of cinematographers, camera operators, grips, and gaffers. Providing adequate lighting, handling the camera in movement, undetectably getting and shifting focus, using a film stock that will ideally capture the situational light and movement: all these are the bread and butter (gluten-free or not) of picture-making, and virtually any filmmaking crew will manage the challenges at all times, whether they are doing "good" work or not. What is difficult involves variables most viewers neither notice nor think they care about: depth of field, lateral movements, eccentric camera placements, focus maintenance in motion, and sometimes the color of lighting (for a startling example of which see Coppola's *One From the Heart* [1982]).

The "good cinematography" cheat, fostered in informal discussion, in media reviews, and officially by the Academy of Motion Picture Arts and Sciences by way of the Oscar competition (the World Series of film), often offers a sense of Marvel!! and WONDER!!!! at what cinematographers would consider normal for film, the day-to-day that goes along with the territory. An equivalent posture might be raving ecstatically about a RADA-trained British actor's crisp enunciation, or giving immense admiration to a concert pianist moving her fingers very rapidly upon the keys to play, say, Chopin's Grand Polonaise. If you can't do fingerwork like that, you don't play Chopin. If you can't enunciate you get off the stage.

The presentation of an Academy Award for cinematography (since 1927) is a firmly grounded incitement to audience admiration, yet admirers often neglect to take into account the salient truth of the Academy Award in general, that, beyond the commercial intentions of producers to make still more money at the box office with an "Oscar winner," it tends to be given only in cases where films are *believably* special; the award plays to a pattern of viewer assumption and expectation and is not awarded where the uninformed cannot see a reason. Reason is crucial, if an audience is to be had for next year's show. Triumph must meet comprehension. If we look at winners, to see what underpins viewers' easy comprehension of Best Cinematography, we find that in almost every case the amazing mastery of some arcane photographic challenge is missing from the list. Instead there are films with very famous and much beloved stars; films depicting ("accurately") archaic situations of historical interest (and fantasy); films containing well-framed but very conventional majestic landscapes, seascapes, or cityscapes; and films much adored because of witty or devious scripts, bizarre plots, and adorable characterizations. The untutored viewer can easily love the comedic fool, for example; the view from a mountaintop; the elegant portrait of ancient Egypt; the Brad Pitt or Leonardo DiCaprio vehicle, without being able to grasp whether any of the images that appear onscreen were serious accomplishments. Given that members of the American Society of Cinematographers (the A.S.C.) make nominations for it (unimmune to studio blandishments), The Academy Award for Best Cinematography will seem to be a professional acknowledgment of superior worth, but will also be comprehensible as such to non-professionals. More than touting the work of a particular cinematographer the A.S.C. is in effect selling itself by way of the Award, since the giving over of the Award will be seen by an enormous audience worldwide.

Here are the winners for the past forty-nine years (at this writing), with my parenthetical comment as to characteristics that would have made the work in question easily readable to the multitudes as "evidence" of "good cinematography," notwithstanding that all of these cases are of course splendid examples of what cinematographers can do. It is to be noted that there are genuinely brilliant moments in these (and other) films, in some of them more than in others, and even on occasion cinematographic work of a pioneering nature (see 1975; 1979; 2009; 2013), but it remains broadly true that in accepting the award-winning as sensible in itself, the eager popular audience did not then, and does not now need to recognize authentic cinematographic challenges and difficulties. It is worth noting how many of the characteristics I note are essentially non-photographic in the first place:

1970: Freddie Young for *Ryan's Daughter* [pure, untouched landscape; cultural charm]
1971: Oswald Morris for *Fiddler on the Roof* [adorable characters, archaic situation]
1972: Geoffrey Unsworth for *Cabaret* [adorable characters, archaic situation]

1973: Sven Nykvist for *Cries and Whispers* [hyperintensive color design]
1974: Fred Koenekamp and Joseph Biroc for *The Towering Inferno* [spectacular setting via effects]
1975: John Alcott for *Barry Lyndon* [shooting by candlelight]
1976: Haskell Wexler for *Bound for Glory* [evocative landscape]
1977: Vilmos Zsigmond for *Close Encounters of the Third Kind* [landscape, situation, pioneering effects demands]
1978: Nestor Almendros for *Days of Heaven* [landscape, effects]
1979: Vittorio Storaro for *Apocalypse Now* [landscape, characters]
1980: Geoffrey Unsworth for *Tess* [landscape, characters]
1981: Vittorio Storaro for *Reds* [characters, effects]
1982: Billy Williams and Ronnie Taylor for *Gandhi* [landscape, powerful central performance]
1983: Sven Nykvist for *Fanny and Alexander* [characters, situation]
1984: Chris Menges for *The Killing Fields* [landscape, situation]
1985: David Watkin for *Out of Africa* [landscape, powerful central performance]
1986: Chris Menges for *The Mission* [landscape]
1987: Vittorio Storaro for *The Last Emperor* [landscape, characters, archaic story]
1988: Peter Biziou for *Mississippi Burning* [situation, characters, "dangerous" story]
1989: Freddie Francis for *Glory* [landscape, situation]
1990: Dean Semler for *Dances with Wolves* [landscape, characters, archaic story]
1991: Robert Richardson for *JFK* [characters, "dangerous" script]
1992: Philippe Rousselot for *A River Runs Through It* [landscape]
1993: Janusz Kaminski for *Schindler's List* [situation, rare b/w usage, "dangerous" archaic story]
1994: John Toll for *Legends of the Fall* [characters, situation]
1995: John Toll for *Braveheart* [landscape, situation, powerful central performance]
1996: John Seale for *The English Patient* [landscape, script]
1997: Russell Carpenter for *Titanic* [effects, situation, characters, pre-established fame of plot]
1998: Janusz Kaminski for *Saving Private Ryan* [landscape, war situation, realistic battle scenes]
1999: Conrad L. Hall for *American Beauty* [script, characters]
2000: Peter Pau for *Crouching Tiger, Hidden Dragon* [newly welcomed foreignness, effects, situation]
2001: Andrew Lesnie for *Lord of the Rings: The Fellowship of the Ring* [already popularized fantasy story, landscape]
2002: Conrad L. Hall for *Road to Perdition* [characters, situation]

2003: Russell Boyd for *Master and Commander: The Far Side of the World* [landscape (seascape), archaic situation]
2004: Robert Richardson for *Aviator* [script, characters, powerful central performance]
2005: Dion Beebe for *Memoirs of a Geisha* [script, situation]
2006: Guillermo Navarro for *Pan's Labyrinth* [script, surreal effects]
2007: Robert Elswit for *There Will Be Blood* [script, characters, powerful central performance]
2008: Anthony Dod Mantle for *Slumdog Millionaire* [script, "exotic" situation, and setting]
2009: Mauro Fiore for *Avatar* [effects, (CGI) landscape]
2010: Wally Pfister for *Inception* [effects, (CGI) landscape]
2011: Robert Richardson for *Hugo* [effects]
2012: Claudio Miranda for *Life of Pi* [effects]
2013: Emmanuel Lubezki for *Gravity* [effects, situation]
2014: Emmanuel Lubezki for *Birdman or (The Unexpected Virtue of Ignorance)* [witty characters, situation]
2015: Emmanuel Lubezki for *The Revenant* [landscape, situation]
2016: Linus Sandgren for *La La Land* [characters, "behind the camera" landscape]
2017: Roger A. Deakins for *Blade Runner 2049* [effects, situation]
2018: Alfonso Cuarón for *Roma* [characters, rare b/w]

If the cheat of "great cinematography!" is achieved through the production of images the audience will predictably appreciate, that audience will have seen similar imagery enough beforehand to have learned the appreciation, to have found and developed the taste. With fabulous *landscapes*, for example: given that we are more and more an urban society, and the capital development is frenetic in the city, relief would come from seeing some vast, virginal territory—Henry Nash Smith's *Virgin Land*, in fact—by way of sweeping topographies uninterrupted by real estate development, dense natural growth as in forests, jungles, or rock formations, or even urban scenes rendered smartly topographical and alluring by being photographed from the air, looking straight downward, or at night when the lights look like diamonds in the dark. A *situation* will seem visually stunning if it involves behavior that is morally stunning. *Effects*—by which we tend to mean computer graphics or other special effects, but not camera effects themselves—will grab attention if they resemble effects, in short, if we have learned already to detect and value them for their own sake. Any abnormal *character*, photographed in close shot or medium shot with a wide-angle lens will seem unbearably interesting and unforgettable, especially if played by a known star.

Actual cinematographic masterpieces, however memorable, may not strike the same chord as do stunning pictures. Many of the above-listed pictures that were sold as stunning photographically were photographed competently, but the drama of the pictures came from acting, from setting, from quirkiness in the script. Two quick examples of cinematographic masterpieces that languished in hiding: in both *Mystic River* (2003) and *Chinatown* (1974) cinematographers had to shoot long important scenes in extremely cramped space, thus being forced to utilize the wide-angle lens; but to shoot without distorting the image so much that the lens choice became visible. The most difficult shot in a film might pass too quickly to gain notice (about which, more to come). One might have stunning success in only a scene or a sequence, and perhaps not a scene in which the drama has built to an audience-absorbing climax. And very often what makes for difficulty in shooting is a trick or two of the light, something about the challenge of rendering light on film, not a composition showing interesting objects together. Jump back for a signal illustration to the still lifes of Paul Cézanne, where we find arrangements of apples, oranges, pitchers, tablecloths, sometimes plants. It is not the objects that make the pictures awe-inspiring, it is the way they are painted. In great cinematography the content of the shot, as composed and balanced as it may be, is often less important for valuation, and less interesting for contemplation, than the inherent difficulty in using the camera to effect it.

What the Academy Awards celebrations help foster, as part of their grand (and celebratory) cheat, is the illusion of the "magical image," the screen presentation that stuns, evokes, persists, even endures because of some arcane formula no one can quite put a finger to but that underpins all of the film images that we cherish most strongly as a culture. *As a culture*: the idea that fantastic cinematography is widely and uniformly appreciated, not dependent on more idiosyncratic variables. And also, the idea that with such broad-based support such imagery must gain for its superiority a kind of definitiveness. In actual fact, beyond certain prerogatives and limitations, say the requirements of the story (what should and should not be carefully shown); beyond the requirements of the director (what kind of image should be crafted for this particular film); and beyond the requirements of the producer (what it costs to set up the shot in the way the cinematographer claims is best), cinematography works essentially in two often disconnected dimensions. It is aesthetic: how the picture should best be framed, what the depth of focus should be, how color could ideally be organized (or the gray tones), what kind of light, harsh or soft, should be used, where and in what way(s) it should be modulated, and what film stock would ideally render a certain type of pictorial beauty. But cinematography is also, and very substantially, technical, involving matters well known in the trade but not part of the vocabulary of the general filmgoing public: how to go for an ideal ASA in particular circumstances; what exact types of lighting to use, Moles, arcs, etc.?, given that there are rental prices involved; how many assistants including the chief gaffer will be needed to idealize the production (and at what cost); the sophisticated challenge of lens choice, given all the variables effective with this one or that one; the nightmare of focus pulling, especially in very long or in moving-camera shots; the relationship between technical equipment required and physical location, with its restrictions and limits (for *The Player* [1991] schlepping cameras, lights, dollies, and other equipment up the vertical slope that leads to Whitley Heights); special working demands of the director or performer; the need to make visual continuities within each shot (this happens, then this, then this, then this) so that later on shots can be cut together by someone else.[1] How to balance the aesthetic demands of the shot with the labor demands of the producer and the unions, since everybody working to achieve the moment of aesthetic beauty is a contracted employee with guarantees and obligations arranged in advance.[2] All of these technical contingencies point to a working environment much more than to a magical one, all would show a canny audience that what is onscreen results from a complex and sophisticated arrangement of labor and does not spring spontaneously out of the blue. But audience engagement—which sells tickets—is favored when attention is kept away from the technical, and the celebration of "good cinematography" is a useful way of setting this distance.

For just a few examples: When Emmanuel Lubezki gets the (much deserved) Oscar for *The Revenant,* nobody says in public that almost the entire live-action portion of the film was shot with available light, an achievement that put onerous demands on both crew and performers. When Vilmos Zsigmond is rewarded for *Close Encounters* it is not part of the publicity that he had ongoingly to make live location shots that would work in combination with extremely high-resolution and high-illumination effects mattes; that the human characters encountering extra-terrestrial life should not diminish in stature visually when they did. What we see touted instead is Leonardo DiCaprio struggling in the wilderness and looking dirty; and a visit to earth of a cool alien starship that perfectly calls up 1970s lightshows.

To illustrate extremely difficult work finely done I choose three examples (none of which earned an Academy Award), knowingly passing over a very great deal of material that could just as reasonably capture our attention here.

---

[1] It is well known about Alfred Hitchcock during his combative days at Selznick International that he retained artistic control (in the face of the aggressive and manipulative David O. Selznick) by "pre-cutting" the film; the shots were planned in advance then made in such a way that *there was only one way to cut them together into the final sequence*. For more on this see Leff.

[2] One example of the constraint placed on cinematographic work by collaborative labor arrangements is Cary Grant's standard contract (he was an independent contractor): it mandated that he would leave the set promptly every day at 6:00 p.m. no matter what, and this sometimes meant working very quickly to complete a shot on time.

[1] *Vertigo, the redwoods sequence.* An uncanny voyage shown as though "by available light" but filmed in a place where available light did not exist since in Big Basin State Park, where this sequence was made, the trees are roughly three hundred feet high and very little light drops down to ground level to become "available." Artificial light had to be used both for figuring the protagonists (James Stewart and Kim Novak) in medium shots and close shots, and for creating the effect of ethereal light rays angling through the giant trunks that recede from view. For creating such effects, only arc lamps would be strong enough and the only way to get arc lamps powered was by means of a portable generator. But once powered, carbon arcs are exceedingly hot, enough to produce a fire hazard (here, in a protected National Treasure). The scene could be photographed only in very brief spates of time, with (expensive) cooling periods between, these long enough to riddle efforts at continuity. We have a scene that might have come straight out of Albert Bierstadt—realistic and utterly stunning, but also an outcome of extreme artistry. It would be easy (and facile) to love the redwoods sequence because it is so beautiful (that is, because viewers were visiting an exotic locale) without seeing labor under stress.

[2] *Pauline à la plage.* Éric Rohmer's *Pauline at the Beach* (1983) required a deeply inscribed summer seaside atmosphere: brilliant, hot, glaring sun; vast sandy spaces; lush Normandy-coast vegetation (hydrangea bushes); a bleaching effect upon the color, as though to see clearly one would need to shade the eyes (a replication, then, of the exact optical experience of being by the sea in the heat of summer). In this place interaction would occur between a small group of young people, ranging in age from about fourteen to about forty. All of them healthy, with fruity skin. The challenge was getting proper exposure on the faces, enough to show not only the identities but also the visual textures (the deliciousness of which motors the plot), in balance with the overexposed backgrounds (yet not so overexposed as to bleach out entirely): to get a sense of radiant, hot airiness, pure Impressionism. Nestor Almendros's (1930–92) work here belongs with that of Boudin (1824–98). With this film it would be easy to revel in the story, the characters and their escapades, the erotic ballet, without ever looking seriously at the light.

[3] *Sweet Smell of Success.* In Alexander Mackendrick's *Sweet Smell of Success* (1957) it was urgently necessary to show midtown Manhattan as a place both enchanting and threatening at once, saturated with "vermin" in the shadows but holding everlasting promise in the highlights. James Wong Howe used a high-key (high contrast) mode of black-and-white photography, with a light bar attached to the camera mount so as to produce precisely aimed glare (which works to special effect on Emile Meyer, Tony Curtis, and Burt Lancaster). The main protagonist (Lancaster) is a master Narcissist and a hawk, seeing everything that lies around him and everything that is buried beneath it as his rightful kingdom. To get J. J. Hunsecker's relentless opticality across to the viewer, Howe rubbed a small amount of Vaseline

onto the lenses of the eyeglasses Lancaster wore, so that his lighting would produce some glare and bring emphasis to his eyes as agents of a surveilling gaze. Since J. J.'s dialogue was written to be sharp, pithy, and aggressive, hearing the voice speak it while being unable to take one's gaze away from those glary eyes made for an unforgettable effect. But at the same time the camera and lighting rig had to move with the character in such a way that no light would fall extraneously on the surround. The film needed to look expressionist, without ever going so far in that direction that it veered detectably away from realism—even though the Manhattan being portrayed was more a fabular than a realistic Manhattan. One could watch this film being wholly impressed by the play of power without giving a thought to the cinematographer's inventiveness.

As one can see by the awards given over the past ten years or so, a taste has developed for cinematography that points to itself in some way, as the recording of elaborate visual effects surely does. This kind of flashiness is not a guarantee of quality, but it does ensure the viewer's non-stop excitement, especially if CGI artists can manage to produce an explosion, a wound, a fragmentation, a firestorm, a whirlwind, or a crash freshly every second.

25

"Picture This"

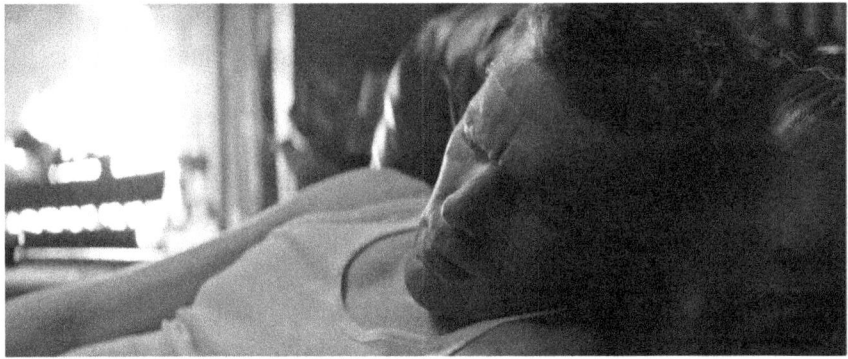

FIGURE 25 *Ethan Hawke in* Regression *(Alejandro Amenábar, Mod Produccciones, 2015).*

Here is a camera challenge that is made to look effortless.

We commence with a cozy wooden shelf in a cozy, softly lit den, and on this shelf a tiny lamp is burning golden. The camera slowly glides to the right. As we move we begin to see, at the extreme right, like a beacon, flames. These become discoverable soon as the flames of a fire burning in a hearth, spiritedly. Between the hearth and the camera, at the right, is an easy chair, and in this chair our friend the detective (Ethan Hawke) is slumbering ... thinking ... meditating ... daydreaming, what have you. We can see only the distal side of his face, the near side dark because the light is emanating from the fireplace on the other side of him and has cast its brilliance there. The shot is about him, not the fire; him, not the chair; him, not the little lamp; him, not the room. The room shows how comfortable and at peace he is at this moment, but the peace is irrelevant next to the fact that it is *his* peace.

In making this pan shot the cinematographer (Daniel Aranyó) has this to consider:

- Every object across which the camera passes—not all of them at the same distance from the surface of the lens—must register clearly as itself, and must do so quickly enough that in the camera's glide it does not vanish offscreen before being known, in this way depositing in the viewer's mind the trace of a disturbing blur, a "what-was-that?," and "I'm-not-absolutely-sure." Consider that in the finesse of viewing, any "What was that?" would obstruct sight by turning the reception, the viewer's alert sense, backward in time toward a vision, already gone, of something that was not only not lit or focused sharply enough in the first place but also *is now recognized in retrospect, swiftly*, as being deficient this way. Every object must register instantly and clearly as itself. This means that the rapidity of this pan—let us say, how many seconds it takes us to travel through an arc of ninety or so degrees—is part of the shot's "equation" and is to be calculated in advance. Once the speed is known, or known roughly, the objects in the room can be placed in such a way that the amount of motion-time resting on each will be known. While we have come to learn of the *flash-pan*, in which space will appear to blur, by design, as it flies by until we hit upon a desired object of focus, this is not intended to be such a thing at all, but something else. Something meditative, relaxed, and dreamy.

- Dreamy, that is: we are already, as viewers, mentally occupying the state of mind we will soon discover our subject is occupying. Perhaps he is taking the lead from us, through some kind of sensation because, as we shall discover, his eyes are closed.

- As this room is a normal room (a normal-looking room of its sort), it is imperative, too, that a proper appearance be given. The place must look (very much) like what it is in the story, a cozy den: there has to be enough light on the set, correctly modulated in every possible nuance, for showing this: showing, that is, making discretely visible. A tiny lamp could be glowing golden on a simple shelf. A healthy fire could be ablaze in a welcoming hearth. A man, presumably at home, could have dumped himself into his favorite chair, and from where we are positioned he would have gained light on only half his face. The composition begs for rational construction of this kind but, as well, the viewer has no problem at all constructing it.

- But it is also true that this picture *looks like a picture*, and while every shot in cinema is in fact a picture only some are "pretty as a picture" and of these only a small number, usually, are intended to declare themselves as such. This shot I point to, its resolution upon the detective at the end of the pan, this shot that is starkly pictorial, is not pretty, however. It merely looks as though some force has paid attention so that the place will show itself, and anyone in it, *off* well. This task no user of his own den would set for himself in the real world. One would be comfortable, but would not strive to give off the appearance of being comfortable. (We can think back to neurotic Larry Renault [John Barrymore] arranging a dramatic light upon himself before committing suicide beside a fireplace in a hotel room, in *Dinner at Eight* [1933].) Had we magically found ourselves in this man's den with him, very nearby so that as he slouched in his chair before the fire we could share his peace and his daydreaming state of mind, *were we to be inside that space*, it is interesting to note that we would not see such a contrast in the fire-lighting with our eyes, the hot, hot, hot glare on the fireplace side of his face and the shadow over here. Our eyes would adjust to even out the discrepancy between the two sides of the face. Given a second or two, the eyes always adjust. The far side would be the brighter still, but not nearly as much more than the near side, as we see in the picture. The camera can be spoken of as analogous to the eye, it can be called The Eye of the Story, it can be thought an "optical" device (not only a device aimed at our eyes but a device that is itself eye-like), but it is not. It does not make this adjustment.

- In order to expose the film stock without adding bounce light to even out the scene, the cinematographer has to take note that the flames will overexpose in relation to the shadow areas; that if one lights and focuses to obtain a clear and realistic portrait of the face, the flames will take over the shot, both being slightly out of focus and being so very bright they offer luminous threat. The shadow areas would be overwhelmed. In this case it would be the fireplace getting the attention (for its brightness), with the result that the man in the chair, brightly enough lit to be visible, would also be insignificant and not so inviting.

- Our picture here looks like a picture because it looks *as though* an artful accommodation has been made by the cinematographer to get a reasonable rendition of the person (detective = central character) in line with a clear and rounded representation of the (difficult) room. Vermeer was an expert at this. Gainsborough.

- However, the cinematographer has used a signal cheat. He has seen to it that the film plays not to our knowledge of the world (our knowledge of what we would see were we there) but to our myths, myths that can be seen to organize our expectation and perception far before we experience:

(a) that the face is essentially a divided one, a space in two, especially in signal cases, such as with a film's star at a critical plot juncture; the dark, the light, the evil spirit, the good one.

(b) that fire is intrinsically interesting in itself and flames here and always make for allure, fire being elemental, fire being Promethean. In practice, flames make a neat photographic effect in themselves, so can reasonably gain focus;

(c) that when we are alive to reality through consciousness, the face brightens; and when we withdraw into meditation, we are in a "darker" mood, because more inward, away from the sun (the fire). Given this mythology, the split face, the crisp flames, and the meditative quality of the dark portion of the face all make sense. The shot is sensible, yet *pictorially so*, quite as though painted. Were we to be there, we would see merely a man lounging next to a fire, and both the man and the fireplace would be noted as connected somehow (this is his fireplace; it is warming his cold doubts). But looking at the picture we get both diegetic information and pleasing harmony and touchstones upon the ancient wisdom (or "wisdom") of our world.

- Cinematography thus concocts and shows off an image of *what the story looks like*, even more, *what the story looks like as we see it*, not an image of the pro-filmic reality. Not the story, but the appearance of the story. We are meant to absorb the image within the framework of a proposition: *It would be like this*. Even that proposition is fabular, one of the fundamental tales the cinematographer must tell. The pan shot is from *Regression* (2015). But the shot is not of Ethan Hawke on a fireplace set, it is of his character at home. Say that visually speaking the shot is its own fiction, just as what it displays is part of the film's fiction, and just in the way that when a character opens his mouth the words that come out, although part of the English language, have meaning only in make-believe.

- Everything in film is meant to *seem to be*, a mountaintop to seem invigorating (*Lord of the Rings: The Fellowship of the Ring* [2001]), a sewer system to seem dank (*The Third Man* [1949]), a library to put one at ease (*Atonement* [2007]), a dinner table to invoke etiquette and propriety (*An Age of Innocence* [1993]). And the photography that makes film is lit to effect that desired and desirable seeming, not to illuminate the facts of life. The camera not being an eye, it is for the viewer only a stand-in. The living eye would stand in the den with Ethan Hawke's detective and see both more and less than the camera shows, more light, compensated for by the iris, yet less information, less enthusiastically hefting a shopping basket filled with all the goodies the storytellers would like us to have.

26

The Angle Angle

FIGURE 26 *Natalie Wood and Christopher Plummer in* Inside Daisy Clover *(Robert Mulligan, Park Place/Warner Bros., 1965).*

Writing of the Dutch still life, Erika Langmuir is brought to consider the height from which objects are seen: "Someone who 'looks down' at us is felt to be supercilious; we ourselves feel superior to whoever 'looks up to us,' while 'to look someone straight in the eye' is to demonstrate sincerity and a desire for intimacy" (54). The cinematographer's so-named "Dutch" angle is not really Dutch but somehow "Dutch" is easier to say than "Deutsch." German Expressivism used this technique frequently, and so when it came into American usage the German word for "German" became part of it. But word pronunciations are brick walls all over the world. In practice now, the "Dutch angle" encompasses a wide range of camera placements in which the world appears to be twisted, flipped to the side, in some other way disoriented, or seen from very high above or below (tilts). When characters are seen through twists, we have through our own projection a sense that their view of things is warping. Drugs, beatings, experimental techniques dramatized will produce "resultant" shots in which we see the world as the affected character presumably does. Shooting characters from on high tends to objectify them through distance, as though we step back to gain a less affected and more clinical view. Usually, further, looking down always seems at least a little dangerous, a view that is chilling. Shooting up can produce figures who seem to loom over the action, dominant controllers such as the Genie (Rex Ingram) in *The Thief of Bagdad* (1940) or the heroic longshoreman (Marlon Brando) defying violence as he marches to work at the end of *On the Waterfront* (1954).

But there is another delicate and wholly cheating use of the upward Dutch angle. This is to shoot an actor, either alone or in shots including others—sometimes even portrait shots—in such a way as to camouflage the fact that he or she is remarkably shorter than the performers around. As women are expected in North America to be shorter than men, and very typically are, it is for shorter male actors that the angle is most frequently used. The tilting camera, especially with a wide-angle lens, changes space so that a second character coming up near, but behind the principal can easily be made to appear the same height. For a fascinating example of a case where this cheat is *not* used, but its absence reveals the presence of a complementary cheat elsewhere in the film, examine the relationship between the body of Barbara Bel Geddes and the body of James Stewart as, in the "alternate" (UK) ending of *Vertigo* (available on the DVD), she walks up and stands in front of him. She is very very short by comparison with him, but throughout the film this disparity in heights is reduced by artful camera placement and image framing.

As to the "Dutch" angle and body disparity, especially when contrary to Western cultural ideals the male in a gendered pairing is shorter than the female: consider the shots involving (shorter) Christopher Plummer and (taller) Natalie Wood in *Inside Daisy Clover* (1965). As Plummer is playing the mogul heading a major Hollywood studio and Wood is one of his ingenues—which is to say, an object he markets for cash—he cannot believably play argument scenes with her if he is looking up either physically or metaphorically. She, in fact, must be reduced in size (and status) just as he is expanded. Shots of (shorter) Claude Rains in wedlock with (taller) Ingrid Bergman in *Notorious* (1946) had to be made this way, too.

While there is an actor/character cheat in play for viewers here, the size of the performer being radically different than that of the character being played, it is not a rare one but occurs throughout cinema in legion ways, inspiring many corrections by lens or CGI touch-up. Increasingly in the age of CGI and mo-cap, actors are not hired on the basis of their size, not that in the case of major stars they ever were. What makes the "Dutch" cheat special is a presumable *character/character* cheat—that the physical world two characters are seen perceiving together, uniform for the two of them in diegesis because singular for us, has been manipulated without their apparently knowing so that it will play "naturally" both with and around their bodies. This needs a little slow unpacking:

- We have a perception of every scene from without. We are looking at the dramatic space from some point of view, in the "Dutch" cheat typically from way above or way below. The action spreads and looms up there or down there, a thundercloud or a Lilliput of possibilities. But at the same time:
- We recognize the characters as they have been spelled out, and part of the spelling is their social status relative to one another. In *Clover*, we know Plummer's Raymond Swan is the studio head and Wood's Daisy is his creation to be used—he thinks--as he pleases, so as we look upward and see him dominating her we also get a social view that accords with the expectations we have borrowed from him and from the Hollywood system.
- Daisy, however, operates differently. She may be a studio employee—a salaried worker—but she is also a major star. She doesn't kowtow to Swan when she interacts with him, she faces him and has at it directly, as does he with her: *directly*—she being a little shorter (as we are shown it) turning her chin up; he being a little taller turning his chin down. For Daisy, Swan is automatically and naturally the man that the camera with its angling has led us to know, the Big Man, whom the system that is exploited in the diegesis has privileged. Yet she is not quite obedient, not quite his slave, not quite not-herself.

We can appreciate her invisible *attitude* (her looking up some) without her having to gesture it; and she is free from gesturing that attitude only because the camera has (invisibly) gestured it for her by means of a "Dutch" angle. The angle invites us to firmly believe that Daisy and Swan are *actually* no more different from one another in height than a "typical" male and a "typical" female. If there is notable upward-gazing signaled in the view, a dramatized "look up," it is *her* angry deference and demeanor: her view.

Shot from below with a wide-angle, a character can dominate monstrously—Orson Welles's Kane (1941) destroying Susan's bedroom, and watched almost from floor level. This same technique is used by Steven Spielberg to give views of the T-Rex in *Jurassic Park* (1993), just to cheat any tendency in the audience to rationalize it as a mere audioanimatronic effect (which is what it is). Seen from above, characters can be diminished in stature or power, made vulnerable, without the actor having to work up an expression: vulnerable Eva Marie Saint in Vandamm's living room in *North by Northwest* (1959), seen by Roger from the balcony above and behind. What we see of characters in these acute views we echo in sentiment, feeling ourselves loom and teeter or shrink helplessly. In the skewed stairway shot in *Rebel Without a Cause* (1955) where Jim sees his mother upside-down as she comes downstairs, we share his confusion, disorientation, imbalance, and vulnerability.

The Dutch shot does some of the performer's work, in that striving with tone or posture or elocution to establish deference or dominance isn't really necessary if the image does that for you.

27

Moving On

FIGURE 27 *Yves Montand in* Grand Prix *(John Frankenheimer, MGM, 1966).*

Cinematographers know that in one special way, and regardless of content, every shot they make will function as a cheat: it will be seen in motion, not only because to show it a strip of film will move through a projector but also because it will be embedded among other shots in a chain the outlaying of which constitutes the film. Every shot will travel past, and with, the viewer's appreciation. One can experience the illusion of presence in a shot where the action is rather tranquil and there is no camera movement, but in film there is no present. In film, as Takeshi Kitano says to Tom Conti in the finale of *Merry Christmas, Mr. Lawrence* (1983), "We go on and on." This brings up two considerations to which cinematographers respond, some of them with reflective spontaneity and some out of educated reflex:

- *I. Panoramic perception.* In his masterful treatise on railway travel, Wolfgang Schivelbusch takes special note of a new kind of perceptual organization that became both necessary and habitual for travelers on trains in the middle of the nineteenth century—roughly in the 1840s—a way of seeing to which, beforehand, they had had no need to accommodate themselves. It is essentially a kind of glance to the side, a view of terrain possible only as one moves laterally through it. Schivelbusch names it "panoramic perception," after Dolf Sternberger:

> Sternberger uses this concept of the panorama and the panoramic to describe European modes of perception in the nineteenth century—the tendency to see the discrete indiscriminately. "The views from the windows of Europe," Sternberger says, "have entirely lost their dimension of depth and have become mere particles of one and the same panoramic world that stretches all around and is, at each and every point, merely a painted surface." (Sternberger 57, qtd. in Schivelbusch, *Railway* 61)

In the train one could see neither where one was going nor where one had come from but only, instant by instant in an unbounded fragmentation, what was here now. "The dissolution of reality and its resurrection as panorama," Schivelbusch writes, "thus became agents for the total emancipation from the traversed landscape: the traveler's gaze could then move into an imaginary surrogate landscape" (64). The signal argument in Schivelbusch's book relates train travel and its mode of perception to modernity itself.[1] Film is, in a way, like a train;[2] and as we watch it (cinematographers all know) no matter our construction of the experience we actually see without recognizing a beginning or an end but only a fleeting ongoingness.

Given that we are not fixating on the image but only glancing at it, the image may work quite well if it contains less information than is supposed by the viewer. A single telltale feature, nicely lit, may suffice entirely. The cheat, then, is that the images invoke, imply, or suggest a field and mode of attention they do not take pains to serve with detail, that they seem to offer a picture of things while in fact offering a glance. Instead, the onward thrust of the story's increasing probability sweeps us forward on a kind of hunch.

- *II. The coup d'oeil*. Ortega discusses the act of looking *in modo obliquo*, rather than *in modo recto*:

The impression of concavity is derived from the *modo recto*. If we eliminate this—for example, by blinking the eyes—we have only oblique

---

[1] I am grateful to Ann Kaplan for pointing me to Schivelbusch's book in London in 2005.
[2] François Truffaut to Jean-Pierre Léaud, in *Day for Night* (*La nuit américaine*, 1973): "Les films avançent comme un train, tu compris?, comme un train dans la nuit."

vision, those side-views "from the tail of the eye" which represent the height of disdain. Thus, the third dimension disappears and the field of vision tends to convert itself entirely into surface. (123)

The cinematographer knows he is making images that will be seen "with disdain," obliquely, in a series of blinks. To follow what is "spelled out" in a film the viewer must be alert to the flying image, able to grasp.

But the grasp is already an accomplishment of a certain kind, one that is tied, wrote Balzac, to the artist (*Séraphita*, qtd. in Benjamin, *Baudelaire* 41). The artist seizes the world in an instantaneous regard.[3] Film makes every viewer an artist in that sense.

The problem of the quick grasp for those who seek to have telling information is that if concentration moves speedily only some aspects of the image can be caught. Cinematographers know that some details will pass unnoticed. And further, in final effect any shot however carefully taken in the first place will be edited in a flow of shots, at some regulated pace (perhaps a very fast one). The viewer of the film will be seizing glances, stitching them much as the editor does, fabricating a somewhat independent view of the continuity. The pictures help, and even go out of their way not to block helping this fabrication, yet when cinematographers, directors, and editors look at assemblages of scenes they all think about what will be most likely to show and what will be likely to pass. One prepares for accident. The shot being a passing vision, every showing is a potential hiding, every point in the field a potential show.

---

[3] A fascination exploration is undertaken of the in situ landscape painting of Frederic Edwin Church, in Gould 90ff.

28

Behind the Camera Behind

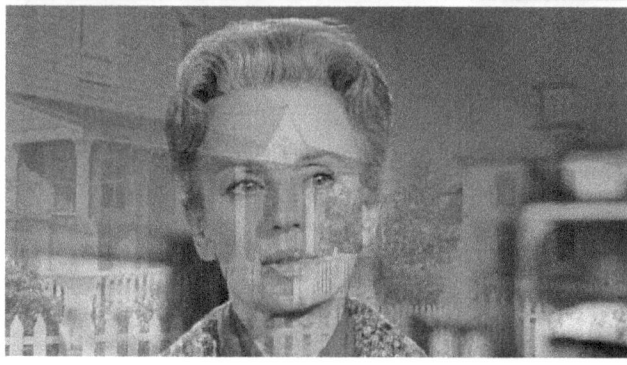

FIGURE 28 *Two lap dissolves. Above, Gregory Peck with Ingrid Bergman in* Spellbound *(Alfred Hitchcock, Selznick International, 1945), effect by Jack Cosgrove. Below, Jessica Tandy in* The Birds *(Alfred Hitchcock, Universal, 1963), effect by Bob Broughton.*

The optical printer was developed by Linwood Dunn. Taken at its most essential, it is a pair of devices fixed near one another in absolute registration within a solid, metallic frame structure. One of these is a standard camera, typically 35 mm although other devices can be subbed in. The second is a projector. The lens of the projector is pointed straight into the lens of the camera. What the projector projects, the camera can record on film. And the two devices can be regulated to operate at variable frame rates—24 fps, which is the Academy norm; 36 or 48 or higher fps for producing slow motion; 18, 12, or lower fps to produce speed-up—as well as being set to count frames; to easily shift movement forward or backward one or more frames at a time; and to accept inserted blocks ahead of the film plane, such as black cards.

Fade. If as film unspools in the projector—any scene at all—the aperture on the camera side is made to close in a smooth progression through the frames, until it is completely closed, what is recorded on film is the *fade to black*. Clearly, this can be done swiftly or slowly, as called for. A *fade-up* would be made by starting with the camera's aperture closed, turning on the units, and as the film unwound ahead slowly opening the camera aperture (again, at variable rates).

Here and in other maneuvers with the optical printer special care will be taken to meticulously clean the two lenses, that of the camera and that of the projector. In final effect, what is produced by the camera is a second-generation record, a film of a film, and it is sometimes possible to see the shift of generation onscreen at fades and so on, since only the tail end of the outgoing and incoming scenes need be used to make the transition and in the print the recorded transition will be spliced in. With optical printer moves that were worked through at the Technicolor laboratory, the transitions were made in the original black-and-white records so that in the final print there was no perceptible shift. With Eastmancolor films processed in studio labs (DeLuxe, Warnercolor, Metrocolor, and so on), this purity was absent.

Dissolve. Scene A is optically printed as though for a fade (see above). The system is stopped. Both the camera and the projector are wound backward to the starting point. Scene A is removed from the projector and replaced by Scene B. Now a fade-up is made on the same receiving stock. The effect will be a *dissolve* from A to B. By varying the rate of film movement in the projector, or the rate of aperture closure or opening, the disappearance of A and appearance of B can be symmetrical or skewed either way. Hitchcock took pains to arrange for dissolves that would remarkably add layers of implication to his stories.

Split. The scene being projected onto the film stock can bear manipulation at the hands of the operator (and many operators in the studio era were exceptionally accomplished). A small black card can be inserted in a slot between the passing film and the lens. The operator can make the card block any part of the frame, and as the projected image moves forward the rate can be controlled, even to one stop-frame at a time so that the card can be adjusted. In this way, only half of a scene can be recorded. When camera and projector are rewound, on a second pass the operator can block the other side. To make films in which a performer exists beside himself or herself onscreen, "double" films, two pieces of film are used in the projector, A with the performer on, say, the right side of the set; B with the same performer, perhaps costumed differently, perhaps not, on the left. When the film is shot on set, clearly the camera has to maintain strict alignment for both sequences A and B, keeping an exactly measured distance from the performers. The material on the set that will appear in the very center of the frame is important and will typically be some kind of vertical structure that is built into the setting, such as the edge of a bench or a tree trunk.

Design. By affecting the projected film with a variety of blockers of different shapes, and controlling the blockage one or two frames at a time, an effect can be created of scene B moving into A and taking over by means of circling, dropping, popping up, arriving through venetian blinds, and a very large array of other possibilities.

Given that both the projector and the camera can be set to turn at variable speeds, and that both have apertures that can be opened or closed to whatever degree, the final effects on the recording film are consummately varied and can be achieved with great clarity. All of this constitutes a cheating mechanism, technical in its base yet used by artists of extreme skill and inventiveness to produce effects that can only be called creative in their falsity. In the dissolve, for example, the viewer is intended to actually "see" one scene wiping, fading, or dissolving into another as though in a world of the dream, where images can transpose in such irrational ways. The cheat is necessary here because although the experience of watching film is dreamlike, it is not a dream. Part of the delight of watching film comes exactly in unpredictable transpositions, and in our ways of interpreting these transpositions in line with our appreciation of the whole. Digital transpositions have their own variety of flexibilities, but both digital and non-digital forms come to life especially in color shifting or grading, such as we find in the *Lord of the Rings* films (2001–03).[1] Optical work allows us to unknowingly see more than the pictures shot by the cinematographer, and although their names do fly by in the credits (usually under "Special Photography") the matte artists, optical printer operators, and color specialists who fabricate what we call "the film" from the filmic materials originally shot, tend to go unheralded and unknown, if they are not simply forgotten.

---

[1] I discuss one very complicated visual morph effected through non-digital color control in *Cinema, If You Please*, Ch. 2.

29

Peek-a-Boo

FIGURE 29 *Audrey Totter in* Lady in the Lake *(Robert Montgomery, MGM, 1947)*.

Perhaps no screen myth addressing the story or the labor behind it is more prominent and also more taken for granted than this: figures of the screen do not know the audience is there watching them. They act, as it were, in a world cut off, a private and untouchable zone, a territory into which we peek at our peril and for our pleasure. The "invisible" effect, if we might call it that, is produced by actors maintaining sight lines that are generally guided *away from the lens*. When the actor doesn't see the camera, the character doesn't see the audience (whose camera it finally is, by adoption).

The actor knows of the existence of the audience, of course, because it is only by virtue of that audience that he eats dinner. As the character only "eats dinner," but never actually eats dinner, nor actually does anything else that might erode a self, she has no need for the box office or the audience who flock there, and thus does not need to understand that she is being watched. For the viewer, there is initially a shocking discontinuity between the active sense of *being in a position to watch* these characters, their continually being watchable; and the retiring sense of *peeking in on people* who are behaving only in their privacies. The film, all its protagonists, all its events—all exist in a privacy we invade (with delight). As one gets older and older watching movies, the hesitancy dissolves and we concentrate on the many wonders of the peephole.

There is always a subtle, only indirectly evoked sense of the screen world being conscious of the audience, of action emanating from characters who vaguely intuit that they are not alone—a sense that, as Wheeler Winston Dixon suggests of cinema, "it looks at you." And certainly as viewers we have a keen sense of that subtle sense, an ongoing awareness that all of what is so elaborately being played out here is being played out for us to see, played out in that strange marriage of voyeurism and exhibitionism (challenged so beautifully by *Psycho* [1960] and *Mon oncle Antoine* [1971]) where the peephole appears to work only one way. Our film watching is mobilized by the tension between, on one side the free gaze, the seeing without responsibility or the obligation to recognize that something is being provided for us to see, and on the other the culpability that comes with knowingly invading the Other's space. Every piquant glance at the facts of production melts away and transforms into a rapturous engagement with the action itself, the action that binds us deeply, as though even without our participation *it really exists*.

It is essential that the flashing awareness of acting dissipate and resolve into a committed bond with fictionality. It is part of the camera's cheat, as much as the writer's and the performer's, that the character's gaze is averted; that no frame be included in which that gaze finds us and shows us that it is finding us. Yet:

In some works of cinema, the character knowingly and pointedly does face the camera and stare directly into the lens, not en passant while meandering down an alleyway but for some protracted spate of time, definitively, unmistakably, confrontationally, as though to say, "I do not just deeply know you are there, viewer; I here affirm that knowledge, and pointedly extend it to you. You know that I know, because I give you a demonstration of my knowing, a demonstration you can avoid only if you also avoid anything else onscreen." Robert Montgomery's *Lady in the Lake* (1947) is a classic example, with continual camera reference by character after character, scene after scene, so that one has the sense of the filmmaker wanting at once to create a film and also to tell us he is there creating one—to bridge cinema to theater. The tension is hard for Montgomery to keep up, and without the murder-divorce-duplicity story and its peculiarities the gazes do not work to fashion a new engagement, except perhaps with the screen bodies *taken in themselves*. *Le Trou* (1960) commences with a very brief address to the camera by Jean Keraudy about his friend Jacques Becker's film (telling a "true story" in which he was involved); that film we are about to see. Samuel Fuller's *The Naked Kiss* (1964) is structured conventionally but at a climactic moment a central character, Kelly (Constance Towers), confronts the lens and dramatically removes the stunning hair that has captivated us all along to reveal that she is in fact bald. Something of an homage is given by Steven Soderbergh in his *The Laundromat* (2019). Jason Reitman's *Up in the Air* (2009) leaves us with the principal character standing at loose ends in front of an airport departure board unsure where his future lies. Swiftly, in a half-blink, he looks at us for guidance. Lewis Gilbert's *Alfie* (1966) is a first-person narrative in which our beloved (and belovedly naughty) hero Alfie tells the story by looking into the camera and addressing us, with a tone of great personal warmth and confidentiality: the confiding is conspiratorial, and from the outset we are cozily wrapped into the conspiracy. The same intermittent cozy attachment is shown in Tony Richardson's *Tom Jones* (1963) by Albert Finney. An even more conspiratorial, and finally diabolical, affiliation with the audience is produced in the original *House of Cards* (1990) by Ian Richardson as Urquhart, winking at us sideways, smirking into our privacy as he makes defamatory comments about other characters strolling blithely around him. It can hardly be that as these characters "see the camera" they also "see us watching," since even if one passes from the character to the actor one can admit only that the actor knows what a camera is, and can have no expectation of meeting any one of us in the dark. This is, then, a curious, even idiosyncratic form of affiliation: the character recognizes himself or herself as a character, not a person; a being put on by a person who works to a camera. That person, as far as we are concerned, recognizes only the "form of" the audience, the audience as a construct.

How can the character's confrontation be understood in light of the tension between our presence and our absence as viewers: between presumed innocence of the production on one side and the production's explicitly catching our eye and ear on the other? If the fleeting knowledge of actorial presence—of our presence onlooking the character's[1]—swiftly flies away in most cases, how can we entertain the experience suggested in the films above, where such flight doesn't seem to happen at all?

The answer to the dilemma is both simple and profoundly troubling.

The onlooking character, that screen figure who "turns to the audience" and winks, emits in seeing us a kind of transubstantiating *ray* that converts

---

[1] On the audience member's capacity as "onlooker," see Goffman, *Frame Analysis* Ch. 5.

us, not only *as* we watch and listen but *by virtue of our* watching and listening, into someone else, another character in the screen extravaganza but one who goes without a name and without an image, one who is a participant not a mere outsider/peeker-in. I might coin a word to match Michel Chion's *acousmêtre* (which functions in the sound by speaking and audible speech from *off*) and suggest that the viewer becomes an *optimêtre*. Sound is something we should not produce in any event, as it would be unconscionably (impossibly) rude to interrupt the proceedings. But we can stand silently and nearby, the servant who makes entrance with the Queen. As *optimêtre* we have full rights to inhabit the place of the drama, to position ourselves anywhere and to move in any fashion, and this, surely, with any filmic arrangement, yet somehow much more particularly, more intelligently when a character gives us the eye. The recognizing, approving, welcoming eye. The *optimêtre* knows what it is to be there, through the secret illumination that comes to him and to all characters by virtue of their placement in the drama. When I am an *optimêtre*, the Queen can talk to me, can confide in me, can whisper endearments or scathing critiques to me, can use me to share her ribald jokes. Because in sharing herself this way the Queen has identified the proximity of her confidant(e), that charged and eager watcher knows her as no other character does, sees and hears the silent soliloquy hiding in every comment she makes.

When one character speaks privately and directly to another character, makes a kind of "inside soliloquy," the same charge is not invoked. We are special, as we watch.

The difference between the *optimêtre* and the *onlooker*:

The *onlooker* is part of the actor's world of awareness, a creature invoked by the performance, akin, in a direct way, to Walker Gibson's "mock reader." The "mock reader" is a persona of the reader's, someone I become when I approach a text; and in order to make such an approach I act as though the language of the writing is familiar enough to me, as though the presumptions made by the author can be taken by me for granted, just as required, and as though my fascinations are those implicit in the textual address. As to the *onlooker*, who exists in the act of cinematic spectatorship, the character neither knows him, nor recognizes him, nor sees that he is there, nor believes in the possibility of him, nor admits him to citizenship in his world. For the character, *it happens that,* without consciousness of it, he lives his expressive life in register with the onlooker's knowledge and expectations: again, by happening but not a happening of which he is aware. If he were asked about it (but who could ask?) the character in all sincerity would be entirely oblivious to how this happens. The actor, however: well, she does know how this happens, being in league with a writer and aiming her performance to a viewer's reception. The actor knows she has created the onlooker, in a way, and created, too, by invocation, another character who is not in the know about onlookers. That character, the *optimêtre*: this "person" *is* known to the character, likely very well known, known and recognized as known, although a being to whom, until the moment of the direct gaze to camera, when the figure of the *optimêtre* is expressly summoned, neither the character nor the viewing audience gives a thought. He is one of those who, in Starobinski's words, "can see to it that his name no longer designates himself. Rather ingenuously he dreams of placing himself in the position of one who sees without being seen" (81), ingenuously because also hopelessly, since at the moment of the character's gaze to camera it is evident that trying to peek without being seen peeking is doomed to fail. The *optimêtre* is a bunkmate, a bosom pal, no matter the tone adopted by he or she who looks straight forward to address him or her. Not a creature who is involved in the action of the drama but a creature in whom the actor's character can confide. The confidant(e) has been in the room all along, silent and standing to the side, and now that he or she is invoked by that character gaze there is felt and assumed a response, an attitude the character can have predicted. (Certainly not an attitude that could shock the character looking out at it.)

When I say "invoked" by that character gaze I am of course tilting the scale a little toward the character as active being when, of course, it is no more than a put-on. Michael Fried writes in *Absorption and Theatricality* of a shift

> from the primacy of absorption toward the primacy of action and expression—more accurately, from the representation of figures absorbed in quintessentially absorptive states and activities toward the representation of figures absorbed in action or passion (or both). The shift, in other words, was in the direction of the values and effects of pictorial drama. (107)

Notwithstanding that Fried is moved to write by the painting of Greuze and other mid-eighteenth century artists, we may find in his thought inspiration to wonder about the character who regards the lens. He may well be scanning us, reaching out, understanding, sympathizing with our plight in being caught up with his appearance; but he may also be absorbed in an entirely private moment of reflection, reflection about something that is not at all, anywhere in the film, brought for our consideration.

Yet, there does seem to be a voice that emanates. "Well, of course *you* know what it's like when things like this happen," the character whispers to the *optimêtre*, and the *optimêtre* conjoins, "O, yes, I see what is going on with you, what has been going on, what you saw, what you were seen seeing, and also what you intended me to see, and you can feel reassured that I see it your way, 'through your eyes,' as it were, and not by way of any other character. Your eyes opening to me lead me to see everything your way. You are my friend. I am yours." I see through your eyes.

Your eyes, now opening only to me.

Of Scenes

{30} No There There
Credibility and incredibility; *Changeling*; *Avatar*

{31} Where Are We?
Yi-Fu Tuan; *The Cabinet of Dr. Caligari*; *The Adjustment Bureau*; *To Catch a Thief*

{32} Walk on the Wild Side
The Man Who Knew Too Much; Kenneth Burke; Henry Bumstead

{33} Happy Trails
Bringing Up Baby; *Six Degrees of Separation*; *The French Lieutenant's Woman*; *Bigger Than Life*; *The Courtship of Eddie's Father*; *North by Northwest*

{34} The Thing
Forbidden Planet; *2001: A Space Odyssey*; *Alien*; *War for the Planet of the Apes*; *Star Wars*; *Jurassic Park*; *The Stepford Wives*; *Life*; *20,000 Leagues Under the Sea*; *Jaws*; *The Blob*

{35} Heist
Moral implications of watching

{36} The Reality Effect
Stanley Cavell; *A Midsummer Night's Dream*; *Detour*

{37} Stand-ins
Barbra Streisand; *Rebel Without a Cause*; *F for Fake*; Kevin Costner

{38} The Superuniverse
Twentieth Century; *Spider-Man 2*; *Darkman*

30

No There There

FIGURE 30 *Daniel Radcliffe in* Harry Potter and the Prisoner of Azkaban *(Alfonso Cuarón, Warner Bros., 2004).*

Either by extraction from the flow of the normal, or by artful concoction, film is made in the stream of everyday life, sometimes secretly on a soundstage, and sometimes relatively openly on location (if with direction signs for the cast and crew that have fake titles on them). Quotidian routine is an essential element in the prepared broth: routine that is either filmed directly (sidewalk crowds, trees in a park) or "directly" (as in documentary—an epitome being Frederick Wiseman's *High School* [1968]), or imitated for fictional realism (*JFK* [1991]), or used as a substrate on which some fantasmal invention rests (*Marriage Story* [2019]). But sometimes a filmmaking team will need to realize an image that cannot be made in the stream of everyday life, a picture of something fabulous and mythical, else a picture in a dangerous circumstance, else a picture of the actor's body yet showing a body that does not look like the actor's actual body to fans who recognize it. And many other things.

Call these "impossible pictures," and consider how making them successfully represents not only a triumph of skill and technique but also a triumph of dramaturgy, since by virtue of these sudden revelations of the extraordinary the audience's sympathy can be very specially engaged. The matte technique is one way of making "impossible pictures"—long in use (since the days of Norman O. Dawn), considerably developed over time, and quite extraordinary in range and power. Very often matting involves a point of dramatic placement, convincing viewers that they are watching events—action in true space—when they are not.

There are essentially two kinds of reasons that motivate the use of mattes in picture-making. I say mattes generally, referring both to hard mattes and in-camera mattes (including, among the latter, mattes produced exclusively in the optical printer). In a matte, some figure or object X appears in a scene set in location L, and moves around the place with some normality. X lives in L. X is visiting L. X is passing through L. X is singing and dancing in L. X could be a person of any type; a non-human figure or object; a sculpture; a yacht; a supersonic aircraft; anything. Any object X in a scene L.

X is in L, but X is not in L.

How? X may be shot in such a way that the recording film (or material) can be manipulated to isolate him or her in the frame, isolate so that everything else shows up with no exposure at all. (Typically the recording material is a very high-contrast film that can be processed to eliminate one end of the contrast range.) Or, two spaces—one a partial studio set, the other a photographic or painted scene—may be conjoined by way of two exposures on the same film, with part of the film blocked off each time. For in-camera matting the object X is positioned against an immense blue screen or green screen or sometimes sodium yellow background. X may stand, or be suspended by cables designed not to show. By use of color correction in camera (typically with filters), everything but the figure can be reduced to an optical nullity on the recording stock. This piece of recording stock is eventually "married" to a second one containing the location. Camera-manipulation matting is complex, yet fascinating: X stands against a neutral ground, usually black, and is caught on high-contrast film processed to render him or her as nothing but a black silhouette with the ground eliminated. This piece of film is sandwiched against another piece containing the scene, in an optical printer, the resultant being a scene with a black human-shaped spot gesturing through it. The original shot is now counter-processed so that the ground does not register and the figure is clearly shown. This is sandwiched against the composite already made and now the figure appears to move through the space against the background.

X and L: Harry Potter (Daniel Radcliffe) aboard a Hippogriff flying over a Loch. Harry is on the Hippogriff. But Harry (Daniel) is actually not on the Hippogriff. There is no Hippogriff. Daniel is hanging by wires from a grid at the top of a sound stage. The animal, the Loch, the mountains, the sky—all these are matted in. Daniel is not above or even near a Loch, he is in a soundstage near London, in the air but not necessarily far off the floor. A by-product: if he is a child actor, he is most likely having the time of his life "flying" in the green world.

The two motives for matte usage are these:

[1] *Credible tale, impossible production.* X being at L not only makes sense in the drama, it makes sense in real life, since people like X really do go to places like L. But there is a serious technical problem. It would be too costly to actually have a shooting day with actors at L, because L is so distant from the general shooting site(s) that flying a crew there with one or more performers would be prohibitive or because L looks marvelous as a possibility but is a very dangerous location, and the insurance wouldn't dream of covering actors working there, or because specific nuances of lighting and sound recording are needed to capture X, the sort best accomplished in a controlled studio setting, and so X must be in studio but L, being so vast, cannot be, or because X(1) is playing a twin, X(2), and both twins cannot be on camera at the same instant, although they must seem to be, or because the actor playing X has refused to travel to L, and his contract insists that all photography must be done within a few miles of the studio, or because the availability of actor X is extremely limited and the most economically efficient and convenient way to get him or her to L is to photograph L far in advance and then do a matte on whatever day(s) the actor can be free, or because a very complex and elaborate set has been envisioned—a long busy street in Los Angeles in the 1920s for Eastwood's *Changeling* (2008)—and it is far more economical, not to say aesthetically interesting, to shoot only part of the image on a stage and matte in the bulk of the design. This last procedure has been in action since Norman Dawn's glass mattes in the early 1910s. For all of the above, dramatically speaking it makes sense to think of X and L being united in a picture, but such a picture cannot be made except through the matte cheat.

[2] *Incredible tale, unthinkable production.* Here there is nothing *sensible* about the merger of X and L, but if it could be accomplished the effect would be astonishing and alluring. Say the film requires a group of figures to be injected by hypodermic into the body of a stranger. Or the film requires a group of hunters to climb into a forbidding cave with a horrifying monster. Or the film requires a person to do extra-vehicular activity in outer space. In all these dramatic situations, and legion more, the locational ground must be both invented and constructed since in the world as we know it there is no place like this, or if there is a place we do not

have a way to go there, or if we can go there we would never find a venturing figure such as must be shown onscreen. The protagonist X and the filmmaking team are acting in a strange world together. This means there are no direct models in the extra-diegetic universe for what we are to see onscreen, except in the loosest possible sense (e.g. riding the flying dragons in *Avatar* [2009] is somewhat like riding a horse in a cowboy movie and something like hang-gliding: one can imagine a designer being urged to imagine hang-gliding on a bucking bronco).

A number of interesting features of the matte cheat:

- Very frequently the actor must move, gesture, and enunciate *as though* other people are present, or as though there is a real narrative space in which she stands—an overarching tree, a precipice, a castle rampart, an airport tarmac, what have you—when she is really positioned alone, often in a sort of vacuous nowhere. The acting must be accomplished on the soundstage without scene partners, who will act later, perhaps also alone, and be matted in themselves. The actor must therefore not only be prepared to be the character in a setting now invisible—already a challenge—but also to imagine the setting and the other players, based on sketches. When a battle is in progress, the protagonist must fight a nobody who will later be matted in as a somebody. One saws the air, promise-cramm'd. This form of acting, akin to mime, is not the talent of all those who work in front of the camera.

- The character is either in a space he or she knows, or in a strange space entirely unfamiliar, and the matting must convey these relations. The exact position of the actor's body in relation to the ground, the color match between the actor's costume and the painted ground, the form of movement and its style, all these contribute to a quality of familiarity or alienation. And these aspects of the performance are frequently planned well in advance. It is one thing to walk into a familiar space, drop one's keys upon the table, put on the coffee, draw out a munchie, take a phone message; but quite another to do all this in an empty green space with nothing at all around except, perhaps, markers on the floor. The rehearsal of action when a number of live actors are at work is a choreography involving timing, posture, and precise placement, but one works against the bodies of one's scene partners. In matte work one very often rehearses with "phantoms." It would be a somewhat similar exercise for actors to rehearse with living teammates who in final production will be wearing elaborate make-up and costumes they are not carrying now, so that one has to shape the enunciation of

dialogue toward these presently non-existent figurations. We are considering here a kind of acting by displacement, including voicing animated characters and recording off-camera speeches.
- And the character must ideally seem really, fully, indubitably to belong in the space; indeed, to be part of the space as we watch. Any evidence of the matte procedure will ruin this illusion. A notable problem was something called the "minus," a very thin but visible line running around the matted-in figure in early matte work. Computer-generated in-camera matting has removed the minus, helping to give the impression that the body of the actor fits perfectly into the space containing it.

Special visual effects are no longer the public secret they once were. Books are in print detailing them with splendid illustrations that will call up fond memories of screen moments one had thought to illustrate one thing when in fact they were based on quite another. The matte technique has been explained in detail, and nowhere better than, in Raymond Fielding's *The Technique of Special Effects Cinematography* (1965). But after 2000 public interest really peaked. From Mark Cotta Vaz and Craig Barron's *The Invisible Art* (2002) to Richard Rickett's *Special Effects: The History and Technique* (2006) to *Editing and Special/Visual Effects*, ed. Charlie Keil and Kristen Whissel (2016), and much more, effects techniques such as mattes are explained, illustrated, discussed, and mused upon. Everyday viewers, not making claims to professional status, continually voice opinion about effects and claim to see failures. They look back with hollow charity on the now disregarded early techniques with which they grew up.

What the matte cheat finally provides is one or the other of two opposing results: a coherent, apparently seamless, aesthetically unified image in which the protagonist seems perfectly to fit and harmonize with the space, quite without the effort of any special construction; or only a hapless attempt to convince viewers that the protagonist perfectly fits and harmonizes with the space without the effort of special construction, hapless because a canny audience, already appreciative of the delicatessen affectionately known as sfx, search for, measure, evaluate, and compare the technique they claim to see in use: see baldly for what it is. When the matte works, the character is *there*. When the matte doesn't work, the character isn't *there*. But in both cases, regardless of the success or failure of the technique, one finds a place, a *there*, to experience and point to.

They are really there, they aren't really there.

But . . . where is there?

There is no there. In front of us is only a "there." Yet the inducement to accept the true thereness of the "there," to think of a there there, is the cheat. And this is, of course, the same cheat as applies in filmmaking that does not use the matte technique, filmmaking altogether, albeit the matte technique when discovered as such raises the cheat to our observation most distinctly, most blatantly. In cinema there is never a there there but to follow along we must surmise that there is. When we watch it is impossible to see the image without conceiving of a there that is not there, without falling for the effect even if one thinks one is watching the magician employ it.

31

Where Are We?

FIGURE 31 *Grace Kelly and Cary Grant in* To Catch a Thief *(Alfred Hitchcock, Paramount, 1955)*.

For ages we have conspired together, with startling uniformity, to envision the human universe as four-directional, with the compass points arranged in fixation, and in physical space we have composed with six vectors, left, right, forward, backward, up, down. All of this is of course entirely arbitrary, but perfectly functional. Yi-Fu Tuan shows how a great deal of this supposition comes from ancient celebratory and declamatory ritual, centers for which

> were oriented skyward, to the sun, moon, stars, and other hierophanies of the sky rather than, as in Neolithic times, downward to the spirits of the earth. With the ritual center, and later the city, human horizons

expanded beyond the local and the fleeting to the cosmos and its orderly cycles. Not only that, priests and kings believed that they could mediate between heaven and earth, impose the former's stabilities on the latter's propensity for chaos. In form, these cities were rectangular, with the four corners oriented to the cardinal points, as with Dur Sharrukin (721-705 BCE) and Borsippa (604-561 BCE), or with the four sides oriented to the cardinal points, as with the historical cities of China. (114)

Our cities and our landscapes, our religions and our sciences have all pointed themselves with regularity in the same "cardinal" ways. More, in *The Return of the Vanishing American*, Leslie Fiedler uses the northern, the southern, the eastern, and the western as the four principal narrative forms, at least in American literature.

Yet cinema is different. It is always a case of, "Where are we? *Here.*" And "Where are we going? *Onward.*" "Where are we coming from? *Before.*" There are no cardinal points, the left and the right of the picture are vacua, above and below simply do not exist and never did, behind the picture is nowhere and in front of it is the unspeakable us.

At the same time, those who view renditions on the screen finally leave the theater and go off to live conventional lives, in which they have dutifully learned the rigors of conventional geographies, a learning by means of which they traveled to the cinema and then traveled home again—even though the map that connects "home" to the "screen world" is nonexistent. When space is designed to create a cinematic place, a setting for a story, homage must be paid to the everyday grid, notwithstanding that shapes may be freely reconfigured to slide away from the limitations of that grid. (Designing *The Cabinet of Dr. Caligari* [1920], Walter Reimann and Walter Röhrig built city sets in modulating proportion, so that buildings would seem to stretch away from the eye.) When we dream, we enter and move through a space that is more like the space of the screen narrative than the space of the territory outside. When we watch film, we move through a space that is like the space of a dream.

Two cheats become evident as laws of design. First, any set design that is intended to call up—to summon—thoughts of any realistic world known or knowable to the viewer will include, however minimally, some tag that connects to everyday perception. A highway marked with road signs. A bathroom with a roll of toilet paper next to the toilet. A conference room with a telephone. A kitchen with a frying pan. We are very often so swayed by the pungent realism of this tag that we neglect to see the plasticity of the overall design: a highway with no vehicles on it (shot on a location, by the aid of a police license for stopping traffic flow); a toilet with an odd figurine standing on its basin (shot on a soundstage, with the help of an artist's construct); a conference room with picture windows giving out upon a prospect of the stormy sea (a stage set, with a stunning rear projection or CGI ground); that frying pan sitting on a stove that has no power. The *real tag* signifies a *real place*. When the real tag is withheld from the design we find ourselves in a *purely fabular* place, somewhere we can admit only through imagination, somewhere we can travel only by imagining. A good example would be that cityscape in Wiene's *Caligari*. It is possible to strike a dramatic unfolding that hovers between dreamscapes and reality, either by using a realistic design and structuring unrealistic action there; or by using an unrealistic design and having characters behave in an ordinary, recognizable way. In *Caligari*, for example, the characters have conversations which model, in their form, their tone, and their linguistic structure the kinds of conversations people have all the time everywhere. In *The Adjustment Bureau* (2011) we move from one to another very precisely photographed, realistic Manhattan location, following people who behave as people do on the sidewalks of New York, while entertaining the thought of secret agents moving through secret doors into secret tunnels that magically connect distant points as though they are adjacent. It is easy enough to see the trouble expended in mounting believable signs over banks, restaurants, hotels, and the like; in painting up police cars to look as though they properly belong to the NYPD, the LAPD, and so on; in decorating the building fronts of studio backlots so the street will not look like only a "street."[1]

In a scene with characters, how do we find ourselves, self-locate as the being we must become to apprehend and appreciate what is shown?

Those characters we follow are in front of us only because they are being screened, occupying there what is depicted as a recognizable sort of place, behaving in a way consistent with at least our imagination of how people like that would act in a place like this (not that we base that imagination on knowledge). The actors are using their bodies persistently to aid in shaping the place, producing angles, stretches, extensions that match the lines of the design: thus, while in an actual setting such as this people might use their bodies much more haphazardly, paying less attention, here the body of the actor is treated as part of the scenic design. The actor as a presence never disrupts the image design. (For an elaborate demonstration, see the ballet sequence in *Singin' in the Rain* [1952]).

And there is to be seen a responsiveness—perhaps even an odd responsiveness—to the qualities of a place in the specifics of performance: a character not just turning off a table lamp but standing beside it for a moment to let a dramatic beat emphasize the gesture, or resting a hand upon a doorknob to give weight to the instant of turning it and walking in. The characters not only fit the place, they become *of the place*, relating to the *locus*, local. We sense appropriateness, belonging, order. A very extreme situation, where, miraculously, there is still fit: in *Cries and Whispers* (1972)

---

[1] Usually the giveaway is the kerb, not forefronted in the shot.

women in sparkling white gowns move slowly around rooms designed entirely in carmine red. In *Le Trou* (1960) the jailbird characters have furtive postures, furtive eyes, so that they seem to have inhaled the darkness we see when they dig beneath the floor of their cell. In *The Greatest Show on Earth* (1952) the many circus performers working under the Big Top with exotic animals and in glittering sequined garments of rich midnight blue and grass green and tropical fuchsia and many other colors are themselves, as it turns out, richly varied emotionally, strongly performative offstage just as they are onstage, and interactionally irregular, just as denizens of the circus are "supposed to be" and just as, beautifully encircled by the three rings of the three-ring circus, they look.

Note that character/place adjustments are cheats. People do not harmonize with the rooms in which they live; they do not sit in a chair so as to reflect in their posture the shape, the familiarity, the appropriateness of the chair here, just here, just for them. Stanislavsky wanted his acting students, in fact, to break with the achievement of harmony I am describing implicitly, and *just sit in a chair*. They found it difficult, having already learned too well, perhaps, how to demonstrate fondness for the "carpet" beneath their feet, how to *indicate* sitting. On film, characters are continually making indications, and these indications are appropriate, that is, in the right place.[2]

A provoking case:

There is a scene in *To Catch a Thief* (1955) that has become much celebrated, mostly because viewers associate it with a tongue-in-cheek sexual reference, a naughty joke, thus gaining an opportunity to laugh freely and later on remembering the opportunity with pleasure. Cary Grant and Grace Kelly are ensconced in a fabulously lush hotel room on the Côte d'Azur, at night. (We are told in the plot that it is the Carlton in Cannes, a small city not more than a few kilos from a larger city, Nice, where, at this time of year, the *Bataille des fleurs* is annually celebrated near the flower market, that also plays in the film.) The place and persons: a small sea of turquoise and lavender light, with shadows at the margins; allure, romance, mystery, exoticism. Pale turquoise French doors giving onto a balcony fronting out to the Mediterranean, with a little bouquet of white chrysanthemums in a vase. A sumptuous loveseat, in the Louis XV style with an elegantly curving polished mahogany frame and luscious silk upholstery. Francie (Kelly) is seated, a pithy diamond necklace beaming from her neck and chest, a diaphanous white gown spread over her. Behind her back, on a high table, stands a Sèvres vase. Her hair is white as the beach sands, her eyes blue

---

[2] The ticquer can be thought of as a person who makes numerous inappropriate indications, as it were signaling out of context and for no appreciable reason. In carefully designed "catastrophic situations" (such as in *A Night to Remember* [1958] or *World Trade Center* [2006]) people frantically gesturing do not seem out of place.

as truth. She is talking to Robie (Grant), who stands patiently nearby in a tuxedo, a tuxedo that is burnished lavender by the light, his tanned face a study in concentration. She is teasing him that she knows he is a jewel thief and is obsessed with the necklace he is staring at, but he, of course, is staring at her. Fireworks explode magnesium white in the black sky (to an unnecessary but thrilling musical cue). He comes to sit beside her and continues the unrelenting gaze. We should note:

- Any possible doubt or viewer hesitation about the social status of the place is quickly resolved by our view of the vase and the qualified light. Darkness is one thing; turquoise or purple darkness is quite another. The tuxedo and the gown also testify. Ceramics from the Sèvres factory are rare, exceedingly valuable.
- The loveseat upholstery, very slightly restrained, is what one would find in an elegant hotel but not, say, in the home of an elegant person such as Francie or her mother, as they would have arranged for a decorator to be expressive on their behalf (being able to afford the luxury) and the fabric would have enunciated more. Here, it must not enunciate, both to seem realistic for a hotel and also to avoid drawing our eye from Francie or Robie. The two of them, too, must not enunciate as they play at each other.
- She sits at left, facing screen right, in a lovely pose, her right arm, long and silky, literally draped at her side, and her left arm resting on the curvature of the wood and, once he is seated there, too, extending behind Robie's neck. In her arm position there is a literal mocking—through imitation—of the curving wood, not only as though she is accustomed to sitting like this in furniture like this in places like this one but also as though she and the loveseat are indistinguishable. Her loveseat for her love, the loveseat that *is* love but also is Francie at the moment, and he is sitting on it/her.
- As he leans over just slightly, to gracefully bend his head deferentially her way, the line of his back echoes the line of the loveseat, too. He is a little less accustomed, a little more sheepish, yet also a body in the act of belonging. Now it is his loveseat just as much as it is hers, they are sharing furniture. Not a bed, perhaps, but furniture. And sharing with extreme grace, the kind of grace we see all over this room.
- The fictional hotel room is reified for us by the continuing visibility of the Grace Kelly face, the Cary Grant face, the gleamy necklace far too twinkly to miss, so that we can hover between realist and oneiric readings. The dream reality includes the exploding fireworks that are manifestly outside but that are easily—perhaps too easily—readable as inside the consciousness of at least one protagonist here.

The fireworks are not only white but also purple, suggesting that the purple in the room comes from some slowly dying ember of passionate radiance that flew off the explosions.

- The fireworks function diegetically as well as aesthetically, and so the open French doors through which we can fully see them and the explosions themselves were requirements, given the story. The Bataille is in progress not so far away. The fireworks are in celebration of that, and thus work to evidence the geophysical setting of the story. Much else in the film works to do the same, as though constant reiteration of our presence on the Riviera is part of the deeper meaning here. The Riviera *as* The Riviera is a central player in the film (from the opening shots onward). The Riviera = glamour = wealth = sophistication = exclusiveness: Francie and Robie, glamorous, wealthy in their two ways, sophisticated beyond belief (especially from the cinemagoer's point of view), exclusive in that they are exclusively ours, just as this room is.

* * *

I have argued above that in watching a film scene like this one from *To Catch a Thief* the viewer becomes an onlooker. I ask now, how has the place been arranged to help the viewer in her effort to become that onlooker? It is clearly a transformation that has to be learned, and that bears constant support and incitement. Here the viewer is an onlooker floating on The Riviera, a peeper who has crept into a private hotel room, a seeker after romance. We need hardly stress that this onlooker is not attending the Cannes Festival while she is watching this film; she is not on The Riviera at all. Three obstacles must be cheated successfully, or the love duet—that is floating near us—will ring entirely hollow from start to finish, top to bottom.

[1] *Stolidity*. The viewer is and remains comfortable and satisfied to be here, both "here" as an onlooker watching and here as a cinemagoer alive in the theater showing this film. There can be no anxiety stemming from the lack of a compass. Bringing a self to the theater, the viewer did not at any point expect to take, and did not make necessary preparations for taking, a voyage to the South of France. (We see the large colorful travel poster in the travel agency vitrine, but we do not have our passports.) We are "staying put." We wish to be in France watching all this happening in France, but basically *not* be in France because that would be troublesome and expensive. We are reticent to move, in a certain sense. Our reticence to move must be addressed, and it is addressed, by virtue of the seductive glamour with which the shots are composed. (Of all the opulent settings we see, this is by far the most opulent.) At this moment, however, the viewer has been infected with no realistic need to be shown a hotel room in turquoise and/or purple light,

with mysterious shadows. A hotel room could have any kind of light, any kind of furnishing, and the scene could be late in the afternoon. Further, sexy as Kelly and Grant are together, this story could be told with any two actors if they were sufficiently competent. Kelly and Grant bring value-added allure.[3] And the romance being sparked here, *possibly*, is something we are not just eager but very hungry to see, so that we are willing to be where we must be to catch the action from the beginning and willing to stay with the characters, follow their actions, to see what will develop. We come to cinema with a stolidity, an idea of a compass, but the film cheat must tease us out of it. To tease us to feel at ease shifting around without palpable direction. As we sit looking at the screen, *where is France,* after all?

[2] *Modesty*. It is unconventional, to say the least, to sit in observation of two people in an actual or potential lovemaking situation. Desire to see as we might, we really tend not to put ourselves in the embarrassing situation of being caught peeping. Conversations, glances, mutterings, and gestures like theirs are considered private. While it is the case that in some ways the entire depiction onscreen is a privacy opened to viewer inspection, this scene is a privacy within that privacy and, again, a privacy without shape, with no up or down, no left or right. But the glimmer and glamour seduce the eye, so that reticence flies off. We can feel reason, in fact, to believe something *else* is happening with these two in this place, and it is entirely reasonable, not to say sensible, for us to pay it heed. The fireworks alone are a spectacle we yearn to watch, and for doing that this room provides such an ideal vantage point. Or the jewelry, especially against that exceedingly idealized Kelly skin. The calm sophistication of the dialogue and poise of the postures, a nice lesson for the imitative spirit. Not to say the much noted (and much exploited) screen modesty of these two stars, who by this point had teased audiences plenty of times so that audiences got used to leaning forward and entering the tease. This scene might get sexy, even naked, with some actors, but with Kelly and Grant in 1955 there is no way it will be anything but properly dignified and properly filled with implication. It is safe to be here watching. We are in the presence of those who observe Decorum. But that presence: *where* in space is it?

[3] *Class*. These are exclusive coordinates: Cannes, the *Bataille* season, the Carlton of all hotels in the world, a huge suite inside it, two rich American women visiting France, a suave man who knows how to handle himself anywhere. The entire construct here is beyond the class of most film viewers, who are principally working-class and middle-class citizens of modernity. The very rich, like Francie's mother or the aristocrats she is imitating, don't go to see movies like this. The Carlton they know inside and out because that is where they stay. They know the Riviera altogether, in the 1950s haunt of the

---

[3]For Kelly's last time onscreen, since while shooting this film she met, fell in love with, and subsequently married Prince Rainier of Monaco (but a short hop from Cannes).

jet set and the mega-rich, Juan-les-pins, Antibes with its yacht basin, Cimiez high above Nice. The chic clothing: Grace Kelly ain't wearin' schmatas. The knowing dialogue. The jewels. The casualness of the seduction, as though it were part of a repeated routine. Here, as in other depictions of wealth in movies, we will be known to be watching out of a kind of resentment, a paining regret that we don't have the resources these two do.

But in the avidness of the watching, cannot our being lost in space be cheated in itself? Is there a doorway out of here? If so (and we don't see one), where does it lead? How far off, and in what direction, is the lobby and the hotel's front door? Does that door face the Mediterranean or away from it? And so on.

Seeing Francie and Robie occupying this room as they do, we have nothing but a firm conviction in their belonging here, nor anything but the very firmest conviction in the fullness, the completeness, and the unquestionability of this *here*. Her hand comfortably, possessively on the wood framing of the loveseat, his graceful body leaning toward her amicably, the opened French doors behind them, the sparkling tranquility—all these are made to appear not so much fabulous, exotic, and exclusive as natural and right and proper. The designer, J. McMillan "Mac" Johnson, has made certain that his hotel room set will have just this kind of space, extending on both sides (but to where?); room for just this kind of furniture as placed by the decorator Hal Pereira; and a coloration scheme that when lit with color filters will produce an ineluctable attraction to the eye.

If, by sharp contrast, we examine the design of a film like Alfonso Cuarón's *Roma* (2018) we find a domestic residence that sprawls shapelessly and in which the camera—the narrative—will be (will have to be) in very constant motion. The home is filled to overflowing with objects appropriate to the bourgeoisie, continually speaking a motto, "Wealth, Privilege, Possession," but the film is about the characters only, mostly servants, this place and its design being onscreen only to identify some of them and designate their social positions. We move from character moment to character moment, passing through the carefully packed and rather generally lit domain but never really taking it in *as a domain* except in the most general way. The same kind of optical unconcern attaches to other film places designed to show off wealth, the home-castle in *Firewall* (2006), the cabin in the woods in *Leave Her to Heaven* (1945), the actress's home in *Imitation of Life* (1954), the New York apartment in *Rosemary's Baby* (1968: our protagonists live in The Dakota!), the Minifer residence in *The Magnificent Ambersons* (1942). These depictions contain in their design an implicit axiom, that we already know the kind of life represented here, know it and are eager to see it, so that in effect it needs only the most general kind of representation, only a cue. In *To Catch a Thief*, the design is the film; the place is the action, yet east and west, north and south are utterly confounded in the image. We can know the directions, perhaps, but we cannot see them.

32

Walk on the Wild Side

FIGURE 32 *Two angles from the restaurant scene of* The Man Who Knew Too Much *(Alfred Hitchcock, Paramount, 1956). Cinematography by Robert Burks. Design by Henry Bumstead.*

It is interesting, if not mind-twisting, to think, "I am but I am not." Sometimes the graphic design of a scene takes us to such a thought.

We are invited to join our protagonists for a special dinner in Marrakech—something "exotic"—by a traveling Frenchman who appears to know his way around the really good spots. (How blissful to find such a person, or to be found by him!) But at the last minute the man begs out. We go anyway. And what a sumptuous place! Very very low tables, people seated on enormous softly cushioned divans. Ornate hand-made tiles literally paving the walls. Sedateness, good taste, even spicy intoxication. As our guests position themselves (James Stewart and Doris Day; an extraordinarily tall man and a glamorous woman), she sweetly placing herself on a divan and he struggling mightily with his gangly legs to find a seat next to her, in which he has no real backrest(!), we watch the buffoonery from, effectively, the matching divan on the opposite side of their table. (This is good; we will be able to smell the food!) We get the following view:

Close-focused long shot of the entire restaurant space with tables stretching out to the back of the shot, the high airy ceiling, the hanging chandeliers, the low table, the cobalt blue and white soft divan on which our friends sit, and the tiled wall stretching on our right all the way past them and alongside all the diners as far back as we can see.

The narrative and physical attractiveness of the two stars is plenty of reason to concentrate on them at any rate, but if we need more reasons we can count on (a) Day and Stewart holding principal status in the Hollywood constellation; (b) Stewart's magical show of stumbling, almost tripping, as he steps over Day with us looking between his spread legs, as well as his innocent Midwest, drawled bumbling as he moves; and (c) the magnificent white and teal dress and matching cape Day is wearing out tonight. We are concentrating on them, nice tidy shot, and thus taking the setting more or less for granted once we quickly verify by sweeping inspection that it is the Moroccan restaurant we have been promised.

Very pleasant. Some slight education about foreign climes. A private entry to this tight American marriage.

A little time goes by.

Now the McKennas, our new friends, meet another couple who are sitting back to back with them, the Draytons. Rather than trying to converse by twisting their backs out of shape, they invite the Draytons to turn around and take their seats, and they move across the table, now occupying the position that the camera (that we) occupied previously. Sharing with strangers—the epitome of hospitality and friendship. The two couples chat amicably.

But . . .

In order to get a better view, to see one couple at screen left, the other at screen right, all in profile and all cheery as pie, we suddenly move to take up a position where just earlier we saw a tile wall. We become, in fact, that wall, and from the position of the wall look down the length of the table to see the McKennas at left and the Draytons at right. Fun to watch them break the bread, try to eat the roast squab in the tajine. And the Draytons are as thoroughly British as the McKennas are thoroughly American, so this is a friendly trans-Atlantic summit.

I here forego all discussion of the content of the discussion and what it might come to reveal in turning the plot of *The Man Who Knew Too Much* (1956), in order to focus on the subtle shift of perspective that has occurred, already, twice in the scene. In the first instance, the camera traded places with two characters. In the second, the camera is trading places with the set. But in both cases we are implicated.

In both cases we are both viewers who can see and viewers who are blocked from seeing. Early on, watching Ben and Jo, we cannot see where Ben and Jo are soon to be sitting. Later, watching Ben, Jo, Lucy, and Edward ("a big noise in agriculture"), we cannot see the restaurant wall that defines the limit of their space.

As to that wall: when the camera (when we) become the wall (take up the position where the wall was) we are caught in a conundrum, because as agents of the film vision we can appreciate the shot composition but as onlooking believers in the restaurant construction we are momentarily stymied. Being positioned where we have just seen a tiled wall we are obliged to occupy its dumb, uncalculating attitude, to be as neutral as it was. Yet because a vision is offered to us here, by the camera, we must also occupy the onlooker's consciousness. Thus, we see (objectively) and we see (personally, because we know the McKennas) simultaneously and at once, in a puzzling stance that opens us to a wholly non-rational, wholly equivocal kind of sight. Four tourists in Morocco; or two people with whom we have bonded and the strangers they have just met. As to the soft divan: when the camera (when we) occupied it and got a long shot of the restaurant stretching past the McKennas, we used our eyes to see the full frame—as much as the film camera ever allows viewers to see. But then the McKennas take up our seat and we must "hop" to the wall (the aisle on the far side being for the waiters to use, not for us).

The view to which we move is produced through a particular design cheat called the "wild wall." When a wall in a set is "wild," it is built so as to be completely, or partially removable, so that the camera can be placed where that wall stood. There are other distinctive "wild" shots like these restaurant shots to be found in Hitchcock, another in the Marrakech hotel room when Dr. McKenna begins by unpacking clothing from a dresser backed up against a wall and continues his action as perceived by us *from that wall*. The legendary *Rope* (1948) is substantially dependent on wild walls that are on rails, able to "swing back," as Hitchcock said, "And the furniture was mounted on rollers" (Truffaut 183). When a filmmaker expressly wants to work without wild walls, as is the case with Clint Eastwood, the camera team must figure a way to use squeezed positions and wide-angle lenses to shoot scenes inside small rooms.[1]

Another feature of the wild wall is that it claims a double identity. As a floor-to-ceiling array of decorative tiles, for example, the restaurant wall is part of the story-scene, an element in a setting declared openly by the story and one that is shown to "establish a kind of realism," inspiring the viewer to think of what she is seeing as a representation of an actual place.[2] At the same time, and in a wholly contradictory way, the array is a pre-designed part of the production, present to the view at one instant while always prepared to be removed at another, but removed not only from view: removed also from story-space and re-placed in production-space. When it is moved the wild wall is part of the production, invisible to audiences. This wall is thus, at each moment whether we are seeing it or not, both present and absent, both a challenge to us and nothing at all. These antinomies make for a very confounding, not to say disorienting mode of vision, and the secrecy of the wildness helps audiences slide (wrongly) to the side of believing they are simply always placed in the ideal position for taking a view.

To be noted: When first we see the tile wall—more accurately, when first we are exposed to it—it functions casually and entirely unobtrusively as a highly ornamental part of a highly ornamental interior design, a story element helping to identify our surround. We do not gaze at it, but we do recognize it instantly, and it belongs to the world of the story, the Marrakech world, the exotic. But when, having taken the second camera position, we think back in realizing that we are positioned where the wall was seen, it has become something that could be manipulated at will, something to do not with a story but with a set design. The divan that the McKennas move over to occupy began for us, an assumed if not quite a presented audience, as a camera position and became the McKennas' seat. As in retrospect we realize that this is where we were positioned to look at the restaurant the divan becomes, now, a signal of the production of the film.

Why, one might reasonably ask, does the viewer typically not pause to see this "many-sided" wall, not pause to consider how the story and the production of the story are intertwined? Because a cheat has been made to glide over the duplication of tasks. But how could such a cheat have worked? To answer this we must briefly look at the restaurant as a good example of Kenneth Burke's grammar of ratios. Here is a *scene* in which

---

[1] I am grateful to the late Henry Bumstead for sharing some of Eastwood's preferences with me, in 1998.
[2] The restaurant, entirely fabricated on a Paramount soundstage, *was* intended to reproduce an actual Marrakech restaurant and, secondly, all the tiles were hand crafted by the designer, Henry Bumstead, after local patterns. More on the film can be found in my *The Man Who Knew Too Much*, and the arrangements for the restaurant are described in detail in DeRosa.

some vital *act* takes place. We are thus confronted with a *scene: act* ratio, for Burke a declaration that this act is (always already) properly the kind of act to be observed (set) in a scene like this one; and that this scene is (always already) properly the kind of place in which one easily and reasonably finds such an act. A unity of movement and place. But the Burke scene: act ratio is not even-sided. In a story film, especially a suspense film like *The Man Who Knew Too Much*, action must always be set in the right place but also always take precedence over that place in the perceptual routine. The place is quickly registered and laid away, so that the behavior can take the spotlight; indeed, the action becomes dominant in this scene, and after we register the identity and nature of the restaurant as a space we dismiss the place from attention. Filmmakers know this pattern. When he designed the restaurant for Paramount's Stage 1, Henry Bumstead was fully aware that he could make a wild wall for Hitchcock, and that if the wall as an object would at first be enticing yet soon it would recede, taking its wildness with it.[3]

Were viewers fixated on cardinal directions and the absolute definition of diegetic space, they would have to map out that restaurant, and the wild wall would be impossible as part of that map since features on non-fictional maps do not toggle between appearance and disappearance. That tiled wall is only to Ben and Jo's left (which is nothing but *screen right*) and then their right (nothing but *screen left*); screen right and screen left, not right and left. And then it vanishes, and then it is nowhere.

---

[3] The restaurant sequence was made June 27, 28, and 29, 1955, the first days at the studio after a substantial filming voyage to Morocco and London.

33

Happy Trails

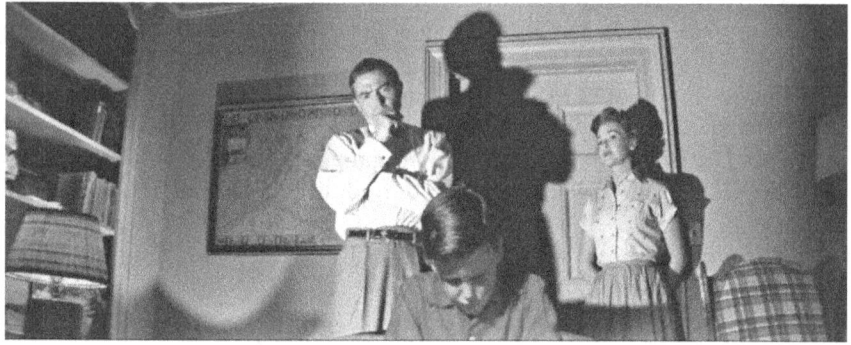

FIGURE 33 *James Mason (l.), Christopher Olsen, and Barbara Rush in* Bigger Than Life *(Nicholas Ray, Twentieth Century Fox, 1956)*.

So compactly and coherently are filmic action and filmic setting unified, when the artists at hand are expert, that one thinks of the two as being not only interrelated but mutually generative in an ongoing way. When, at the end of *Bringing Up Baby* (1938), Cary Grant's David has finally found his cherished dinosaur bone and is climbing up a scaffolding to place it in the culminating position on that massive skeleton, the massive skeleton happens to be there waiting for him, and so does the scaffolding: the latter looks just flimsy enough to give us the barest hint that it might not be as sturdy as poor David would like, and the former looks like a catastrophe waiting for its moment. When, in *Six Degrees of Separation* (1993) Flan (Donald Sutherland) wants to impress his guest Geoffrey from South Africa (Ian McKellen) by taking him aside and showing him a transparency of a Cézanne he intends to have, the warmly lit study is there for them to be alone in, a haven, silent, plushly lit, and the Cézanne transparency, provided by props, looks perfect when held up to the light in this place: so perfect, in fact, that when Flan says he plans to have it and turn it around for a quick sale, anybody who loved Cézanne would be chagrined. When, in *The French Lieutenant's Woman* (1981), the nineteenth-century Dr. Grogan must be presented in his private study, the study is there for Leo McKern to walk into, jammed with skeletons, glass cases, weighty tomes, magnifying glasses, and such like, and all of the furniture looking as though it has been there forever inside these sanctified walls that, bordered by nicely painted trim—trim lit by candles—treasure the deepest past. One has the feeling of the designer and the director confabulating in a corner, the actors fully made up in role standing by patiently yet with extreme eagerness to inhabit the scene, though of course the confabulation happened long in advance of the actors' presence, possibly before they were even hired.

What could it mean to speak of a unity of action and scene, in film? Proportion, for one thing. That the space in which characters move seems to fit them, and they it; trees larger than humans, but not so much larger that the humans become insects (unless, as with the *Vertigo* forest, that is the effect). Rooms appropriate to a social class. Modes of transportation believable for the characters at the moment, containing within them a believably sized space. Further, spaces that are "designed" in the diegesis should fit the character's apparent taste. All of this is carefully done in such a way that it is clearly and variably photographable, in short no touches that cannot show up on camera. And a scene, as well, magnificent enough to apprehend, so that it captures the viewer's attention; yet not so magnificent that it abstracts the attention away from the character at a key moment. A character can stand at a plate glass window, for example, looking out upon a splendid lake with mountains and a sunset, but all of the terrain must recede when we see the side of the gazer's intentful face.

A collaboration of filmmaker and film designer. But this collaboration is largely cheated. Audiences are not to detect it. The scene is "naturally" this way. The character is here, but the here is merely present for the character to inhabit. Nor the place itself but its face. Not the redwoods as used for Kim Novak and James Stewart but the way those redwoods are made to look, since, like a place, a scene is not a space (see Tuan, *Space and Place*). The awesomeness of the *Vertigo* redwood forest is distinctive, even unforgettable; but it is not the same as the awesomeness of the actual redwood forest, what Novak and Stewart would actually have experienced in making Madeleine and Scottie experience the "redwood forest."

In practice, the director-designer arrangement tends to work this way:

Having carefully read, annotated, and thought about the script, the designer knows what diegetic "locations" will be needed. Let us take Nicholas Ray's *Bigger Than Life* (1956). (1) An elementary school classroom where Ed Avery (James Mason), finishing up a day's teaching with a sweet but slow-witted student, prepares to leave; also set here will be a night-time parent-teacher session later on. (2) The teachers' lounge in the same school, where he meets a few colleagues and reminds them about the party at his house tonight. (3) The Avery house, with a front yard, a back yard grassed over (in which some action will occur), a living room, a den, a kitchen, a hallway with a staircase up to the bedrooms, an upper landing. (4) The Averys' bedroom upstairs. (5) The upstairs bathroom. (6) The taxi depot where Ed is moonlighting. (7) A medical consultation facility with, among other things, a fluoroscope. (8) A doctor's office for discussions. (9) A department store where Ed can buy his wife an expensive dress she protests she does not need. (10) A church for a Sunday morning service. (11) A hospital room where Ed, seriously overdosed with cortisone, lays in agony and finally recovers. (12) The hospital corridor outside this room. The designer is getting a rough idea of places, not exact behavioral movement that will occur in them and how broadly that will be choreographed. He will build every space to be a choreographable space and the director will use it as he will.

The designer is thinking, which of these are interior spaces and which exteriors? Translated: how many scenes can be shot on hunted-out real locations, how many will require sets to be built on soundstages? And regarding the latter, which soundstages, that is, which studio? The designer is familiar with all the soundstages at the major studios and many at the legion minor studios in the Los Angeles area, the New York area, the London area, the Vancouver area, and so on, and what he doesn't know he can fairly easily learn, since the studio will offer up a map with specifications for each stage: height, length, width, grid structure, whether or not there is a removable floor, whether there is a pool. *Bigger Than Life* is a Paramount production: will the set-building be on-lot at Paramount (5555 Marathon Street, Los Angeles) and if so, which exact stages will be rentable for the designer's use (the designer will have preferences)?[1] For each interior "room" in the diegesis: is it connected to any other space and must passage between the spaces be possible for the actors or will those movements be handled through matching edits (in which case the two sets can be miles apart)? For making exterior shots that include part of the house, how much of the house will have to be built, and what arrangements made so that this part matches against interiors built elsewhere?[2] How big will the location *appear* to be in the story, measured, say, in feet, and how big would the set have to be so that the camera could give the impression of that diegetic size, using a

---

[1] The floor being removable there to yield an extra ten feet of height, Paramount's Stage 18 was ideal for the single set of *Rear Window* (1954) and later for the sorority house of Jerry Lewis's *The Ladies Man* (1962).
[2] In *North by Northwest* (1959) the memorable Vandamm house (in the Frank Lloyd Wright style) is a matte painting. The on-set build included the very lowest beams only and a separate piece for a balcony and a railing. Cary Grant never gets very far off the studio floor here.

50 mm, a 75 mm, a 100 mm, a 40 mm, a 35 mm, and a 28 mm lens? (The designer will not have been forewarned about lens size.) How big would the set have to be (each set) for accommodating the camera and necessary crew? Since usually in advance one cannot know whether the camera will be stationary or moving or both, how much room should be "reserved" for it? Can any portions of the sets be joined so that a single construction allows for movement and shooting in more than one place in continuous action? This last because it costs money to rent a studio soundstage and saving unnecessary expense is always a concern.

Now the production manager is called in to see the set list and two sets of estimations are made in writing. The cost of each construction and of each outside location rental; and the ideal way of scheduling use of all the built sets in one phase of the shooting process and all the outside locations in another. This latter calculation tends to have little to do with the designer's needs directly except that it will dictate the order in which sets need to be used (thus, built). It is more dependent on the actors' required scenes (alone or with others) and work contracts. Typically all the scenes involving one particular supporting player (in this film, Walter Matthau, flown in from New York) will be scheduled back to back on as few shooting days as possible; but how many, and which, different sets would be needed to make that possible? Those would all have to be ready for camera on the specific dates that have been arranged for him to be in Los Angeles (at a hotel the producer is paying for), and given that it takes time to build sets the building would have to start considerably in advance of the actor's presence. Will any diegetic "damage" be done to the set in any part of these scenes? If so, and if the set is to be used "clean" later on, how much time and cost will be involved in undoing the "damage"—that is, how can the "damaging act" be set up so as not to really antagonize the design? As for set construction, one feature the producer has to worry over is the sound stage space needed for building each set, since all the stage costs—a portion of the studio's heating and electricity; a portion of the film budget's total overhead—need to be absorbed in the budget, and they vary with stage size. Can the Avery living room and the Avery dining room, one on either side of the central hallway, all be built together on one stage? What proportion of the stage is needed for this—could the schoolroom be built in another part of the same stage? Studio charges are for the entire sound stage, with all its built-in amenities (listed for producers' consideration).[3]

Then design sketches, benefiting from the work of the studio's Research Department ("What does a hospital corridor in a small town look like?"); consultation with the producer as to cost and the director as to feasibility

---

[3] MGM's "Munchkinland" occupied only one corner, about one sixth, of their Stage 27. The village of Brigadoon took up the whole place.

for the storytelling and the cinematographer and costumer in terms of colors and textures. Then calculating the time required in the studio's carpentry shop, the materials, the labor for building, the labor for delivery to the stage and erecting, and also the labor for striking and removing when the shooting is done. Is it possible that all the scenes of the classroom can be shot at one time (regardless of cast), so that after a few days that set can come down and be replaced, on the same stage, with another one?

But now a more delicate, more penetrating problem, once all of the carpentry cheats have been accomplished, all external locations have been spotted and legally arranged for (a written contract for each one with the owner or supervisor of the property). Where will the director put his camera? What will the camera see and not see of this interesting place? That is, what has to be made perfect for camera, what can be left undone? (Will the bedsheets be pulled down?) Sets can theoretically be built only partially, to work for the *scene the camera will frame*. (Most Hollywood sets are built without ceilings, for just one example, but doorways can lead nowhere, tables have nothing in their drawers, the kitchen cupboards, like Mother Hubbard's, be bare.) Some set designers work with meticulous knowledge of where the camera will be for every shot made on a set they are building and what will and will not be seen there, the director having thought this through long in advance and given consultation. In other cases the director comes onto the set, often alone, and figures out what will be done today, and how, right in the space itself. On top of all this, if painted backings are to hang behind portions of the set (viewed through windows or doorways, for example: an extremely typical tactic, used considerably also in television and made-for-tv movies), what colors will the scenic painters use for those backings and what adjustments to the colors on set will be needed—or, for economy, will preexisting skyscraper or other backings be used? Such things are available. What film stock will the cinematographer be using and what will that stock do to shift the colors as finally printed: Technicolor (before 1956), Eastmancolor, Fujicolor, Agfacolor—these all work differently.

Some designers work on the basis of an overriding principle: that they do not know now, and will never know, what the director will want to see or what the actors will want to do, so the entire set must be made for show, including the backs of doors, the area behind furniture, the inside of desk drawers! Nothing—but nothing—left out. The director has freedom to go where he will, show what he desires, no limit. The designer knows that he will not be at the director's side.

He will not be at the director's side because he is several days to a week ahead of the director all through the production, busy planning, making, and setting up designs that won't be used until later, by which point he will have moved on again. The director and actors, the cinematographer, the support crew will arrive for work early one morning and find the story world they need ready and waiting for them to inhabit. It will be built to work, and they will work it.

So effectively will the designed world seem to have been arranged, so considerately designed, so artfully crafted, so tastefully surfaced and textured and painted, and so easily will the characters move about there as we watch, that the thing seems nothing less than real, and real, too, seems the characters' involvement with the place. In *The Courtship of Eddie's Father* (1962), a kitchen with paneled cabinets *filled with tea cups and food items*. In *The Manchurian Candidate* (1962) and *E.T.* (1982), a kitchen equipped with a modern refrigerator that will teem with food and drink when the door is dramatically opened. It is certainly part of the actor's talent to give the impression of comfort and ease in a place never known until now, and she will walk around and rehearse if necessary in order to "learn" the place; but unless the place is designed to offer comfort first, the actor cannot do the work.

North by Northwest is an excellent example of set cheats, because Robert Boyle, the designer, had a keen eye for realistic detail and because he intimately knew Hitchcock's framing. The lobby of Roger's office building on Madison Avenue, a built set. The Oak Bar of the Plaza Hotel, a built set. The Townsend mansion interior, a built set. The Plaza Hotel's room 796, a built set. The lobby and delegates' lounge of the United Nations, built sets. The dining car of the 20th Century Limited, a built set. Eve's sleeper, a built set. Parts of the cornfield recreated on the rear-projection stage. The Shaw & Oppenheim auction house, a built set. The interior of Midway Airport, a built set. Portions of the Mt. Rushmore monument, a built set. The interior and close-up exterior of the Vandamm residence, a built set. The viewing platform and visitors' center of the Mt. Rushmore monument, built sets. Roger's hospital room, a built set.

The cheating designer, hard at work building what will seem a real place of one kind when in truth it is a real place of another, must have fidelity, and show that there is fidelity, in two matters:

First, making the specially built nature of the set disappear behind utter conventionality of design, so that instead of looking like a design the set looks like an actual place: in short, faking style. In Billy Wilder's *Sabrina* (1954) we are treated to an executive boardroom with attached kitchenette and high windows looking out at the Hudson River. Hal Pereira and Walter Tyler give us a mammoth polished table (ideal for William Holden to go sliding on after Humphrey Bogart lands him one on the kisser). The kitchenette is used briefly, but not centrally in frame. The window plays urgently, but we never get a good enough look outside to determine the fakery of the painted backing that hangs there. The whole place is dressed "expensive," as it belongs to a corporation run by a fabulously wealthy family and they apparently spare no expense: viewers have likely never been in such a place and so if it is large enough to hold the action, the engaging action by major movie stars who take our eye, it will be fine.

Secondly, the designer is completely covering up the fact of the faking, a matter of key importance, just as actors cover up the fact of the acting. The picture in all its aspects seems to flow off the screen in a golden aura of not just authenticity but *spontaneous* authenticity. Albeit there are times when a film set looks somewhat like a film set, because it has been designed to look precisely that way: one will find this frequently in the Hollywood musical, where ongoingly the set supports the action and the action is more oneiric than practical.

34

The Thing

FIGURE 34 Life *(Daniel Espinosa, Columbia, 2017)*.

It may well be that the fighting forest in Baum's *The Wonderful Wizard of Oz* (1900) gave inspiration to Walt Disney for his 1932 animated film *Flowers and Trees*, but it certainly led to the forest sequence in MGM's 1939 film. The inanimate (or imperceivably animate) becomes—surprisingly—animate. The trees sprout mouths and make language of a kind, using their branches as arms to encircle our friendly quartet. Here is a primary example—though, given Lang's *Metropolis* (1927), not the first example—of the object becoming characterological. Think of *The Mummy* (1932) rising from the dead, the dinosaur bone at war with the terrier in *Bringing Up Baby* (1938), the controlling, perhaps malevolent power of the "dingus" in *The Maltese Falcon* (1941), the unholy power of the box in *Kiss Me Deadly* (1955), the living playroom in *Tom Thumb* (1958), the mobilizing force of the slab, a font of intelligence, in *2001: A Space Odyssey* (1968), the creature disguising itself as conduits and storage space in *Alien* (1979), the talking stone wall in *The Princess Bride* (1987). I avoid mentioning the numerous occasions in the Harry Potter saga when some *thing* behaves as though it is an embodied consciousness, a significant object upon which canniness, motivational design, and purpose have been inscribed. The thing made "flesh."

Less disturbing somehow but equally products of the systematic animation of matter are robots, advanced computers, and alien tools: HAL in *Space Odyssey*, Robbie the Robot in *Forbidden Planet* (1956), Gort in *The Day the Earth Stood Still* (1951), the velocitor in *This Island Earth* (1955), R2-D2 and C-3PO, bless them. A smartness, a power, and a plan that gain dramatic potency by apparently superseding what human agents can do.

Achieving the hybrid characteristics of these creature-devices, these device-creatures, requires a design cheat. The object in question must be made to look on first examination like a product of human or alien engineering, and this examination, as choreographed in the flow of narrative cinema, is not likely to be slow and patient. A surface of metal, usually polished (a signal that atmospheres will offer no resistance). Controls, often illuminated (the power room of the Krell in *Planet* is a spectacular array of lights). Mechanical (rhythmic, unstoppable) agencies: arms, grapplers, magnets, emitted rays, moving parts (Robbie the Robot being quite hilarious because of the contradictory direction in which some of his parts move simultaneously—a sign of delightful confusion). Essential is that the Thing be conveyed as fully and swiftly as possible in the form of the inhuman, a being that was born of no mother—this orphanage, so to speak, being the root of the affecting pathos in the finale of *2001* when HAL sings his "kindergarten" song and introduces his "parents." No human birth, at least not a normal one, yet also nothing spiritual in the sense that we accord in legends of Jesus, also not born of mother in a normal way. This inhuman birth makes for a coldness and inhospitability, a calculation, a mathematical soul. The thing as machine, then. The machine as un-alive.

But also the Thing as touchingly animate. A discernable personality, a spirit of good or evil to mobilize action, a ferocity or gentleness that sensitive human characters find affecting. Also, a diligent capability that trumps human skill: objects can be hurled at greater speed and frequency, chemistry can be converted, sinews can be manipulated, a ringing metallic voice can issue commands impossible not to follow. To get at this we must see some simulacrum of the dominating face, or an arrangement that we can willingly and pleasurably choose to interpret as a face. By presenting the mechanical surface *first*, and in some telling detail, the photography allows for the animated qualities—the suddenly appearing control surfaces—to be seen in light of mechanism, thus, not life per se but a machine that seems "alive," as well as *seeming to seem*. Yet also consider the formula exercised in reverse, something first seen in light of the fully human, a person who turns out—that turns out—to be a machine. Consider the death of the science officer

Ash (Ian Holm) in *Alien*, as, his head struck off by a fierce blow he continues to flail, finally making it clear that he was, all along, (only) robotic. This is a human become mechanical, a degradation. The machine become human, like the animal become human(oid) (Caesar in *War for the Planet of the Apes* [2017], who, as we all know, is mo-capped by Andy Serkis), is climbing the "ladder," doing what evolutionary theory tells us we all did a long, long time ago. Doing what we did, the Thing becomes like us, conspecific in a way, recognizable. "This thing of darkness I/acknowledge mine."

The animate mechanism as graphic subject runs the risk of bringing laughter or dismissal. Robbie the Robot works powerfully because, although his plexi head allows us to see desperately whirring mechanisms (puppy learning new tricks) he is still a major player in more than one scene of violent aggression where he shows amazing brute force. But the animus, the spirit of what had been a stationary, immobile thing is tricky because it can seem to come out of nowhere, which means, of course, out of some designer's toolbox off-camera. If sympathetic characters fall under machine power and are threatened there; or if they accept benevolent but "living" machines as friendly forces, we can be persuaded to take the things very seriously indeed: this happens over and over, both for good and for trouble, in *Jurassic Park* (1993) and its sequels. It is a recurring trope in war films where an endangered flyer seizes the controls of a damaged aircraft and saves the day (this apotheosized by Luke in the starfighter at the climax of *Star Wars* [1977]).

What considerations come into play when mechanism or solid objectivity comes "alive" believably onscreen?

- In effect, the now living thing will become a character, like all other characters in a fictional zone. One danger is that, only because of its physicality, it might come to seem much more interesting than human characters, more compelling even than the stars of the film. The viewer is therefore, quite intentionally, given limited access to this Thing, and access only at dramatic points when the involvement of the creature is central to the story either as action continuity or as comic relief. The Thing is given an introductory scene of its own, so to speak, but then relegated to secondary status. Even in conflictual conclusion sequences, where a heroic human must battle the Thing, the human gets more camera time, which means that the shots of the Thing must be very carefully calculated to be specially informative. Arnold Schwarzenegger concluding his battle with the alien in the finale of *Predator* (1987).
- But what we will be encouraged to forget or dismiss as irrelevant is this: that before it was characterized, the Thing was part of the setting, a kind of mass ornament, *mass* in the sense adduced by Kracauer describing telltale cultural formations (as he writes, of

Weimar culture) that arise but not from the people and are without a "current of organic life." There is in the character-object a kind of "linearity":

> The more the coherence of the figure is relinquished in favor of mere linearity, the more distant it becomes from the immanent consciousness of those constituting it. Yet this does not lead to its being scrutinized by a more incisive gaze. In fact, nobody would notice the figure at all if the crowd of spectators, who have an aesthetic relation to the ornament and do not represent anyone, were not sitting in front of it. (77)

The Machine-Thing was an element in the place, finally turned in nature so that it could ground a principal (but also wholly human) action. Now the set itself has come to life. This thought alone is so potentially disturbing, at least so confusing, it is easier for the viewer if the camera pulls in from the set to concentrate (in close shot) on a particular item ready for conversion. In the brain-dismantling scene of *2001*, the pull-in gives us to view first small arrays of white information cells, then reveals, closer, only a few. But the computer is the entire room, totally surrounding the hero. The fading voice gives accompaniment to the diminishing size of the array made visible. Yet, too, the non-organic white cells are already, if only vaguely, like any human, in that a keenly directed touch can have profound effect on them.

- In being characterized, the Thing will have attributes similar to those of other characters, attributes just such as characters in film dramas possess generally. Yet on balance it can never be quite the magnet the human characters are. It will be motile. It will be "conscious." It will have particular dexterities (and, useful for plot termination, particular deficiencies as well). And it will have—or through audience invocation will be read as having—personality. The distinction between human and non-human characters being a central maintenance problem, the personality of the Thing will be described in much more limited, much more superficial (again, "linear") terms. If at crisis moments the robot seems precisely as human as human characters do, it actually *is*, functionally speaking, never quite a human character. Robbie the Robot can hilariously make bourbon for Earl Holliman, but he never understands what he is doing, why he is doing it, or what the effects will be, even though he suffers some of them! HAL-9000 is not at first shown to be as manipulative, as conniving, or as confused in motivation as the astronauts he taunts, and he has a cajoling, persuasive voice (thanks to Douglas Rains) but finally he is a cipher-brute. In *The Stepford Wives* (1975) the suburban women finally discovered as much less human than they looked are reduced qualitatively by inclusion in a massive group of such beings, all of them more or less identical and thus only superficially personal.

- Often the Living Thing will ultimately suffer degradation at the hands of human characters, being relegated in that way to a status closer to that of objective matter than that of human life. Or (again in reverse) it will come out of extremely elemental, simplified (say, amoebic) matter and grow into a "personality," as we see in Daniel Espinosa's *Life* (2017). Moderating during the film between the elemental and the mature, the material and the sophisticated, it will conclude in regression to its origins, or at least notably in that direction, as happens to the alien Thing in *Alien* at the very end, when Ripley (Sigourney Weaver) triumphs over it; or to HAL when Dave (Keir Dullea) dismantles him; or even to Robbie, who becomes wholly (and happily) a pet aboard the starship when Altair-4 disintegrates.

- Yet, too, the pure Thing-ness of the Thing is hardly sufficient to mobilize audience fears, and at some critical moment in the story it will show itself more venomous, more irrational, more capable of negativity than any other character around, if inexplicably so. Structurally in the story the final victory over the Thing is achieved as revenge for some earlier destruction, when it abuses, degrades, tortures, and dispenses with a disposable human character, beloved to other characters. This theme of vengeful destruction and unbounded Thingish capability is carried to exciting extremes in *Life*, where the initially tender and innocent cell grows into a giant and malevolent Entity, horrifically terminating crew members aboard a spacecraft in which it is running loose.

- A general testament to, even paean to technological progress typifies Thing stories. Very typically, first deployed as a machine or device created by people but magically gaining more power than they accorded it, the Thing proceeds along a destructive line growing in stature and malevolence as the story unwinds. Finally, however, the human capacity for invention—the same capacity that gave birth to, that animated, the object in the first place—stands over the Machine's power, either destroying or stalling or freezing or expelling it. We can always go further, the film says. We will build a better Thing next time. But there will surely be a next time, and when it happens we will be there. Technological advancement as eternal life.

- *Or wholesale disguise.* The Thing, immensely powerful and a Force of Nature in itself, made into what it is, perhaps, through ignorant human agency (Godzilla) or by an organic world far more complex than man has understood (*Prometheus* [2012]), never appears at all as an object to be transformed; but meets our gaze instantly and wholly as a fully articulate Golem, promising to control the world. I have in mind that splendid special-effects creation, the giant squid in Disney's *20,000 Leagues Under the Sea* (1954), a matter of puppeted tentacles detached from any clearly visible central body. Or the now much celebrated (and much dismissed) shark in *Jaws* (1975) which appeared when the film was released in a bubble of such terrifying presence that audiences tried to recoil in their seats. Irvin Yeaworth's blob worked much this way in *The Blob* (1958), particularly because, as was arranged later by Spielberg for his shark, the Thing got very little, and only the most dramatically significant, camera time. Things like these are objective and material, but are not presented that way at all, the illusion (cheat) being effected upon (and for) us that the animation we see is real, that in truth the Machine is alive. Thus is sung and sung again the ballad of material progress, the melodic reassurance that once the Things have us, once we are converted, we will find immortality.

35

Heist

FIGURE 35 *Anne Bancroft and Dustin Hoffman in* The Graduate *(Mike Nichols, Lawrence Turman/Embassy, 1967).*

Especially—but not only—in contemporary cinema (adventures, action comedies, etc.), we experience something that could easily be morally perturbing. Extreme violence, for example, including radical depictions of dismemberments and bodily fragmentations (worked through, we are not always comforted to know, with expensive makeup). Medical or other death scenes. White collar crime of a high order, say drug cartels holding hundreds of millions of dollars and more (and associated bloodshed). Vituperative, hateful, scornful, demeaning, and unpoetic language used with staccato repetition, to "simulate real social conditions." Extremely direct portrayals of sexual encounters.

It is not a matter of prurience to consider the moral implications of such material, since in our everyday lives we do so all the time, at least by implication. From extreme gun violence we turn a moral eye, or, enacting both self-preservation and morality, we flee; from bombs we keep distant if we can, and we do not condone their usage excitedly, notwithstanding the aesthetic "fireworks" effects we might imagine. Deaths of strangers we respect by not watching. Sex we relegate to our imaginations, and eschew opportunities to visit and observe those engaged in it. Crime we neither see nor expect to see when it is managed at a high level, since part of the management is evasion of detection. Mary McIntosh: "When he is working, the thief aims not to be noticed by his victim and to look, if he is seen at all, as if he has other and legitimate business" (105). As to abusive language, when it races in torrents we might attempt to shut the ears against the flow: is this a person in desperation? Is this a ticquer?

Yet in cinema we avidly attend.

Attend with ongoing fascination, expanding feeling, expectations of climaxes that never quite come. One might easily have the impression that the climax has actually not been slotted into the shooting schedule: the actual effect of gunshot wounds; the actual outcome of death scenes; the actual big payoff in big-time crime; the orgasmic pleasure; the effect on user and victim of vituperative language. These fulsome factualities are elided, but the scenes invoking them are played out, again and again, always with the same conventional structure and only slight decorative variation. Even drug highs are pointed to only obtusely, as with Peter Fonda in the relatively spectacular LSD scenes in *The Trip* (1967); but withdrawal, coming back to the norm, can get extreme treatment, as in the long "cold turkey" sequence with Gene Hackman in *French Connection II* (1975).

Such blissfully painful, penetrating, provocative, private moments: how is it that while modesty, shame, or dignity prevent us from watching them in the everyday, should they present themselves, and hold us back from seeking to find them, we can be so ready to see them depicted onscreen? Moments of the loss of self.

[1] One argument, essentially a psychoanalytical thesis, is that we do very much wish to watch, deeply, madly, truly—scopophilia—but repress the desire in the name of civilized propriety, propriety as to behavior with other people, propriety as to approvable seeming. The gawking urge is always there, but held back, held down. As the film we are watching doesn't constitute behavior with other people, not really, not exactly, here in the cavern, our deep desire can be released in the dark. In watching filmic sex and violence, we are doing what we secretly wish we could be doing all the time everywhere—watching, digesting the world's culture—and one signal value of cinema (such an argument maintains) is that it offers this opportunity for undoing the repression in a safe, which is to say controlled, environment. As different people with differing life backgrounds have different buried tastes, film scenes that reveal the interior of life, as it were, will not be universally appealing; some may even put some viewers off while turning other viewers, a few seats down, on.

[2] Another argument is that nobody takes any of these direct intimate scenes, as they are portrayed on film, the least bit seriously in the terms they offer. We recognize that we are being given only passing nibbles, leading us to a sensible moral resolution in which the good will end well, the bad unwell, and the world will remain intact. We must witness a very dirty moment indeed so that the hero can be in a position to *appear heroic* by making things clean. This is essentially a dramaturgical argument: the violence is structurally necessary as a set-up for the sanctified retribution. Sanctification, order, permanence—these are the principal targets, not characters, feelings, or storylines. And not hidden drives or pathologies.

[3] A third argument, very popular in the second decade of the twenty-first century, is that sex, violence, hard language, wounding, death, and rampant crime are quotidian attributes of the world in which we live.[1] The world has become this way, wake up and try to smell the artificial roses. Back in the 1920s and 1930s and 1940s the world was an entirely different kind of place (say viewers too young to have been there). The film is merely reaching for realism in the spirit of *not hoodwinking its audience*, telling a truth, revealing the everyday to us in a light that will help us see it more clearly. Call this the pedagogical argument. Without scenes of hardness and cruelty, without dark penetrations, a film would be only juvenile fluff, indeed hype. Fluff, I should add, as abounds, these critics claim, in purportedly discardable Hollywood films of the 1920s, 1930s, 1940s, and 1950s. Fluffy, nonsensical, unreal.

>Unreal city,
>Under the brown fog of a winter dawn,
>A crowd flowed over London Bridge, so many,
>I had not thought death had undone so many.
>
>(T. S. Eliot, "The Waste Land")

These three arguments about the depiction of the secret, the blistering, the agonizing, the violent, and the private onscreen can all be countered, and without making roundabout voyages.

- *The educational argument* [3]: First, the world in which we live actually doesn't look as things do onscreen, not at all. The participants are far less ably choreographed in everyday life and far less distinctive to look at, since unlike screen performers, who must labor to be where they are, the folks we see on the street haven't worked with a choreographer and haven't

---

[1] A world, Bertrand Russell told Romney Wheeler in 1952, in which (already) it was very difficult for an old man (he was approaching 80) to live. He said, too, that he thought no one who was born after 1914 could possibly understand what it had been for him to grow up (in the late nineteenth century).

sat in the make-up chair. Further, everyday action is subtler in most cases, harder to grasp quickly and easily (as we must be led to do by the cheats of the camera). Action is subtler, more unresolved, often unresolvable, often unclear, but onscreen each instant must have clarity, even the instant of narcotized unclarity. Another way to put this: the viewer must never be lost at the point of the punch line. But then the punch line and what cacophonies lead up to it are not so very much like our lives. The images of life given on the daily news are constructed to appeal the way film images do, directly, bluntly, in high contrast. Life is not life dramatized.

• *The dramaturgical argument* [2]: Taken alone, this is not off-center but is finally too simple. Film stories don't follow a single roadmap, nor is the screen giving over only a story. A film can be structured in many ways, including a hypermoral situation leading to a criminal one, not the other way round. Nor, in cases of holy retribution, is our nobly vengeful hero ever shown to experience serious pleasure, release, or moral contentment for having erased the dirt. That the hero would redeem a sacred world in eliminating evil—that the dirty evil is placed in the film to permit this—is an assumption that makes for a difficult reading of, say, *The Godfather* (1972), or even, examined closely, *The Wizard of Oz* (1939).

• *The psychoanalytical argument* [1]: The proposition that we gawk only or principally because we deeply want to see what we "should not" has a deep (yet untestable) logic, but those who support it make the mistake of taking representational realism as a given, the dirty image onscreen as a double for some dirty display in the everyday. Their case always rests on the idea that outside the theater, just as inside, violence and darkness are what we secretly wish to look at, that going to the movies only heightens, polishes, and extends the action in which we are already always engaged. But the screen image isn't quite a window on things, and the relentlessness in the presentation of screen violence belies a social world in which many kinds of activity take place, not all of them enticing our secret desires. If scopophilia is engendered very deeply in the human condition, this insatiable craning of the spirit toward sight, it is hardly directed only at the taboo, only at the prurient, only at the shameful, and is therefore hardly always problematic. The hunger for vision applies to even the most casual and peremptory seeings, the ornamental lights in the lobby of the movie theater, the screen depictions of grass growing. Yearning to see is not elementally bound to the urge to discover what has been held back.

What if we acknowledge that as settings for film stories, violence and sex are fake, and palpably so? Either viewers in the know see the open duplicities, or ignorant viewers realize that what they see is part of a film. No one watching a murder onscreen, for instance, believes (a) that a real murder took place before the camera and therefore that (b) they are, by watching, accomplices. No one watching what is purported to be sexual intercourse feels moral qualms, thinking that what's onscreen is reality, since the framing, the timing, the rhythm, the musical treatment, the lighting, and the specific viewing angles are far too contrived. What if instead of claiming to be hoodwinked by the fake, taken in, robbed of the real by illusion, we confess that we know all along we are getting paste? More: getting a paste is what we adore. Then:

Secondly, what if part of the appealing fakery, as we see and appreciate it, is the very sophistication of its production, the sheen, the high-resolution frame captures, the gorgeous lighting? What if we come to believe we are seeing not merely a fake but a fake of the highest quality, the kind expressly designed to deceive *hapless others who do not have the perceptual acumen that we do*? It is a deception, *but for them*. We are not deceived because we would not fear deception. In this way we become virtual appraisers of art, priests who offer (or hesitate to offer) authentication. Knowing the screen image is fake, but also recognizing it is such a magnificent fake we have no compunction admitting to being pleasured seeing it, we become cognoscenti, true connoisseurs of the new visual high cuisine. Yet this is cynical. It is possible that in accepting the cheat for what it is we are making a profound acknowledgment, coming to a fuller appreciation of the cinematic process.

A third term in the equation. We not only know fakery when we see it, and have learned to appreciate first-class fakery, but then, growing into film watching by way of screenings and discussions online and offline we come into the desire to catch the best fakes possible, like getting the best pizza in town, snagging the put-up shows that come closest to what we call "the real" without actually going all the way. We are not only connoisseurs; we are like art thieves whose great pleasure it is to nab from the grandest museum, in the thick of night and amid confounding truckloads of buffoonish police, some utterly refined sculpture that is the museum's great treasure, worth a fortune *but also—and only we have the advantage of knowing this—a complete and utter fake*, made originally as such and placed on the pedestal to replace an actual treasure so priceless no one is given access to it. This action is spelled out through the mythology of "the story" in William Wyler's *How to Steal a Million* (1966), but the assumptions behind it, the way it mirrors a possible general attitude, is left unexplored there.

What if cinema has made all of us appraisers, specialists with an eye for fakes and especially brilliant fakes? Or if not an eye, a heart?

If the cheat is a theft of credulity, a kind of heist, rather than clinging to "the authentic," whatever that is, we can admire the cheat; become aficionados of all those delicious heist movies with an adorable crew—not only George Clooney but George Clooney *and* Brad Pitt; not only them *but also* Matt Damon; and also and also—aiming for the gargantuan gleaming emerald, the last painting of the great French Impressionist Henri-Charles du Parc de la Vallée, the contents of the casino vault, the storehold of the Bank of England, the night's take in Las Vegas's five biggest casinos all at once (as in the original *Ocean's 11* [1960]). In fact, we can come to see, by way of admiration for the skill involved in cheats, that all movies are heist movies. And that authentic treasure, that treasure that was authenticity, stored by so many viewers diligently in the secret vault inside the vault inside the vault, has no ultimate value at all.

The cheater's greatest challenge: images that only look as though they are only trying to look real.

36

The Reality Effect

FIGURE 36 *Mickey Rooney as Puck in* A Midsummer Night's Dream *(Max Reinhardt, Warner Bros., 1935).*

"What happens to reality," Stanley Cavell pithily asks, "when it is projected and screened?" (*World* 16). But later he has a more worrisome comment: "We do not know what our conviction in reality turns upon" (189). One conclusion is that "In screening reality, film screens its givenness from us; it holds reality from us, it holds reality before us, i.e., withholds reality before us. We are tantalized at once by our subjection to it and by its subjection to our views of it" (189).

My question—born, I sometimes think, of Cavell's (and of William James's) and born, too, I think at other times, of some stormy condition, doubt or wonder, that originates beyond mankind and has affected Cavell and me (two students, at different times, of the same teacher)—is this: not "What is reality?" but "What is it that motivates, urges, presses us to consider certain qualities and experiences 'real,' in the first place?" James wanted to know under what conditions we call things "real." I want to know, with Cavell, what moves us to do so, conditions notwithstanding. For James, we do not consider something real because it is real before we consider it. What it is, is indeterminate, and we sometimes use the word "real." If the name sticks (if many others use the name this way) a thing becomes real, at least to those who speak about it, and the world that subtends it becomes reality. Names stick when they are applied by the forceful, the deeply respected, the dominant agencies of power.

But why do we find it necessary or helpful to use the word "real," especially when we think of film? Surely the candy can be sweet, the poison bitter, no matter how real. "Everyone," writes James, "knows the difference between imagining a thing and believing in its existence, between supposing a proposition and acquiescing to its truth" (283). What is the profound ontological pleasure that flows our way when we aver that something we see onscreen bears a striking resemblance to, copies, faithfully represents "reality"? It is to be presumed that when we see something unworthy of this claim—take as a good example Mickey Rooney cavorting in the spangly ferns as Puck in Max Reinhardt's *A Midsummer Night's Dream* (1935)—at least the sane among us would grasp that it is not to be called "real" and that the world of the film is not to be believed as "reality," yet does such a categorical denial actually describe, arrange, clarify matters in some vital way? Our seeing "reality" in movies is not as simple as film reconfiguring onscreen, to some marked degree of exactitude, what we have already configured somewhere else in the eye, both because much of film is not for the eye alone and because only using a 50 mm lens makes it easy to roughly approximate the form of normal ocular experience. To pin everything of film to our prior experience is to take ourselves more seriously than the films we watch and also to not carefully watch those films. Further, finding "reality" in experience would seem to privilege the experience of the finder, if it is indeed worthwhile to make such a call; and once the privileging is in place, once we find reality on the front lawn, claiming the existence of a replicating agency, film, is wholly unnecessary. In Bob Rafelson's *Five Easy Pieces* (1970), we can see Jack Nicholson's "smartness and sarcasm" at a diner table when the waitress won't bring him whole wheat toast, but as I have sat at such a table and had trouble getting whole wheat toast myself, the "reality" of his experiencing the problem is not value-added for me, does not elevate what I see by likening it to my own experience. And surely my experience is my experience whether we call it "real" or not.

What I have called "the reality effect" sums to our accepting and labeling depictions as "real," as well as our fierce penchant for doing so, with all the circumstance that flows after. "Reality" is a hot topic. There are legion films now where some character's "sense of reality" is seriously challenged (he suddenly awakes to find that he is not where he thought he was, and so on), sometimes by means of mechanical arrangements that are arcane and indescribably complex, yet always the resolution of the riddle is the "ground" of the everyday, always he finds where to put his feet in a world that is called "real," and furthermore, usually at the point when he finds this "sacred" ground, the story is over. Why need that ground be "real" in order for it to be resolving or culminating or apotheotic? Why the apparent need for a double tag, "real ground," when one might think "ground" would be sufficient in itself? Why does a place need to be real if it is to be somewhere that, when a person can neither remember nor find it he searches through legion difficulties, and finally, with a glow, "really" discovers again? That is a serious question, but it misrepresents the query I pursue. That question stands upon the presumption that something can be—is—real, that such a condition as reality exists, and asks why the label tagging it should be applied in a present instance. I am not interested here in whether reality exists or not. I want to know why we wish to use the word (as though it does) and what the outcomes are.

I am not meaning here to follow strictly in William James's steps and ask of the attributes of the "real," the features of an object or situation that would lead us to place it in the category of the "real," which category we already believe in, fundamentally. I mean instead to ask how it serves to believe in such a category enough that we will speak of it. How by virtue of belonging to the "real" an experience gains elevation and importance it apparently did not have to begin with, quite as though experience is not enough. What I am calling the "reality effect," then, is not an attribute of things or happenings that leads us a certain way, but a condition of our own experience, a kind of addiction to a form.

Do we believe, as Cavell has suggested, that we have a wish to be present—not only present, I might add, but authorial!—at Creation?

Cavell's Cartesianism: when we are present at Creation, we believe in it fully, we acquiesce to its truth, because, like Descartes (and Cavell would agree, I think) we do not think a Great Deceiver has constructed a Great Deception in order to waylay us. James was meticulously describing a kind of "mechanism of realization," the operative psychological gearing, whereas Cavell seeks the spirit within, our reaching toward occasions we can understand as real. We can note that at least in popular discourse to see a filmic moment as real brings a special treat: not only, perhaps, that a moment of creation is before us and we are, as Cavell suggests, present but that this present moment is made special by being thought, not creation alone but, "real" creation, so finely danced, so sumptuous, so radiant.

(For instance, the "real Creation" at which we might be "present," a purity of purities, would not be a movie set.)

A commonplace understanding of cinematic cheats is that they help convince the viewer that what she sees onscreen is real, when it is not. Or by contrast, that the cheats detail and define ways (as we find in the Reinhardt film) that something is not real, thus by omission citing, bounding, and arguing some presently absent real. A man is bleeding from the neck, but he is not really bleeding from the neck. Well, if the bleeding looks authentic do I not respond in either case? (Or do I stand and test the reality until the poor person collapses in front of me?)

The cheat artist—make-up person, set designer, cinematographer, acting coach, costumer, publicity agent—works against film's limitations and flaws, and also against the suspicion viewers can harbor when they watch. I am driving down a highway with a man (say, Ulmer's *Detour* [1945]) but at the same time I am not, except I am waylaid from paying attention to how I am not. The cheat dresses up the cutaway car, the background set, the lights, and by dressing them converts them to a vehicle, a passing landscape, lamp posts. But let us take this little example a step further. The artistic cheats work together to "put us" in the car on the highway, say, at twilight, and we see lights, and passing cacti, and what have you. (a) The actor pretending seriously to be handling a steering wheel when he isn't. (b) Rear projection showing passing territory, which isn't there. (c) A fake partial structure pretending to be a car interior when it isn't. We are "in the car." At that point we see all of the following:

- the wholesale appearance of a car interior;
- driver-like and/or passenger-like behavior, "realistic" because a "faithful copy of" what we know having ridden in cars;
- a time of day (consistent from shot to shot, ideally);
- a territory, possibly quite beautiful, possibly lonely, surely made through pathetic fallacy to jibe with the action of the moment;
- concerned, devoted, serious facial expression and body posture;
- the car consistently remaining itself over time;
- the landscape in motion, or us in motion through the landscape.
- all of this rendered for the eye in very accomplished black and white, with profound shadow, eerie highlight, modulations of surface—a picture that we can never think anything but a picture while we consent to forget that it is a picture.

(Once again, every single one of these elements is worked at least partly through a cheat.)

The moment brings a certain satisfaction, a certain doubt, an eagerness to keep watching, a keen attention to the setting, a matter-of-fact acceptance of the maneuvers made upon the car's steerage. "Yes," we can say with enthusiasm, "a car scene!"

Yes, a car scene. Yes, a conversation in a car. Yes, two people conversing. Yes, the car moving forward. Yes, the sun setting. Yes, the steering wheel controlling the car.

We can see, approve, even find some delight in this. Certainly the humdrum normalities of car driving do not surprise or engage us in themselves, not the way they did the very first time we were taken somewhere in a car.

But given the scene in *Detour*, so fulsome, so present, so detailed, so engaging, so exciting, so mysterious . . . then . . . then . . . why do we take one step further and claim it all looks "real," and then, thinking through the manner in which it has been made to look this way, think to ourselves, "It was the cheats that made for the look of 'reality.'" The word "reality" couched in such a shroud of sanctity the word "cheat" now looks abysmal. Why does the cheat achieve "reality" rather than a pleasurable delusion? Pleasurable—more pleasurable, considerably more, than would be possible without the cheat. *Thanks to the cheat, this is gorgeously fake.* The driver, let us say: he sits woodenly at the wheel doing nothing and saying nothing. We get it, he's there, we're there with him. But somehow if he turns the wheel a little, stares through the windshield, talks to the passenger, we like it more. Do we (have to) like it more *because now it seems real*?

Do we not trust our liking, in and of itself?

Consider the driver's action here—I hope it is clear that each element of this exemplary picture could be examined this way. The driver's action brings delight, and we could examine the mechanism of that transaction, his movements, our experience. The moving body portends a future, we are more easily wrapped into an event when we think it is going somewhere. If the hand moves the wheel the driver is gesturing: presence, thought, reaction, sensation, even desire. Seeing this movement we see ourselves. We have come to the birth, the creation of the gestures, the moment of their inspiration (and then perhaps the moment of our own inspiration, too). The humanness and the impending futurity the performer suggests by "acting like a driver" bring a peculiar thrill of recognition, a release of doubt, a quickening of the breath. Let us go so far, even, as to suggest we might come to feel fear, chills up the spine, desire for union, eagerness to find a coffee shop, anything at all. Feeling, emotion, commitment, and delight. In a package.

In a unified package.

But how does it add to think of that package as "reality"? Everything we see of the driver is what it is, surely, yet by invoking some "domain of the real" and positioning our current experience there, do we add a layer of identification, a bringing the driver into our presence and a bringing of our presence toward the driver? Even if we know we are watching cheats artfully applied, still we are brought to yet another, higher-order "reality," the truth behind the false image, and like other "realities" this truthful one is worth a visit. How and why? For whether we name this place of residence, where the image shines and we are shined upon, "reality" or "unreality," the same cheats brought us there. We could call it art.

Once we have raised up the "reality" tent, regardless of how deliriously colored its stripes, the guy lines assume command: proper dispensation of resources, of living beings, of space, of time. Inventive transformations—dirt roads into railways. Proper enunciation of principles, reasons for living, pathways to success, what to hope for After. Another tent will go up nearby, to be sure, and soon enough we will have struggles of "reality" facing off against "reality," struggles followed by skirmishes, skirmishes followed by wars, all in the name of whose "reality" should be officialized as truth. Breakdowns in the method for examining reality: chemical reality, historical reality, dramatic reality, political reality, psychological reality, biological reality. And we have indices and representations, which by our compulsion to adhere to the structures of "reality" use "proper" proportions, in order to acknowledge instead of expressing. Hence the weight of ("unreal") caricature to dismember elites and forms and institutions that could be called pernicious. And the desire for a glowingly "true" and "real"—as we take it—vision of the way things are.

Reality gets in the way of experience, however. Cheats could be understood as leading not to something pretending to the *real* but to something avowing the beautiful:

> When old age shall this generation waste,
>   Thou shalt remain, in midst of other woe
> Than ours, a friend to man, to whom thou say'st,
>   "Beauty is truth, truth beauty,—that is all
>   Ye know on earth, and all ye need to know."

37

Stand-ins

FIGURE 37 *Barbra Streisand with chorus in* Funny Girl *(William Wyler, Columbia, 1968).*

When we touch one particular and delicious rose, do we find in it a discreet and lonely thing, a creation only to itself, possessed of its own identity and history and life cycle as distinguished from all others? Or do we take seriously the familiar, generalizing epithet, "a rose," familiar because familial, because belonging to a category by which this one blossom and "all blossoms like it" are to be named; and do we use that epithet to abstract away everything that is peculiar and unique in order to locate, elsewhere, in a formal zone, the "essential" traits and probable futures this thing—as a thing of its kind—shares with a wholesale collection, called, if you like, members of its genus and species? Is this flower a member of the category of roses, or is it itself? To me it seems plainly evident that holding the flower between our fingers we are first experiencing a thing in itself, but our way of organizing language promotes the category. Our conceits, linguistic and otherwise, are advertisements for generalization, for advantageous multiplications, for building edifices.

At issue is the problem of substitution, which plagues dramatic representation to the heart, because in categorizing we make what is diffuse substitute for what is specific. We do this by mentally traveling away from the moment of action to what we would prefer to think a discerning (objective) remoteness, not a perception but a reflection; but this new position denies the most complex aspects of what it purports to examine. I am walking down Tottenham Court Road and two young men, approaching me, are having a chat. They come within hearing and one of them literally bursts into laughter, his whole body thrown into the spasm of pink delight. I have no idea what they have been talking about. It is certainly easy enough to say, "That was a laugh," and then to say, "A laugh that will take up only two seconds of the eternity that is this man's life," and then, "Therefore a laugh that seems bold and emphatic but is actually, in the course of things, trivial," and finally, "What a show of enthusiasm that fellow allowed himself to put on, given how perfunctory the whole thing must have been." But of course for the two interlocutors that laugh was, at the moment, everything. For them, nothing could substitute for that laugh, and my substitutive disclaimer thankfully does not exist. My analysis—any analysis—is a substitute for conditions. To sail from Yi-Fu Tuan's port, analysis is the space in which we live; conditions form the place we make of it. This place. Here. Now.

Substitution. Every performance is given by an actor pretending to be—substituting for—a character, to our manifest delight. And every dramatic scene is shot in a particular space substituting for another: a soundstage for a restaurant, a manor house for an embassy. The location scout will find a postmodern building, a museum, say, with an exit to the street that looks very much like the doors to an arrival hall at an airport, so he tells the designer to put up the sign ARRIVALS and the museum is converted. In the film for all the characters involved, and in the audience as we are involved with the film, the building *is* an airport, never less than an airport, never hinting at a museum. In *One From the Heart* (1982), Francis Ford Coppola plays with this substitutive removal by making an airport out of stage flats and having a cardboard airplane take off overhead. Most buildings lack an intrinsic being-in-the-world. A museum may look very much like an airport terminal, an airport terminal like a museum. Nothing about the look of museums designates them, classes them inevitably as museums; their character as museums isn't common, save that they bear a public name. If a bank is to be diegetically robbed in a film story, the management may take a dim view of a film crew shooting their actual facility in connection with a robbery; and so another building will substitute. In a similar manner, stunt personnel will substitute for actors, as will musicians and athletes. In biopics actors substitute not only for characters but also for other people living now or in the past. Barbra Streisand isn't the movie character Fanny Brice;

but she is also not the person Fanny Brice who is being mocked up by that character. Of course neither was Fanny Brice, the performing phenomenon, this or any character or person, as Fanny Brice, because historically she was a woman named Fania Borach. "Fanny Brice" was a product she sold, a substitution with which she came to identify.

In substituting one shooting location for another, filmmakers need only take care to ensure that any specific reputation attaching to the substitute does not read over into the drama, or a quality of the actual place leak through the curtain of the substitution. Caution will be exercised in proximity to recognizable landmarks, lest they creep into the shot. Or, by contrast, caution will be exercised to include the landmark if it can help seal the identification of a location that is actually disconnected from it (against the dictate of the fiction). In *Rebel Without a Cause* (1955), for one example, the concluding sequence calls for the three protagonists to assemble at night at a huge mansion adjacent Griffith Park and within short running distance from the observatory. But the sequence was shot at the Getty Mansion at 6th and South Irving, quite a long way off and with no particular view of the observatory at all. But thanks to careful framing and careful editing the diegetic connection can be made. The edit as a geographic join is all over cinema.

When the viewer experiences an accomplished substitution—one place for another; one person for another—the principal effect is an unrecognized but calculated misdirection. One could gain considerable insight here from a viewing of Orson Welles's *F for Fake* (1973). The ersatz is exchanged *as the authentic*, a situation considered seriously problematic in the economy of material acquisition (the art world) but somehow not only permissible but entirely regular in the economy of fictional transaction (the world of film). In watching film, we never really expect the goods on offer to be what they claim to be, indeed the irony produced by the gap between what they seem and what they are (what they are identified as elsewhere, by those in the know) is a major source of our thrill. We relish fabrication, knowing all along that it is fabrication but being held away from a view of the technique in the wings. "I am fooling you," is a trumpet call we love to hear, but "Let me show you how I'm doing it" is a threat of ruin.

An elementary question: *How is it that we can entertain such pleasure at the patently inauthentic?* What is the relationship between our consciousness of inauthenticity and our devotion to the presence of the moment?

The conception of a visual narrative is a process different from its reception and appreciation, in that a different scale of values is invoked and a different mode of consciousness implied. The material effect being worked through in both production and viewing is the same effect: a showing of the crowd of the everyday, the myriad minute articulations that are life itself (as "conceived" by the characters) at the same time as they are the substance of rational cataloging (for those seeing the surface). In the act of conceiving, it is necessary to block out character types, on the presumption that instead of an uncountable variety of characters viewers should find a far more limited collection of sets, each member of any set being, for all intents and purposes, interchangeable with the others. Sam Spade, Mickey Spillane, Phillip Marlowe, and Hercule Poirot are all the same as types, but differ radically as personalities. If one can manage to apprehend the shared performative characteristics of set members one can replicate them easily, and a recognizable[1] character can emerge—a character observable and comprehensible in terms of the "telling" qualities of the set. This makes not only casting but also direction more fluid and less time-consuming (time having economic weight and thereby constituting a central problem for filmmakers). If one hired Kevin Costner, for instance, to play a pitcher on a baseball team, one would not have to give him the full experience of being one so that he could play the role: anxiety, sleeplessness, arm pain, the rigor of constantly keeping in shape, the difficulties of memorizing statistics on all the opposing batters, and so on. He would need to be thinking of himself as (a) an athlete (type); (b) a baseball player (type); and then (c) a pitcher (type), all of these being generalized and available for inspection on many fronts, not to mention inspection in the files of his own memory since he has played one. Any actor knows there is no way for him to become a particular individual other, but he can establish the form, and this is true, more crucially, even in biopics. There the claim is made and, with labor, supported that the being we watch *is* either the person who is the subject of the film, or an acceptable representation, in short, that a specificity is being performed when the actor and writer are really contriving to effect—since in creating any character for the screen there are no other options—a diffuseness, a generality, a decorated type.[2]

The viewer's moment of appreciation and involvement is of another, more discrete and more incomparable quality, enthusiasm, perhaps, linked to a pervading relaxation into being, a more or less non-conscious devotion to feeling at the moment, even in those odd somewhat cool moments when inspired to distanced rational observation. The viewer becomes enflamed. Norman O. Brown:

> The apocalyptic fire: "Meditate on the make-believe world as burning to ashes, and become *being above human*." (Dante, *Inferno* I, 118–20, qtd. in Brown, *Body* 179)

We sense a world fluttering around, and ourselves in motion there, each passing breath a direct and uncalculated simulation of our sense of presence.

---

[1] The ease of recognition is profitable, and the ease of replication is cost saving, two principal effects of genre filmmaking in the 1930s and onward. See Schatz.
[2] As used here, the terms "specificity" and "diffuseness" are borrowed from Parsons.

The actor must do the same. By virtue of infusing generalized thoughts about a character's type with his own spirit of temporal presence, his pulse of sensitivity, a spirit he always carries about, the actor jettisons the technical categorization scheme out of which he began to fashion the character and now by both reaching and relaxing brings the character to life. That is, "life": fleeting sensibility with all its foibles and snorts.

We are enthused by performance because of this liveliness, exactly. We accept our knowledge of its categorical construction, but then eclipse that knowledge by touching the manifest expressiveness of a being who is tasting time.

38

The Superuniverse

FIGURE 38 *Christian Bale in* The Dark Knight Rises *(Christopher Nolan, Warner Bros., 2012).*

Production cheats have the power to modify intelligence. An example: one of the fashions prevalent in 1930s Hollywood filmmaking, something that made it delicious and imitable, was a recurrent snappy, smart, ironically angled, and poetically flip "patter" dialogue, something born of the (New York) stage. When you are dealing with a stage production there are no close-ups. Some of the viewers are a long way off. What happens of dramatic significance must be made acoustic, and in order to keep up a pace (a tempo) one strikes certain notes with force in imitation of the staccato chain of terse, pregnant, linguistically ornamental speech.[1] Stage writers were brought west to write for Hollywood. In a case like Howard Hawks's *Twentieth Century* (1934), one is sped downriver on a thrilling torrent of Ben Hecht and Charles MacArthur's histrionic jabber.

Film lovers might well try talking in a pithy staccato in everyday life. Language becomes more and more colloquial over the decades, saturated with caustic metaphors and bouncy circumlocutions. The increased pace of social change, broadly speaking, lends to a curtailment of enunciation, a jargonizing and telegraphy. Everyday life soon dominates over the arcing romance of fiction. And fuggedaboudit.

If we consider the Superhero Universe, the Superuniverse, now unboundedly popular by virtue of Marvel Productions, we find a world in which feelingful experience is systematically abbreviated or curtailed; in which commentary and visuality marry—body hurled against plate glass window; face chemically distorted beyond recognition; eyes glued to LED monitors. Heightened contrast is pervasive: dark dark dark dark darkness, bright bright bright stunning brightness. As with patter dialogue and so many other felicities of film production, this universe and its attributes constitute a colossal cheat, one commercially packaged as such, an alluring distraction of thought away from the recognition that (a) as they live people really do feel; (b) there is very often, and not only onscreen, an ironic disconnection between what things look like and what people say; and (c) the world is not a high-contrast zone, broadly speaking. Regarding the last, in working with color cinematography it became necessary for filmmakers to abandon any simplistic ideas about the dark-light black-white contrast, and this is why when we look at neo-noirs (like *Chinatown* [1974]) we find moral extremity embodied in characters and character responses whereas in noir, moral contrast could be expressed instantaneously through lighting (a wondrous example is *Sudden Fear* [1952]). In watching superhero films over and over (as many people do), and gradually becoming so accustomed to, addicted by, the Superuniverse—*whichever* Superuniverse one would care to cite, since structurally they are similar—one picks up these three assumptions about feeling, disconnection, and contrast and begins, as a way of adding weight to one's predisposition, to think of the world as conforming. Politics starts looking like a comic book story, a battle to the death between cold and unfeeling, morally black or white, lying myrmidons. Those who take action seem to do it as feelinglessly as the heroes and villains onscreen. Irony is replaced by incongruity.

---

[1]Reflecting on the casting process for *Six Degrees of Separation* (Vivian Beaumont Theatre, November 8, 1990) John Guare wrote, "We used that time of casting to discuss the play, to understand the rhythm of the play, to hear what the play wanted to be. All I knew about the play was that it had to go like the wind" (xi).

The Superhero cheat is effected through a combination of optical design and scripting; and since a great deal of Superhero cinema is made through CGI, the optical design is seriously saturated, intensified, extrematized. If you have lots of money you can get a computer with enormous memory, and if you have that you can make pictures with a vast number of pixels, and once you can do that you can animate virtually anything, including the reflection of a face in a teardrop. In *Stairway to Heaven* (1946), there is a very, very, very significant teardrop, shown in close-up, and there is no animation of reflections in it, and it touches the viewer to the bone. Because CGI springs from a technology that every day becomes more expensive (as well as more efficient), the rule of thumb is, if you *can* do an effect you *should*. That is, use the technology: what else is it for?

Felt experience. Because the superhero story is an action story, it can contain as subject only action that flows toward action, events that flow swiftly by, that are themselves transported at starcruiser speed. While a character may be required to show emotion—Bruce Banner (Eric Bana) blowing up in greening anger until he becomes The Hulk (2003)—the film will avoid the obstacle of delving into the subtle aspects of feeling, the complications, the troubling contradictions, the unavoidable costs, except as any of these can be compacted into a tightly visualized descriptive glyph. Anger>>{morph}>>Hulk. Angry Hulk >>>> Fist-smashing Hulk. Clark Kent has conflicted, confused feeling about being raised on a farm with gentle people unrelated to his own parents now distantly dead, but we are given to see him only in a cartoonish reference: he stares into the twilit sky, but there is no elaboration of his farm boy's life, a life of chores accommodated to; nor of the city life he will lead at the Daily Planet (the planet that is invented daily; the news as planetary; a body that revolves around a non-solar star, Superman). The simplest way out of addressing the felt experience of the character is by way of concentrating on power, usually some technical capability that can be publicly tested and splendidly revealed. Doc Ock (Alfred Molina) in *Spider-Man 2* (2004) scaling a skyscraper with his tentacles in full public view. He touches the building but the viewer does not touch him. A pose chain thus replaces a tactile exploration.

Visual talk, spoken image. The superhero-film character, most assuredly the villain, will speak in language especially crafted for pungency, shock value, metaphorical twist: heightened expressivity. But this heightening is shaped to balance the extremity of the visualization, not in order to reveal the confounding depths of the character (as happens in Sophocles and Shakespeare and Eugene O'Neill). Much is left unsaid, so that the audience is forced to imagine fill-ins, such as explanations, stabilizations of placement in context, motives. We catch repetitive use (artful syntaxing) of proper names, created for this genre of filmmaking with special attention to musicality, oddity, articulatory sharpness. SPYYY-derr-MAAAAANNN. Peter Parker (picking a peck of pickled peppers profitably). In the superhero film, much as the picture is sharpened for bizarreness of content, angularity of structure, and density of configuration so is language sharpened for percussive, tonal effect. The sound overall might seem Wagnerian.

Contrast. Both the image and the spectrum of evaluation are pushed to extremes, notably stuffed and running over with: blinding incendiary bursts of all sizes (a relatively early, very comely one in *Darkman* [1990]); flashing, even outlandish saturated colors leaping out from bits of muscularized Spandex (see *Green Lantern* [2011]); monstrous shadows lurking around monstrous corners (*Batman* [1989]); looming objectivities—mechanisms, flying bodies—racing toward the viewer's face (*Star Trek Generations* [1994], *Avatar* [2009]); a tightly defined and highly publicized system of honor and social justice (*Sin City* [2005]); a face with seemingly unbounded expressive powers, made hideous for some spectacular reason or entirely obliterated from view in a "brilliant darkness" that reveals covering but no essence (*Watchmen* [2009]); demonstrations of exceptional strength, agility, endurance, and couth (*Superman* [1978]) or the stark opposite, debilitation, degradation, weakness, and fear (*Batman Begins* [2005]); bloody victimization of well-behaved and wholly unmilitaristic civilians (*Superman Returns* [2006]); possession and ostentatious use of exorbitantly expensive high technology (*X-Men Origins: Wolverine* [2009], *Avengers: Infinity War* [2018], *Deadpool* [2016]); uniformed social control teams disabled or revealed to be insufficiently smart (*The Dark Knight Rises* [2012]); bold transformations at once miraculous and scientific(!) in which organic forms are radically altered temporarily or permanently in massive machines that radiate colored light (*Hollow Man* [2000]); and so on. Dreams of power, yet power beyond the human. Never the power to understand, but the power to keep a jet aircraft from falling out of the sky by holding it by the nose or to vaporize buildings or to brainwash.

There is a preponderance of gloom, depression, and panic proudly disrupted by the hero's entrance in high illumination, rampant color, shapely form, sonorous voice, and with a smile to win elections. The darker the scene the more the hero glows in it.

The cheat in superhero movies is strict sidestepping of a colossal truth, the open telling of which would malform or destroy the pleasing process of watching: namely, that there are no superheroes, the Superuniverse does not exist, there are no giant machines injecting a purple fluid that turns some everyday bloke into a musclebound masked Agent of Good. In these so very palpably hyper-theatrical stories, these evidences of arbitrary decision-making and expense, with people obviously addicted to dressing up, flying, swinging, emerging garishly from flames, and clawing the world apart as well, the production conceit works hard to keep viewers from losing interest by focusing expansively and urgently on the figures as constructs and keeping away from the deep logic that supports them. Action flies past in a half-breath, advanced modes of transportation on earth and in space race to a problematic future, the superhero's ultimate prettiness (beneath the mask) fills us with admiration. Yet, too, it is all throbbing toward a finale. Finale is everything. Finale as apocalypse.

All this ranting and racing takes place in a tailor-made setting where gimmicks will always work.

The reminder is offered that the Superuniverse is created for children, that it delivers the sharply delineated moral spectrum as a pedagogical tool, that the color and speed and flash are for uncultivated delight. Yes, but. But it is not because of the ticket-buying children that the Superuniverse nets in untold hundreds of millions of dollars.

Of Joins

{39} Believe in Me
King Kong (1933); *King Kong* (1976); *The Seven Year Itch*

{40} Over Thames
Location selection and usage; plot contrivance and setting; setting and plot fills; *Survivor*

{41} Sequitur
Edit as cheat; spatial/temporal transitions and continuous or discontinuous movement; Hitchcock and Kuleshov; the cheat of causation; *Rear Window*

{42} *Veni creator spiritus*
L'Avventura; viewer consciousness of the filmmaker's presence

{43} "Bite the Dust"
Actors and stunt shots; facial recognition as code; acted characters as individuals; *Baby Driver*; *The Train*; *Gravity*

{44} Reflect On That
Editorial control of shot length and character formation; Bette Davis; *Empire of the Sun*; perspectival shift and involvement

{45} Presence and Presentation
Presence without presentation; presentation without presence; *Eyes Wide Shut*; *Spider-Man*; Robert Walker and *My Son John*; *E.T. the Extra-Terrestrial*

{46} By Contrast
Complexity and simplification; *The November Man*; resolving moral muddles; resolving resilience muddles; *Shane*; *Body of Lies*

{47} The Blood Effect
Leave Her to Heaven; *The Wild Bunch*; *The Godfather*; *Sabotage* (2014); the "blood is everywhere" effect; *Carrie*; *Hamlet*

* * *

{Epilogue: Our Cheating Heart}
Escapes from reality; rejection of performance; *The Thief of Bagdad*; being taken for a ride; *Love Is a Many-Splendored Thing*; *An Affair to Remember*; screen "here" and screen "there"; getting lost; dance; boundlessness; *The Red Shoes*

39

Believe in Me

FIGURE 39 *Jessica Lange in* King Kong *(John Guillermin, Dino DeLaurentiis Productions, 1976).*

A momentary exhalation in Dino De Laurentiis's *King Kong* (1976) when the young and very beautiful Dwan (Jessica Lange), having been seized and carried off by him, stands tremulously in the palm of the megalithic hand of the Great Ape.[1] Start with proportion: were she standing in the palm of my hand and I Kong (I permit myself this odd fantasy) she would be roughly as tall as my index finger is long. That means I would be several times her size, and our Kong is at least that. Very large. Quite hairy. One could imagine rather odorous. And with a face so far up in the clouds she would not really be able to see it well.

---

[1] A July 2019 conversation with Kat Zabecka prompted this meditation on Kong.

As this creature gazes down at her she is a Lilliputian daydream, save that, being no Swift reader, he has no education to help him recognize Lilliput or to imagine whether instead he might be in Brobdingnag. She is both small and quaint and delicate, let us say a kind of doll, yet alive. (As with George Lucas having his Princess Leia emerge from R2-D2's projection, a holographic miniature, this is something of an homage to the projected Altaira in *Forbidden Planet* [1956].) Dwan excites Kong's curiosity, even, if it would not be too bold to imagine this, his quasi-scientific curiosity—and why not fully scientific curiosity—because he concentrates on her frame, her movement, her coloration, her size as though she is a specimen he has recovered. With the other hand he stretches out an index finger to feel her butterfly surface. The fiction of the tale (here and in the earlier *King Kong* [1933]) is that capitalistic adventurers have journeyed to the hidden, remote island where Kong lives in order to follow hints of a mysterious Other; but here it is evident Kong himself is journeying to follow at least the smell of his own mysterious Other, that he is as bent on discovery as his pursuers are. He teases her by bringing her close enough to a waterfall to get soaked. To him Dwan is ineffable.

Are we to suspect, as pop theorizing insists, that he is harboring a throbbing sexual motive? The wild beast and the tender maiden, the *nouveau* dragon and the princess? He would have to come down in size, an unthinkable challenge not only because of his nature but also because the story of strange monumentalism would collapse if he did. It can only be a fascination that leads to Pure Love, the love that brings adoration and surpasses the flesh, a sanctified dream. She has become his beckoning spirit, although it is clear enough that from her point of view beckoning is quite out of the question.

Now, a coup de grâce. The ape exhales, and his warm breath shudders downward and flutters her clothing so that we have a brief echo of Marilyn Monroe (another blonde) in *The Seven Year Itch* (1955). Monroe is on a subway grating, Lange is on a leathery palm; for Monroe the air comes from below, a subversive tickle, while for Lange it drops from above, something of weather. The breath, the flutter, the contact, the deep and unforgettable knowledge.

How on earth did they persuade Jessica Lange to stand in the palm of a giant ape this way? Without visible fear, with only hesitation. How did they find an ape, indeed, whose hand was so large—the palm alone about six feet long or more? Where could such a creature be found? (We might remember with ironized pleasure that the hunters in *Kong* are seeking to make a movie, too; so the thought of our own movie-makers seeking an exoticism for their camera to eat is not such a strange thought.[2]) The answer, of course, and in a word: cheats.

---

[2]The eager, hungry camera is taken to exciting extremes in Pirandello.

This is not Kong's palm. (An incredible statement, because this is Kong, always forever, and here we have his palm.) It is not any kind of palm, medically speaking. It is a large plastic and fabric device with an internal system of hydraulic tubes all powered from without, puppeted. The fingers twitch on command. As she stands there, she is in a set, not a hand. The wrist, the forearm extending upward are parts of the mechanism. There is actually no Kong face exhaling Kong breath. A fan flicked on and off will do the trick, Lange will competently fill in with the appropriate response. Today a realistic palm would be created digitally, and the Lange image matted onto it. In 1976 such a process was as yet unperfected and the mechanical palm was a crest-of-the-wave effects form. A special-effects hand, at any rate, masquerading as a living one. Not so very hard to do, assuming the audience is unfamiliar with giant apes and their hands.

The potential trouble with such a cheat lies in a bent for denial confronting any viewer's deep conviction and belief in the story—the willingness to believe is part of the lure that brings viewers to the theater—a denial insistently affirming that in our world, the world pictured onscreen, there are no giant apes and Kong is nothing but a fabrication for narrative purposes. This hand we see cannot possibly be a real ape's hand. Yet at the same time the viewer takes the position, easily and without consideration, that the girl is a real girl, youthful, vivacious, hungry, radiant. Thus a reality and an unreality are combined for view, the oil not quite mixing with the water. A jarring dysjunction keeps separating the female figure from the mechanical support. She is effectively jolted into hyperperception with every tiny indication falsely imported to the hand: the line of the hand embedded in the leathery "skin," the thing's magnitude and its radical disproportion, even the caution with which the fingers move in a kind of robotic learning curve. How to overcome these subtle yet not so subtle challenges?

The shot will not be long enough to permit objections to mature into arguments. Here, on the page, they can mature a little, but the shot doesn't even last as long as it took you to read these two sentences. Also, Lange's clothing will be designed not only to *feature* her admirable body but also to *appropriately cover it*, to offer rags that seem, in their weird way, fashionable upon her at this instant, and also teasing, both a revelation and a secrecy. She will become, for only the spate of Kong's breath, a fashion model, a figure who arrests the eye and brings focus.[3] Next, the "breath" fluttering that garment will seem to touch her skin, too, a thrilling glaze, and any reaction to this on the viewer's part will take attention away from doubt. The same can be said for the marvel of the disproportion as it fully hits, since in all of the interaction between Dwan and the ape we have never yet seen a measurable comparison like this. And then a factor that effects artists can

---

[3] Not strangely. In the early 1970s, Jessica Lange was a fashion model in New York.

always knowingly count upon, that a voice inside the viewer beckons her to go along with the story development no matter what, to move forward, to push aside any looming obstacles to such motion, else the pleasure of the entertainment will be hopelessly lost. Believe in Kong. Otherwise the dark tunnel of doubt that leads to the depressing daylit realization that one was a fool buying a ticket to be here. One can see easily that with the advent of widespread and intensified exhibition outside of theaters, on a basis that does not call for quid-pro-quo payment film by film, the problem of belief and denial is exacerbated, and effects must be hyped.

Indeed, all of *King Kong* requires that we believe in Kong. Wonder about him, love him, care for his future. Consider now, just for a quick juxtaposition, the final moments in the 1933 original. Having escaped from the Broadway stage(!), the ape has rampaged through the city (fifteen blocks in reality) and climbed the tallest tree he can manage to find in this jungle, which is, of course, the Empire State Building.[4] Perched at the top vulnerably, proudly, in torment, he can do nothing but succumb to the air force. And although when he falls the long shot utterly fails to mobilize sympathy, since it is only a scientifically calculated demonstration of an object taking a long fall through space, the body upon the ground stirs us to the heart, not just because Kong has been killed by modern civilization (what else could happen?) but because here and all along he was our pet. We were attached to him, artificial as he seemed, and so we believed. We loved the artificial-and-living Kong, or the toy that simulated life, much as when we are children we loved our own favorite mechanisms and endowed them with both life and consciousness. Speaking to our toys we believed in them, and when he lies dead we finally speak to Kong. When he lies dead, having returned from the dead and died again, we speak to Kong.

---

[4]In the 1976 film, the setting is updated from the Empire State Building to the World Trade Center, a technical problem for Peter Jackson and crew making another remake in 2005. They again used the Empire State Building as a model of triumphalist height.

40

Over Thames

FIGURE 40 *Aerial view of the Thames over Waterloo Bridge in* Survivor *(James McTeigue, Millennium, 2015).*

James McTeigue's *Survivor* (2015) is an elaborate wild goose chase, with an international assassin of high social standing(!) hired to knock off a young American intelligence officer working in the Visa Department at the Embassy in London. The handsome Pierce Brosnan, being evil for a change; the charming and purposive Milla Jovovich. Neither her pals at the Embassy, Dylan McDermott, Robert Forster, and Frances de la Tour nor the American ambassador Angela Bassett prove of any help—of course. We jitter around Bloomsbury and the West End, mostly at night, and Kate Abbott, our smarty-pie but wholly innocent heroine, narrowly escapes explosions, bullets, knives, and what have you. All this is somehow in aid of a master plot to make use of a profoundly disgruntled, vengeful European scientist (Roger Rees), whose wife died because the Americans kept insisting on more paperwork before giving the visa that would permit her to have proper medical treatment in the United States. Dr. Balan (anagram: banal), as he is known, is an expert in mixing gases, and we discover to our presumable chagrin that he plans to pump full the twinkly ball that descends in Times Square on New Year's Eve. *Think of all the death!!!!*

It therefore seems inevitable that the action must speed by air—through airline checkpoints not a single one of which manages to filter strangers as they are intended to do—from London to New York. The pretext was present from the beginning, since we learned then, from Kate and her chums, that "tomorrow" is December 31. New Year's is presumably synonymous in the domain of movie terrorism with Times Square ("There are a million people there! You saved all of them!"). Thus, we can hardly expect the finale to take place (not that it actually does *take place*) anywhere else. We can hardly expect the matted-in footage to show any other mountaintop.

Why, then, so much action in London ("She was assigned to London—that's a high-ranking post!")? Why so much at night (when visual details are hard to pick out)? Why is the rehearsal (the killer has a long-range rifle he can use to shoot at the target "bomb" from anywhere) set in London, not in New York? Why the presence of the London police (abysmally inept)? Why the constant invocation of the Home Office?

All of the footage is tidily scenarized, competently photographed, straightforwardly it not even musically edited, and, as may be expected of such films, generous as a handsome travelogue for those interested in London (New York does not get such treatment): but the production could have been set anywhere. Even in New York itself.

Producers will often push scripts to define locations in which it is both convenient and inexpensive to shoot; in which closure of streets and perhaps subway tunnels (a long tunnel scene occurs), crowd control, and location transformation are all possible with relative ease and in which the shooting fees are minimal. New York is not such a place. Indeed, very little footage was needed there to invoke the place. And shooting London by night makes it easier for the designer-cinematographer team to hide revealing signs, alleys, windowfronts, etc. that could intrude on the action. Moreover, there has been developed and broadcast a certain teleological cachet about London: a place where meticulous language will be used consistently by slightly pompous bureaucrats who prove inutile; an imperial sedateness that makes a perfect background for disruptive action; a high-tech communications dreamspace, with CCTV cameras ready to record on every corner (yet not catch the villain, who always knows how to stand out of view, else the film will be done in fifteen minutes). In America, for all its cultural alertness, things are slacker and more haphazard, not a proper setting for the erudite Brosnan and the athletic Jovovich to play in. To ice the cake, the American never quite *belongs* in London in the way that the British do (and all British persons here are typically considered and dubbed Londoners); the American is too casual, too energetic, too brash, too inventive, too disrespectful of formality. Thus, the home secretary, whoever he or she is, will be wholeheartedly disattended; the British police barked at; the calmly ordered London streets (London is a paragon of social order) strewn with explosive detritus or raced through with no concern for the rules of the road. In placid Hyde Park a nice murder can take place, with the astute British population standing around filming it on their cellphones.

When I note that the production could have been set anywhere I am stymied by one startling shot, that works to wash away that hypothesis and propose London as not only an ideal but also an essential site. Between two sequences of differing action, we have a simple transitional shot, something intended—as are so very many shots of this kind, in films these days—to vaguely suggest the passing of time, languidly and serenely, in a notable, beautiful place while turmoil and angst jitter anxiously in hiding all around. This one is taken from the air at pitch of night, looking down onto the Thames from the East and gliding from the City toward the South Bank, with the twinkly cobalt blue chain of the Jubilee Bridge at screen-top, the London Eye all blue-lit at left, and Waterloo Bridge far off, blanketed by light from Westminster. The Embankment is a strand of genuine pearl. This shot is the edit cheat that stitches London tightly into the picture, makes London instantly identifiable and inevitable as the scene of action, even though we flit off to Manhattan for the explosive—or not-quite-explosive—finale. To be noted:

- Diegetically speaking, this transition shot is as entirely unnecessary as London is to this film. It moves us from one time of day to another, from one place to another, in an abstract, contemplative way, yet virtually any shot made for aesthetic consideration and kept onscreen for a few seconds could accomplish this purpose.
- It establishes our presence in London, but in a way that all of the action scenes heretofore have not managed. We have been relentlessly caught up in action, and to the end of following action we have taken our views of London navigationally: what sort of place is this?, how might we flee from here to safety somewhere *else* (but not necessarily in a location we can be expected to recognize)? This transitional shot says *London . . . world capital . . . withdrawal into perspectival stability.* Withdrawal, as in pulling away, lifting up, ascending over the fray, looking down on the battlefield to estimate the tactical advantages here and there. Yet also reveling in the dark of night when no battle is in progress, quite as though one were scouting the terrain of a performance—a set—before stepping onto it. Robert Wise, Jerome Robbins, and cinematographer Daniel Fapp originated an aerial perspective-as-stable-withdrawal shot at the beginning of *West Side Story* (1961), giving over a very peaceful and meditative shot of the Bronx where, once we zoomed in, teenage angst would dance. Here there is no such zoom.

- More than a place of potential action in the dark, this twinkling urban space suggests pure meditation, light arrayed against the absence of light, geometrical form (the Eye; the river) for the appraiser's evaluation. But also:
- A place unmistakably in London, thus unmistakably in the United Kingdom, and removed from America. The watcher can easily be persuaded that London is important to the story—London, the Royal imperative, the withheld insult, the cuppa tea—whereas ultimately it is not. Even if we examine the action in London we find that the settings are arbitrary, as though economically sensible from the producer's point of view more than diegetically sensible from the writer's. English spots, English manners, English characters are all *written in*, but we could be seeing Americans in Chicago, just as well.
- Our principal hero, Kate, is an American citizen and American-trained specialist discovered at an American embassy working visa applications. Why London, there are American embassies all over the world? Because she has been seconded to London, a *prime appointment*, for her special expertise. Special, expert, careful, responsible, meticulous, now "British"—verrry nice cuppa tea! We could as well find her in Paris, Tel Aviv, Buenos Aires, Toronto. Are the rates good in London? Further,
- The London connection allows the film to ring with both British hierarchical stiffness and decorum and British elegance, wealth, power, and stiff lip. Brosnan, not only a much experienced player in action cinema but a fine character actor as well, hails from Ireland and spent his youth in England. He echoes a suave European flair, self-transforming into a Man of the World with inestimable cultural groundings and devotion to refinement and precision. A dangerous enemy. The battle between him and Jovovich will be a traditional USA-UK match, her feisty no-nonsense can-do against his polished technique and diabolical perseverance. European types like this villain can be found sipping their cuppa anywhere, though. Clive Owen plays an interesting one in *The Bourne Identity* (2002) and Vincent Cassel in *Jason Bourne* (2016). The stand-off could occur in San Francisco, Mexico City, Hong Kong. But not with the accompaniment of:
- A dignified, tranquil, patiently reflective, and deliriously distracting sense of *being in London*, London to which the world comes in wait, London Queen of the Empire, London historical, London classical. Espionage London, torture London, labyrinthine London. Ye olde London. And therefore,

- *Not—America.* A film that is (a) about America and American iconography, (b) a military threat against American interests, (c) a reminder of 9/11, the American Tragedy, exponentially larger than which the finale will prove to be, if it is not heroically thwarted, (d) fueled by American intelligence and military power, that is, the ambassador and the president and other invisible types who communicate by omnipresent telephones, (e) arranged to depict, finally, a quintessential American scene, Times Square on New Year's Eve; all this, and yet at the same time a film that gives all appearances of being about Britain. Gives appearance because of, yet not only because of, this transitional nighttime reverie, a reverie that brings to focus, assembles, conjoins, even melds all of the English references in the film thus far into a single coherent—if also rather empty—image of sedate, orderly, long-enduring cultural thrust.

41

Sequitur

FIGURE 41 *Claude Rains (l.) and Humphrey Bogart in* Casablanca *(Michael Curtiz, Warner Bros., 1942)*.

Edmund Husserl wrote of time in 1905, the year Einstein published his Special Theory of Relativity:

> From an Objective point of view every lived experience, like every real being [*Sein*] and moment of being, may have its place in the one unique Objective time—consequently, also the lived experience of the perception

and representation [*Vorstellung*] of time itself. . . . It may further be an interesting study to establish how time which is posited in a time-consciousness as Objective is related to real Objective time, whether the evaluations of temporal intervals conform to Objective, real temporal intervals or how they deviate from them. (22–3)

Françoise Dastur observed that for Husserl, time "constituted the most crucial problem for philosophy. This problem marks the limits of its enterprise of intellectual possession of the world" (179). As we attempt to apprehend cinematic time, thinking back to Husserl, we can note not only that the cinematic work is ongoing in its essence but also that within it, through editing, various manifestations of contextually external time are offered for consideration. One is causality, in which some B eventuating after some A is considered to result from it, to be caused by it, even to be impossible without the prior eventuation of A. There is an instant in Jim Jarmusch's *Dead Man* (1995) when William Blake (Johnny Depp) is struck in the chest by a bullet, and what happens thereafter is a sequence of journeys he makes into the wilderness that end with his expiration. Here is a separation of A from B by an intermediate parade of events, but we never have doubt that his death, B, eventuates from his being shot, A, although the intermediate events accrete upon one another in fascinating arrays and overlayerings. Causality may come up as a thought, then. That B comes from A. And this can be nicely confounded if by means of a flashback technique we do not actually see A until after we have seen B. In diegetic exposition B leads to A, but we take the exposition to be in reference to an Objective time in which A of course preceded B. Mervyn LeRoy's *Random Harvest* (1942) gives a very beautiful example. But causality is a relatively determinate calculation, a thought that has limited utility.

Eventuality itself is another possibility. The arrival of things after things, the ongoingness of the world. When Merleau-Ponty writes,

> If time is the dimension in accordance with which events drive each other successfully from the scene, it is also that in accordance with which each one of them wins its unchallengeable place (457)

he does not specify, but with his antimony clearly means, that the placing of events is provisional, that any event winning an unchallengeable place will later be driven successfully from the scene by another event winning another place. The ongoingness of cinema, perpetual, is its sense of time, its acknowledgment of eventuality. That B appears after A, and that in seeing the movement from A to B thanks to some method of editing we can have the sensation of a flowing forward, with or without causality. It is the "afterwardness" that strikes us, the sequentiality. Time in the film seems to be unspooling just as the film itself does, moving forward so that events precede and then flow after each other. Rick (Humphrey Bogart) and Renault (Claude Rains) stride across the gleamy tarmac by night, heading for a new friendship, and this happens, this can only happen, after Rick puts a bullet into Col. Strasser (Conrad Veidt) who is trying to make a phone call (*Casablanca* [1942]). Sugar Kane (Marilyn Monroe) confides to Daphne and Josephine (Jack Lemmon, Tony Curtis) in her train compartment after she is seen by them striding down the platform to get onto the train (*Some Like It Hot* [1959]). Even two eventualities posed as "temporally contiguous" need not bear an implication of causality yet there is flow: spoiled Veda (Ann Blyth) doesn't want her mother Mildred (Joan Crawford) to kiss her goodnight, "It's sticky," and then she turns away to sleep but with her eyes hungrily open (*Mildred Pierce* [1945]). And when in a diegesis a configuration is put forward of two eventualities happening "simultaneously" in different locations (the desperate radio conversation at the beginning of *Stairway to Heaven* [1946]), there is no way for cinema to *offer* the simultaneity other than a flowing forward, excepting arbitrary use of effects (like split-screen) seen through the viewer's knowing assumption that without them, simple forward progression would have been the only way (*Pillow Talk* [1959]). Even in the split-screen, the sides of the "simultaneity" have to be optically curtailed, one following the other, to aid focus.

Yet also, the production of editorial sequencing, indeed of filming itself, occupies a time quite separate, a time lived in the editor's or cinematographer's experience and quite prior to the existence of the filmic sequentiality that can affect us. When we watch a film, we do so without consciousness of the temporal relation between watched eventualities in the Objective time of the filmmakers. Which scene was shot before which scene. Which scenes were cut together before which others. Which performer, indeed, was hired before which other performer and was waiting on the set to give a welcoming hello. Our opportunity while watching film to assess temporal flow, sequence, eventuality, even causality, is all produced through a cheat.

Every edit is a cheat of sorts. It is a way of joining two pieces of film, which amount to two fragments of experience, so as to make them seem intrinsically bound in a continuity which stands upon a unity. Even the tactic of cutting across space and time, as cinema is so pronouncedly capable of employing, brings together vastly separated zones into what is felt as a harmonic and fluid march. Film's unspooling makes every advance a continuity.

Every discontinuity a continuity.

We have all heard the Hitchcock hymn to Kuleshov:

> You have an immobilized man looking out. That's one part of the film. The second part shows what he sees and the third part shows how he reacts. This is actually the purest expression of a cinematic idea. [Vsevolod] Pudovkin dealt with this, as you know. In one of his books on the art of

montage, he describes an experiment by his teacher, [Lev] Kuleshov. You see a close-up of the Russian actor Ivan Mosjoukine. This is immediately followed by a shot of a dead baby. Back to Mosjoukine again and you read compassion on his face. Then you take away the dead baby and you show a plate of soup, and now, when you go back to Mosjoukine, he looks hungry. Yet, in both cases, they used the same shot of the actor; his face was exactly the same.

In the same way, let's take a close-up of [James] Stewart looking out of the window at a little dog that's being lowered in a basket.[1] Back to Stewart, who has a kindly smile. But if in the place of the little dog you show a half-naked girl exercising in front of her open window, and you go back to a smiling Stewart again, this time he's seen as a dirty old man! (Truffaut 214–15)

Here, speaking into the ear of François Truffaut, Hitchcock is being puckish as well as informative. His clear fascination is for the exact effects a filmmaker can cause through shot manipulation by editing: the placement of shots in a linear row, one before another. Eyes>>baby>>Eyes: Eyes>>soup>>Eyes for Kuleshov (fond, perhaps, of babies and soup) and Stewart>>doggie>>Stewart: Stewart>>half naked girl>>Stewart for Hitchcock (fond, perhaps, of both doggies and half-naked girls). What Hitchcock does *not* trouble to elaborate, but what calls urgently for elaboration, is the very principle implicit in the forward movement of the edits.

This is a matter of huge interest to those who make and those who study "slow cinema." A subsequence can seem no different than what it is subsequent to.

Normally we are given to read any B as ensuing from, reacting to, even caused by an A that preceded it, even when B is a retreat to an earlier diegetic time and therefore diegetically the cause of A. (Coming diegetically first, our B is truly an A.) As we read forward, all the words that emerge from the text *refer back to*, take their meaning from, and keep the rhythm of the words that came earlier. The Kuleshov "experiment" works exactly because we are prepared, or willing, to think that if we see a man looking and then see an object, that object is the thing that man is looking at. Immaterial that a crafty writer-editor team can fool the audience's calculations by breaking that formula sleekly; the point is that there is a formula to be broken.

There is a formula dictating that one thing leads to another. One thing has been led to by another.

(Continuity is a requirement for cinema because frames come one after another.)

---

[1] Hitchcock is here chatting with Truffaut about *Rear Window* (1954).

Except that one thing does not lead to another. Experience is hardly so simple. In the realism of cinema we reduce experience to simple, digestible arrangements. A woman reaches out to a door handle, turns it, opens a door and walks forward. After a cut we see her emerge from a doorway (from the other side of that door: *that* door, the door I have just mentioned) into another space. The rationale of editing would teach us that the two rooms are contiguous, that the door leads from Room 1 to Room 2 straightforwardly; but also that in making that move, nothing at all is happening for the woman beside taking herself out of one place and inserting herself into another. Since movement is all we see, movement is all there is. Cute narrative games can be played here. When she arrives in Room 2, looking the same, in fact a year has passed and all the conditions of her existence have changed. Or in Room 2 she loses her whole memory of Room 1 and cannot figure out how and why she is here. A forward edit: being somewhere, then later forgetting that one was there. Or in Room 1 she forgets why and how she is there, but she reaches forward, turns a doorknob, and moves into Room 2, where suddenly she remembers being in Room 1.

The logic of the forward edit is meant to apply to the viewer more than to the character. When in *Rear Window* Stewart looks out of his window, *we* look out of his window. And when "Stewart sees" a half-naked girl dancing, *we* see that girl. We look, we see. As though nothing else intrudes, nothing else is subjected to consideration, no daydream, no reflective thought, no sideways glance, no retrieval of memory. Look>>see>>be. We look before we see. Or do we see before we look? Is it possible to look without having seen?

Considerable work has been done by filmmakers who are broadly considered "experimental"—Stan Brakhage, Paul Sharits, Maya Deren, Michael Snow, Hollis Frampton, R. Bruce Elder, to name only some—to the end of producing cinematic motion with edited pieces but without building in the essentially formulaic dictate of causality, eventuality, process; or, more broadly, to the end of invoking a greater process, more poetic and less journalistic, more natural and less arbitrary. But the narrative edit is always a kind of cover blinding us to the world of happenstance, reflection, consideration, dream, by offering a direct map to eventualities, forthcomings, finales. A map cheat.

Hitchcock uses *Rear Window* to explore its own system of cheating at a crucial moment when Jeff (James Stewart) becomes so enraptured watching Thorwald (Raymond Burr) across the courtyard (a man he suspects strongly of having butchered his wife) that he takes his eyes away from another apartment down below, where Miss Lonelyhearts (Judith Evelyn), a middle-aged woman he was spying on a moment before while she was disappointed on a date, has now apparently downed a bottle of pills. Hitchcock's point at this instant, yet also throughout the film, is that many things are going on at the same time all around, the apartment structure (elaborate and expensive) mainly a mechanism for setting before the camera (before Jeff, who uses a camera, too) a manifold spread, manifold but at the same time a spread only a part of which can be taken in at any one moment. With every act of gazing we may establish connections, discover clues, as Jeff does; but with every act of gazing we are taking our eyes away from something else, possibly equally potent, possibly dire. To do otherwise we would need a greater eye, the eye that is shown in close-up (to our horror) in *The Fly* (1958).

Anyone would know that the solitary reality under consideration at any moment is not the only reality, that one's logic does not stand alone in the world. And yet the cinematic process, by way of the editor's cheat, makes us sense ourselves bearers of such an omnipotent logic, sole, solitary, independent, floating, unless (as with *Rear Window*) some direct notice is given that we are not. Always, with or without notice, something vital is happening here, now, that I do not see.

42

Veni creator spiritus

FIGURE 42 *Gabriele Ferzetti and Monica Vitti in* L'Avventura *(Michelangelo Antonioni, Cino del Duca, 1960).*

And indeed, something is happening directly before my eyes, while I am watching, exactly while I am watching, and it escapes me. Evades my watch.

Michelangelo Antonioni's *L'Avventura* (1960) has a small group of wealthy familiars escaping for a while to a little volcanic island. Rocky, boldly sunlit, in a tranquil Mediterranean. A very *little* island, this; "the volcanic stump of Lisca Bianca" (Sinclair 107). Certainly as old as 4000 BC. They clamber about, like so many happy crabs. Our principals: the beautiful Anna (Lea Massari), her boyfriend Sandro (Gabriele Ferzetti), her chum Claudia (Monica Vitti). We follow the action, sparkling black and white, hot blazing afternoon, prehistoric rocks. Anna is suddenly gone.

Anna is gone.

Where can she be, Anna? Anna? Anna?[1] An aggressive search, every crevice, every sea-washed nook, the foamy waters all around, the blazing sun. Can she have gone into the water to swim away? Away where? To death? Is there a hidden cave?—no, there is no hidden cave. Anna has gone. This is early in the film, within the first twenty minutes or so. The story continues for about another two hours. Anna never reappears. Is Claudia concerned all this time? Is Sandro always everywhere endlessly searching for Anna, no matter what else comes into his life?

Might Anna have been an illusion in the first place, an illusion considerably more potent than the illusions of cinema, even? The film seems grounded in the practical, not in illusion. Sandro has his feet on the ground, physically if not morally.

We ride the boat. We come to the island. We hop onto the rocks. We explore. We laugh. We tease. We run and we climb. Always forms, shadows from the hot sun, glare, more forms, old forms, rocks from a billion billion years ago, the sea, the everlasting sea. Where and when can she have disappeared? She was here, before our eyes, and now she is not here.

There is, then, a Force beyond the social forces at play in the story, the class, the attitude, the aspiration, the regret. Name the force Antonioni; name it God; name it Creator Spirit. *Veni creator spiritus!* This force is in action over and above—entirely independent of—our seeing the results; it causes happenings and it erases happenings; it places before us, like so many gifts to the emperor laid out on a fabulous carpet, all the creatures we need to see, with their anxieties, their questions, their hopes, their abject fears. Vitti's character (as so very often in Antonioni's work) is a notable case of pent-up anxiety covered over by smooth grace. Everything is forcefully (if calmly) laid out, all the conditions carefully spelled, the whole temperature of the afternoon's fun dictated firmly by the quality of the sunlight and the forms of the rocks. If everything is here, if everything has been *given*, then . . .

Then Anna's absence is also here.

The emptiness is also given.

But here Antonioni executes a masterful plan. He does not play with the conventions of the edit, the way one shot leads to another, the way we are led first to feel expectations mounting and then to make a detection on the basis of those expectations. He simply waits for a shot to terminate—any good reason: the film runs out, the sun hides momentarily behind a solitary cloud, a wind comes up blowing the women's skirts, anything—and when

---

[1] "Massari suffered a heart attack and was unable to complete a swimming sequence. The assistant director, Franco Indovina, pulled on a petalled cap and bikini to double the passage between pleasure boat and shore" (Sinclair 107).

the camera is off he simply rescues Massari from the film. Ultimate Force, he reaches into the narrative ongoing before him and he withdraws one of the beings, simply. "Grazie. That is all for you."[2]

Anna/Massari vanishes not behind a rock, not in the waves, not on the far side of the island, but in a pause made by the Creator Spirit, a pause placed off-camera. Her vanishing makes us starkly aware of the camera, the island as setting, the Creative Force operating all this while at the same time lingering before our sensibility like a vagrant perfume. So: not everything that happens in a film needs to be seen happening. Not everything we see is a happening. There are two worlds, one before the lens and another behind it, two worlds, two horizons. Anna not only exists in both; she moves from one to the other. And for the filmmaker, conscious of the twinning of his world, she never dies.

---

[2] "And please remain nearby for twenty-four hours so that we can be assured no re-takes will be necessary before you fly off," would be the typically understood farewell on a real set.

43

"Bite the Dust"

FIGURE 43 *George Clooney in* Gravity *(Alfonso Cuarón, Warner Bros., 2013)*.

When the action gets swift the body almost always disappears. The editor's problem when the story launches into a hot-blooded pursuit, a precipitous dangle, a fight, a horseback chase, an extra-vehicular activity, the climbing of a construction crane—the problem and the challenge is to find a way to do two things, apparently at the same time, although in practical effect different shots are made and very skillfully cut together. First, quite beside the long shot that will show the terrain, the complexity, and the challenge—*why fear has a place here*—be certain to feature the principal character, clearly identifiable, and heroic in deed. Next, keep the actor who is playing that character from having to do anything at all, since a recognizable character doing something is intrinsically interesting in herself but here it is the pulse that is important.

Why must the actor be kept out of the stunt shot? A question that has become too innocent for words in the wake of the 1983 death of Vic Morrow while filming *Twilight Zone: The Movie* for John Landis (and not staying out of a stunt shot). Stunt work has a dangerous edge. While it is true that in any movie shot accidents can happen, in stunt shots special safeties are put in play:

- Stunt performers are expert at what they do, and can be differentiated according to expertises with different kinds of action. They have performed the actions in question more than anyone else on the set; they have learned the inside tricks.
- Stunt performers work with directors and cinematographers to plan out the precise action of every single shot, so as to place maximal advantage on their own safety.
- Crew members are generally sensitive to stunt work and its inherent difficulties, and work hard, if necessary with numerous takes, to get a shot right, injury-free.
- Stunt performers are insured differently than actors are, and part of the complexity of the stunt shot is the producer's need to have it accomplished with no untoward extra costs to the production, beyond the specialized equipment needed.
- Given the planning, the detailed labor, and the knowledge involved, generally speaking stunt shots are not at all as hair-raising or life-threatening as they appear onscreen. Much (cheated) exaggeration can be produced through lens choice, camera speed, and filming angle; as well as through sound editing. We tend to see what we hear. Sound editing is a fascinating aspect of the driving shot, because cars move much more slowly than they are posited as moving in the story. The sound of revving motors covers (cheats) the actual movement. Where there is no reason for diegetic sound, a music track works effectively as cover.

Stunters and stand-ins are selected for reasons of physique: in a medium-long or long shot, dressed in matching costume, with a wig if necessary, the performer will be indistinguishable from the star as long as he or she is in motion and the shot is relatively brief (Karen Sharpe supposedly climbing out of the window of a moving city bus, in high heels, in *The Disorderly Orderly* [1964]). This leads to a dialectic worth considering. Seen up close, we have a star persona with recognizable features supporting the affection of a fan base (eager to buy tickets). The character has already, by this point, become identical to the star, identical at least to some modulated (made-up) version of the star playing this particular role. Because of the star identity more than because of the writing, we are moved to love the character, feel for the character, engage with the character, and *care about* the character's life chances and safety. In this way we are set up to be concerned about the character moving through quick action and courting danger. The courting is performed by a stand-in, that is, comes from the behavior of not an actor/character but a stranger/character we can reasonably believe to be the actor/character; yet at the same time reasonably hope is not, since the actor would get hurt and this stranger is inviolably magical in talent and stamina.

While the action flows—and typically the editing is accomplished with very short pieces of film, running as briefly as a quarter of a second—we feel a certain comfort in relaxing away from the screen and mapping the movement (for which process designers assist us by dressing the protagonists in either especially visible colors or easily detectable body suits). We sit back, we ease into the rhythm of the action, we generalize the antagonism, drawing it further and further away from Hero/actor vs. Villain/actor until it is wholly morphed into the moral panorama of Good vs. Evil. As long as we find ourselves watching a competitive "sport" between two discernable teams, and as long as we are comfortable rooting for one of them, we can lose our anxious fear that the hero will be hurt *as an individual*. Any wound produced will be diegetic, a "hurt" that facilitates the plot (Luke Skywalker losing his forearm in *The Empire Strikes Back* [1980]). To keep stoking that fear between moments of release, to produce a fearful-relaxed-fearful-relaxed-fearful-relaxed pattern, an ideal pattern for hooking the suspicious eye, editors will cut back and forth between medium-long or long shots of the motion (including vehicles, stunt actors, and background with intensified scenic illumination) and matching very close shots meant to indicate that the player we have been watching is "really" the star we love. The star we love, now amazingly a race driver, a mountain climber, a skydiver, an acrobat.

Some moments of performer disappearance are without intrinsic threat. The character and some associate are to be seen driving swiftly down a road, with enough of the road visible that the car and the passengers are very small. Here, stand-in stunt drivers are used (they cost less per day than the star does). In car chase scenes, we move back to the close/distant paradigm I discuss above, some particularly challenging and, for many, pleasurable examples being the car chases in Paul Greengrass's Bourne films. In these, the intercut shots of Matt Damon as Bourne are very swift, sometimes of a hand on a gear knob for only eight or nine frames. The head shots typically show expressions of extraordinary intensity, but only to lead into long shots of a vehicle operating entirely outside the rules (such as driving against oncoming traffic on the wrong side of a busy road).

The action sequence tends to be arranged in such a way that the viewer must make a trade-off. To get the full value of the *attractions* phase, the shots of cars flipping or exploding, mountains crumbling, helicopters bursting into flame, shots looking down on dinosaurs or on faces smashed in or on marksmen grimacing as they eye their scopes . . . the payoff must be a thrill, not a recognition: one temporarily relinquishes a hold on the star/character as a discrete individual. One must be ready to do this, and a common strategy for handling the cognitive dissonance (as Leon Festinger called it) is to deny that the star/character is being taken away. The denial is effected through wholesale acceptance of the stunt substitute as character, this allowing for a continuity of belief that the same person we see behind the wheel in a close shot is the one driving the car off a cliff. "The star vanishes." = "The star cannot vanish." In this curious way, stardom with all its accompaniments is congealed with attraction, the flamboyance of personality with the flamboyance of the screen as a whole (because that screen flamboyance is essentially what the action sequence achieves for the viewer's pleasure).

Ansel Elgort's spectacular driving sequences in *Baby Driver* (2017) perfectly exemplify the action problem, while at the same time humorously mocking stunt driving itself, since Baby drives as though his dream in life is to be a stunt driver in the movies. Here we must cut between clear shots of the actor at the wheel, or using his hand to yank the emergency brake as he turns, and shots of the car speeding down the road balletically with "Baby" at the wheel, Elgort here supplanted by a stunt driver. It is possible nowadays to photograph inside a moving car with a hand-held camera so that rear-projected backgrounds are not needed, but the car cannot be moving so quickly that the world outside becomes only a blur.

The conventions of action design and editing notwithstanding, a very elegant ornament can be played upon the "disappearing star" theme. Given our expectation, once it has been cultivated, for seeing star portraits and action long shots in alternation, and for knowing or suspecting that doubles are being used in the long shots, a filmmaker might try something daring, something we may think a cheat of a higher order. The star could be asked to shoot the entire passage, yet in such a way that, relatively invisible in them, she *appears not to inhabit* the long shots and be replaced by a stunt double, *while in fact this is not the case*. (For obvious reasons this couldn't be done in shots posing actual danger.) In such a construction, the star-character identity does dissolve in the longer shots, to be replaced by a stunter-character identity, except that the actor is the stunter. Given poor visibility (strategized in any number of ways), the star face is not visible as such. The viewer thus experiences the same alternation between recognition and calculated observation, recognition of the star up close and calculation of the trajectory of the act seen at a distance, as in conventional action sequences, *without realizing fully* that there are no substitutions being made. Again, the viewer is tricked.

One can see this system in place very dramatically in the locomotive sequences of John Frankenheimer's *The Train* (1964), in which Burt Lancaster does all the engine-driving shots himself. Lancaster was an athlete before he was an actor, however. He had the training for moving skillfully in undoctored space, such as the cabin of an engine or the river area beside a railway track. But a very elegant passage illustrating the apparent absence but continuing presence of the star is the Kowalski death sequence in Alfonso Cuarón's *Gravity* (2013). Here, the extensive and complex use of animation effects, elaborate body rigging, and flexible camera movement make possible stunts that are only "stunts." I use the asterisk (*) to indicate character moments that will seem to be played by stunt doubles, since the identificatory face is not sufficiently visible; yet the entire sequence was shot with the principal stars:

[1] A long shot (14 sec.) of Ryan Stone* (Sandra Bullock) in full spacesuit outside her capsule, black space in the background, as she plummets toward the camera writhing desperately. (Treble high-tech static soundtrack.) As she somersaults her leg is caught in some floating cabling attached to the vessel. She comes toward, then past the camera, moving swiftly so that the face inside the helmet is not identifiable. She flies off screen-right as the camera turns to show the earth beneath her. She comes to the end of the tether and is drawn to the side, first across a land mass and then across several strands of cloud. CUT.

[2] Picking her up on the return, as with the earth below she approaches us again. When she is close, and we can see the Bullock face inside the helmet, she is reaching forward (toward us) with her extended right hand. Her hand fills the upper left of the screen. (7 sec.)

[3] CUT TO her view, with that hand at screen right reaching. The vessel is in the background with *Kowalski (George Clooney) heading her way on his own tether as the camera rotates. He is upside-down to her alignment, and their hands graze each other but do not connect. Upside-down he moves away as they still reach. Her extended hand grasping nothing signals the desperation of the moment. His tether extends from lower screen left. He becomes smaller as, with one hand and then the other, she keeps reaching. (8 sec.) CUT.

[4] MATCHING SHOT, her hand at screen left, *Kowalski twisting against the background of the earth in the distance, flailing. Her hand, foreground, has his tether. (2 sec.) CUT.

[5] *Him appearing to glide off. (1/4 sec.) CUT.

[6] Ryan has his tether in hand, ship behind her, being drawn forward across the screen. (2 sec.)

[7] EXTREME LONG SHOT. Fragment of capsule at left, fragment of earth at right, black space filling the screen. **Two very tiny creatures, the left one tethered to the ship and holding the tether of the second. (2.5 sec.)

[8] With tether extending from screen left, Kowalski looking forward at Ryan and both twisting and yanking with a shout. (1 sec.)

[9] With tether at right, Ryan's reaction, being yanked. (1 sec.)

[10] Closer shot of Kowalski, looking up at her. He is muttering, as he fills the screen, and is being pulled toward us. (3 sec.)

[11] AS IN [9]. She is being pulled toward and then over camera. As torso disappears we see the tether wrapped around her left foot and lower leg. (4 sec.)

[12] AS IN [10]. "Hold on," she says off. "Going to bring you in."

[13] AS IN [9], with camera further back from her so we see full body. "Just hold on!" (2 sec.)

[14] AS IN [10]. "... pull you in!," in continuing voiceover from her. KOWALSKI: "Ryan ... Listen ..." She says again, "Pull you in." He is serious. "You have to let me go." (3 sec.)

[15] AS IN [13]. "No!" She hears him argue, "I'm pulling you with me." (2 sec.)

[16] AS IN [10]. Reaching up to the hook to untie himself. "You have to let me go. Or we both die." (1.5 sec.)

[17] AS IN [13]. She is being tugged past camera, grunting. "Not letting you go, we're fine!" She flies past camera, which turns to show both of them, *Kowalski quite far away, Ryan moving off. (4 sec.)

[18] AS IN [7], EXTREME LONG. Ship at left. Earth curving across screen bottom. **Two tiny figures floating. "Ryan, let go," we hear him say, although they are hundreds of yards away. (5.5 sec.)

[19] Face-on to Ryan in her suit, filling most of the screen. She is shaking her head. (1.5 sec.)

[20] Close on Kowalski. "It's not up to you." Unfastening himself. (1.5 sec.)

[21] Close on Ryan, shaking her head. (1.5 sec.)

[22] Close on Kowalski, unhooking, staring at the hook in his hand while clasping the tether with his other. (5 sec.)

[23] Closer on Ryan. Shaking her head. (3 sec.)

[24] On Kowalski. "You're gonna make it, Ryan." He lets go, with her calling after him, off-. Looking into camera he recedes into space. (11 sec.)

[25] MEDIUM-LONG on *Ryan, as she recedes back toward the ship, the tether waving after her. (6 sec.)

[26] LONG on *Kowalski, alone against the blackness, slowly turning, receding. (9 sec.)

Whenever a stunt performer "bites the dust" in order that the star's character may appear to do so, a fundamental postulate of cinema is invoked, one well known to insiders and camouflaged from the public by cheats: that a star is not always a star. Effectively others may appear in the star's place, not only adequately filling in but fully appearing to be the star in action. Thus, the action sequence does not augment or diminish the star persona nearly as much as transmogrify it. The actor and character become together a new creature with and without a face, with and without gestural skill, technically adept while being innocent.

44

Reflect On That

FIGURE 44 *Christian Bale in* Empire of the Sun *(Steven Spielberg, Amblin, 1987).*

A wonderful editorial cheat of classical cinema:
    The film tended to be written by one or more craftsmen, members of an exclusive cadre of former stage writers or fictionalists who had a particular flair for characterization and dialogue. When their characters spoke, every line echoed and was something to reflect upon. Very often the talk was happening not to rationalize or support some rapid forward story movement, to effect an action cinema, but to round out both personae and moment, to socially embed behavior so that it would mirror, simply and directly, broader social structures enduringly present.

The speech was to hear and think about, but one could do this only when some still riper riposte did not instantaneously follow onscreen (as happens incessantly in *His Girl Friday* [1940], thanks to the sound work by Lodge Cunningham). The principal agent controlling the pace of story procession, instant by instant, was the editor. When an actor had been shot in close-up uttering a precious line, film would be exposed before the utterance and after it, making a head and a tail. It was finally up to the editor (here, Gene Havlick) how much of either to use in the cut.

By controlling the "space" around a speech, the editor can modulate the pace at which the actor's body would seem to move from one point to another, and the juxtaposition of talk against that movement, thus fashioning a character for which the actor had provided only working material. Assuming, for a quick example, that a portrait shot of a woman saying something while she sits in a chair is made with a longish tail, the "tail" being continuing silent footage as she remains where she is after delivering the line, the editor can make her seem to reflect on what she has just said, and urge us to reflect, too, by using two or three seconds of that tail. When Bette Davis was encountered by Rudi Fehr, the man who had edited most of her pictures, she said, "Rudi, you're *it!*" (Bell 139). She knew with surety what he had done to the work she had offered in front of the camera to give it pace, duration, echo, and pause. The editor is also in control of how long we will wait before a speaking companion rejoins in a conversation. And of much else that we see and hear. The impression generally given in cinema is that, magically and unseen, the lens has recorded all of what happened before it, *that what we catch here happened as recorded*. But the editor systematically cheats that impression, and cheats the real action on-set in order to produce, to sculpt, to create the scene as we see it.

Let us look at a very moving scene in a late 1980s film made with a classical grammar, the moment in Steven Spielberg's *Empire of the Sun* (1987) when young Jamie (Christian Bale) witnesses the United States Air Force attack on the Japanese prison camp in which he is interred. Shot after shot shows planes racing across the sky, sometimes heading for the camera and swooping away, other times seen in lateral motion across the screen, and with quick cutaways to all the principal protagonists: Julianne Moore and Peter Gale staring up through a window; John Malkovich and Joe Pantoliano doing likewise; Nigel Havers coming into the fresh air and staring up in shocked anxiety; Masatô Ibu, the commandant, looking up with fear and concern. Jamie has been seen already racing up the staircase to the balcony of a building, suitcase in hand. He has reached the balcony:

[A] (*Camera at floor level, looking up at Jamie, full body, standing at a red-painted railing.*) Jamie's mouth is agape with wonder. Excited he races off, screen-right, dog tags jingling from his neck. He moves all along the balcony (*as camera pans*), arriving at the [our] right end and staring off-right. CUT TO:

[B] (*A longer shot from behind Jamie, seeing the camp beyond him.*) He runs back, to his right again, back where he came from, staring out intently. Then runs halfway back left. A plane coming left-to-right down the runway strafes it. Plane moves off-right and Jamie runs right to follow it with his gaze. An explosion in the far right distance. A plane soars toward him, up and overhead, motor buzzing. CUT TO:

[C] (*Medium-close shot of Jamie*) He stands at the railing, seen face-on, with his hands raised to his temples and a look of anxious fear on his face. Eyes furrowed. (*Theme music strikes up extra-diegetically.*) Jamie crosses his arms over his chest as he steps back. Another step back. A step forward. A smile beginning to crease the boy's face. Stepping to his right (screen-left) with the smile growing. Turning to look to his left and stepping a little that way. (*Theme ascending.*) CUT TO:

[D] (*Long shot. Fighter jet coming our way, very low, flying at the same height as Jamie's balcony.*) (*Vocal humming in the sound track, ethereal, magical.*) Wings tilting the plane comes forward. THIS SHOT HAS BEEN FILMED WITH CAMERA CRANKED UP AND PROJECTS IN SLOW MOTION. CUT TO:

[E] (*Medium shot of Jamie staring off at the plane.*) (*Vocal music continuing.*) Frame cuts off top of boy's head but he ducks down squinting forward. CUT TO:

[F] (*Close-focused long shot, Jamie's back in foreground, jet at left moving to pass him.*) CUT TO:

[G] (*Medium-long of Jamie, with camera lower than in [A], looking up at balcony and boy with arms out excitedly at his sides.*) THE CAMERA SWOOPS IN SOME, AND SWIFTLY GLIDES LEFTWARD (imitating the plane's movement). CUT TO:

[H] (*Medium-close of plane passing left to right.*) Pilot is looking at Jamie, giving him a brave wave of the hand.[1] "Tugboat" is written behind the propeller. THIS SHOT IS MADE FOR SLOW MOTION (*with vocal humming continuing*). CUT TO:

[I] (*Extreme close shot of Jamie, frontal.*) His eyes explode with joy, he stretches out his arms, he throws back his head, and yells at the top of his lungs: "Wowwww! (*Music harmonically echoing his voice.*) Go! B-51! Cadillac of the sky!!!"

---

[1] The shot was created using a miniature plane with the flyer matted in. My thanks to Linda Ruth Williams for pointing this out.

Note these fascinating editorial effects, each presenting an opportunity and a situation apparently intrinsic to the story but in practice created ad hoc through an editor's decision:

- Between [A] and [B] we shift for a fluid storytelling rhythm, but in the reality of the situation as configured here, the diegetic *detail*, we have no clue how long Jamie "stares off right" before moving back to where he was. The move back does seem to flow logically from spending himself in the stare, and yet the extent of his suspension in staring is entirely editorial. The shot runs a second or two longer than it needs to if all we need to learn is that in [A] Jamie has gone to the end of the platform for a good look. And at what point in the photographed action of [B] does the editor choose to pick the boy up? This is a matter of shaving one frame, two frames; very precise to catch a *hesitation* in his movement. Shot [B] does not begin with him serenely standing, as we see in [A].

- When as [B] ends we see the plane soar above us (Jamie's perspective), up, up, and away, how much does he think, consider, meditate, worry before, jumping to [C], we catch him standing with hands to temples? (His hands were not at his temples as we left him in [B].) Again, the story moves ahead fluidly, but through what kinds of possibly jerky contractions and expansions of "time"? Are we looking at realistic time or at dream time, given that evidently Jamie is in a reverie on this balcony?

- When at the end of [C] we cut to what Jamie is staring at "out there," and find the fighter jet approaching in slow motion, we might well have the impression that, as though in swift order, as with an invocation, he (i) reaches the end of the balcony, (ii) looks out, and (iii) *presto!*, a fighter jet is approaching *just as he hopes here and always*. (Jamie has been carefully established in the story so far as a kid obsessed with airplanes.) But is that plane answering his desire in the diegetic reality, or is he conjuring it? It cannot be flying slo-mo in diegetic reality. If Jamie is slowing it down through his diligent examination, might he not also be slowing down the entire sequence of events, stretching out and unfolding each part as a glorious shawl of momentarity? The editor's question: he has Bale in portrait staring out; how long to hold on the end of that shot [C] before cutting to [D], the plane? The plane is going to instantaneously resolve the unresolved probability of the end of [C], so how long to hold off that instant of resolution? (How far should the boy's desire be shown to expand onscreen?)

- Movement from [E] to [F]: he ducks and squints forward, then we see the plane passing. The speed of the cut from [E] to [F] suggests that the plane passes just as he catches his breath, that one needs—that Jamie needs—to race if he is to see it. That racing feeling, added in by the editor who would have had plenty of film to work with either way, allows us to share Jamie's eager sensibility. Many have written about Spielberg's career at this point being one in which he relishes the pleasures of his child characters; but the editing here shows precisely how he displays that relished pleasure and entices us to share it by means of the viewing we are given to have.

- When we cut to [G] we are suddenly below Jamie again, looking up in wonder at him looking up in wonder (the Wondering Boy as cause for wonder). He stands in for the thing he is looking at (he looks up; we look up at him looking up) and our looking at him becomes a sympathetic adjunct to, or substitute for his looking. [G] is a more exciting, more stimulating shot than [F], the long shot from behind; the rapidity with which we are brought from [F] to [G], from behind Jamie to a low spot in front of him, is an indication of the editor's decision to bring us a thrill without making us wait for it. It is as though Jamie is whispering, "Hurry, love this!"

- [H] is an interesting shot technically, because once the film has been exposed with the camera cranked up it can be worked in the optical printer to project at virtually any desired rate: a normal 24 fps projection of film shot at, say, 48 fps would lead to conventional slo-mo; for film shot at 36 fps, say, slightly faster if still slow; 20 or 18 fps notably slower; or any number of frames per second at all. That is, the hovering, floating, dreamy slowness of the thing as the pilot waves is under aesthetic control. This shot directly addresses and mirrors Jamie's feeling as he sees the plane. The longer the shot can last, the longer the boy's thrill of contact with the pilot, for him a true hero of the sky, the person he has dreamed of being. Jamie is meeting his dream self.

However, the technical virtuosity hides itself. Given that [H] is a matte, there are actually two pieces of film that must be composed together, in the optical printer, one of them a shot of a model with the camera's reverse motion simulating the plane's forward motion; the other a shot of the pilot making his move. To make this matte seamlessly is a challenge to begin with, but here and now it must be done at an accelerated frame rate—for both pieces of film—thus giving the optical printer or digital compositor more frames to work with (and potentially more frames with which to make a mistake).

- The cut into the close-up portrait [I] can come at any point during the plane's movement in [H] as long as the pilot's wave is registered first (and that wave can be calculated, given the length of film exposed and the speed of projection). It must interrupt our reverie with the plane (Jamie's reverie) as an explosion of joy no longer containable.² The precision of the dialogue just evidences the boy's detailed knowledge of planes (matched in the film by no other character, not even the pilots we see).

* * *

If one saw this tiny sequence again, but in a re-cut form, say with all of the shots [A] through [I] in the same order but cut so that each ran the exact same number of frames (with [H] multiplied by two, to get the slo-mo effect but for no longer than any other shot), the impression of the scene would be radically altered. Our emotional attachment is struck, shaped, modified, heightened because of the way the editor, Michael Kahn, is lengthening and shortening the shots, our experience, and film time.

---

²Joseph McBride offers an astute comment about Jamie and airplanes: "Preparing Bale for Jim's separation from his mother, Spielberg said, 'I think the reason I want you to have a plane in your hand is because you need to make a choice between your mother's hand or your airplane, which drops, and you choose your airplane. You let go of your mother to get the airplane and your mother is swept away in this force'" (397).

45

Presence and Presentation

FIGURE 45 *Rick's American Bar in* Casablanca *(Michael Curtiz, Warner Bros., 1942). Design by Carl Jules Weyl. Decoration by George James Hopkins. Humphrey Bogart at right. Dooley Wilson left of him.*

For a breath, let us return to Jamie on the balcony with that slowly passing B51, "Cadillac of the sky!!!" It is plain enough that a passing aircraft is being *presented*, that is, shown to a character and in such a way that it is also shown to us. But as the item was filmed as a miniature, authentic B51s being unavailable, with a pilot matted in, one could argue the plane was never *present:* not for Jamie, not for Spielberg, not for us. Screen *presence*—as in, the condition of being directly present—involves the entirely extra-diegetic relation an object or person can have with a camera, beyond simply existing in and of itself; whereas *presentation* involves the entirely diegetic relation an object or person can have with a character's eyes (and with ours--sometimes in film we see what a character sees, sometimes not).

Spielberg's diegetic "airplane" has presentation but not presence.

We could imagine a condition in which something or someone had presence but not presentation. In Hitchcock's *Dial M for Murder*, the painted canvas of a bucolic scene hangs on the wall in almost every other shot of the film, always decorating the space but never featuring in it. This canvas is entirely present in itself, but is never actually presented. A nice equivocal case occurs in Martin Scorsese's *The King of Comedy* (1982) as Rupert (Robert De Niro) entertains Rita (Diahnne Abbott), a girl he wishes to impress, at lunch by paging (ostentatiously) through his autograph collection for her. They are at a table very near the camera. His boorish straining to catch her whim takes our attention, as does her somewhat interested (in the names) but also somewhat disinterested (in him) attitude. Far in the background, at a table all by himself, sits a man who has obviously been watching these two and who is entertaining himself by mocking all of Rupert's gestures in sync (Chuck Low). There is no presentation shot of this man, yet he is very evidently present. One could appreciate the nuances of the scene without noticing him at all. The Hitchcock wall decoration works in the space, too, but its working is never made part of the show.

Thanks to the "magical" cheat of special effects the bulk of what appears on camera is a presentation without presence. We are meant to think—encouraged to think—of such material as having presence, most notably by the care with which it is shot in order to convey the effect of realism. One important presence that is established with care but almost never made the subject of presentation is what could be called "design tone." When a number of different sets must be constructed for a film, the reality "tone" established in the first one we are to see in the final edit will call for replication in the others, and designers know that by establishing the scene at first in a certain key they will be required to keep "in harmony" in succeeding sets. For a good model of this "key retention," see *Blade Runner* (1982), designed by Lawrence Paull. The apartment interiors could be exterior alleyways, and vice versa.

But painted backings open another possibility for presentation without presence. When a film scene is shot in studio in front of a large painted backing the seamed canvas, sometimes more than 40 feet high and as much as 180 feet long, is drawn and filled in such a way that from a distance the eye sees it as real. The paint used is specially manufactured at the studio not to suffer under intense illumination. And for illuminating the field, gaffers use round dish lights called "skypans," mounted at the top of the backing and uniformly lighting it. The cornfield in *The Wizard of Oz* (1939) and the poppy field are painted backings; the surface of the moon in *Destination Moon* (1950), seen in numerous differing shots, is one, too. The Scottish hills around Brigadoon (1954); the atmosphere and mountains of Altair-4 in *Forbidden Planet* (1956); the Triboro Bridge (now the Robert F. Kennedy Bridge) visible through the windows of the delegates' lounge at the United Nations in *North by Northwest* (1959); the black star field in *2001: A Space Odyssey* (1968); much of "Las Vegas" in Coppola's *One From the Heart* (1982); that spreading city one so frequently sees through the plate glass windows of skyscrapers. The painted backing, expertly done, gives a very strong sense of presentation and works to convince the viewer (falsely) of presence, too. Painted mattes work similarly, as we see in numerous films from *Gone with the Wind* (1939) and *The Thief of Bagdad* (1940) through *Star Wars: The Empire Strikes Back* (1980) and *An Age of Innocence* (1993) and *Titanic* (1997), to the *Lord of the Rings* films (2001, 2002, 2003) and onward. As we believe the action to be occurring in a place, and believe ourselves to share that place, we must accept the presentation as flowing from direct presence if we are not to witness an artisanry that, being explicit, yanks us out of engagement.

Obviously fill-in performers of all kinds affect to give a presentation without announcing an actor presence, although we are usually tricked (cheated) into finding presence where there is little more than physical occupation of a space. When in *Tootsie* (1982) we see in long shot Dustin Hoffman's Dorothy Michaels stumbling on high heels through a sidewalk crowd, Hoffman is present and also presented (via Michaels). But the thousands of streetwalkers moving around him are only presented. While we recognize that of course those people must have been there, their *being there* does not register as a palpable fact for us in the way that Hoffman does; they are merely streetwalkers (that is, the diegetic characters they are playing to crowd the scene).

Two paradoxes:

- *Presentation Without Presence.* That everything presented cannot always be present was true as far back as the Keystone Kops and Harold Lloyd and Charlie Chaplin and continued forward through sci-fi space epics and highly charged, but in the everyday world impossible, action sequences. Tricks of one kind or another are unavoidable, even at the very most basic level in dramatic film. An actor plays a character who delivers a pungent line—"Here's looking at you, kid"—and his character seems to reverberate in our screen consciousness as he speaks. But a real presence is hidden here, as neither Rick nor Bogie composed that line, although both of them act to animate it, Bogie with his embodied self and Rick with his coherent surface. The line actually comes from Julius and Philip

Epstein, who do not make an appearance of any kind save by way of the melody that they wrote to come out of Bogart's mouth. Certainly in its enunciation the line is present, but as a composition it is not. We could say the presence is partial, since the Epsteins have presence only through Bogart's agency.

Increasingly, film stories have been challenged to include displays of the impossible or improbable, events that took place a long time ago now reconstructed (say, in Clint Eastwood's *Changeling* [2008]) or events that have not taken place nor could they. A space ship descends from the sky (*The Day the Earth Stood Still* [1951]; *Invaders from Mars* [1953]; *Close Encounters of the Third Kind* [1977]) or a gargantuan monster emerges (*Frankenstein* [1931]; *Godzilla* [1954]; *Alien* [1979]). These eventualities are designed to arouse, shock, confront, and finally threaten with their apparent presence in elaborated presentations often costing enormous sums and employing legions of workers to achieve. But neither flying saucers nor monsters have the presence we are offered in science fiction and horror.

Even the complacent and tedious will be subject to unseen transformations that subtract or radically alter the presence behind presentation. In Stanley Kubrick's *Eyes Wide Shut* (1999) Tom Cruise strolls the sidewalks of New York, but no. He is walking a treadmill in front of a rear-projected image, largely because Kubrick, who lived in London and did not fly, refused to work in America. In *The Man Who Knew Too Much* (1956), James Stewart and Doris Day walk a treadmill in front of a rear-projected noontime Marrakech not because the filming could not happen on location—in fact it did—but because getting the kind of control of sound and lighting for an adequate portrait shot required studio shooting. Day and Stewart seem present and are present, along with their characters. But Marrakech's Place Djemaa el Fna, which also seems present, is a presentation (it is there for the characters, but not for the actors).

With more contemporary extravaganzas comes a curious twist on presentational trickery. Take *Spider-Man*, the first version (2002), with Tobey Maguire gooing his way through Manhattan by using stickum to hook up to the top of one skyscraper after another as he zooms up the avenues. Viewers may watch a scene like this *wishing* they were flying along with Spidey, catching glimpses of his thrilled excitement and noting with respect his gradually improving talent, but they do not believe it. What they believe, if pressed, is that an actor has been dangled in front of a green screen in a harness attached to cables; and that the whole panoply of gestures has been matted into separately photographed footage of New York or even into a computer-generated artist's version. For viewers who see the film this way, the presence is special effects, which can still remain romantic and mysterious—just as for decades acting was thought to be, before the age of Capitalist Realism (when characters mumble and gunfire for Big Profit replaces speech). Special effects are mysterious because though it is widely known they are there it is widely *not* known how and through what combination of labors they work.

Presentation can be separated from presence in another, more chilling way. Between October and December 1950, Hitchcock filmed *Strangers on a Train* (1951), using numerous locations some of which were in Washington D.C. A principal shot shows the villainous Bruno (Robert Walker) standing on the steps of the Jefferson Memorial looking out to eye another character. The film, assembled by Rainbow Productions, was released by Paramount. Walker was signed to film Leo McCarey's *My Son John* (1952) afterward, mostly between August and October of 1951. This was also a Rainbow Productions film, released by Paramount. But on the 28th of August 1951, Robert Walker died (from an improperly administered drug, in hospital), thus being unavailable to film all his scenes for McCarey. Some of the footage of *Strangers* is copied into *John* with the diegetic context entirely altered. The copying was unobstructed because the footage was owned by Rainbow and was available from Paramount, both companies having made both films. When we see the Jefferson Memorial shot from *My Son John*, for one example, we are watching a presentation without a presence.

While it was not a secret, the death of Robert Walker also did not gain broad publicity, and the edit substitutions in *My Son John* were not broadcast. A far more notable and popularly recognized case of presentation without presence was the opening, October 29, 1955, of Nicholas Ray's *Rebel Without a Cause*, starring the meteoric James Dean. Dean had been killed in Cholame, California one month before, when his Spider was demolished in a road accident. As Dean's reputation was already keenly established because of his electric performance as Cal Trask in Elia Kazan's *East of Eden* (April 10, 1955) the news of his death spread, so that with *Rebel* and then with George Stevens's *Giant*, which opened in November 1956, the stark mismatch between a vibrant character scuttling through the drama with intense emotion on one side and the entirely absent performative spirit on the other could not have been more evident. Viewers at the time were as saturated with news of Dean's untimely death as they were deeply moved by the performances they saw. Vivacity married to morbidity.

When I say "viewers at the time" I am touching on the tip of what seems to me a very great iceberg indeed. When today we watch a film that has been made "today," that is, within the past year or so, in the great majority of cases we read the actor beneath the character as a living person, just such as we are, presently at work on some other film or at home with family or friends somewhere: enjoying a life. We acknowledge that we have no access to the privacy of the actor, yet also that there is such privacy and it coexists with our own in time. There is thus a kind of depth to the screen images we see, a penetration from the surface characterization through to the working actor through to the citizen under-standing that actor in society. Presentation and presence inextricably coupled. And in cases where a performer suddenly leaves the scene, where presence is severed abruptly from presentation, there is a kind of chill (that produces waves of reverberation in, say, social media). Our viewing of films from the past works quite differently, however, albeit that when those films opened in theaters they had the kind of vitally engaged spectatorship I have just described. For us now these are bygone presentations—long bygone—supported by the work of actors not only not present but altogether forgotten *outside of the fact that they are seen in a film like the one we are watching*. The world in which they had current presence is as relinquished, as left in the wake of time, as their lives in it. Only legends support a belief in the actor as present; biographical accounts, historical acknowledgments, the living memories of old-timers who sometimes go public (and feed the scripts Ben Mankiewicz speaks on TCM). When more than sixty years afterward we see an uncannily vital spate of screen acting—Dean in *Rebel*—the vitality leeches onto the performer construct; we imagine to ourselves *now* that Dean was the sort of person he embodied in that film, or at least the sort of person who could embody that Jim Stark. But this is a kind of imagination on the part of the viewer quite different from the imagination in play when she watches, say, Ben Affleck and Rosamund Pike in *Gone Girl* (2014), imagining a living Ben Affleck and a living Rosamund Pike who made the film. We know Dean *only was* alive, whereas Affleck and Pike *are*. The past world Dean inhabited, as seems to us today, and the present world we inhabit with the living actors of our recent films, taste differently.

All of what we call "old film," "classical film," "historical film" constitutes presentation without presence in that whatever "presence" is involved is nothing like the presence we can feel knowing that an artist is with us somewhere in the world. "Former presence" is not exactly "presence."

- *Presence Without Presentation*. Further, it is not the case that everything that is present can be presented. The screen is bounded, not only informationally but also aesthetically. When the eye looks at the screen rectangle in a fictional film, two conditions come into play at once:

[1] The optical rectangle of the screen image is brought into both technical and cognitive focus through a differentiation of the relative values of objects (in this case, bodies and things) in sight. A selection is made that establishes something as central, crucial, important, special, valuable against other things that necessarily recede at the same time. The camera's focus is almost always a guide to meaning, and when the focus changes during a static shot our "composition" of the screen is altered to fit—that is, we follow the guide. Following means, among other things, not reading presentational status onto every presence before us. Fixation of vision can be aided by a

sharp musical cue, too—a kind of downbeat, but one sounding a torturous orchestration so as to alarm.[1] As to the problem of rectangular boundary, when they are worrying about what might be sliding over the edge or kept out of frame the default tendency among film viewers is to trust that the camera has captured the relevant rectangle inside the broader diegetic space. Innumerable rectangles are theoretically possible, *but this rectangle* is the optimal one, here, now. (Clearly, in horror film a very great *frisson* can be produced by the filmmaker who is willing to play with this formula.)

When we concentrate on two bodies engaged in conversation, put before us in medium shot, say, we take anything either of them says as being centrally relevant to the moment; and we let our concentration bleed away from the walls, the curtains, the hung pictures, the fireplace, the door. *One cannot see everything*.[2] Yet at the same time a set will be fully decorated so that no telling lacuna gives away that singular dispiriting fundamental fact, that this is always, and always was, only a set built of plywood and painted up, an emptiness filled in with décor. Unless the camera picks out some design element for us to focus on, we take the whole as a coherent presence without expecting a highlit presentation of detail. And if there is a highlit presentation of detail, we fold the detail into our consideration of diegetic value and importance. The little piece of notepaper on the desk . . .

[2] But in addition, the cinematographer's lighting crew will select out some particular features of the scene for special highlighting in circumstances where a shot is to be made that will later be adjoined in editing to another one, in order that a pulsing sense of plot movement be given. Since screen shots are complex to begin with, and since they last but a very short time, the viewer must be given aid in selecting out the feature that will most relevantly afford a sense of direct continuity when connected with a design feature upcoming. The chase sequence at the end of *E.T. the Extra-Terrestrial* (1982) gives a brilliant illustration. We see shot after shot of chase vehicles (from an unidentified federal agency, possibly the F.B.I.) racing after a pack of kids on dirt bikes through the unfinished construction of a hilly Los Angeles suburb. The action is fast, and the cars are meant to be speeding, swerving, jamming to a halt at a sudden precipice, and so on. But the screen is continually composed using the flashing front bumpers of the cars, as they race across the screen, to catch our eye and lead to the next flashing item in the next shot. In effect the screen is an empty canvas on which Spielberg and team are inscribing first one sweeping abstract line (the front of the car moving in), then another but contradictory one (with another car on the other side;

---

[1]The limiting case here is Bernard Herrmann's screeching violins during the shower scene in *Psycho* (1960), inspired, I am reliably told, by the sound of a violin tuning up.
[2]Those who work with pausable media, able to stop on a frame, back up, and repeat several times see, at least, more than their predecessors.

or a low shot of the bicycles speeding away, the pumping feet constituting the match). Pretty much everything else has to be taken as read, since the eye is taken up following the brightest parts of the screen: the bumpers, the bike fenders, the dirt base.

And in this *E.T.* sequence the screen composition is gracefully managed so that by looking straight forward at the screen the viewer can be offered all the relevant moving objects *seriatim*, each swooping into a fixed field of vision in turn. The filmmaker constantly reminds us that he knows we can only look straight ahead in the theater. There is no other field. Therefore what he needs us to see, what he needs to present, must be arranged so that it will be seen directly and frontally, will have a presence that dissipates the presence of other things that are also there and not being presented. The scene itself, taken as a diegetic space, has presence; but only what is relevant to the story at each instant will be presented there.

46

By Contrast

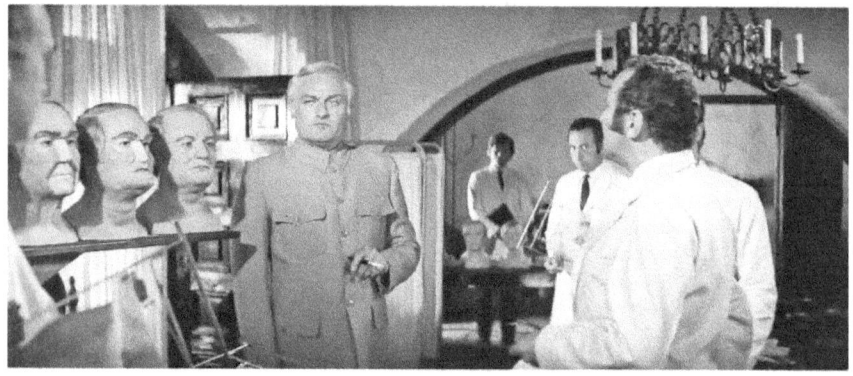

FIGURE 46 *Charles Gray in* Diamonds Are Forever *(Guy Hamilton, Eon Productions, 1971)*.

Since the mid-1990s, it has become fashionable to create action stories overflowing with characters, many of whom look like one another, share talents for whipping out cell phones, changing SIM cards, tossing "burners" into trash cans (in cities where there purportedly still are trash cans), downing copious amounts of alcohol, using a firearm brutally, and running almost as quickly as a camera can move on a dolly track. The multiple storylines, multiple locations, multiple encounters, arcane (e.g., "smart") dialogue, esoteric motivations, gleamy technology, perfectly coordinated movement, and, of course, spurting, dribbling, oozing, blanketing blood make following the line of action in detail something of a challenge, not to say a wild goose chase, since the story as surfaced almost always turns out in the end to have been a mere subterfuge for something darker and more hidden, plain clues to which were supposedly offered at the very beginning (and too casually disattended).

Roger Donaldson's slick *The November Man* (2014) has Peter Devereaux, a cast-iron CIA man (Pierce Brosnan), brought out of retirement by Hanley, an old friend (Bill Smitrovich), so that he can seek out and handle Arkady Federov, a Russian bureaucrat waiting to become president (Lazar Ristovski). On the way we meet a Russian contract killer (a woman with long hair) (Mediha Musliovic); a much-violated Serbian woman whose family were exterminated by the soon-to-be president and who was for two years raped by him (a woman with long hair) (Olga Kurylenko); a young CIA officer trying to show the older one how good he is (Luke Bracey); an American case officer, more or less impotent (a woman with long hair); a newspaper reporter, sweet-mannered and doomed to a hideous death (Patrick Kennedy); a CIA director, taciturn and slimy (Will Patton); and countless nameless Slavic-looking thugs not one of whom can shoot straight. Who is on what side here? What, in fact, are the sides? Will Brosnan's Peter Devereaux manage to escape from all the different sorts of folk who want to kill him? Will he be reunited with his twelve-year-old daughter (a very young girl with long hair) who has been kidnapped to keep him at bay? Will the would-be president become president? To get an extremely vague sense of the quality of this film, a film which is in so many ways like countless others of its type, all of them starring actors like Pierce Brosnan, travel back to the beginning of this paragraph and read it aloud as fast as you possibly can. When you come to the end, stand on a pretty parapet overlooking a beautiful river on a nice, sunny day and deeply inhale.

The filmmaker and his team are trying to do two somewhat contradictory things here, of necessity. First, make a story both involving *and complicated* enough to convince even the most cynical viewer (in an audience now filled with cynics) that the picture has something to say, was worth making, and deserves both attention, the restricted rating it will most surely be awarded, and fifteen dollars at the box office. Secondly, take this exceedingly complicated and heavily ornamented tale and find a way to simplify it, in a way that is undetectable (because the cynics will be put off by simplicity) but also indelible (so that viewers unaccustomed to the form, viewers half sleeping, viewers with much else on their minds can manage to follow well enough to be satisfied—or at least think they ought to be satisfied—by the conclusion, and thus willing to pay at the box office still again for more fare like this). Signpost it, but subtly.

If you don't signpost it, the viewer may get lost or lose interest—certainly sit back without involvement and watch the thing rather like a kaleidoscope. If you signpost it too much you risk giving away the show.

There are two major muddles:

- *The moral muddle*: Who is ultimately on the side of Good, who ultimately on the side of Evil? Imperative that the nature of the Good not be explored in depth. Goodness must be taken entirely for granted (thus showing off its hegemony). The good characters die sadly, the bad ones perfunctorily. The good *shouldn't die* and the bad *should* (just as Oscar Wilde suggested[1]). What is involved here politically is the problem of economic and military alignment and the power imbalance that must occur when alignments shift. At this writing, for instance, Turkey is threatening to "unfriend" America in the name of a "bond" with Russia. In the sense that the film's characters will be spread across a moral spectrum they in effect constitute opposing teams, teams each suffering the possibility of infiltration by spies pretending to be bona fide members. The action film, the western, the crime film, and the adventure film all work by aligning the viewer's moral compass and desire for satisfaction with the heroic side, but the game will be all the more extensive and challenging if the villain and company are not just threatening but interesting and also in disguise.

To clear the moral muddle, any or all of these cheats will be employed, part of the basic language of writers, directors, and producers but entirely *unhighlighted* (as cheats will be):

[1] Have the hero brush his or her teeth. Only good characters brush their teeth. Brushing the hair doesn't work: liars brush their hair sometimes. Another equally effective ploy is to have a sensitive character (almost always a woman, although in *Kiss of the Spider Woman* [1985] a man) tend to a heroic character's open wound. Heroes must be guarded from infections.

[2] Have the hero spare a critical moment to look upon some severely wounded innocent, as though showing regret for stray bullets or, in the case of a compadre, as though trying against all odds to prevent a death. The key here is that time must slow almost to a halt as the hero bends down to look, to touch, to care, to speak, to press on the wound. "Stay with me! Stay with me!" Thus, when we have a hospital scene with doctors and nurses caring for the brutally wounded, these medical folk are not defined as good by virtue of their occupational action; they are not taking time out. Goodness stops the clock. And "bad guys" never stoop to comfort fallen comrades. Humaneness is entirely a property of The Good.

[3] Have the hero avoid sexual culminations, or, for that matter, sex altogether. The hero must be reserved for instantaneous physical combat, and the exhaustion produced by orgasm is disempowering

---

[1] "The good ended happily, and the bad unhappily. That is what Fiction means" (*The Importance of Being Earnest*).

in that regard (Samson and Delilah). The hero may be shown to be on the cusp of having sex, and this kind of show works best at the very end of a film (the standard finale of James Bond films); and if, for viewer titillation, the hero does have a sexual engagement it must never be exhausting. More simply: the hero must never experience exhaustion, period. When asleep, he or she must awaken like a sprite, very often with pistol under pillow. "I am ready!":

> If it be now, 'tis not to come; if it be not to come, it will be now; if it be not now, yet it will come: the readiness is all.
>
> (*Hamlet* V.ii.221–4)

[4] If the hero becomes engaged in romance it will always, definitively, be a heterosexual one, usually with a partner who begins by being eminently distrustful but whose life is saved by the hero and who slowly warms. The deepening goodness of the hero is indexed by the gradual warmth of the romantic other. Homosexual encounters are permitted onscreen, more and more frequently now, but are reserved, typically, for secondary characters or, as has long been the case, villains, unless the hero pretends to a same-sex affair in some kind of tactical subterfuge.

[5] The hero eschews ornament in general, so that any piece of jewelry or fancy piece of clothing will be rationalized as necessary to the action or as a sentimental treasure rescued from a horribly tortured past. The dandy cannot be heroic (a condition Wilde's writing twists).

[6] The villain will smile at inappropriate moments. Some off-kilter internal mechanism causes this person to find humor in bizarre situations that others would cringe at. Thus, the villain's smile is not only not to be trusted, not only malevolent, but also psychopathological (a nice case being Donald Pleasence's 1967 performance as Blofeld in *You Only Live Twice*).

[7] The villain will speak volumes, showing either a verbose or a hyperpolite self, or both. The vocal etiquette will rise in proportion the closer the villain comes to hurting the hero. That is, torture is unthinkable absent elaborate discourse. The lesson for young people here, unfortunately, is that verbal articulateness is to be shunned as morally questionable. Very unlike what happens in Shakespeare, the hero will be incapable of making long, prolix, shining statements.

[8] The villain will typically manifest clearly demarcated (brilliantly lit or focused) signs of control and power, thus rationalizing his or her reign over a realm of thugs. Movement in a slick limousine, access to live, in-the-moment computer scanning and tracking, accompaniment almost everywhere by a specially unctuous factotum who is designed to be unforgettable (bald with scars, overdressed, linguistically odd). In *Die Hard* (1988) the flunkie Karl (Alexander Godunov) flashes extremely long, flaxen, Goldilocks hair.

[9] When the hero makes demand for something technical—information, equipment, backup—it is almost always unavailable or insufficient, thus forcing innovation, strain, and ennobling sweat; while the villains are instantly satisfied by (hyperloyal) servant types.

[10] If at film's end the villain should end up in the back seat of a police car, he or she will be given a close-up for a remarkably ironic and pointedly ugly facial display; and should the villain die, the death will be spectacular in its own right, something especially and unimaginably horrendous. The hero will seem—because heroes are—immortal.

[11] Except in parodies ("I do it for Her Majesty!"), the hero will avoid explicitly naming the moral source on behalf of whom or which he acts. The villain will proclaim a desire for world domination but the hero will not stand as representative of a nation or tribe.

- *The resilience muddle*: The hero and villain (and their separate crews) must seem radically different not only morally but also because of the strengths they possess and demonstrate, physical, spiritual, or intellectual. Thus, heroism cannot be claimed simply to exist as a principle but must be demonstrated ongoingly, must be claimed to flow from a cultural base widely acknowledged and accepted; ditto villainy. In *Shane* (1953), to take a good example of a morally bifurcated universe onscreen, the hero (Alan Ladd) rides into the picture from the East, locus of high culture, connector to Europe and the Old World. He makes not only his cleanliness but also his origins clear in his tailored clothing and in his mannerly dialogue with Marion Starrett (Jean Arthur). The archvillain Wilson (Jack Palance), by contrast, also attired with taste and at expense, thus perhaps also from an Eastern city, has not picked up sociability. We see him excluded from the group, leering at others, smiling obnoxiously, without grace. He is a man bought on command, a mercenary type, whereas Shane has solid working-class values as well as couth, knows how to ask for a job and how to work hard for his pay. Wilson uses his tricks but never works hard. Yeoman vs. charlatan.

Here are cheats for clearing the resilience muddle:

[1] The hero will not only tolerate but appreciate cultural expression (expression, not over-expression), even showing an ability to drop a significant keyword. In *November Man*, again, Devereaux is resting in her apartment with Alice Fournier (Kurylenko), and at one point she sits at her grand piano and begins to play one of Erik Satie's "Gnossiènnes." He stands beside her, focused and patient, his ears open. "Satie!" he says quietly. She admits Satie is one of her favorites. We quickly imagine him as a teenaged boy, studying music in a conservatory!

[2] While villainous display of etiquette will be oily, overcooked, and often out of place, heroic etiquette will be precise and appropriate and quiet. Jason Bourne (Matt Damon) is in flight with Marie (Franka Potente) (*The Bourne Identity*, 2002), and it becomes necessary that her hair be changed. We see him gently massage color into her hair in a sink, his technique exceptionally tender and considerate. When he uses scissors on her, he touches with the most exquisite combination of affection and care. The villainous Al-Saleem (Alon Aboutboul) in Ridley Scott's *Body of Lies* (2008) speaks with false, troubling quietness and a pleasant (too pleasant) smile as he interrogates Ferris (Leonardo DiCaprio) chained to a table. Slowly, pacifically he walks up. Then in an abrupt move takes a hammer and slams it down to break Ferris's finger.

[3] The villain will have recourse to nefarious weaponry all through the story but the hero shows goodness by using weapons only as a last resort or when in an equivocal situation, facing a small army to be cleared through. When he does become physical, however, regardless of how evenly or unevenly matched he is against his opponent, it becomes startlingly evident that he is straining more, urging himself toward some superhuman (divine?), hitherto unattained goal. Tries harder. He will escape, for instance, from a cloistered imprisonment in a secret, dark place or from a lethal stranglehold being laid on by a very muscular, much bigger enemy. Or he will have to realign or reorient some physical construction, a door, a safe, a wall, a builder's crane, an aircraft, showing remarkable ability to handle almost any equipment without training (as though before being a hero he held odd jobs as a crane operator, an elevator boy, a paver of roads, a pilot, etc.). The hero will be notably less than successful until the finale moment, when his "spontaneous" success will "save the world."

More than handling equipment, heroes and villains have signal contact with their immediate environment, working the world.

For the Good Man, the whole is malleable, giving, yielding, a true material out of which salvation can be forged: cell phones without service suddenly have service, door locks can be jimmied, shackles can be opened and knots untied, light can emerge into darkness. By contrast the Evil One, the one under whose command the mechanism of the story is at some key point shown to operate, finally cannot save himself, cannot escape the all-consuming explosion, cannot find an escape through the forest of the city. Stubborn to the wicked, kind to the beneficent is the world. An ambiguous environment. Unless (as in *Alien* [1979]), a sequel is in the works . . .

[4] The "world," indeed, becomes a salient locus for the villain, who almost invariably has concocted an expensive and tricky plan to control Everything, to "Take Over the World," to "DOMINATE." At the end of *November Man* the villainous Hanley lectures Devereaux on how elevating Federov to the Russian presidency will "change the world" because Russia will be joining NATO! This because Federov (along with all the commitments and engagements to which Federov is attached) is under *his* thumb. All James Bond villains are World Dominator wannabes. The hero demonstrates goodness by "saving the world" but this is, in a way, inadvertent; he holds back, stymies, or defeats a villainous type who wants to "endanger the world" and thus the world comes into question. Beyond that the hero's concerns are always local and situational. The hero is local, the villain is global; the more global the more villainous.

[5] At a critical story moment, the villain will bluntly insult, deprecate, and verbally diminish the hero, whom we know already to be of superior mettle and thus a very model of dignity easily sloughing off the insults as empty and inappropriate. At the end of *The Train* (1964) the neurotic and desperate Nazi commander Von Waldheim who has been trying to run a train filled with the treasures of French art to Germany (Paul Scofield) confronts the French resistance hero (Burt Lancaster) with a blunt sneer. "Labiche: You are nothing." This comes at a point when we have already seen, as has the bitter Von Waldheim, that Labiche is anything but nothing.[2]

* * *

---

[2]The villainous deprecation of the hero works as well in historical epics. *The King* (2019) has a brief confrontational moment between King Henry (Timothée Chalamet) and the Dauphin of France, who wishes to antagonize him. He comments that the king has big balls but a tiny

What is worth noticing about all these cheats, the cheats that join the two sides of the moral coin into a cubist treasure, is not their identity, since in effect these, and other cheats, constitute nothing other than the generic identity of a kind of film. What is significant is the filmmaking team's ability to employ these flags without permitting them at any point to actually look like "flags," a possibility only partly because viewers know the formula. With ever more sophistication and richness as time goes by, the hero covers his exquisite etiquette by saying, "Umm." The villain covers his covetousness in myriad silent macro-close-ups where he is evidently pondering: a thinker, a philosopher. And so on. The effect of the secretion of cheats is a kind of glorious brilliance. The film takes on the quality of a rich and energetically charged story (failure to follow along with which would be unthinkable) but not what it more practically is: a necklace of repeatable tropes (stemming, often, from melodrama) expressed through gestural dances of intent and poetic songs of regard. We may find pleasure in remembering that while the villain will feel free to slur the hero—"You and your preposterous attempts . . ."; "You will never have the stamina . . ."; "I pity you"—the hero does not slur the villain at all, much like St. George, who did not curse his dragon.

---

penis, and he wiggles his pinky finger. Henry looks at him quizzically, as though to ask, "What on earth can you possibly mean?" but says absolutely nothing.

47

The Blood Effect

FIGURE 47 *Neil Patrick Harris in* Gone Girl *(David Fincher, Twentieth Century Fox, 2014), with Rosamund Pike.*

Ironically, while the cause of a blood loss tends to be painful—bullet hit, knife slash or stab, organ puncture—the loss of blood itself brings no pain at all. Indeed, medically speaking, the rupture is one thing and the bleeding another, since the rupture involves skin breaking, thus nervous, muscular, and/or dermatological stimulus (and likely degradation), while it may signal internal malfunctioning as well, whereas bleeding affects blood pressure, respiration, consciousness. In most medical addresses blood loss, unless very minor, will be treated as a priority. The circulatory system, in effect the flow of blood itself, is concerned with oxygen transfer; unless there is severe organ damage as well, breaks in the skin of one kind or another can be treated in first aid, washed, made antiseptic, bandaged, but lost blood needs to be replaced, leaks in the circulatory system swiftly patched.

The issue is the violent act and its way of joining the victimized body.

Early film violence involved, principally, the strike: a character subjected to a punch or series of punches, a slap, a swat with an object, or even a structure crumbling on top. The body, if trampled, was, if broken, still, largely uninvaded, and actors would indicate wounding through mockings-up of various debilities: staggering, collapsing, holding the self. Bullet hits in 1930s and 1940s westerns are like pantomimes, yet perhaps sincere as such, since when a person is hit by a bullet the energy for dramatic display of the arms and torso is usually absent; but these pantomimes were read by audiences, and taken seriously, as real enough. Since other subjective experiences also needed to be demonstrated in drama, one wanted to be as sure as possible that one's "pantomime of complaint," as Jonathan Miller named it, was somewhat idiosyncratic, unmistakably the result of an attack from without, rather than, say, inebriation, which a wounded staggerer might seem to be experiencing instead. (There are plenty of scenic "gags" in which a character stumbles in drunk, but is soon discovered to be, instead, severely wounded.) In the 1930s, 1940s, and 1950s, bodies were still treated integrally, however, generally woundless as far as things looked, and after violence some pantomime of debility or recovery was required for cogency and continuity. In 1930s westerns, "cowboys" would shoot marauding "Indians," and one would see a body fall from a swiftly racing horse, hit the ground, and perhaps roll, but nothing more (special stunt performances from horse wranglers). In *Leave Her to Heaven* (1946), Gene Tierney throws herself down a flight of stairs but the major wound is the early abortion of a pregnancy—entirely internal and thus offscreen. When he is gunned down at the end of *White Heat* (1949), Jimmy Cagney folds into himself and collapses dramatically. At the conclusion of Hitchcock's *I Confess* (1953), we see a husband and wife both killed by gunshot, each giving a simple bodily collapse. Even in the celebrated shower scene of *Psycho* (1960) one sees rivers of blood, and also a naked body, but a naked body without wounds through which that blood has flowed.

It was 1969 before, in Sam Peckinpah's *The Wild Bunch*, gun shots to the body were depicted with make-up squibs electrically signaled by a technician offscreen. Tiny explosions burst hidden "blood" packs and one saw "blood" spurting out. It was the first time the bullet was indicated onscreen as a projectile that would penetrate the body, leave a distinct hole, then most likely damage an artery or vein thus causing bleeding. Blood swiftly became an element de rigueur in shooting scenes, the challenge for make-up artists being to solve the problem of showing gunshot effects to uncovered body parts (where squibs would have to be hidden under some form of makeup), like the head, as we see with Sterling Hayden in the restaurant scene of *The Godfather* (1972). It is commonplace now that the word "violence" associated with a film means quite specifically "bloodshed," a feature effected, of course, without the actual shedding of blood. For blood, a dye-glycerin mixture is used, made up to order and variably viscous depending on how much flow the director wants. David Ayer's *Sabotage* (2014) has a large number of sequential, bizarre, unimaginably brutal, and exceedingly bloody killings, in which whole or partial slain bodies are shown swimming in, caked in, dripping with, or altogether saturated with blood; there are also countless lesser killings where much blood is shed, but rapidly. If the bloodshed is to be put on camera, the viscosity could help determine the required length of the shot. It would not be an overstatement to say the shedding of characters' blood has gone rampant in film, with the blood effects swollen more and more as time goes by. In military or quasi-military plots, a member of a tightly bonded fraternal team takes a bullet hit and bleeds profusely (from a vital location, such as the point where the neck meets the shoulder); a compadre rushes up and presses on the wound, but through the helpless fingers blood fountains out. Or a noxious villain is machine gunned, half a dozen or more bullet holes being produced in the torso. Blood is everywhere. In *Some Like It Hot* (1959) the Mafia hits are intended as comedy (the entire film is intended as comedy) and so explicit blood loss is avoided.

Two considerations:

- Blood isn't actually anywhere in the peridiegesis, the production area surrounding the photography space, at least not as a matter of routine. At the same time, within the diegesis it abounds. Blood simultaneously present (to extremes) and absent. This of course raises the issue of dramatic conviction and audience engagement, fertile ground for planting cheats, and raises it with special acuity since the loss of blood is potentially lethal, thus serious, and bloody circumstance must therefore be sharply set off as fictional. Indeed, climactic or semi-climactic. Of all fakeries onscreen, the blood fake has a special power because when we see blood flowing from a character we know instantly that it cannot be real (unless injury was intentionally produced on set: unthinkable). The dramatic fiction—involving the dissolution of the actor's presence and the actor's habitation of the character—is vulnerable variably but never so much as when blood flows. Blood in our lives is not only distinctively real; it is life-sustaining. And, of course, from a cinematographer's point of view, especially in color, quite a visible substance.

This vulnerability may well be one reason why in an age where filmmakers strive harder and harder for social realism, efforts are undertaken to make bloody scenes as extensive as possible. Extensive, as in "beyond the bounds simple fakery could achieve." Every stretch of the ribbon, every extra bullet hole increases the odds of a moment of credibility. The viewer's "How did they do that?" has to be rapidly multiplied with numerous grotesque bullet hits, and finally becomes lost, therefore moot. One buys into the fiction by default, since the labor of calculating the multiple effects is just too great to achieve speedily. The helicopter massacre in Brian De Palma's *Scarface* (1983) nicely illustrates, as does the Nice car chase in John Frankenheimer's *Ronin* (1998).

One diegetic strategy that adds reality to the blood effect is a character's "sudden" discovery of a blood-saturated victim and shocked withdrawal in disgust. "I'm OK," protests a character, who then collapses and is seen to have sustained a massive and fatal abdominal wound. This is a variant of the play-within-the-play, in which however mocked-up the performance (the victim's body) may be it gains authenticity by virtue of the belief demonstrated by on-scene watchers.[1] In *Sabotage* there is a scene where Olivia Williams and Arnold Schwarzenegger discover the body of Sam Worthington folded up inside a refrigerator. The throat has been slashed, and the entire figure is saturated with red. Williams jumps back in horror, and the shot is held so briefly we do not have time to rationalize the "corpse" as either a posing actor in make-up or a latex model. Coroner scenes are played obversely: the doctor examines the (now somewhat cleaned) body of a brutally murdered character, but instead of pulling away physically exhibits professional rationale, a much experienced and well-trained calm objectivity, often using ambiguous humor as a way of pulling "back" without pulling back.

- In "bloodbath" scenarios, blood is everywhere, or so it seems, and the audience is meant to take the presence, the quantity, and the spread of blood seriously as indicative of gravity, that is, as actual. (Consider the character who calls himself a "painter" in Martin Scorsese's *The Irishman* [2019].) But viewers know that movies are made by people and that all the people one ever sees onscreen are always already full of blood. Even in film stories where no blood is shed, one is watching "blood everywhere" all the time, yet it does not manifest itself. A good deal of the horror of diegetic "bloodshed" is thus not the simple presence of blood in the world of the scene, but its actual appearance outside the body in clearly specified spots we think to be blood free: on clothing, furniture, walls, floor, ceiling. Blood has come out of hiding in the body and now stains the setting. *Macula* as drama. *But not*: blood has come out of the body and therefore the body cannot support life. That is true but insufficient. What is needed is blood as a stain in the fictional world, leading us to imagine it as a stain in the everyday world, too. Blood as optically rendered substance, not only red but slick, not only

---

[1] On audience belief and the play-within-the-play see Goffman, *Frame Analysis* 475 and my discussion of *Gone Girl* (2014) in *Virtuoso* 241–5.

slick but contaminating. Other "problematic" substances work in roughly similar ways, without having the added charge of vitality: mud, sewage, polluted swamps. There is a scene in Joe McGrath's *The Magic Christian* (1969) in which a bevy of London City stockbroker types, in bowler hats and with umbrellas, jump into an enormous vat of ordure to collect some pound notes that have been scattered there: a distinct quality of pollution for the viewer. In *On Chesil Beach* (2017) Saoirse Ronan reacts on her wedding night by withdrawing in abject horror when her young husband's seminal fluid touches her thigh; this is something of an homage to Candy Clark's catatonic withdrawal under similar circumstances with David Bowie's alien character in *The Man Who Fell to Earth* (1976). In Brian De Palma's *Carrie* (1976), Sissie Spacek is mocked at the school prom by having porcine blood dumped on her.

The "tactility" of screen blood both adds to its realism, helping to induce us toward belief, and makes for good screen business, indicating a material actors can have their characters attend to and react against.

- Part of the emotional thrust of bloody scenes has to do with the abject nature of blood in Western society, its confinement, both physical and cultural, to proper embodiments; its use, say, substituted by wine, in ritual celebrations; the broad-based sense of its vitality and preciousness, its symbolic representation of life. Violent bloodshed in drama breaks with social form, aggravating conditions in the name of drama. In *Hamlet*, bloodshed, signally diffuse in the dramatic population by story's end, elevates the tragedy to heroic proportions. The violent police thriller or criminal adventure film uses substantial blood flow for the same elevation, lifting shooters above victims and the force of authority who finally shoots the shooters, above everybody. As Kurt Vonnegut Jr. writes in *The Sirens of Titan*:

Any man who would change the World in a significant way must have showmanship, a genial willingness to shed other people's blood, and a plausible new religion to introduce during the brief period of repentance and horror that usually follows bloodshed. (176)

The religion is, of course, action cinema's neoliberal capitalist patriarchy, very typically celebrated through a close culminating portrait of the heroic savior's satisfied, now peaceful face positioned in a beautiful composition, as far away from the bloody world as possible.

Epilogue:

Our Cheating Heart

FIGURE 48 E.T. the Extra-Terrestrial *(Steven Spielberg, Amblin, 1982)*.

Hip, penetrating, extensive, articulate, and persuasive, if also superficial, have been endless critiques of movies and other popular imagery as "escapes from reality." This "reality" from which we purportedly "escape" is almost always interpreted as one or another socio-economic formulation with political overtones and undertones, a particular hegemony which rules the everyday experience of vast multitudes in order to aggravate the benefit of the very few and in the wearying process alienates, frustrates, angers, and certainly disenfranchises the audience who become (quite sensibly) eager to escape. Escape from this by all means. Escape truly and wholly, if only for a few hours. In this light, a film like *Escape from Alcatraz* (1979) or one like *Escape from L.A.* (1996) becomes a shining allegory. Who in his right mind wouldn't want to get out of here?

But escape to where? And with what consequences, particularly? And gaining access to the forbidden territory along what pathway, using what passport, with what kind of duration, toward what quality of what new experience? So much has been unsaid.

Can it be thought the same thing, escaping from reality by way of Gene Kelly and Judy Garland in *The Pirate* (1948), as by way of Joan Crawford in *The Women* (1939), or Laurence Olivier in *Richard III* (1955), or Monica Vitti in *La notte* (1961) or Brando in *The Godfather* (1972) or Wallace Shawn in *My Dinner With Andre* (1981), or Minnie Driver in *Good Will Hunting* (1997), or Elizabeth Taylor in *Who's Afraid of Virginia Woolf?* (1966), or Tilda Swinton in *I Am Love* (2009), or Armie Hammer in *Call Me By Your Name* (2017)? Is there only one tunnel of escape, no matter the painted hieroglyphics on its walls? And when we go, if we go, do we head into a substitute present or a substitute past, and if a past, whose past, what kind of a past, a past that is liberating *how*?

The argument that cinema offers an "escape from reality" may or may not have genuine weight, but even if it does it goes only part way toward an understanding of our experience with the screened image. Cinema does many things to many people, as many people do many things to make cinema. The implication throughout these pages has been that one of the most serious allures of film, taken for granted and thus unheralded, is its absolute guarantee of offering pleasing lies, by means of which, of course, it comes around to offering unspeakable truths (secret truths, perhaps, or truths for which words do not suffice, or truths that cannot be sung). We are attracted to, enchanted by, always hungry for more of cinema's many cheats, those devious little workings that, knowably false still put forward an inviolable presentation of life, coherent and apparently seamless, angled for participation and lensed for startling clarity: clarity of the clear, clarity of the less than clear. It makes no difference to be aware that the pictures we watch are pictures only, instead of the things they are pictures of, because we have no difficulty substituting the pictures for the things, which is to say, believing that the pictures picture things reliably and fully, and more: that the pictures are for us, as we watch them, better than the things. It makes scant difference to know that moving pictures are made through fakery of one kind or another as long as we wish to gaze at them and in gazing find some hitherto undiscovered territory in ourselves. *As long as we wish.*

The cinematic cheat is one of cinema's principal attractions, then:

- That all these lively characters, seeming to be intensively present, are not really there, that the characters are only "such stuff as dreams are made on," made round and given flesh by the unseen actors who bring them before us. We follow characters, we accept the premises of their experience, we note the circumstances of their lives, we are caught up with their fates, although they are nothing, we know; and knowing they are nothing does nothing to displace us from our satisfaction, nothing to prod us away from the vital path they lead as we follow. The character is through and through a cheat, but not only a cheat we would not wish to do without; also a cheat we choose to love.

- That the happenings we see played out are very often concoctions made up through the use of expertises we neither recognize nor understand. It is raining on Gene Kelly as he dances, but it is not really rain. And the puddles he steps into, so rhythmically, have been created in advance—concrete depressions that will hold water and also give solid footing. That Harry Potter skimming through the air upon the Hippogriff is really a boy hanging by invisible guy wires from a grid against a green screen. That a splendid drawing room, such as we see in *Dinner at Eight* (1933), for example, is painted plywood flats and antiques from the MGM prop house set in place. That in the back seat of a Rolls Royce in the underhold, Leonard DiCaprio and Kate Winslet are not really aboard the Titanic as it hits an iceberg; nor are they in an actual Rolls Royce; nor are they really making love.

- That the fluidity of process by which we glide onward from place to place, gesture to gesture, instant to instant, light ray to light ray is entirely and arbitrarily constructed, for our delight—a delight we feelingfully experience—by way of an artful combination of camera placements, lighting arrangements, and editorial moves. We go to the movies and lose our sense of regular time (say, that we will be in the dark for roughly two hours) picking up instead a procedure of fictional time, a formula of "this-and-then-this," outplayed in a variable tempo that has been pre-designed. (A director will know how long he wants a scene to play, how speedily he will want the actors to respond to each other's agency.)

- That the very look of screen reality is artfully effected to entrance us (as it does). The sets are painted or decorated a certain way to look like this and not like that under particular patterns of lighting. The very paints used are selected for endurance and reflectivity. The film stock (about which viewers remain blissfully unaware) is chosen to register light and color in one way rather than another, on a shot by shot basis. The cinematographer thinks about historical models, in earlier film, in painting, in sculpture. The lens is chosen to shape screen space with a particular stretch, bloating the faces or thinning them, spreading objects outward or bringing them together.

- The viewer's expectations, on the basis of which much judgment may later be made to stand, are cultured, even dictated to, by advance publicity: the graphic image of the star(s), the coloration of the narrative space, the explosiveness of the action shown in fragments in trailers, the topological placement meant as attraction—the swamps of Florida, the peaks of the Alps, a starfighter in outer space, a submarine beneath the Pacific—and also the spicy and somehow mystical language, not unambiguous, not plain, not everyday, especially when discourse is abruptly cut into or out of. A group of decisions will be made when a film goes into production to shape it one way rather than another; but after the rough cut is available, another group of decisions will be made about how to sell this thing, even, perhaps, what to call it. What manner of beast shall we say it is, because it can be twisted (spun) this way or that? How troubling will we make it for the viewer to gain access to its cage?

- And more.

Here are five ways the film viewer finds accommodation and excitement not in the pathways cinema openly affords but in its cheats. Not the supposed realities *as putative realities* but the supposed realities *as pure suppositions*.

[1]   *Act for me.*

There is an urgent, intense, perhaps very longstanding desire for seeming rather than being. That is, a vital part of our being (*Sein*) is a craving for being elsewhere, with others, in another world (*Dasein*). Gertrude wants to know why Hamlet is so particularly obsessed with (his father's) death, since death is "common." In that case, she presses, "Why seems it so particular with thee?" and he ripostes (in all the productions I have seen, with some overt irritation), "Seems, madam! nay it is; I know not 'seems'" (I.ii.76). This Hamlet rejects performance??? Or this Hamlet is *performing* rejecting performance?

But this Hamlet is not watching a character in a play, with enthusiasm, in the way that we are watching him berate his mama. This Hamlet *is* a character in a play, perhaps a being *like* you or I, yet surely in his presence a creature we watch for pleasure (brighter pleasure, darker pleasure) through his very fictionality. We would rather watch Hamlet (let him be Laurence Olivier, Kenneth Branagh, David Tennant, anyone) than look in the mirror. That he seems *so very real* at the same time as he is *palpably not real*, that *we know* he is not real but love to pretend that he is. (Playing with dolls.) Hamlet unendingly fascinates (let him be Mel Gibson, let him be Benedict Cumberbatch, let him be Innokentiy Smoktunovskiy). This particular fascination, for the *ersatz* not the *echt*, for the pretense, we will find onscreen with any and every Hamlet, each actor bringing forth a body and a breath which signify life and instantiality yet behaving in a way that is crafted for seeming. And then, after every Hamlet, every everyone who lives in the screen world.

What we seek in film stories, then, from those who engender them, is performance at least as much as action, perhaps a great deal more so. The sharp and articulate tongue (such as no one of us can muster on the street corner); the graceful sweep of the arms and consummate, dancer's balance; the replete vocabulary of gestures, small and huge; the diva's capacity to modulate the voice for subtlety and extensivity; the uncanny sense of spontaneous presence (that Nicholas Ray found to his great delight in James Dean). The green glare of the eye. The pause between words, for emphasis, for rhythm. The sweeping exit (none better than by Bette Davis). In *The Fantasticks* (1960) the old actor regales his listeners about his long career and how audiences particularly favored his various ways of dying. "Do it again, Oliver!," he says they cried, "Do it again!" To see what seems real in the full and reassured knowledge that it is not. *Encore!!!* To intimate consequence when we know the consequence is only false. To see gravity when if there is gravity it is elsewhere.

So that no matter the assiduity with which an actor can race through his paces, no matter the blunt accuracy with which he can deliver his lines, a bad performance still, and always, stinks. It leaves us wanting, but surely not wanting the factualities of the imposture, the gun pulled, the threat chewed out, the awkward hesitation, the finger on the trigger . . . these may be not enough as cooked, but it is something more that we want. We want the glory of the fakery. As Gene Hackman puts it in *Heist* (2001), eyeing a character who is pointing a gun into his face, "Don't point that if you're not going to shoot it. It's so insincere." We need the sincerity of the character seeming to be alive in his moment, not secretly alienated from it through some puppeteer's manipulative consciousness smartly denied us. We need Hamlet to be suicidal while not being suicidal. We need Romeo and Juliet to be lost in the madness of young love while not being lost. We need Lee Marvin in *Point Blank* (1967) to be hell bent on revenge, at all costs. We need Geraldine Fitzgerald in *Interiors* (1978) to behave as though nothing on the face of the earth is more crucial than placing each piece of furniture at exactly the right spot in a well-designed room. We need Sean Connery as James Bond to be absolutely relaxed in his confidence in his well-trained strengths. We need Elliott Gould in *The Touch* (1971), eyeing the termites eating the wooden statue of the Virgin from the inside, to be shaken, while not being shaken at all.

Luke Skywalker is not really fighting Darth Vader, you know, with his light saber. This is not really a battle to the death.

"Yes, yes! But I want to see!" (And if, as did not happen in 1977 but by this time is very likely to happen, one sees the arcing, flashing light sabers as "effects" not light sabers, the whole performance starts to stink. One must will to believe it all real, while knowing it is an effect.)

One must will to believe.

And being given we want still more. That the character, unlike folk of the everyday, should at each instant be at a peak of emotion or form, never less than spectacular, never in front of a mirror getting ready to seem that way. Even waking up and crawling out of bed, the character must act with brilliance, even brilliant stupor. Even the before-the-mirror moments must be spectacular in themselves (see David Warner checking himself out in his gorilla suit in *Morgan: A Suitable Case for Treatment* [1966]). No stumbling that is not dramatically wonderful in itself (Van Johnson in *23 Paces to Baker Street* [1956]). No speech troubles that are not sweet and attractive, or poignantly indicative (Patty Duke in *The Miracle Worker* [1962]). No song but eloquent song (Julie Andrews in *The Sound of Music* [1964]; Jerry Lewis in *The Delicate Delinquent* [1957]).

And we want the kind of grace it would be naïve or churlish to expect in the world of the everyday, that every streetcar arrives with its doors open at the precise instant the desperately fleeing heroine needs a ride from Berlin Alexanderplatz; that the multiple bodies spinning, leaping, and vocalizing in bravura color never collide, never even brush or accidentally touch things that have been arranged so much like a Swiss clockwork (the opening number of *La La Land* [2016]). A symphony of movements expressing the height of style (Brando in *Streetcar* [1951]) and, too, the high aeries of emotionality (Wendy Hiller in *I Know Where I'm Going!* [1945]). There is a delicious moment in Michael Powell and Emeric Pressburger's *The Thief of Bagdad* (1940) when in his ornate pink palace the Sultan of Basra (Miles Malleson) is being visited by the (evil) wizard Jaffar (Conrad Veidt) and he decides to regale his guest with a little tour through his collection of toys. One of these is a tiny theater, with a stage and a curtain. A group of acrobats are set to perform, tiny figurines, but the Sultan makes the toy operate and the figures "come to life," going through a whole beautiful routine: no accidents, no flaws, no bumping, no falling. This has been achieved with a matte-in of an acrobatic routine filmed life-size on a stage against a black curtain, and before optical printing the matte image has been several times reduced in size—because we do see at least one shot of the Sultan standing beside the theater looking at it with awe. This little fakery-within-a-fakery has a lesson: very like these tiny acrobats are the figures (figurines) of cinema, mechanically placed and constructed, moving according to plan, everything seen and foreseen, everything polished, everything sized to fit the screen. Everything a joy.

Give me someone who is saying something, anything, so very believably, with such generosity of feeling laid upon each breath . . . something he or she doesn't believe at all, since he or she has no mind, no belief, and a writer wrote all this. Give me that absent writer through the shining body of this bewitching genius. Give me puppets.

Let me see a growing up that isn't growing up, a dying that isn't dying, a love that isn't love, devouring a chicken leg that isn't real devouring, inebriation that I can trust is sober, malevolent intent that is only a puff. Give me *brilliantly choreographed* fear and desperation (the car chase), give me startling intelligence from a being who, were I to encounter her or him in the everyday world, would seem only pleasant, polite, and pale. Or would seem, indeed, supremely gracious and sweet (I have found many very celebrated performers to be this way) but not as scathingly expressive, as chilling as they were onscreen. (They don't go through real life with a writer at the side.) Give me a realm that is another realm, filled with creatures of superhuman proportion and form, unearthly expressivity, color to bleach the rainbow.

[2] *Take me along.*

It was in the 1960s that film productions began remorselessly to use location exteriors and often location interiors, rather than studio set-ups. Call it social realism, call it economy, since studio space rental was not cheap. A very frequent tactic was to shoot set-ups and exteriors on location (sometimes with a second unit) and do the interiors on soundstage sets. The idea of giving the viewer a location to view bloomed in the 1950s, of course, with exotic, often Technicolor epics set in such desirable spots as postwar Rome, Hong Kong, Paris, Istanbul, and London. The idea of a lush travel experience, fostered on land through such agencies as *Gourmet* magazine and onscreen in films such as *Three Coins in the Fountain* (1954), *Topkapi* (1964), *An Affair to Remember* (1957), *Love Is a Many-Splendored Thing* (1955), *The Man in the Gray Flannel Suit* (1956), *Love in the Afternoon* (1957), *The Barefoot Contessa* (1954), *Light in the Piazza* (1962), *The Roman Spring of Mrs. Stone* (1961), *Midnight Lace* (1960), or *To Catch a Thief* (1955) accustomed audiences to the expectation of being taken somewhere by film, taken in luxury and shown only the richest sights of the territory. The act of viewing thus entailed the viewer taking as given a description of narrative space, its geographic identity flashed onscreen through a title card. One cherished authenticity as regards architecture, quality of light, human and vehicular traffic, language, and cultural emphases. One did not recognize what was in fact playing out through the images:

- A story scripted in the United States, mostly Hollywood, by writers familiar with foreign customs (because of their own wartime experience, often; or their own travel) or else deftly based on a detailed published fiction (deriving from the same kinds of source), and very meticulously researched by studio departments with enormous library and personal resources.
- Scenarios imaginatively but tactically set in foreign locations, usually very specific foreign locations, such as the hilltop hospital in Hong Kong where Dr. Han Suyin (Jennifer Jones) works in *Many-Splendored Thing* or Rome's Trevi Fountain in *Three Coins*.
- Visions of splendid—for many North American viewers, hitherto inconceivable—panoramas effected by special photography or

second-unit crews sent off from the studio in advance of principal photography and working for supervisors in Hollywood very typically under the guidance of local advisers. Photographed landscapes or interiors were usually so artfully managed, so spectacularly encompassing, and so richly colorful that deprecating them to second-quality status was unthinkable to viewers caught up in the sight.
- Canny insertion into the script of specific linguistic identifiers, tinting the situation with credible sound. *Bon giorno! Aloha! Mais, quoi?*
- Sensitive make-up effects meant to hint at foreign physiognomy without disconcerting disrespect, as was considered at the time: Jennifer Jones's eye make-up in *Many-Splendored Thing* or Paul Muni's in *The Good Earth* (1937), in both cases to Orientalize. Film has grown from conditions we would not blithely accept today, but we were not there with our astute and discerning critique.
- Specific casting of local actors to bring genuine vocal and ornamental tone to "foreign" locales, such as Rossano Brazzi in *Contessa* or *South Pacific* (1958), Khigh Dhiegh in *The Manchurian Candidate* (1962), Pedro Armendáriz in *The Hidden One* (1956), and Katy Jurado in *High Noon* (1952).
- Knowing and artful set design and interior decoration to establish European or other non-American interiors on Hollywood stages. A good example is Cathleen Nesbitt's hilltop home in *Affair to Remember*.

All of the above have signal effect in "exoticized" travelogue dramas of the 1950s and 1960s, but the audience's purchase on setting, the belief in the transportational quality of cinema, the willingness to be taken along all function strongly in other films, too, since a fundamental proposition of the cinema is that we should be elevated by it and removed to a special place where notable things happen. The War Room with its fluorescent giant screen in *Dr. Strangelove* (1964), Astaire and Horton's hotel suite in *Top Hat* (1935), the Miami Beach hotel in *Written on the Wind* (1956), the Jamaican quay in *Dr. No* (1962), the viewing platform at the top of the Empire State Building while three goofy sailors dance out their happiness at being on leave in *On the Town* (1949), not to mention very contemporary concoctions like the "Shanghai" skyscraper from which Tom Cruise does a (matted-in) nocturnal jump in *Mission: Impossible III* (2006). We want to believe we are going, and so we "go," all the while knowing deeply that we are in a theater the lights of which have been strategically dimmed, a theater for entrance to which we have paid, a theater also occupied by myriad strangers. The scenic, script, performance, and editing cheats that carry us "abroad" we accept and digest with eager joy—even, ironically, when the screen depicts a darkened room filled with strangers staring at a bright screen (*The Dreamers* [2003], *Play It Again, Sam* [1972], *Sabotage* [1936]).

To be "not here" but "there," and further, to be "there" in a space we are substantially imagining, building up through kenning acceptance of clues embedded for us to find, is a strange, even surreal experience if we give it serious consideration, but in order not to be troubled by such disruptive thought we accept the whole package without proof; move without a map. There are so many advantages, indeed, to traveling by motion picture that actual travel can seem laborious and tedious by comparison. We move from signal spot to signal spot, with no cumbersome intermediary treks, in fact flying effortlessly through an ether not even hinted at. We are given the most glorious points of vantage, selected ideally so that anything interesting that happens will be in full visual range, unobstructed. If cinema cheats by offering such delights, take pleasure in the cheats. The cheats offer a magical fulfillment of dream desire. We need not change money at the bank, pay for the tram, negotiate our way from the airport, put up with seasickness, find a decent restaurant, avoid being pickpocketed, learn enough of the language to converse with the most appealing conversationalists. We need not learn to read a map for fear of getting lost, *because in cinema we never get lost*. If we "get lost," even that is part of the pleasure, a design but not a fact.

[3] *Make more happen.*

In the everyday, we move in and out of sharp consciousness, entertaining reflections, daydreams, empty pauses, anxious preparations, self-reminders, and so on. Our consciousness of events happening around is thus interrupted and spasmodic, and anything at all might call up a vague blur of memory, a line of dialogue rising from the past that one cannot place, a smell. In filmic narratives, notwithstanding that in a very eventful, intensively pictured way a character might be posed as having a memory, an anxiety, a daydream, coherence and continuity are simpler, fuller, and purer. The characterological daydream onscreen is far more evenly eventful than actual daydreams, which are themselves interrupted, fragmented, repeated, jumpy, and variably focused. In film we are shown a cue that signals "daydream," or "anxious fear," or whatever arcane internal state, and then the material onscreen is very capably presented for clear focus and swift understanding. It is as though the viewer is being told a tale from a great distance, arrangements having been put in place to ensure constantly that every nuance, every syllable, every frame comes across plain and simple as an a-b-c. But being told a tale this way is especially enchanting.

As we watch film, there is a much clearer sense than we have as we live our lives outside, that one thing inexorably and directly leads to another, the facts flow on; this is because in cinema there is only continual process, a leading and a leading and a leading (even toward a precisely calculated confusion). Eventfulness is primary. Yet very often as we go about our banal everyday routines, it is difficult if not altogether impossible to be sure what leads to what because events in themselves are so diffuse. In cinema, the story and the visual presentations are cheated so that nobody has opportunity to get actually lost, so that clarification is heightened, so that some specially noted feature centralizes and focuses each moment, and so that the transitions are made so probable, instantly now or instantly in retrospect.

Onscreen there is also a preponderant and weighty tendency toward significance, whereas we live in a world where if anything might be significant relatively few things are. In film, there can be no insignificance, not as we perceive—even if apparent significances turn out later to have been false ones—essentially because, five seconds of screen time costing an arm and a leg and necessitating the sophisticated organization of many people's labor simultaneously, time is not to be wasted on what does not contribute to the construction. Because many shots are taken but only some are used; because film is edited and re-edited and re-edited again; because it is watched dozens and dozens of times by the makers before it hits the screen, there are no mistakes to be seen. Mismatches are routinely covered, continuity errors routinely patched. What we see is *happening*, boldly and frankly; our seeing is a *happening upon a happening*; and as we see relentlessly, film events relentlessly happen, blossom without letup. It is inconceivable to think film might pause upon itself, daydream for a moment, fly away. Imagine in Disney's *Peter Pan* (1955) the flying boy stretched out on a fat tree branch of a lazy afternoon, muttering to himself, "Oh wow, what an exciting time I'm having here in Neverland!" Imagine Rick (Humphrey Bogart) in *Casablanca* (1942) sitting morose at his shady office table doodling on a pad in thick black ink, "Ilsa, Ilsa, Ilsa, Ilsa, Ilsa, Ilsa, Ilsa." Imagine Professor Charles Xavier in *X-Men* (Patrick Stewart), sitting by himself one evening in his wheelchair and muttering, "Oh my God, I'm so alone. All those fabulously inventive young people I teach have gone off to the movies. What will happen if I try to go downstairs and my chair crashes and I'm caught underneath it?!" Imagine May Welland (Winona Ryder) in *An Age of Innocence* (1993) watching her husband Newland Archer (Daniel Day-Lewis) chatting with Ellen Olenska (Michelle Pfeiffer) at a dinner party and thinking to herself, "Oh! He is in love with her! Or wait—is he? I *think* he is. But maybe he isn't. I'm wrong so much of the time. Am I wrong now? How would I ever figure that out? Should I do anything about this, or just let it go? I'd better make sure to see my attorney tomorrow morning!"

Fred Astaire in *The Band Wagon*, a private moment: "Gee, I have a big dance soon, I'd better get some practice in."

Cinematic narrative flows onward, a river that is not a river, with no times-out, no intermissions (even when a long film actually has an "intermission"), no coffee breaks. And we would have it no other way, would find lacunae—

if there were any—intolerable, as though, flying through the air with the greatest of ease we had suddenly come upon a patch where all the oxygen was missing. To get the intensified eventfulness, scripts are drafted and redrafted countless times, scenes polished or curtailed or eliminated, establishing shots dropped away, lines of dialogue clipped, editing rhythms established, clues planted about what lies ahead down the road and then some object is sent barreling down the road soon afterward, lest the audience forget about having been given clues. All of this cheats authenticity, but creates the believable surface, and the believable surface is everything.

As we watch, authenticity—actual authenticity, if we could ever determine what that was—is of no value.

[4] *Dance*

We are not given access, by cinema, to performers and artists as they train or prepare. Fred Astaire's long, long, long hours of off-camera practice, refining those splendid dance moves to perfection . . . impossible even to know which direction to point the compass to find him doing this. Hein Heckroth mixing his paints to do the sets of the *Ballet of the Red Shoes* (1948) for Powell and Pressburger—unthinkably hidden. Vittorio Storaro getting ready to shoot scenes of *One From the Heart* (1982) for Coppola and testing out various theatrical gels to see what effect they will have on various film stocks with certain patterns of lighting: all backstage. Leonardo DiCaprio or Meryl Streep or Pierce Brosnan or Ian McKellen (born Los Angeles; New Jersey; Ireland; Lancashire) learning how to put on believable South African accents (for *Blood Diamond* [2006], *Out of Africa* [1985], *Survivor* [2015], *Six Degrees of Separation* [1993]). McKellen doing makeup tests for *Lord of the Rings* (2001), *Apt Pupil* (1998), *X-Men* (2000), or *Mr. Holmes* (2015). Johnny Green re-populating and re-seating and rehearsing the MGM Orchestra to record for *An American in Paris* (1951).

Without access we are led to take the realized performance as a spontaneous outpouring, and this spontaneity, this unprepared spirit is what we come not only to believe we are always seeing in cinema but also to desire to see, again and again. (Desire does not spring from a vacuum; "Nothing will come of nothing.") We much prefer the cheated gloss to the untouched, and would not choose the latter over the former if given free opportunity (even in documentaries, which have their own backstage). We wish not to see labor but to revel instead in the fruits of labor, success. This even in the many strange, utterly ironic cases where labor, not performance, is openly given onscreen as the content of the performed dramatic moment: the prisoners' work laying bricks in *One Day in the Life of Ivan Denisovich* (1970), the actor's dressing-room labor in *The Dresser* (1983; 2015), the engineer's control of the train in *The Train* (1964), the botched rehearsals of a wannabee diva in *Florence Foster Jenkins* (2016). We happily see the elegantly performed botched dance rehearsal (*The Band Wagon* [1953]) or the elegantly performed clumsy work-up to a complicated heist (*The Italian Job* [2003]), without wishing to see the inelegant rehearsal for, or work-up to, filming such scenes.

[5]   *Project without bound*

We want to believe that all of the lines composing all of the spaces we see can be projected further than the limit of our sight, on and on, so that a corner becomes a neighborhood, a neighborhood a city, a city a portion of a state, the portion the state, the state the country, the country the hemisphere, the hemisphere the planet, and on and on until the end of time.[1] That space is both fluid and continuous, that the border does not really exist, that fragmentation is a theoretical construct but not a fact of life. The truth is that outside what is depicted onscreen, very little exists of the scene involved, not the ceiling, not the other side of the bedroom. The qualities of screen space end not very far from the camera's framing. On the other side of the door to the office is a storage space full of boxes and rolled canvas and spare light bulbs. The skyscrapers we see through the office window are painted on a backing that is thirty-seven feet high, and from the top of that upward one finds only ropes, hanging work lights, a fixed grid. Everything of cinema is built to appear perfect *in the frame* but is not built the way the world is built, except, of course, that what is built for the camera *is* in the world. And when something is made to fit a frame, the designers think about how long the shot might be on the screen, whether the camera will be in motion, which colorations will stand out and which recede, how much that is already familiar to the viewer will be filled in by the imagination and need not be constructed. In *The Wizard of Oz* (1939), Dorothy, Toto, the Scarecrow, the Tin Man, and the Lion go dancing off on the yellow brick road, away, away, away from the camera, diminishing, diminishing, and then quickly the scene dissolves to another. Just at the last point of the shot, before the dissolve begins, the dancers were only inches from the painted backing that showed the road continuing onward as far as one could see; but that backing was only twenty or so feet from the camera. What is built as a set is what will be seen by the camera, not what would exist in a world such as the world depicted (suggested) in the frame. Thus, cinema has its own geometry, but the cheat of the medium is to convince viewers they are looking at some natural geometry instead, the mountains receding, the distant clouds.

---

[1] André Bazin wrote, "What the screen shows us seems to be a part of something prolonged indefinitely into the universe" (166). One might add, indefinitely and perhaps not without form.

And in the contest between fake and real geometry, watchers want the fake to win.

*   *   *

Moreover, we know all this.

We know of the arbitrary constructions of cinema. But we choose instead to revel in our suppositions, that the star after walking past the camera keeps going down the street, turns the corner, climbs onto a tram. The cheat is not a negation of cinema, not a withdrawal from the viewer's bank account of sympathies, but a pillar of the temple. It is not the filmed story that we want, truly, madly, deeply: it is the lie that gives the story over to us.

And yet, can it be said that we wish for a bold-faced lie?

Do we want the deceiver to wear his identity on his sleeve, and prance with it before our eyes? "Here I am, TOM CRUISE pretending to be Ethan Hunt!!! Watch me do this fake leap!!!!!!!" And the answer to that piquing question is no, definitively. We want to know that we are being confronted with fabrication, and at the same time be deceived, be unable to discern the cheat as such. I know there is a trick, but . . . how? We do not—we cannot and must not—adopt the belief of fools and come into the conviction that onscreen we are witnessing actual reality. On the other side, we cannot and must not see a rank charlatan hiding his cards up his floppy sleeve. That would be demeaning to critical judgment. "Not even the best magician in the world can produce a rabbit out of a hat . . . if there isn't already a rabbit in the hat," the impresario Lermontov (Anton Walbrook) says in *The Red Shoes* (1948). Yes, surely, because, first, the magician cannot embody a living rabbit out of thin air (any more than can Nature). But: *Where* was that rabbit in the first place? Where in that infernal hat? Because if we can see the creature in its hiding place there is no marvel in its sudden appearance.

The cheat will be enchanting when it is accomplished by workers of great accomplishment, smoothly, as it were effortlessly, swiftly enough to pass criticism, blended artfully with its scene. We want the actor to put it on, but not show us her putting it on. We want the scenic designer to fool the eye, but not jab us with the information that he is fooling the eye: that set design of Heckroth's for the *Ballet of the Red Shoes*—it looks precisely like a stage design for a ballet, ready to be incorporated into a film that shows that ballet; that and only that; and since the "designer" is a character in the film, Ratov (Albert Bassermann), it must look like the kind of set this man would have prepared. The non-balletic sets in *The Red Shoes* are glorious, but they do not seem to have been designed by this same man; they can have been designed only by the designer-behind-this-designer, Heckroth, who (also designed the ballet, and) neither makes himself visible nor identifies himself except through his work.

The cheats multiply, far beyond what I have pointed to in these pages. Punch cheats, rooftop chase cheats, language cheats, makeup cheats, cheats upon cheats upon cheats. Should we be embarrassed or ashamed to confess our delight with all these? Should we be upholding the search for truth and only truth, and decry all these cinematic fabrications or opiates? Or should we accept ourselves, and accept the cinema we so deeply wish to accept? To put it differently: reality isn't truth, so the imitation or cooking of reality through "reality"-making is no evasion of truth. "Human kind cannot bear very much reality," sang T. S. Eliot.

As concluding example, I take a cinematic moment of trite sentimentality, yet one that seized and transformed a generation of filmgoers and still, repeated as it has so often been, manages to lift the spirit. Note: the thought of it does not lift the spirit. The knowledge about it does not lift the spirit. But as we actually watch it onscreen we are lifted. There can be no question of how blatantly inauthentic it is, nor any doubt that the inauthenticity bears the least weight of importance. This is the iconic instant in *E.T. the Extra-Terrestrial* (1982) when basketed in the boy's mini-bike, with little Elliott frantically pedaling, E.T. causes the device to fly in front of the full moon. Obviously an animation—yet caused when, where, how, and by whom we are not to see. The musical theme, already stirring, is here soaring over its highest harmonic Alp. The moon is notably gigantic, silver yellow, both radiant and mysterious and confounding. It is the moon over Los Angeles, thus the movie moon, the moon that illuminates and substantiates the transformative magic we are watching. The bike and its two riders are fully, and only, a silhouette, thus a call-back to the nineteenth century as much as a call forward to the future. The movement is the movement of liberation, snapping one's tether to conventional reality and to budgetary constraint and to moral proscription and to the rule-guided business of the everyday. It is also, of course, escape from noxious people who were quite prepared to use rifles on the creature and on Elliott. And ultimately, it is proof positive—within the narrative constraints, always present yet always invisible—of the alien's awesome power, his freedom from gravity, his ability to protect against all evil, his beneficence without bound here shown in a notably unbounded glyph.

Movie cheats are contingencies finally, always kept in treasure but always lost. They hauntingly invoke the strange and plastic yesterday. They bravely summon a strange and plastic tomorrow.

WORKS CITED

Albers, Josef. *Interaction of Color*. New Haven: Yale University Press, 2013.
Almendros, Nestor. *A Man with a Camera*. London: Faber & Faber, 1985.
Altick, Richard D. *The Shows of London*. Cambridge, MA: Harvard University Press, 1978.
Altman, Rick, ed. *Sound Theory, Sound Practice*. New York: Routledge, 1992.
Alton, John. *Painting with Light*. Berkeley: University of California Press, 2013.
Arthur, W. J. G. Ord-Hume. *Clockwork Music: An Illustrated History of Mechanical Musical Instruments*. London: Allen & Unwin, 1973.
Bartsch, Shadi. *The Mirror of the Self: Sexuality, Self-Knowledge, and the Gaze in the Early Roman Empire*. Chicago: University of Chicago Press, 2014.
Bazin, André. *What Is Cinema?* Vol. 1. Trans. Hugh Gray. Berkeley: University of California Press, 2005.
Beck, Jay. *Designing Sound: Audiovisual Aesthetics in 1970s American Cinema*. New Brunswick: Rutgers University Press, 2016.
Bell-Metereau, Rebecca. "Searching for Blobby Fissures: Slime, Sexuality, and the Grotesque," in Murray Pomerance, ed., *BAD: Infamy, Darkness, Evil, and Slime Onscreen*, Albany: SUNY Press, 2004, 287–300.
Belton, John. "Technology and Aesthetics of Film Sound," in Elisabeth Weis and John Belton, eds., *Film Sound: Theory and Practice*, New York: Columbia University Press, 1985, 63–75.
Benjamin, Walter. *Charles Baudelaire: A Lyric Poet in the Era of High Capitalism*. Trans. Harry Zohn. London: Verso, 1997.
Benjamin, Walter. *The Arcades Project*. Trans. Howard Eiland and Kevin McLaughlin. Cambridge, MA: Harvard University Press, 1999.
Berger, Peter L. and Thomas Luckmann. *The Social Construction of Reality: A Treatise in the Sociology of Knowledge*. Garden City: Anchor, 1967.
Berman, Marshall. "Too Much Is Not Enough: Metamorphoses of Times Square," in Terry Smith, ed., *Impossible Presence: Surface and Screen in the Photogenic Era*. Chicago: University of Chicago Press, 2001, 39–69.
Bordwell, David. "Intensified Continuity: Visual Style in Contemporary American Film," *Film Quarterly* 55: 3 (Spring 2002), 16–28.
Brewster, David. *Letters on Natural Magic, Addressed to Sir Walter Scott, Bart*. London: John Murray, 1834.
Brown, Norman O. *Love's Body*. Berkeley: University of California Press, 1966.
Brown, Norman O. *Apocalypse and/or Metamorphosis*. Berkeley: University of California Press, 1991.
Burke, Kenneth. *A Grammar of Motives*. Berkeley: University of California Press, 1969 © 1945.

Carey, John. "Temporal and Spatial Transitions in American Fiction Film," *Studies in the Anthropology of Visual Communication* 1: 1 (1974), 45–50.
Cavell, Stanley. *The World Viewed: Reflections on the Ontology of Film.* Cambridge, MA: Harvard University Press, 1982.
Cavell, Stanley. *Little Did I Know: Excerpts from Memory.* Stanford: Stanford University Press, 2010.
Chion, Michel. *Audio-Vision: Sound on Screen.* Trans. Claudia Gorbman. New York: Columbia University Press, 1994.
Chion, Michel. *La toile trouée.* Paris: Éditions de l'Étoile, 1996.
Chion, Michel. *The Voice in Cinema.* Trans. Claudia Gorbman. New York: Columbia University Press, 1999.
Clark, Kenneth. *The Nude: A Study in Ideal Form.* New York: Pantheon, 1956.
Crafton, Donald. "Pie and Chase: Gag, Spectacle and Narrative in Slapstick Comedy," in Kristine Brunovska Karnick and Henry Jenkins, eds., *Classical Hollywood Comedy*, New York: Routledge, 1994, 106–19.
Dastur, Françoise. "Phenomenology of the Event: Waiting and Surprise," *Hypatia* 15: 4 (Autumn 2000), 178–89.
DeRosa, Steven. *Writing with Hitchcock: The Collaboration of Hitchcock and John Michael Hayes.* N.P.: CineScribe Media, 2011.
Dixon, Wheeler Winston. *It Looks At You: The Returned Gaze of Cinema.* Albany: SUNY Press, 1995.
Durkheim, Émile. *The Division of Labor in Society.* Trans. W. D. Halls. New York: Free Press, 1997 © 1933.
Durrell, Lawrence. *Justine.* London: Penguin, 1991.
Ellis, Bret Easton. *Glamorama.* New York: Vintage, 2000.
Eyman, Scott. *The Speed of Sound: Hollywood and the Talkie Revolution 1926–1930.* New York: Simon & Schuster, 2015.
Fielding, Raymond. *The Technique of Special Effects Cinematography.* New York: Focal Press, 1965.
Fiedler, Leslie A. *The Return of the Vanishing American.* New York: Stein & Day, 1968.
Fiedler, Leslie A. *Freaks: Myths and Images of the Secret Self.* New York: Simon & Schuster, 1978.
Fried, Michael. *Absorption and Theatricality: Painting and Beholder in the Age of Diderot.* Chicago: University of Chicago Press, 1980.
Galsworthy, John. *The Forsyte Saga.* Auckland: The Floating Press, 2009.
Garfinkel, Harold. "Passing and the Managed Achievement of Sex Status in an Intersexed Person, Part 1," in *Studies in Ethnomethodology*, Englewood Cliffs: Prentice-Hall, 1967, 116–85.
Gay, Peter. *The Naked Heart: The Bourgeois Experience Victoria to Freud.* New York: W. W. Norton, 1996.
Gay, Peter. *Pleasure Wars: The Bourgeois Experience: Victoria to Freud.* New York: W. W. Norton, 1998.
Gibson, Walker. "Authors, Speakers, Reader, and Mock Readers," *College English* 11 (1950), 265–69.
Goffman, Erving. "On Cooling the Mark Out: Some Aspects of Adaptation to Failure," *Psychiatry* 15: 4 (1952), 451–63.

Goffman, Erving. *Stigma: Notes on the Management of Spoiled Identity*. New York: Simon & Schuster, 1963.
Goffman, Erving. *Frame Analysis: An Essay on the Organization of Experience*. Cambridge, MA: Harvard University Press, 1974.
Gould, Stephen Jay. "Art Meets Science in *The Heart of the Andes*: Church Paints, Humboldt Dies, Darwin Writes, and Nature Blinks in the Fateful Year of 1859," in *I Have Landed: The End of a Beginning in Natural History*, Cambridge, MA: Harvard University Press, 2011, 90–109.
Gross, Kenneth. *Puppet: An Essay on Uncanny Life*. Chicago: University of Chicago Press, 2012.
Guare, John. *Six Degrees of Separation*. New York: Viking, 1990.
Gunning, Tom. "The Cinema of Attractions: Early Film, Its Spectator and the Avant-Garde," in Thomas Elsaesser (with Adam Barker), ed., *Early Cinema: Space Frame Narrative*, London: BFI, 1990, 56–62.
Husserl, Edmund. *The Phenomenology of Internal Time-Consciousness*. Trans. James S. Churchill. Bloomington: Indiana University Press, 2019 © 1964.
James, Henry. *What Maisie Knew*. London: Penguin, 1966 (1897).
James, William. "The Perception of Reality," in *The Principles of Psychology*. Vol. 2. New York: Henry Holt and Company, 1890, 283–324.
Keating, Patrick. *Hollywood Lighting from the Silent Era to Film Noir*. New York: Columbia University Press, 2009.
Keating, Patrick. *The Dynamic Frame: Camera Movement in Classical Hollywood*. New York: Columbia University Press, 2019.
Keil, Charlie and Kristen Whissel, eds. *Editing and Special/Visual Effects*. New Brunswick: Rutgers University Press, 2016.
Kolker, Robert. "*2001: A Space Odyssey* (1968)," in Jeffrey Geiger and R. L. Rutsky, eds., *Film Analysis: A Norton Reader*, New York: W. W. Norton and Co., 2005, 650–69.
Kracauer, Siegfried. *The Mass Ornament: Weimar Essays*. Cambridge, MA: Harvard University Press, 1995.
Langmuir, Erika. *A Closer Look: Still Life*. London: National Gallery, 2010.
Leff, Leonard J. *Hitchcock and Selznick: The Rich and Strange Collaboration of Alfred Hitchcock and David O. Selznick in Hollywood*. Berkeley: University of California Press, 1987.
Marchetti, Gina. *Romance and the "Yellow Peril": Race, Sex, and Discursive Strategies in Hollywood Fiction*. Berkeley: University of California Press, 1993.
McBride, Joseph. *Steven Spielberg: A Biography*. Second ed. Jackson: University Press of Mississippi, 2010.
McIntosh, Mary. "Changes in the Organization of Thieving," in Stanley Cohen, ed., *Images of Deviance*, Harmondsworth: Penguin, 1973, 98–133.
Merleau-Ponty, Maurice. *Phenomenology of Perception*. Trans. Colin Smith. London: Routledge, 2002.
Miller, Ron. *Special Effects: An Introduction to Movie Magic*. Minneapolis: Twenty-First Century Books, 2006.
Ortega y Gasset, José. *The Dehumanization of Art and Other Essays on Art, Culture, and Literature*. Princeton: Princeton University Press, 1968 © 1948.
Osborne, John. *Look Back in Anger*. Woodstock: Dramatic Publishing, © 1957.
Parsons, Talcott. *The Social System*. Glencoe: The Free Press, 1951.

Perkins, V. F. *Film as Film: Understanding and Judging Movies*. New York: DaCapo Press, 1993.
Pirandello, Luigi. *Shoot! (Si gira): The Notebooks of Serafino Gubbio, Cinematograph Operator*. New York: E. P. Dutton, © 1926 (Chicago: University of Chicago Press, 2005).
Pomerance, Murray. *An Eye for Hitchcock*. New Brunswick: Rutgers University Press, 2004.
Pomerance, Murray. *The Eyes Have It: Cinema and the Reality Effect*. New Brunswick: Rutgers University Press, 2013.
Pomerance, Murray. *The Man Who Knew Too Much*. London: BFI, 2016.
Pomerance, Murray. "Bells Are Ringing: Rear Projection and Audience Engagement," *Film International* 15: 4 (February 2018), 37–55.
Pomerance, Murray. *Cinema, If You Please: The Memory of Taste, the Taste of Memory*. Edinburgh: Edinburgh University Press, 2018.
Pomerance, Murray. *Virtuoso: Film Performance and the Actor's Magic*. New York: Bloomsbury, 2019.
Rickitt, Richard. *Special Effects: The History and Technique*. New York: Billboard, 2007.
Ryave, A. Lincoln and James N. Schenkein. "Notes on the Art of Walking," in Roy Turner, ed., *Ethnomethodology*, London: Penguin, 1974, 265–74.
Sacks, Oliver. "The Lost Mariner," in *The Man Who Mistook His Wife for a Hat and Other Clinical Tales*, New York: Simon & Schuster 1998, 23–42.
Salt, Barry. *Film Style and Technology: History and Analysis*. Second ed.. London: Starword, 1992.
Schatz, Thomas. *Hollywood Genres: Formulas, Filmmaking, and the Hollywood System*. New York: McGraw-Hill, 1981.
Scheff, Thomas J. "Audience Awareness and Catharsis in Drama," *The Psychoanalytical Review* 63: 4 (Winter 1976–77), 529–54.
Schivelbusch, Wolfgang. *The Railway Journey: The Industrialization of Time and Space in the Nineteenth Century*. Berkeley: University of California Press, 1986.
Schivelbusch, Wolfgang. *Disenchanted Night: The Industrialization of Light in the Nineteenth Century*. Trans. Angela Davies. Berkeley: University of California Press, 1995.
Sinclair, Iain. *American Smoke: Journeys to the End of the Light*. New York: Farrar, Straus & Giroux, 2013.
Solomon, Matthew. "Laughing Silently," in Murray Pomerance, ed., *The Last Laugh: Strange Humors of Cinema*, Detroit: Wayne State University Press, 2013, 15–29.
Starobinski, Jean. *The Living Eye*. Trans. Arthur Goldhammer. Cambridge, MA: Harvard University Press, 1989.
Steimatsky, Noa. *The Face on Film*. New York: Oxford University Press, 2017.
Sternberger, Dolf. *Panorama, oder Ansichten von 19. Jahrhundert*. 3rd ed. Hamburg: Claassen & Goverts, 1946.
Strachey, Lytton. *Eminent Victorians*. New York: G. P. Putnam's Sons, 1918.
Sudnow, David. *Ways of the Hand: The Organization of Improvised Conduct*. Cambridge: M.I.T. Press, 1993.
Swift, Jonathan. *Gulliver's Travels into Several Remote Nations of the World*. London: J. Walker, 1815.

Truffaut, François. *Hitchcock*. Trans. Helen Scott. New York: Simon & Schuster, 1984.
Tuan, Yi-Fu. *Space and Place: The Perspective of Experience*. Minneapolis: University of Minnesota Press, 2001.
Tuan, Yi-Fu. *Romantic Geography: In Search of the Sublime Landscape*. Madison: University of Wisconsin Press, 2013.
Vaz, Mark Cotta and Craig Barron. *The Invisible Art*. San Francisco: Chronicle, 2002.
Vonnegut, Kurt Jr. *The Sirens of Titan*. New York: Dial Press, 1998.
Weis, Elisabeth and John Belton. *Film Sound: Theory and Practice*. New York: Columbia University Press, 1985.
Worth, Sol and John Adair. *Through Navajo Eyes: An Exploration in Film Communication*. Bloomington: Indiana University Press, 1972.

INDEX

Note: Page numbers in italic signify images.

Abbott, Diahnne 301
About a Boy (Chris Weitz and Paul Weitz, 2002) 4
Aboutboul, Alon 313
À bout de souffle ([*Breathless*] Jean-Luc Godard, 1960) 170
Abraham, F. Murray 84
Absorption and Theatricality (Michael Fried) 209
Academy of Motion Picture Arts and Sciences 183
  Academy frame rate 203
  Oscar (Academy Award) 65, 183–4, 187
Ace Ventura: Pet Detective (Tom Shadyac, 1994) 106
Adair, John 139 n.2
Adam, Ken 164
Adam's Rib (George Cukor, 1949) 92
Adjustment Bureau, The (George Nolfi, 2011) 221
Adorno, Theodor 69
ADR (additional dialogue recording) 129, 140
Adventures of Robin Hood, The (Michael Curtiz and William Keighley, 1938) 100
Affair to Remember, An (Leo McCarey, 1957) 327, 328
Affleck, Ben 305
Affleck, Casey 151
Africa, veldt, as setting 159
Age of Innocence, An (Martin Scorsese, 1993) 194, 330, *see also* Hollywood, mattes
Agfacolor 236

Alcott, John 185
Alexander, John 160
Alfie (Lewis Gilbert, 1966) 29, 207
Alice in Wonderland (Tim Burton, 2010) 150
Alien (Ridley Scott, 1979) 86, 87, 150, 239–41, 243, 303, 314
Allen, Karen 144
Allen, Woody *121*, 125
Almendros, Nestor 169, 185
  Claire's Knee 169
  Paris vu par 170
  Pauline at the Beach 169, *182*
Alps, the, as setting 323
Altick, Richard 86
Amadeus (Milos Forman, 1984) 84
America 41, 67, 89, 94, 161, 165, 195, 196, 220, 225, 228, 229, 273, 274, 276, 277, 303, 309, 310, 327, 328
American Beauty (Sam Mendes, 1999) 185
American in Paris, An (Vincente Minnelli, 1951) 132, 175, 331
American Society of Cinematographers (A.S.C.) 184
American Standards Association, ASA ratings 168, 187
Anderson, Judith 3
Andersson, Bibi 77
Andress, Ursula 165
Andrews, Julie 95, 326
Animal Kingdom (2016) 104–5
Ann-Margret 95 n.1
Annie Hall (Woody Allen, 1977) *121*

INDEX

Antibes   226
Antonioni, Michelangelo   285
Antony and Cleopatra (William Shakespeare)   144
Anwar, Gabrielle   105–6
Apocalypse Now (Francis Ford Coppola, 1979)   100, 185
Apollo 13 (Ron Howard, 1995)   163
Apt Pupil (Bryan Singer, 1998)   331
Aranyó, Daniel   192
Argentina   3
Aristotle   73, 158
Armendáriz, Pedro   328
Arnaz, Desi   35–6
Arnold, Malcolm, "A Grand, Grand Overture Op. 57" (1956)   66 n.2
Arsenic and Old Lace (Frank Capra, 1944)   *81*, 160
Arthur, Jean   312
Arthur, W. J. G. Ord-Hume   86
Artists and Models (Frank Tashlin, 1955)   138
Asner, Ed   138
Asphalt Jungle, The (John Huston, 1950)   10
    lighting   169
Astaire, Fred   3, 4, *55*, 57ff, 74, 175, 328, 330, 331
Asther, Nils   90
Astin, Sean   100
Astor, Mary   99
Astronaut's Wife, The (Rand Ravich, 1999)   *143*
At the Circus (Edward Buzzell, 1939)   83
Atherton, William   50
Atonement (Joe Wright, 2007)   53, 111–12, 194
Avatar (James Cameron, 2009)   186, 216, 265
Avedon, Richard   90–1
Avengers: Infinity War (Anthony Russo and Joe Russo, 2018)   265
Aviator (Martin Scorsese, 2004)   186

Baby Driver (Edgar Wright, 2017)   72, 76, 138, 175, 177, 290
Bach, J[ohann] S[ebastian]   129
Badejo, Bolaji   150, 152
Baker, Kenny   85
Bale, Christian   4, 4 n.2, 100, *262*, 294, 295ff, 299 n.2
Ball, Lucille   35–7
Bana, Eric   264
Bancroft, Anne   *245*
Band Wagon, The (Vincente Minnelli, 1953)   4, *55*, 57–63, 330, 332, *see also* Hollywood, studios, MGM
Banlieue 13 ([*District B13*] Pierre Morel, 2004)   27, 29
Bannerjee, Victor   162
Barefoot Contessa, The (Joseph L. Mankiewicz, 1954)   4, 67, 327, 328
Barnes, George   171
Barry Lyndon (Stanley Kubrick, 1975)   185
Barrymore, Drew   3
Barrymore, John   3, 193
Bartsch, Shadi   128
Bassermann, Albert   333
Bassett, Angela   273
Bates, Alan   18 n.2, 52
Batman (Tim Burton, 1989)   265
Batman Begins (Christopher Nolan, 2005)   265
Bazin, André   332 n.1
Becker, Jacques   207
Beckinsale, Kate   106
Beebe, Dion   186
Bel Geddes, Barbara   196
Belle, David   29
Bellini, Adriano   128
Belton, John   46
Ben-Hur (William Wyler, 1959), chariot race   175
Benjamin, Walter   51
Bergman, Ingrid   101, 196, *201*
Berlin Alexanderplatz   326
Bierstadt, Albert   189
Bigger Than Life (Nicholas Ray, 1956)   232, 233ff
Big Store, The (Charles Reisner, 1941)   134
Bill of Divorcement, A (George Cukor, 1932)   67

Birdman or (The Unexpected Virtue of Ignorance) (Alejandro G. Iñárritu, 2014) 186
Birds, The (Alfred Hitchcock, 1963) 134, *201*
Biroc, Joseph 185
Bisset, Jacqueline 89, *167*
Bitter Tea of General Yen, The (Frank Capra, 1932) 90
Biziou, Peter 185
Blade Runner (Ridley Scott, 1982) 301
Blade Runner 2049 (Denis Villeneuve, 2017) 186
Blanc, Joann 106–7
Blanchett, Cate 150
Blob, The (Irvin S. Yeaworth Jr., 1958) 244
Blood Diamond (Edward Zwick, 2006) 331
Blow-Up (Michelangelo Antonioni, 1966) 23, 24–5, 46 n.1, 117
Blyth, Ann 280
Bobrinskoy, Alexei 41
Body of Lies (Ridley Scott, 2008) 313
Body Snatchers (Abel Ferrara, 1993) 106
Bogart, Humphrey 4, 146, 237, *278*, 280, *300*, 302, 303, 330
Bonanova, Fortunio 76
Bonham Carter, Helena 150
Bordwell, David, intensified continuity 50 n.3
Born Yesterday (George Cukor, 1950) 140f
Borsippa 220
Bösendorfer piano 136
Boudin, Eugène 189
Boulding, Kenneth 28 n.3
Bound for Glory (Hal Ashby, 1976) 185
Bourne Identity, The (Doug Liman, 2002) 276, 313
Bourne Supremacy, The (Paul Greengrass, 2004) 31, 177, 289

Bourne Ultimatum, The (Doug Liman, 2007) 161, 289
Bowie, David 84, 320
Boyd, Russell 186
Boyle, Robert 237
Bracey, Luke 309
Brakhage, Stan 282
Branagh, Kenneth 89, 324
Brando, Marlon 99, 100, 175, 196, 322
Braveheart (Mel Gibson, 1995) 185
Brazzi, Rossano 328
Break, The ([*La trêve*] 2016) 106–7
Breathe (Andy Serkis, 2017) 150
Brewster, David 86
Brice, Fanny [Fania Borach], characterized 258
  as person 259
Bridge on the River Kwai, The (David Lean, 1957) 162
Brigadoon (Vincente Minnelli, 1954), 235 n.3, 302, *see also* Hollywood, studios, MGM
Bringing Up Baby (Howard Hawks, 1938) 232, 239
Broderick, Matthew 29
Brokeback Mountain (Ang Lee, 2006) 144
Brosnan, Pierce 273, 274, 276, 309, 331
  childhood 276, 331
Broughton, Bob *201*
Brown, Jeffrey 21 n.1
Brown, Norman O. 98, 260
Brown, Steve 85
Browning, Ricou 150
Bucquet, Harold 90
Buenos Aires 276
Bullitt (Peter Yates, 1968) 26, 157, 175, 176 n.1
Bullock, Sandra 291–3
Bumstead, Henry 140, 227, 230 n.1, 230 n.2
Burke, Kenneth, ratios 135 n.2, 161, 230–1

Burks, Robert   *182, 227*
Burr, Raymond   282
Burton, Richard   18 n.2, 144
"By Myself" (Arthur Schwartz and Howard Dietz)   57, 59ff

Cabaret (Bob Fosse, 1972)   184
Cabinet of Dr. Caligari, The ([*Das Cabinet des Dr. Caligari*] Robert Wiene, 1920)   220, 221
Caesar salad (Caesar Cardini)   36
Cagney, James (Jimmy)   317
Caine, Michael   29, 160
Call Me By Your Name (Luca Guadagnino, 2017)   322
Cannes Film Festival   224
Caravaggio (Michelangelo Merisi da Caravaggio)   168
Carey, Harry   91
Carey, Harry Jr.   91
Carey, John   73
Carlton Hotel, Cannes, as setting   222ff
Carpenter, Russell   185
Carrey, Jim   106
Carrie (Brian De Palma, 1976)   106, 320
Casablanca (Michael Curtiz, 1942)   131, 278, 280, *300*, 330
Cassel, Jean-Pierre   89
Cassel, Vincent   276
Cavell, Stanley   76, 251–3
Cedergren, Jakob   162
Cerusico, Enzo   128
Cézanne, Paul   169
    painting as prop   232–3
    Provence canvases   169
    still lifes   187
CGI   100, 196, *see also* Hollywood, cinematography tricks
Chalamet, Timothée   314 n.2
Chalfen, Richard   155
Chaney, Lon, "Man of a Thousand Faces"   82–3, 85, 152
Changeling (Clint Eastwood, 2008)   215, 303

Chaplin, Charles   36, 302
Charade (Stanley Donen, 1963)   160
Chicago   276
Chickering piano   136
China, historical cities of   220
Chinatown (Roman Polanski, 1974)   93, 94, 96, 97, 187, 263
Chion, Michel, *acousmêtre*   47, 131, 208
Cholame, California   304
Chopin, Frederic, "Grand Polonaise Brillante in E-Flat, Op. 22" (1830–1834)   183
Christie, Julie   52
Chronicles of Narnia: The Lion, the Witch and the Wardrobe, The (Andrew Adamson, 2005)   150
Church, Frederic Edwin   201 n.3
CIA (Central Intelligence Agency)   309
Cimiez, *see* Nice
Circle, The (James Ponsoldt, 2017)   86, 164
Citizen Kane (Orson Welles, 1941)   30, 32–4, 51, 65, 66, 73, 76, 197
Claire's Knee ([*Le genou de Claire*] Éric Rohmer, 1970)   169
Clark, Candy   320
Clark, Kenneth   108 n.2
Clayton, Alex   34 n.6
Clift, Montgomery   93, 94–7
Clooney, George   249, 287
Close Encounters of the Third Kind (Steven Spielberg, 1977)   185, 303
Cody, Andrew "Pope"   105
Colbert, Claudette   172
Cole, Finn   104–5
Collateral (Michael Mann, 2004)   174, 178
Comingore, Dorothy   32
Conlin, Jimmy   160
Connery, Sean   165, 325
Conti, Tom   199

Conversation, The (Francis Ford Coppola, 1974) 163
Conway, Jack 90
Cooper, Gary 90, 165
Cosgrove, Jack 201
Costner, Kevin 260
Côte d'Azur 222ff
Cotten, Joseph 64, 65, 66
Courtship of Eddie's Father, The (Vincente Minnelli, 1962) 237
Coward, Noël 58, 58 n.2
Crafton, Donald 28
Craig, Daniel 105
Crawford, Joan 32 n.3, 280, 322
Creature from the Black Lagoon, The (Jack Arnold, 1954) 150
Cries and Whispers (Ingmar Bergman, 1972) 185, 221–2
Cronenberg, Brandon 151 n.1
Crouching Tiger, Hidden Dragon ([*Wo hu cang long*] Ang Lee, 2000) 185
Cruise, Tom 3, *174*, 303, 328, 333
Cuarón, Alfonso 186
Cumberbatch, Benedict 324
Cunningham, Lodge 295
Curtis, Tony 91, 131 n.1, 189, 280
Cusack, John 180

Damon, Matt 105, 161, 249, 313
Dances with Wolves (Kevin Costner, 1990) 185
Daniels, Jeff 21 n.1
Daniels, Leroy *55*, 58
Daniels, William 171
Dark Knight Rises, The (Christopher Nolan, 2012) *262*, 265
Darkman (Sam Raimi, 1990) 265
Dastur, Françoise 279
David and Lisa (Frank Perry, 1962) 135
Davis, Bette 181, 295, 325
Davis, Judy 162
Davitt, Theodora 139
Davy, Humphrey 170
Dawn, Norman O. 214, 215
Day, Doris 40ff, 156, 227, 228ff, 303

Day for Night ([*La nuit américaine*] François Truffaut, 1973) *167*, 173
Day-Lewis, Daniel 330
Day of the Locust, The (John Schlesinger, 1975) 45
  studio catastrophe scene 50–1, 173
Day the Earth Stood Still, The (Robert Wise, 1951) 32, 65, 66, 303
  Gort 240
Dead Man (Jim Jarmusch, 1995) 279
Deadpool (Tim Miller, 2016) 265
Deakins, Roger A. 186
Dean, James 304, 305, 325
  death 304
De Balzac, Honoré, artist 201
De Banzie, Brenda 227
Debussy, Claude
  "Arabesque No. 1 in E" (1888) 134
Deer Hunter, The (Michael Cimino, 1978) 100
De la Tour, Frances 273
Delicate Delinquent, The (Don McGuire, 1957) 326
Dench, Judi 46, 84
De Niro, Robert 15–16, 100, 301
Depp, Johnny 65, *143*, 144, 150–2, 279
Deren, Maya 282
Dern, Bruce 179
Descartes, René [1596–1650], deception 48, 253
Destination Moon (Irving Pichel, 1950) 302
Detective, The (Gordon Douglas, 1968) 83
Detour (Edgar G. Ulmer, 1945) 254, 255
Deulen, Eric 105
De Vaucanson, Jacques 86
DeVito, Danny 100
Dhiegh, Khigh 328
Dial M for Murder (Alfred Hitchcock, 1954) 301
Diamonds Are Forever (Guy Hamilton, 1971) *308*

INDEX

DiCaprio, Leonardo   4, 4 n.12, 184, 313, 323, 331
Die Hard (John McTiernan, 1988)   312
Dinner at Eight (George Cukor, 1933)   193, 323
Disney, Walt   239
Disorderly Orderly, The (Frank Tashlin, 1964)   180, 288
Dixon, Wheeler Winston   206
Dmytryk, Edward   94
Doctor Zhivago (Boris Pasternak)   72
Doctor Zhivago (David Lean, 1965)   72, 73, 75
Dombasle, Arielle   182
Don Juan DeMarco (Jeremy Leven, 1994)   99
Donnie Brasco (Mike Newell, 1997)   65, 66
D'Onofrio, Vincent   100
Doyle, Arthur Conan   69
Dragon Seed (Harold S. Bucquet and Jack Conway, 1944)   83, 90
Dreamers, The (Bernardo Bertolucci, 2003)   48, 67, 106, 329
Dresser, The (Peter Yates, 1983)   331
Dresser, The (Richard Eyre, 2015)   331
Dreyfuss, Richard   101
Driver, Minnie   322
Dr. Mabuse the Gambler ([*Dr. Mabuse, der Spieler*], Fritz Lang, 1922)   68, 71
Dr. No (Terence Young, 1962)   69, 164–5, 328
Dr. Strangelove or: How I Learned to Stop Worrying and Love the Bomb (Stanley Kubrick, 1964), War Room   328
Duke, Patty   4, 4 n.2, 326
Dullea, Keir   243
Dunaway, Faye   93, 99
Dunn, Linwood   203
Durkheim, Émile, organic solidarity   31 n.1
Durrell, Lawrence   113–14
Dur Sharrukin   220

"Dutch" angles ("Deutsch" angles), *see* Hollywood, cinematography tricks
Dutch still life   195
Dynamic Frame, The (Patrick Keating)   168 n.1

Easter Parade (Charles Walters, 1948)   3, 74
Eastmancolor   236, *see also* Hollywood, optical printing
East of Eden (Elia Kazan, 1955)   304
Eastwood, Clint   131, 230, 230 n.1
"Eating Machine", *see* Museum of Contemporary Art
Editing and Special/Visual Effects (ed. Charlie Keil and Kristen Whissel)   217
Edward Scissorhands (Tim Burton, 1990)   150, 151
Einstein, Albert   77 n.2, 278
  Special Theory of Relativity   278
Elder, R. Bruce   282
El Dorado (Howard Hawks, 1967)   138
Elephant (Gus Van Sant, 2006)   105
Elephant Man, The (David Lynch, 1980)   82 n.2, 84, 99
Elf (Jon Favreau, 2003)   106
Elgort, Ansel   72, 76, 138, 139, 290
Eliot, T.S.   334
Elizabeth: The Golden Age (Shekhar Kapur, 2007)   150
Elswit, Robert   186
Empire of the Sun (Steven Spielberg, 1987)   4, 52, 294, 295–301
Empire Strikes Back, The (Irvin Kershner, 1980)   162, 289, *see also* Hollywood, mattes
England   274ff, *see also* London
English Patient, The (Anthony Minghella, 1996)   185
Entertainer, The (Tony Richardson, 1960)   74–5
Epsom salts   136
Epstein, Julius   302–3
Epstein, Philip   302–3

Errand Boy, The (Jerry Lewis, 1961) "dubbing studio" sequence 139
Escape from Alcatraz (Don Siegel, 1979) 321
Escape from L.A. (John Carpenter, 1996) 321
E.T. the Extra-Terrestrial (Steven Spielberg, 1982) 237, 306, 321, 334
Evelyn, Judith 282
Expression of Emotions in Man and Animals, The (Charles Darwin) 85
Extras (2005) 1
Eye for Hitchcock, An (Murray Pomerance) 2
Eyes Wide Shut (Stanley Kubrick, 1999) 303

FAA (Federal Aviation Administration) 49
Fabray, Nanette 57ff
Face Off (2011) 84 n.4
facial recognition aphasia 13–15
Family Plot (Alfred Hitchcock, 1976), downhill car sequence 140, 179
Fanny and Alexander (Ingmar Bergman, 1982) 185
Fantasia International Film Festival 151
Fantasticks, The (Harvey Schmidt and Tom Jones, Sullivan Street Playhouse, New York, May 3, 1960) 325
Fapp, Daniel 275
Farrell, Nicholas 46
Fehr, Rudi 295
Fellini Satyricon (Federico Fellini, 1969) 73
Ferris Bueller's Day Off (John Hughes, 1986) 29
Ferzetti, Gabriele 284, 284
Festinger, Leon, cognitive dissonance 290
F for Fake (Orson Welles, 1973) 259

Fiddler on the Roof (Norman Jewison, 1971) 184
15:17 to Paris, The (Clint Eastwood, 2018) 163
Film as Film (V. F. Perkins) 73
Finney, Albert 89, 207
Fiore, Mauro 186
Firewall (Richard Loncraine, 2006) 226
Fitzgerald, Geraldine 325
Five Easy Pieces (Bob Rafelson, 1970) 252
5,000 Fingers of Dr. T., The (Roy Rowland, 1953) 159
Florence Foster Jenkins (Stephen Frears, 2016) 331
Florida, swamps as setting 323
Flowers and Trees (Burt Gillett, 1932) 239
Fly, The (Kurt Neumann, 1958) 283
Flynn, Errol 100
Foch, Nina 175
Foley tracking 140
Fonda, Peter 246
Fontaine, Joan 3
Forbidden Planet (Fred McLeod Wilcox, 1956)
   Altair-4 302
   Altaira projection 270
   Krell power room 240
   Robbie the Robot 240–3
Ford, Harrison 144, 164
Foreign Correspondent (Alfred Hitchcock, 1940), umbrella sequence 163
Forster, Robert 273
Forsyte Saga, The (John Galsworthy) 109
Forsyte Saga The (2002) 117ff
Foster, Jodie 155, 162
Foxx, Jamie 174
Frampton, Hollis 282
Francis, Freddie 185
Frankenstein (James Whale, 1931) 26, 82, 303
Freed, Arthur 56
   Freed Unit at MGM (*see* Hollywood, Studios)

French Connection II (John Frankenheimer, 1975)   246
French Lieutenant's Woman, The (Karel Reisz, 1981)   233
Frost, Alex   105
Fugitive, The (Andrew Davis, 1993)   69, 164
Fujicolor   236
Full Metal Jacket (Stanley Kubrick, 1987)   100
Funny Games (Michael Haneke, 2007)   161
Funny Girl (William Wyler, 1968)   *257*

Gainsborough, Thomas   193
Gale, Peter   295
Galvani, Luigi (1737–98)   33
Gandhi (Richard Attenborough, 1982)   185
Garai, Romola   53
Garbo, Greta   171
Gardner, Ava   4, 57, 59
Gardner, Virginia   105
Garfield, Andrew   150
Garfinkel, Harold   2
Garland, Judy   3, *20*, 65, 74, 96, 322
Garrel, Louis   67, 106
Gay, Peter   120
Gazzara, Ben   7
Gemora, Charles   83
General Died at Dawn, The (Lewis Milestone, 1936)   83, 90
Georgia, as setting   162
German Expressivism   195
Gervais, Ricky   1, 2
Gettysburg Address   110 n.4
Ghost Story, A (David Lowery, 2017)   47, 151
Giant (George Stevens, 1956)   304
Gibson, Mel   324
Gibson, Walker, "mock reader"   208
Girl With the Dragon Tattoo, The (David Fincher, 2011)   69
Glamorama (Bret Easton Ellis)   108 n.3
Glory (Edward Zwick, 1989)   185

Go-Between, The (Joseph Losey, 1971)   52–3
Godfather, The (Francis Ford Coppola, 1972)   144, 163, 248, 317, 322
Godunov, Alexander   312
Godzilla (Ishirô Honda, 1954)   150, 243, 303
Goffman, Erving   34–5, 95
Golem   244
Gone Girl (David Fincher, 2014)   305, 316, 319 n.1
Gone with the Wind (Victor Fleming, 1939), *see* Hollywood, Mattes
Good Earth, The (Sidney Franklin, 1937)   328
Goodman, John   162
Good Will Hunting (Gus Van Sant, 1997)   48, 322
Gould, Elliott   98, 325
Gourmet magazine   327
Graduate, The (Mike Nichols, 1967)   174–5, 245
Grand Prix (John Frankenheimer, 1966)   27, 155
Granger, Farley   134
Grant, Cary   90, 107, 173, 188 n.2, 219, 223ff, 232
Graves, Peter   103
Gravity (Alfonso Cuarón, 2013)   186, 287, 291–3
Gray, Charles   308
Grazer, Jack Dylan   105
Greatest Show on Earth, The (Cecil B. DeMille, 1952)   222
Greek sculpture, *see* Hollywood, lighting techniques, bounce light
Green, Eva   48, 67, 106
Green, Johnny   331
Greuze, Jean-Baptiste   209
Gross, Kenneth   128
Guard, Dominic   52
Guare, John   263 n.1
Guess Who's Coming to Dinner (Stanley Kramer, 1967)   10, 144

Guilty, The ([*Den skyldige*] Gustav Möller, 2018)   162
Gulliver's Travels (Jonathan Swift)   156 n.1, 197, 270
Gunning, Tom   33
Gyllenhaal, Jake   144
Gypsy Moths, The (John Frankenheimer, 1969)   142

Hackman, Gene   246, 325
Hagen, Jean   *137*, 140
Haigh, Kenneth   18 n.2
Hale, Alan   100
Haley, Jack   20
Hall, Anthony Michael   106
Hall, Conrad L.   185
Hall, Kevin Peter   *149*
Hall, Thurston   57
Halloween (David Gordon Green, 2018)   105
Hamill, Mark   94, 95 n.1
Hamilton, Margaret   20, 21
Hamlet (William Shakespeare)   47–8, 65 n.1, 320, 324
Hamlet (Kenneth Branagh, 1996)   46
Hammer, Armie   322
Hanks, Tom   49
Hardy, Tom   181
Harris, Barbara   179
Harris, Neil Patrick   *316*
Harry Potter films   240
  Harry Potter and the Prisoner of Azkaban (Alfonso Cuarón, 2004)   *213*, 323
Harvard University   48
Havers, Nigel   295
Havlick, Gene   295
Hawke, Ethan   111, *191*, 194
Hayakawa, Sessue   162
Hayden, Sterling   317
Hayes, Rita   139
Hearst, William Randolph   32 n.4
Hecht, Ben   263
Heckroth, Hein   331, 333
Hedren, "Tippi"   134
Heisenberg, Werner, uncertainty principle   134
Heist (David Mamet, 2001)   325

Hellboy (Guillermo del Toro, 2004)   84
Hemingway, Tom   34 n.6
Hemmings, David   *23*, 46 n.1, 111
Hepburn, Audrey   160
Hepburn, Katharine   92
Hercules, Samson & Ulysses (Pietro Francisci, 1963)   128, 129
Herrmann, Bernard   41 n.1, 65, 306 n.1
Hidden One, The ([*La escondida*] Roberto Gavaldón, 1956)   328
High Noon (Fred Zinnemann, 1952)   328
High School (Frederick Wiseman, 1968)   213
Hiller, Arthur   141
Hiller, Wendy   89
Hindenberg, landing of   110 n.4
His Girl Friday (Howard Hawks, 1940)   295
Hitchcock, Alfred   40ff, 41 n.1, 42, 43, 44, 57 n.1, 124 n. 1f, 136 n.3, 188 n.1, 229, 281, 281 n.1, 282
  framing style   237
  and Kuleshov   280–1
Hitchcock (Sacha Gervasi, 2012)   105
Hochheim, Frieder   168 n.2
Hoffman, Dustin   84, *98*, 124, 139, 163, *245*, 302
Holden, William   140, 237
Holliday, Judy   140
Holliman, Earl   242
Hollow Man (Paul Verhoeven, 2000)   265
Hollywood
  body negotiations in film work   122
  car scenes   176–81
    in classical era   179
    rear projection (process plates) in   177, 179
  cinematography tricks
    CGI   190, 221, 264
    "Dutch" angles   195ff
    mo-cap   196, 241

nylon stocking   171
rear projection   177, 179,
   220–1, 303
second unit crews   327–8
sfx and audience
   reception   217, 272, 301,
   303, 304
slo-mo   294ff
split-screen   156, 181, 280
tilts   195
Vaseline   171, 189–90
classical   262
   star images in   171
code (Production) era   119
design tricks, "wild" wall   229ff
editing   294ff
golden age   57, 89, 102
laboratories
   DeLuxe   203
   Metrocolor   203
   Warnercolor   203
latex effects in cinema of   83–4
lighting techniques
   arcs   170, 189
   barn doors   170–1
   bounce light   171, 193
   cookies   171
   Moles   187
   skypans   170, 301–2
   Styrofoam   171
mattes   214ff, 271, 274, 296 n.1,
   298, 300, 326, 328
   glass mattes   215
   green screen   303
   in *Gone With the Wind*   302
   in *Lord of the Rings* films   302
   "minus"   217
   painted, in *An Age of
       Innocence*   302
   in *Star Wars: The Empire Strikes
       Back*   302
   in *The Thief of Bagdad*   302
   in *Titanic*   302
musical canon   58
noir cinema   169, 169 n.3,
   170, 171
optical printing
   and color grading   204

designs   204
digital and non-digital
   transpositions   204
dissolves general   203
dissolves and
   Hitchcock   *201*, 203
   and Eastmancolor   203
fades   203
high-contrast film   214
lap dissolves   *202*, 202ff
and mattes   214ff
optical printer design   203ff
special considerations with
   Technicolor   203 (*see also*
   Technicolor)
split screen   203–4
transformations   204ff
Oscar (Academy Award)   65
painted backings   170, 236,
   301–2, 332
research in   327
stage writers and   263
studios
   Marvel Productions   263
   MGM   90
      The Band Wagon (Vincente
         Minnelli, 1953)   4, *55,*
         57–63, 330, 332
      Brigadoon (Vincente Minnelli,
         1954)   235 n.13, 302
      Freed Unit and musicals   56
      Munchkinland   235 n.3
      musicals   60, 63, 238
      orchestra   331
      prop house   323
      Stage 27: *The Band Wagon*
         (Vincente Minnelli,
         1953)   4, *55,* 57–63,
         330, 332
      The Wizard of Oz (Victor
         Fleming, 1939)   *20,* 83,
         85, 162, 239, 248, 332
   Paramount Pictures   234, 304
      Stage 1   231, 231 n.3
      Stage 18   234 n.1
   Selznick International   188 n.1
   Twentieth Century Fox   90
   Warner Bros.   90

cartoons   36
ranch   165
Road Runner cartoons   26
stunt work in   138, 141, 142, 176, 176 n.1, 177, 179, 258, 287ff, 317
with animal wrangling   287
system, social class in   197
Hollywood Lighting from the Silent Era to Film Noir (Patrick Keating)   168 n.1
Holm, Ian   240–1
Holt, Tim   73
Hong Kong   276, 327
Hopkins, Anthony   99
on Instagram   103
Hopkins, George James   300
Horton, Edward Everett   328
Hospital, The (Arthur Hiller, 1971)   141
Hoult, Nicholas   4, 4 n.12
House of Cards (1990)   207
House of Games (David Mamet, 1987)   7
Howe, James Wong   189
Howitt, Barbara   41 n.1
How To Steal a Million (William Wyler, 1966)   249
Hudson, Rock   156
Huffman, Felicity   7
Hughes, John   165
Hugo (Martin Scorsese, 2011)   186
Hulk (Ang Lee, 2003)   264
Hume, David   14
Hurt, John   84, 99
Husserl, Edmund   278–9

I Am Love ([*Io sono l'amore*] Luca Guadagnino, 2009)   322
Ibu, Masatô   295
I Confess (Alfred Hitchcock, 1953)   317
I Know Where I'm Going (Michael Powell and Emeric Pressburger, 1945)   326
Il provino/Prefazione ([*The Screen Test/Preface*] Michelangelo Antonioni, 1965)   89 n.1

Imitation of Life (Douglas Sirk, 1954)   226
impressionists, French, *plein-air* lighting   169
in cinematography   189
Inception (Christopher Nolan, 2010)   186
Incredible Shrinking Man, The (Jack Arnold, 1957)   162
Indovina, Franco   285 n.1
Ingram, Rex   196
Inside Daisy Clover (Robert Mulligan, 1965)   144, *195*, 196
Inside Man (Spike Lee, 2006)   69
Interiors (Woody Allen, 1978)   325
Invaders from Mars (William Cameron Menzies, 1953)   303
Invisible Art, The (Mark Cotta Vaz and Craig Barron)   217
Ireland   276, 331
I Remember Mama (George Stevens, 1948)   15
Irishman, The (Martin Scorsese, 2019)   319
Istanbul   327
It (Andy Muschietti, 2017)   105
Italian Job, The (F. Gary Gray, 2003)   332

Jackson, Peter   1, 272 n.4
Jacobs, Jason   108 n.3
Jaffe, Sam   10
Jamaica, as setting   328
James, Henry   51 n.4
James, William   251–3
James Bond films   26, 27, 69, 164, 311, 314
Japanese lighting techniques   172
Jason Bourne (Paul Greengrass, 2016)   276
Jaws (Steven Spielberg, 1975)   87, 101, 244
Jesus, legends of   240
JFK (Oliver Stone, 1991)   185, 213
Johannson, Scarlett   105
Johnson, J[oseph] M[a]cMillan "Mac"   226

Johnson, Van   326
Jolie, Angelina   99, 111
Jones, Chuck   26
Jones, Jennifer   327, 328
Jones, Tommy Lee   164
Jovovich, Milla   273, 274, 276
Juan-les-pins   226
Judgment at Nuremberg (Stanley Kramer, 1961)   93, 94–7
Jurado, Katy   328
Jurassic Park (Steven Spielberg, 1993)   197, 241
Justine (Lawrence Durrell)   113–14

Kahn, Michael   299
Kama Sutra   110
Kaminski, Janusz   185
Kaplan, Ann   200 n.1
Karloff, Boris   150, 152
Kazan, Elia   175
Keach, Stacy   94
Keaton, Diane   *121*, 125, 144
Kelly, Gene   65, 322, 323
Kelly, Grace   171, *219*, 222ff
Kennedy, Patrick   309
Keraudy, Jean   207
Keystone Kops   26, 302
Khoshabe, Iloosh   128
Killing Fields, The (Roland Joffé, 1984)   185
King, The (David Michôd, 2019)   314 n.2
King and I, The (Walter Lang, 1956)   162
King Kong (Merian C. Cooper and Ernest B. Schoedsack, 1933)   270
King Kong (John Guillermin, 1976)   *269*, 269ff
King of Comedy, The (Martin Scorsese, 1982)   *13*, 15–16, 102, 301
Kingsley, Ben   3
Kino Flo   168 n.2
Kiss, The (Edwin S. Porter, 1900)   *143*
Kiss Me Deadly (Robert Aldrich, 1955)   239
Kiss of the Spider Woman (Hector Babenco, 1985)   310

Kitano, Takeshi   199
Kitchen sink drama, British   18 n.2
Klein-Rogge, Rudolf   68
Knightley, Keira   53, 111
Kodak (Eastman Kodak), *see* Technicolor
Koenekamp, Fred   185
Kolker, Robert   37
Korsakov's Syndrome   14, *see also* "The Lost Mariner"
Krabbe, Jeroen   69
Kracauer, Siegfried, mass ornament   241–2
Kramer, Stanley   94
Kramer vs. Kramer (Robert Benton, 1979)   124
Kray brothers, characterized   181ff
Krugman, Jack   95
Kubrick, Stanley   37, 303
Kuleshov, Lev   280–1
Kurylenko, Olga   105, 309, 313

Ladd, Alan   312
Ladies Man, The (Jerry Lewis, 1962)   161, 234 n.1
Lady Eve, The (Preston Sturges, 1941)   7
Lady for a Day (Frank Capra, 1933)   177
Lady in the Lake (Robert Montgomery, 1947)   *205*, 206–7
Lahr, Bert   20
L'aîné des Ferchaux (Jean-Pierre Melville, 1963)   32 n.3
La La Land (Damien Chazelle, 2016)   186, 326
Lancashire   331
Lancaster, Burt   91, 96, 142, 189, 190, 290, 314
Lange, Jessica   *269*, 269ff, 271 n.3
Langlet, Amanda   182
Langmuir, Erika   195
La notte (Michelangelo Antonioni, 1961)   65, 66, 322
LAPD (Los Angeles Police Department), *see* Los Angeles
Lap dissolve, *see* Hollywood, optical printing

Last Emperor, The (Bernardo Bertolucci, 1987) 185
La toile trouée (Michel Chion) 25 n.2
La trêve, see The Break
Laugh, Clown, Laugh (Herbert Brenon, 1928) 82 n.3
Laundromat, The (Steven Soderbergh, 2019) 207
Lavallee, Eric 151
L'Avventura (Michelangelo Antonioni, 1960) *284*, 284
Law, Jude 105
Lawrence, Gertrude 58, 58 n.2
Lawrence of Arabia (David Lean, 1962) 20–1
Lean, David 20
Léaud, Jean-Pierre *167*, 173, 200 n.2
Leave Her to Heaven (John M. Stahl, 1945) 226, 317
LeBrock, Kelly 106
Ledger, Heath 144
Legend (Brian Helgeland, 2015) 181
Legends of the Fall (Edward Zwick, 1994) 185
Lego 56
Leigh, Janet, characterized 105
Lemmon, Jack 280
Leslie, Joan 165
Lesnie, Andrew 185
Le Trou (Jacques Becker, 1960) 207, 222
Levant, Oscar 57ff, 131, 132
Lewis, Damian 117, 120
Lewis, Jerry 84, 161, 180
Lewis, Juliette 144
Life (Daniel Espinosa, 2017) *239*, 243
Life of Pi (Ang Lee, 2012) 186
Light in the Piazza (Guy Green, 1962) 327
Lisca Bianca 284
List of Adrian Messenger, The (John Huston, 1963) 5
Little Big Man (Arthur Penn, 1970) 84
Little Did I Know: Excerpts from Memory (Stanley Cavell) 76

Livesey, Roger 74
Lloyd, Harold 160, 302
Logan Airport (Boston) *1*
Lombard, Carole 3
London 111, 200 n.1, 215, 258, 274ff, 303, 327
   Bloomsbury 273
   Buckingham Palace (Buck's House) 52
   CCTV in 274
   City, the 275, 320
   Home Office 274
   Hyde Park 274
   Jubilee Bridge 275
   Kensington Gore (*see The Man Who Knew Too Much*)
   London Eye 275, 276
   Mermaid Theatre (Regent Street) 46 n.1
   Mermaid Theatre (St. John's Wood and Blackfriars) 44 n.4
   Royal Albert Hall 39, 44 n.4 (*see also The Man Who Knew Too Much*)
   South Bank 275
   Thames 273, 275, 276
   Thames Embankment 275
   Waterloo Bridge 273, 275
   Waterloo Station 160–1
   West End, the 273
   Westminster 275
Lonedale Operator, The (D. W. Griffith, 1911), parallel editing in 75
Long, Long Trailer, The (Vincente Minnelli, 1954) 34–7
Long Goodbye, The (Robert Altman, 1973) 98
Long Island 125
Look Back in Anger (John Osborne; Royal Court Theatre, London, May 8, 1956) 17, 18, 18 n.2
Look Back in Anger (John Osborne; Lyceum Theater, New York, October 1, 1957) 17, 18
Look Back in Anger (Tony Richardson, 1959) 18 n.2

Lopez, Jennifer   176, 180
Lord of the Flies (Peter Brook, 1963)   163
Lord of the Rings saga (Peter Jackson, 2001–2003)   100, 204, 331, *see also* Hollywood, mattes
  Lord of the Rings: The Fellowship of the Ring (Peter Jackson, 2001)   185, 194
  Lord of the Rings: The Two Towers (Peter Jackson, 2002)   84
"L'origine du monde" (Gustave Courbet, 1866)   48
Lorre, Peter   146
Los Angeles   60, 235, 331
  Getty Mansion   259
  Griffith Park   259
  Griffith Park Observatory   259
  LAPD   164, 221
  as set   94, 215, 306, 334
  Whitley Heights   188
  Wilshire Blvd.   178
Lost Horizon (Frank Capra, 1938)   162
"Lost Mariner, The" (Oliver Sacks)   14–15
Louis XV, furniture style   222ff
"Louisiana Hayride" (Arthur Schwartz and Howard Dietz)   62
Love, Simon (Greg Berlanti, 2018)   106
Love in the Afternoon (Billy Wilder, 1957)   327
Love Is a Many-Splendored Thing (Henry King, 1955)   327, 328
Lovejoy, Ray   37
Low, Chuck   301
Lowery, David   151
Lubezki, Emmanuel   186
Lucasfilm (Marin County)   48
Lugosi, Béla   83, 152

MacArthur, Charles   263
Machinist, The (Brad Anderson, 2004)   100
Madame Sousatzka (John Schlesinger, 1988)   132

Magic Christian, The (Joe McGrath, 1969)   320
Magnificent Ambersons, The (Orson Welles, 1942)   73, 226
Maguire, Tobey   303
Magus, The (Guy Green, 1968)   161
Malkovich, John   295
Malleson, Miles   326
Maltese Falcon, The (John Huston, 1941)   239
Manchurian Candidate, The (John Frankenheimer, 1962)   237, 328
Man in the Gray Flannel Suit, The (Nunnally Johnson, 1956)   327
Mankiewicz, Ben   305
Man of Property, The (John Galsworthy)   118–19
Mantle, Anthony Dod   186
Man Who Fell to Earth, The (Nicolas Roeg, 1976)   84, 320
Man Who Knew Too Much, The (Alfred Hitchcock, 1956)   227, 228ff, 303
  Albert Hall sequence   39, 40–4, 44 n.4
  kitchen scene   136 n.3
  Marrakech, as setting   41, 228, 229, 230, 230 n.2, 303
  Place Djemaa el Fna   303
  restaurant scene   227, 228ff, 231 n.3
Man With a Camera, A (Nestor Almendros)   168 n.1
Marathon Man (John Schlesinger, 1976)   163
Marchetti, Gina   90
Marriage Story (Noah Baumbach, 2019)   149, 213
Martin, Dean   89
Martin, Steve   7
Marvel Productions, *see* Hollywood, studios
Marvin, Lee   325
Marx Brothers, The   83
  Chico   134
Mason, James   65, *232*, 233–4

Massari, Lea   284, 285 n.1, 286
Massey, Raymond   81
Master and Commander: The Far Side of the World (Peter Weir, 2003)   186
Mastroianni, Marcello   65
Matthau, Walter   235
McAvoy, James   53, 111
McBride, Joseph   299 n.2
McCarey, Leo   304
McDermott, Dylan   273
McIntosh, Mary   246
McKee, Gina   117, 120
McKellen, Ian   1–2, 4, 232, 331
McKern, Leo   233
McQueen, Steve   176 n.1
Mediterranean Sea   222, 284
Melville, Jean-Pierre   32 n.3
Memoirs of a Geisha (Rob Marshall, 2005)   186
Menges, Chris   185
Menjou, Adolphe   92
Merleau-Ponty, Maurice   279
Merry Christmas, Mr. Lawrence (Nagisa Ôshima, 1983)   199
Metropolis (Fritz Lang, 1927)   239
Mexico City (Ciudad de México)   276
Meyer, Emile   189
Miami Beach, as setting   328
Midnight Cowboy (John Schlesinger, 1969)   98, 139, 163
Midnight Lace (David Miller, 1960)   327
Midsummer Night's Dream, A (Max Reinhardt, 1935)   251, 252, 254
Mildred Pierce (Michael Curtiz, 1945)   280
Miles, Bernard   40ff, 44 n.4, 227
Miles, Vera   160
Mill on the Floss, The (George Eliot)   120
Miller, Jonathan   317
Miller, Ron   83
Minnelli, Vincente   36

Minority Report (Steven Spielberg, 2002)   70
Miracle Worker, The (Arthur Penn, 1962)   4, 326
Miranda, Claudio   186
Mission, The (Roland Joffé, 1986)   185
Mission: Impossible (Brian De Palma, 1996)   3
Mission: Impossible III (J. J. Abrams, 2006)   328
Mississippi Burning (Alan Parker, 1988)   185
Mitchell-Smith, Ilan   106
mo-cap (motion capture)   196, 241, *see also* Hollywood, cinematography tricks
Molina, Alfred   264
Mon oncle Antoine (Claude Jutra, 1971)   206
Monroe, Marilyn   90–1, 270, 280
Monte Carlo   27
Montgomery, Robert   207
Moore, Dickie   165
Moore, Julianne   295
Moreau, Jeanne   65
Morgan!: A Suitable Case for Treatment (Karel Reisz, 1966)   150, 326
Morris, Oswald   184
Morrow, Vic   287–8
Moscow   31
Moses   56
Mosjoukine, Ivan   281
Mr. Holmes (Bill Condon, 2015)   331
MSNBC   103
Müller, Robby   168 n.2
Mummy, The (Karl Freund, 1932)   150, 239
Muni, Paul   328
Murder on the Orient Express (Sidney Lumet, 1974)   73, 89
Murder on the Orient Express (Kenneth Branagh, 2017)   46, 89
Murders in the Rue Morgue (Robert Florey, 1932)   83
Museo del Historia Natural y Cultura (Mexico City)   14

Museum of Contemporary Art (Hobart, Tasmania), "Eating Machine" 87 n.5
Musliovic, Mediha 309
Musso and Frank's Grill (Hollywood) 103
My Dinner with Andre (Louis Malle, 1981) 160, 322
My Son John (Leo McCarey, 1952) 304
Mystic River (Clint Eastwood, 2003) 140, 187

Nakajima, Haruo 150, 152
Naked Kiss, The (Samuel Fuller, 1964) 207
Naked Prey, The (Cornel Wilde, 1965) 29
Nalder, Reggie [Reginald] 40ff, 44 n.4
Nantucket, as filming location 101
National Archives (Washington D.C.) 140
NATO (North Atlantic Treaty Organization) 314
Navajos, studied by Worth and Adair 139 n.2
Navarro, Guillermo 186
Neill, Ve 84 n.4
Neolithic era 219
Nesbitt, Cathleen 328
New Jersey 331
New York 49, 162, 235, 262, 271 n.3, 274, 303
  broadway as setting 272
  broadway theater 62, 95, 262
  Bronx, the 275
  Central Park 8
  Dakota, the 226
  Empire State Building 272, 272 n.4, 328
  42nd Street 58, 59, 61, 62
  Grand Central Station 57, 59, 62
  Hudson River 49, 237
  La Guardia Airport 48, 49
  Lincoln Center (for the Performing Arts) 163
  Little Italy 163
  Manhattan streets, as location 160, 189–90, 275, 303
  NYPD 221
  Spanish Harlem 47
  Times Square 60, 62, 274, 277
  Times Square on New Year's Eve 274ff
New York, New York (Martin Scorsese, 1977) 179
New Zealand 1
Nice
  Bataille des fleurs 222, 224
  Cimiez 226
  flower market as setting 222
Nicholson, Jack 93, 94, 96–7, 252
9/11 277
Noir cinema, *see* Hollywood
Noises Off . . . (Peter Bogdanovich, 1992) 161
"Non, je ne regrette rien" (Charles Dumont and Michel Vaucaire) 67
Normandy, beaches of 53
North by Northwest (Alfred Hitchcock, 1959) 107, 197
  cornfield sequence 162
  sets constructed, listing 237
  Triboro Bridge (Robert F. Kennedy Bridge) 302
  United Nations Delegates' Lounge 302
  Vandamm house 234 n.2
Notorious (Alfred Hitchcock, 1946) 101, 196
Novak, Kim 189, 233
November Man, The (Roger Donaldson, 2014) 309, 313, 314
Nutty Professor, The (Jerry Lewis, 1963) 84, 100
Nykvist, Sven 185
NYPD (New York Police Department), *see* New York

Ocean's 11 (Lewis Milestone, 1960)   83, 249
Oldman, Gary   84, 86
Olivier, Laurence   3, 74, 160, 163, 322, 324
Olsen, Christopher   232
On Chesil Beach (Dominic Cooke, 2017)   320
"On Cooling the Mark Out" (Erving Goffman)   6 n.3
On Dangerous Ground (Nicholas Ray, 1951)   44 n.2, 67
One Day in the Life of Ivan Denisovich (Caspar Wrede, 1970)   331
One From the Heart (Francis Ford Coppola, 1981)   73, 183, 258, 302, 331
O'Neill, Ed   8
O'Neill, Eugene   264
On Her Majesty's Secret Service (Peter R. Hunt, 1969)   28
On the Beach (Stanley Kramer, 1959)   4
On the Town (Stanley Donen and Gene Kelly, 1949)   328
On the Waterfront (Elia Kazan, 1954)
  car conversation scene   175
  finale   196
Operation Finale (Chris Weitz, 2018)   3
Orfei, Liana   128
O'Rourke, Heather   157
Ortega y Gasset, José   200–1
Oscar, *see* Academy of Motion Picture Arts and Sciences; Hollywood
O'Toole, Peter   21
Out of Africa (Sydney Pollack, 1985)   185, 331
Owen, Clive   276

Pacific Ocean   65, 324
Pacino, Al   144
Painting with Light (John Alton)   168 n.1
Palance, Jack   312
Palm Beach Story, The (Preston Sturges, 1942)   99
Panic Room (David Fincher, 2002)   *155*, 162
Pan's Labyrinth (Guillermo del Toro, 2006)   186
Pantoliano, Joe   295
Paper Moon (Peter Bogdanovich, 1973)   7
Paramount Pictures, *see* Hollywood, studios
Paris   276, 327
  1968 student revolution   67
  Palais Royal   160
Paris vu par (Claude Chabrol, Jean Douchet, Jean-Luc Godard, Jean-Daniel Pollet, Éric Rohmer, Jean Rouch, 1965)   170
Parker (Taylor Hackford, 2013)   176, 180
Passage to India, A (David Lean, 1984)   162
Patton, Will   309
Pau, Peter   185
Pauline at the Beach ([*Pauline à la plage*] Éric Rohmer, 1983)   169, *182*, 189
Paull, Lawrence   301
Peck, Gregory   *201*
Pereira, Hal   226, 237
Perkins, Anthony   89
Perkins, Victor   73
Perret, Nellie   51 n.4
Personal Shopper (Olivier Assayas, 2016)   98, 163
Persons, Mark   85
Peter Pan (Clyde Geronimi, Wilfred Jackson, and Hamilton Luske, 1953)   87 n.6, 330
Pfeiffer, Michelle   330
Pfister, Wally   186
Phantom of the Opera, The (Rupert Julian, 1925)   85
Phoenix, Joaquin   90, 94
Piaf, Edith   67
Piano Teacher, The (Michael Haneke, 2001)   132
Pigeon, Rebecca   *1*, 7
Pike, Rosamund   305, *316*

Pillow Talk (Michael Gordon, 1959)   24, 156, 280
Pirate, The (Vincente Minnelli, 1948)   322
Pissarro, Camille   169
  Pontoise canvases   169
Pitt, Brad   184, 249
Pitt, Michael   48, 67, 106
Plagal cadence   65
Planck, Robert   32 n.3
Player, The (Robert Altman, 1991)   188
Play It Again, Sam (Woody Allen, 1972)   329
Pleasence, Donald   311
Plowright, Joan   74
Plummer, Christopher   69, *127*, 132f, *195*, 196, 197f
Poe, Edgar Allan   68
Point Blank (John Boorman, 1967)   325
Poitier, Sidney   144
Polanski, Roman   94
Polglase, Van Nest   34
Polito, Sol   181
Poltergeist (Tobe Hooper, 1982)   157
Potente, Franka   313
Predator (John McTiernan, 1987)   86, *149*, 241
Preiss, Wolfgang   68
Price, Vincent   131 n.1
Princess Bride, The (Rob Reiner, 1987)   240
Private Lives (Noël Coward; Times Square Theater, New York, January 7, 1931)   58, 58 n.2
Prometheus   194
Prometheus (Ridley Scott, 2012)   244
Psycho (Alfred Hitchcock, 1960)   105, 160, 206, 306 n.1, 317
Pudovkin, Vsevolod   280–1
Puppet: An Essay on Uncanny Life (Kenneth Gross)   128
"Put Me Among the Girls" (Johnny Wakefield and C. W. Murphy)   74
Pythagoras   47

Quantum of Solace (Marc Forster, 2008)   105
Queen, The (Stephen Frears, 2006)   52
Quinn, Anthony   131 n.1

Rachmaninoff, Sergei   129
RADA (Royal Academy of Dramatic Art)   183
Radcliffe, Daniel   *213*, 214–15
Raging Bull (Martin Scorsese, 1980)   100
Raiders of the Lost Ark (Steven Spielberg, 1981)   144
Railway Journey: The Industrialization of Time and Space in the Nineteenth Century, The (Wolfgang Schivelbusch)   199ff
Rainbow Productions   304
Rainier of Monaco   225 n.3
Rains, Claude   101, 196, 278, 280
Rains, Douglas   242
Raintree County (Edward Dmytryk, 1957)   94
Random Harvest (Mervyn LeRoy, 1942)   279
Ransom! (Alex Segal, 1956)   162, 163
Ray, Nicholas   325
Raymond, Gary   18 n.2
Rear Window (Alfred Hitchcock, 1954)   171, 234 n.11, 281 n.1, 282–3
Reason, Rex   162
Rebecca (Alfred Hitchcock, 1940)   3
  West Wing sequence   171
Rebel Without a Cause (Nicholas Ray, 1955)   198, 259, 304, 305
Red Desert (Michelangelo Antonioni, 1964)   160, 170
Redford, Robert   68, *144*
Redgrave, Vanessa   53, 89
Red River (Howard Hawks, 1948)   94
Reds (Warren Beatty, 1981)   185
Red Sea   56

Red Shoes, The (Michael Powell and Emeric Pressburger, 1948)   331, 333
   Ballet of the Red Shoes   331, 333
Rees, Roger   273
Reeves, Keanu   105
Regression (Alejandro Amenábar, 2015)   99, *191*, 191–4
Reimann, Walter   220
Remember (Atom Egoyan, 2015)   *127*, 132
Renoir, Pierre-Auguste   168
Return of the Vanishing American, The (Leslie Fiedler), and American literature   220
Revenant, The (Alejandro G. Iñárritu, 2015)   186
Reynolds, Debbie   65, *137*, 140
Richard II (William Shakespeare)   2
Richard III (Laurence Olivier, 1955)   322
Richardson, Ian   207
Richardson, Robert   185, 186
Richter, Dan   37
Ringwald, Molly   106
Ristovski, Lazar   309
River Runs Through It, A (Robert Redford, 1992)   185
Riviera, French, *see* Côte d'Azur
Road Runner cartoons   26, *see also* Hollywood, studios, Warner Bros.
Road to Perdition (Sam Mendes, 2002)   185
Robbins, Jerome   275
Robinson, Nick   106
Rohmer, Éric (Maurice Schérer)   21 n.1
Röhrig, Walter   220
Roma (Alfonso Cuarón, 2018)   186, 226
Romance and the "Yellow Peril" (Gina Marchetti)   90
Roman Spring of Mrs. Stone, The (José Quintero, 1961)   327
Rome   327
   Trevi Fountain   327
Romeo and Juliet (William Shakespeare)   325

Ronan, Saoirse   53, 111–12, 320
Ronin (John Frankenheimer, 1998)   319
Rooney, Mickey   *251*, 252
Roosevelt, Teddy, characterized   160
Rope (Alfred Hitchcock, 1948)   229
Rosemary's Baby (Roman Polanski, 1968)   226
Ross, Katharine   144
Roth, Tim   161
Rousselot, Philippe   185
Rush, Barbara   *232*
Ruskin, John   27
Russell, Bertrand   247 n.1
Russia   310, 314
Ryan's Daughter (David Lean, 1970)   184
Ryder, Winona   330

Sabotage (Alfred Hitchcock, 1936)   329
Sabotage (David Ayer, 2014)   71, 318, 319
Sabrina (Billy Wilder, 1954)   237–8
Sacco, Dan   100 n.1
Sacks, Oliver   14–15, 17
Saint, Eva Marie   107, 197
Sandgren, Linus   186
San Francisco   48, 276
Santa Barbara, as location   180
Satie, Erik   313
   "Gnossiènnes" (c. 1895)   313
Saturday Review, The   120
Saving Private Ryan (Steven Spielberg, 1998)   185
Scarface (Brian De Palma, 1983)   319
Scheff, Thomas   23 n.1
   "ladder of awareness"   42, 48
Scheider, Roy   101, 163
Schell, Maximilian   94
Schindler's List (Steven Spielberg, 1993)   185
Schivelbusch, Wolfgang
   light   167–8
   panoramic perception   199ff
Schlesinger, John   51
Schwarzenegger, Arnold   100, 319
Scofield, Paul   314
Scorsese, Martin   15–16
Scott, Campbell   *1*, 7

Scott, George C.   141
Scott, Ridley   150
Seale, John   185
Sedaris, Amy   106
Selznick, David O.   188 n.1
Selznick International, *see* Hollywood, studios
Semler, Dean   185
Sergeant York (Howard Hawks, 1941)   165
Serkis, Andy   84, 241
Seven Year Itch, The (Billy Wilder, 1955)   270
Sèvres pottery   222, 223f
Shakespeare, William   264, 311
Shakespeare in Love (John Madden, 1998)   84
Shane (George Stevens, 1953)   312
  and Europe   312
  and Old World   312
Shanghai, as setting   328
Shape of Water, The (Guillermo del Toro, 2017)   84
Sharif, Omar   21
Sharif, Tarek   72
Sharits, Paul   282
Sharpe, Karen   288
Shawn, Wallace   322
"Shine On Your Shoes" (Arthur Schwartz and Howard Dietz)   55, 58ff
Siberia (Matthew Ross, 2018)   105
Siddig, Alexander (Siddig el Fadil)   103
Silent Running (Douglas Trumbull, 1972)   85
Simmel, Georg
  city life   129
  tertius gaudens   114, 145
Sinatra, Frank   83, 89
Sin City (Frank Miller and Robert Rodriguez, 2005)   265
Singin' in the Rain (Gene Kelly and Stanley Donen, 1952)   65–6, 137, 140, 323
  ballet   221
Sin of Harold Diddlebock, The (Preston Sturges, 1947)   160

Sirens of Titan, The (Kurt Vonnegut Jr.)   320
Sisley, Alfred   169
  Bougival canvases   169
Six Degrees of Separation (John Guare; Vivian Beaumont Theater, New York, November 8, 1990)   263 n.1
Six Degrees of Separation (Fred Schepisi, 1993)   232, 331
Sixteen Candles (John Hughes, 1984)   106
6 Underground (Michael Bay, 2019)   26, 175, 178
Skarsgård, Stellan   69
Sleuth (Joseph L. Mankiewicz, 1972)   160
Slumdog Millionaire (Danny Boyle, 2008)   186
Smith, Dick   83, 84
Smitrovich, Bill   309
Smoktunovskiy, Innokentiy   324
Snow, Michael   282
Snowpiercer (Bong Joon Ho, 2013)   84
Solomon, Matthew   82 n.3
Some Like It Hot (Billy Wilder, 1959)   10, 280, 318
Sophocles   264
Sound of Music, The (Robert Wise, 1964)   326
South Africa, speaking accent   331
Southampton (Hampshire)   48
South Pacific (Joshua Logan, 1958)   328
Spandex   265
Spanish Prisoner, The (David Mamet, 1997)   1, 7–10
Spark, Cheryl   85
Special Effects: The History and Technique (Richard Rickett)   217
Spellbound (Alfred Hitchcock, 1945)   *201*
Spider-Man (Sam Raimi, 2002)   303
Spider-Man 2 (Sam Raimi, 2004)   264
Spielberg, Steven   101, 298, 301
  child characters and   298, 299 n.2, 306–7

Stairway to Heaven ([*A Matter of Life and Death*] Michael Powell and Emeric Pressburger, 1946)   264, 280
"Stairway to Paradise" (Arthur Schwartz and Howard Dietz)   62
Stanislavsky, Konstantin   89, 222
Star Is Born, A (George Cukor, 1954)   65, 66
Starobinski, Jean   209
Starship Troopers (Paul Veroeven, 1997)   104, *110*
Star Trek Generations (1994)   265
Star Trek VI: The Undiscovered Country (Nicholas Meyer, 1991)   48
Star Wars (George Lucas, 1977)   84, 85, 241, 270, 325f
   C-3PO   240
   R2-D2   240, 270
State of the Union (Frank Capra, 1948)   92
Statham, Jason   180
Steiger, Rod   175
Steimatsky, Noa   89 n.1
Steinway piano   134, 136
Stepford Wives, The (Bryan Forbes, 1975)   242–3
Stern, Bert   91
Sternberger, Dolf   200, *see also The Railway Journey*
Stewart, James   131, 189, 196, 227, 228ff, 233, 281, 303
Stewart, Kristin   98, *155*, 162
Stewart, Patrick   330
Stewart, Paul   32
Stigma: Notes on the Management of Spoiled Identity (Erving Goffman)   95
Sting, The (George Roy Hill, 1973)   7
Stolen Life, A (Curtis Bernhardt, 1945)   181
Storaro, Vittorio   185, 331
"Storm Clouds" (Arthur Benjamin; D. B. Wyndham-Lewis, 1934; 1956), *see The Man Who Knew Too Much*

Strangers on a Train (Alfred Hitchcock, 1951)   304
   Jefferson Memorial (Washington D.C.)   304
   shooting   304
   Washington D.C. locations   304
Strauss, Johann II. "The Blue Danube" (1866)   37
Streep, Meryl   124, 331
Streetcar Named Desire, A (Elia Kazan, 1951)   326
Streisand, Barbra   257, 258–9
Strike (Sergei Eisenstein, 1925)   174
Stuart, Gloria   54
Sudnow, David   130
Sully (Clint Eastwood, 2016)   48–9
Sunset Blvd. (Billy Wilder, 1950)   170
Superman (Richard Donner, 1978)   265
Superman Returns (Bryan Singer, 2006)   265
Survivor (James McTeigue, 2015)   273, 273ff, 331
Suspicion (Alfred Hitchcock, 1941)
   Aysgarth home atrium   169 n.3
   milk sequence   173
   train sequence   169 n.3
Sutherland, Donald   232
Suyin, Han, Dr., characterized   327
Swanson, Gloria   170
Sweet Smell of Success (Alexander Mackendrick, 1957)   91, 189–90
Swing Time (George Stevens, 1936)   175
Swink, Gary   168 n.2
Swinton, Tilda   150, 322
Synecdoche, New York (Charlie Kaufman, 2008)   161

Taking Lives (D. J. Caruso, 2004)   111
Taking of Pelham One Two Three, The (Joseph Sargent, 1974)   31 n.2
Talented Mr. Ripley, The (Anthony Minghella, 1999)   105
Tamiroff, Akim   83, 88, 89–90
Tandy, Jessica   *201*

Taylor, Elizabeth   144, 158, 322
Taylor, Ronnie   185
TCM (Turner Classic Movies)   305
Technicolor   168, 236
  epics   327
  Kodak recording film for   168
  lighting for   168
  three-strip process   168
Technique of Special Effects Cinematography, The (Raymond Fielding)   217
Tel Aviv   276
10 Cloverfield Lane (Dan Trachtenberg, 2016)   162
Tennant, David   324
Tennessee, homestead, as setting   165
Teran, Manuel   29
Terminal, The (Steven Spielberg, 2004)   163
Tess (Roman Polanski, 1979)   185
Testament of Dr. Mabuse, The ([*Das Testament des Dr. Mabuse*] Fritz Lang, 1933)   68
There Will Be Blood (Paul Thomas Anderson, 2007)   186
Theron, Charlize   143
They Live By Night (Nicholas Ray, 1948)   176
Thief of Bagdad, The (Michael Powell and Emeric Pressburger, 1940)   196, 326, see also Hollywood, mattes
Third Man, The (Carol Reed, 1949)   64, 65, 66, 194
Third Reich   95
This Island Earth (Joseph M. Newman, 1955)   31 n.1, 162
  velocitor   240
Thomas Crown Affair, The (Norman Jewison, 1968)   155
1,000 Eyes of Dr. Mabuse, The ([*Die 1000 Augen des Dr. Mabuse*], Fritz Lang, 1960)   68
Three Coins in the Fountain (Jean Negulesco, 1954)   327
Three Days of the Condor (Sydney Pollack, 1975)   68
Tierney, Gene   317

Tijuana   29
Time Machine, The (H. G. Wells)   47
Time Machine, The (George Pal, 1960)   73–4
Time Machine, The (Simon Wells, 2002)   73–4
Titanic (James Cameron, 1997)   48, 54, 185, 323
  Rolls Royce   323 (*see also* Hollywood, mattes)
To Catch a Thief (Alfred Hitchcock, 1955)   219, 327
To Kill a Mockingbird (Robert Mulligan, 1962)   51
To Kill a Mockingbird (Aaron Sorkin; Shubert Theater, New York, December 13, 2018)   21 n.1
Toland, Gregg   34
Tolkien, J[ohn] R[onald] R[euel]   2
Toll, John   185
Tom Jones (Tony Richardson, 1963)   207
Tom Thumb (George Pal, 1958)   239
Tootsie (Sydney Pollack, 1982)   302
Top Hat (Mark Sandrich, 1935)   328
Topkapi (Jules Dassin, 1964)   83, 327
Torn Curtain (Alfred Hitchcock, 1966)   57 n.1
Toronto   276
Totter, Audrey   205
Touch, The (Ingmar Bergman, 1971)   77, 325
Touch of Evil (Orson Welles, 1958)   83, *88*
Toumanova, Tamara   57 n.1
Towering Inferno, The (John Guillermin, 1974)   185
Towers, Constance   207
Tracy, Spencer   92, 96
Train, The (John Frankenheimer, 1964)   142, 290, 314, 331
Treasure Island (Bernard Miles and Josephine Wilson; Mermaid Theatre, London, 1961–1962)   44 n.4
Trifonov, Daniil   132
Trip, The (Roger Corman, 1967)   246
"Triplets" (Arthur Schwartz and Howard Dietz)   62

Triumph des Willens ([*Triumph of the Will*] Leni Riefenstahl, 1935)　32 n.4
Truffaut, François　200 n.2, 37, 281, 281 n.1
Truman, Ralph　40
Tuan, Yi-Fu　219–20, 258
Turkey　310
Turner, J[oseph] M[allord] W[illiam], 168
Twentieth Century (Howard Hawks, 1934)　3, 263
Twentieth Century Fox, *see* Hollywood, studios
20,000 Leagues Under the Sea (Richard Fleischer, 1954)　244
23 Paces to Baker Street (Henry Hathaway, 1956)　326
Twilight Zone: The Movie (Joe Dante, John Landis, George Miller, and Steven Spielberg, 1983)　288
Twins (Ivan Reitman, 1988)　100
2001: A Space Odyssey (Stanley Kubrick, 1968)　37, 47, 51, 239, 302
　brain dismantling　242
　HAL　240, 242, 243
2012 (Roland Emmerich, 2009)　180
Tyler, Walter　237

Ularu, Ana　105
Umberto D. (Vittorio De Sica, 1952)　73
Unholy Three, The (Jack Conway, 1930)　83
Unsworth, Geoffrey　184, 185
Up in the Air (Jason Reitman, 2009)　207

Valli, Alida　64, 65, 66
Vanet, Charles　32 n.3
Vanity Fair　90
Vaseline, *see* Hollywood, cinematography tricks
Veidt, Conrad　280, 326
Venezuela　8

Vermeer, Johannes　168, 193
Vertigo (Alfred Hitchcock, 1958)　10, 42
　alternate (UK) ending　196
　Big Basin State Park　*182*, 189
　redwoods sequence　189, 233
Victor/Victoria (Marquis Theater, New York, October 25, 1995)　95
Victorian era　117ff
Vienna　44 n.4
Virgin Land (Henry Nash Smith)　186
Virtuoso: Film Performance and the Actor's Magic (Murray Pomerance)　116 n.6, 146
Vitti, Monica　170, *284*, 284, 285, 322
Voight, Jon　*98*, 139
Von Sydow, Max　68, 70
Vonnegut, Kurt Jr.　320

Wagner, Richard　132
　Wagnerian sound　265
Wainberg, Lory　*127*
Walbrook, Anton　333
Walken, Christopher　100
Walker, Robert　304
War for the Planet of the Apes (Matt Reeves, 2017)　241
Warner, David　150, 326
Warner Bros., *see* Hollywood, studios
War of the Worlds, The (Byron Haskin, 1953)　83
Watchmen (Zack Snyder, 2009)　265
Watkin, David　185
Watson, Emma　164
Watts, Naomi　161
Wayne, John　91, 138
Weaver, Sigourney　243
Webster, Ferris　34
Weimar culture　241–2
Weinstein, Harvey　122
Weird Science (John Hughes, 1985)　106
Welles, Orson　30, 32, 34, 73, 89, 99, 197
"We're a Couple of Swells" (Irving Berlin)　3

Westmore dynasty (Hollywood make-up) 84 n.4
Westmore, Michael 84 n.4
West Palm Beach, as setting 180
West Side Story (Robert Wise and Jerome Robbins, 1961) 47, 275
Wexler, Haskell 185
Weyl, Carl Jules 300
What Maisie Knew (Henry James) 51, 51 n.4
What's Eating Gilbert Grape (Lasse Hallström, 1993) 4, 144
Wheeler, Romney 247 n.1
White Heat (Raoul Walsh, 1949) 317
Whiteout (Dominic Sena, 2009) 106
Who's Afraid of Virginia Woolf? (Mike Nichols, 1966) 144, 158, 322
Widmark, Richard 94, 96
Wieth, Mogens 41
Wild Bunch, The (Sam Peckinpah, 1969) 317
"wild" wall, *see* Hollywood, design tricks
Wilde, Oscar 310, 311
Williams, Billy 185
Williams, Linda Ruth 296 n.1
Williams, Olivia 319
Willy Wonka & the Chocolate Factory (Mel Stuart, 1971) 163
Wilson, Dooley 300
Winkler, Margot 13, 15–16, 179
Winslet, Kate 323
Wise, Robert 32–4, 275
Wiseman, Joseph 164–5
Wisenhunt, Larry 85

Wizard of Oz, The (Victor Fleming, 1939) 20, 83, 85, 248, 302, 332, *see also* Hollywood, studios, MGM
Woman's Face, A (George Cukor, 1941) 32 n.3
Women, The (George Cukor, 1939) 322
Wonderful Wizard of Oz, The (L. Frank Baum) 239
Wood, Natalie 94, 144, *195*, 196, 197
World Trade Center 272 n.4
Worth, Sol 139 n.2
Worthington, Sam 219
Wright, Frank Lloyd 234 n.2
Written on the Wind (Douglas Sirk, 1956) 328
Wycherly, Margaret 165

X-Men (Bryan Singer, 2000) 330, 331
X-Men Origins: Wolverine (Gavin Hood, 2009) 265

Yeelen ([*Brightness*] Souleymane Cissé, 1987) 159
York, Michael 89
You Are There (1953) 110 n.4
Young, Freddie 184
You Only Live Twice (Lewis Gilbert, 1967) 311
YouTube 132

Zabecka, Kat 269 n.1
Zabriskie Point (Michelangelo Antonioni, 1970) 164
  going-to-work sequence 178
Zsigmond, Vilmos 185

www.ingramcontent.com/pod-product-compliance
Lightning Source LLC
Chambersburg PA
CBHW070010010526
44117CB00011B/1489